QUEEN OF DIAMONDS

The Tiger Stadium Story

By Michael Betzold and Ethan Casey

Foreword by Harold Seymour, Ph.D.

A&M

Altwerger and Mandel Publishing Company, Inc.

West Bloomfield Michigan

Key to Photo Credits
(B) — Burton Historical Collection of the Detroit Public Library
(FP) — Detroit Free Press
(M) — Manning Brothers Commercial Photographers, Inc.

Published by
A&M
A&M Publishing Company, Inc.
6346 Orchard Lake Road, Suite 201
West Bloomfield, MI 48322

ISBN 1-878005-34-0 (cloth)
ISBN 1-878005-35-9 (paper)

Library of Congress Cataloging-in-Publication Data

Betzold, Michael.
    Queen of diamonds : the Tiger Stadium story / by Michael Betzold
and Ethan Casey. — 1st ed.
        p.   cm.
    Includes bibliographical references and index.
    ISBN 1-878-005-34-0 (cl) : $25.00. — ISBN 1-878005-35-9 (pbk.) :
$14.95
    1. Tiger Stadium (Detroit, Mich.) — History.   I. Casey, Ethan.
1965-   .   II. Title.
GV416.D488B48 1991
796.357'06'877434 — dc20   91-30612
                                                                      CIP

First Edition 1992

Designed by Mary Primeau

To Anne and Joseph, Patrick and Bridget, and all children young and old who like to eat hot dogs and watch heroes in the sun.
And in loving memory of Isaac Robert Muchmore, 1980–1989.

CONTENTS

Foreword *by Harold Seymour, Ph.D.*   ix

About This Book   xi

Introduction: The Turnstile, *by Michael Betzold*   1

1. Day In, Day Out   7

2. The Charlatan   13

3. Woodbridge Grove   21

4. Bennett Park   29

5. Navin Field   39

6. The Briggs Era   55

7. We're All Behind Our Baseball Team   77

8. The Riverfront Dome Scam   85

9. Billy and the Bird   101

10. The Thirty-Year Commitment   107

11. Tom, Kirk, and Bubba   113

12. The Grand Old Lady   127

13. Renovation: Stop Making Sense   147

14. Obstructed Views   179

15. Empty Seats and Scapegoats   195

16. Shackled to a Rusted Girder   209

17. The Empty Threat   223

18. What This City Needs Is More Millionaires
and Low-Paying Jobs   237

19. The People's Consent   255

20. Ballpark Voices   261

Conclusion: Heading Home   275

Afterword: Self-interest and the Tiger Stadium Fan Club,
by Ethan Casey   279

Appendix 1. Chronology of Michigan and Trumbull   289

Appendix 2. Attendance at Michigan and Trumbull   297

Appendix 3. Hall of Famers at Michigan and Trumbull   303

Appendix 4. Ten Silliest Reasons for Tearing Down
Tiger Stadium   309

Sources   311

Index   315

FOREWORD

Big-league baseball parks are bound up with baseball history. Like the teams, umpires, and owners, they represent our connection to a dynamic part of our past. The baseball park at Michigan and Trumbull in Detroit has soaked up nearly a hundred years of the national game and absorbed large chunks of the lives of millions of fans. But will it survive the attempts to destroy it and to wipe out the memories associated with it?

It will if Michael Betzold and Ethan Casey can help it. In this affectionate portrait of the ballpark and brisk analysis of the issues surrounding the controversy over whether the park should be saved, Betzold and Casey show us what the park really is: a landmark, an asset to city life—especially to the lives of those who live in the neighborhood.

Americans love to travel abroad to exclaim over the antique and even ancient structures of the past, but in their own country they seem bent on annihilating mature and venerable buildings, replacing them with shoddy, characterless imitations in which nobody takes pride and for which nobody has any real feeling.

Must everything be new? Is new always better? Fathers ought to be able to tell their children that it was here that Cobb, Veach, and Crawford performed, here that York, Goslin, Kaline, Gehringer, and Greenberg achieved their fame. Taking the new generation to a park in which nothing has ever happened, a park that has no grand associations, gives the older generation nothing to bequeath.

In baseball the tendency to prefer the new takes the form of permitting the solid structures of the early part of the century to be demolished in favor of cavernous, airtight, skyless, grass-free colossi that bear little resemblance to the homey parks of the past with their distinctive features, places where fans can really feel a part of the game, unique places with strong roots.

Like Betzold and Casey, and like millions of other Americans, I grew up as a baseball fan, and a large part of my youth is linked with one of those parks. For me, it was Ebbets Field, where in the 1920s and 1930s I not only watched famous players perform but for three summers even acted as batboy. Ebbets Field was the outstanding entity of my Brooklyn neighborhood and a critical part of my growing-up years. There, after games, fans hurrying from the park were met by gangs of neighborhood boys asking "Who won? How many hits did Wheat get? Who pitched?" and a string of other questions that showed the importance to everyone in the neighborhood of what went on in that park.

And now Ebbets Field has disappeared. My baseball park—the park of millions of Brooklyn boys—has been annihilated. Worse yet, my team, like that of many other communities, is gone, too.

Will Tiger Stadium be next? The issues involved in whether to replace, restore, or demolish the park, or move it out of the city, as Betzold and Casey show, are not as complex as many of the disputants represent. It all boils down to a question of value.

A fine old ballpark is a treasure. It warrants our esteem, not our disdain. It's a prize that, once gone, cannot be regained.

—Harold Seymour, Ph. D.

ABOUT THIS BOOK

In the spring of 1991 the long debate over the future of Tiger Stadium reached a turning point. Defying strong popular support for renovating the historic ballpark, public officials were formulating a plan to build a new stadium for the Detroit Tigers. With a public-relations blitz over a few short months, Wayne County officials forged a consensus of the rich and powerful to bulldoze a national landmark for the sake of short-term private profits.

It seemed likely that the battle over Tiger Stadium soon would reach a public vote. Clearly, it was time to tell the story of this neglected civic treasure.

Late in May, I took a leave from my job as a reporter at the *Detroit Free Press*, assembled clippings on the stadium controversy, and plunged into the project. In 1988 I had written a booklet on Tiger Stadium's history. That became a starting point for this more ambitious project.

I enlisted Ethan Casey, a writer from Washington, D. C., who I knew was well versed in stadium controversies, to join the project as principal interviewer and coauthor. Ethan did some interviews in Washington and Chicago, and arrived in Detroit near the end of June. He plunged into a whirlwind schedule of interviews, while I devoted most of my time to expanding the history and writing a chronology of the most recent years of controversy.

Our two main goals in interviews were to augment the written chronicle of Tiger Stadium's history with personal memories, and to probe civic leaders, baseball officials, members of the Tiger Stadium Fan Club, and ordinary fans for their views on whether Tiger Stadium should be preserved or replaced, and why. Ethan did most of the interviews, bringing to the task a valuable outsider's perspective and a keen awareness of priorities.

The persons we talked to include: Hank Aguirre, Marc Alan, Roger Angell, Philip Bess, Gunnar Birkerts, Walter Briggs III, Walter Briggs IV, Lois Briggs-Redissi, Peter Brink, Jim Bristah, David Brooks, Major

Brooks, Scott Brooks, Bob Buchta, Jim Bunning, Paul Carey, Alex Clunis, Katherine Colias, Ted Colias, Alice Conway, Bill Craven, Tom Cross, Catherine Darin, Robert Darvas, John Davids, Judy Davids, Peter Dembski, Tom Derry, Bill Dow, George Dumka, Gary Dutton, Vicki Dutton, Jeff Ellison, Michael Ferber, Michael Funke, Anita Gammicchia, Dan Gaule, Catherine Gaule, Anthony Gholz, Bert Gordon, Ruth Goslow, Jim Gray, John Grindstaff, Mike Gruber, Bill Haase, Rosemary Hogan, Jim Holley, Doug Jerome, John Kelly, Christopher Kittides, Max Lapides, Beth Lawles, Mildred Layer, Elmore Leonard, Maryann Mahaffey, Eugene McCarthy, Matthew McKinnon, "Baseball John" Miramonti, Charles Moon, Pat Muldoon, Mario Muscat, Eva Navarro, Eric Neumann, Jeff Odenwald, Joe O'Neal, Dave Osinski, John Pastier, Ron Prebenda, Dennis Prewozniak, Frank Rashid, Mike Ridley, Dorothy Rivard, Sasha Roberts, Carl Rollyson, Peter Rosen, Doug Rutherford, Bret Saberhagen, Mike Selis, Stewart Selis, Don Shapiro, Thom Sharp, Thomas Shull, Tim Slagle, Royce Smith, B. Ward Smith, Tim Springstead, Tina Stoneburner, Brian Tremain, Patty Warner, Randy Westbrooks, and George Will.

On July 11 Ethan Casey attended Eugene V. Debs Memorial Kazoo Night in the Tiger Stadium bleachers and spoke to Eugene McCarthy, Maryann Mahaffey, and a host of Debs attendees. We are especially grateful to the fans met that night and on July 13, when we met radio crews who were conducting interviews at Tiger Stadium. Many thanks to Don Gonyea, Jerry Stormer, Roger Adams, Gretchen Millech, Doug Johnson, and Sean Fox.

Also included in the book are the taped reminiscences of Bill Stevens.

Many, many other people were on our interview list, but our tight timetable did not permit us to make connections with everyone. There were many people we tried and failed to reach, and many others we did not have the time to contact. We apologize to the many important people who have been left out of this book.

Because of their key roles in the stadium controversy, we made special efforts to interview several prominent people in the Tiger organization, in local government, and in baseball.

We tried several times to reach Commissioner of Baseball Fay Vincent and American League president Bobby Brown. Brown refused any comment, and Richard Levin, director of public relations for Major League Baseball, failed to return our calls seeking an interview with Vincent.

ABOUT THIS BOOK

After several phone calls to the office of the Wayne County executive to schedule interviews with executive Ed McNamara and his deputy, Michael Duggan, we succeeded in scheduling a meeting. Duggan's office canceled the interview the day before it was to have taken place. Ethan made several subsequent calls to Duggan's office; a woman on his staff told him that she would try to reschedule the interview. She never got back to him.

Robert Berg, Mayor Coleman Young's press secreatary, never responded to several phone calls and a letter requesting an interview with either Berg or Young.

Tom Monaghan's assistant replied that "due to time constraints, Mr. Monaghan is unable to take part in an interview."

Tiger CEO Jim Campbell did not respond to a letter requesting an interview.

A letter was sent to Tiger president Bo Schembechler requesting an interview, which he passed to vice president Bill Haase, the team's "point man" on the stadium issue. Haase's secretary said that Schembechler was unwilling to be interviewed.

John McDevitt, president of Thomas S. Monaghan, Inc., replied through an associate that he would be unable to speak to us.

Tiger broadcaster Ernie Harwell declined to be interviewed.

Given extreme time constraints, we could never have completed this project without help. This book would not have been possible without crucial contributions from Kathy Burke, Ken Mogill, Mike Gruber, Jerry Lemenu, Dale Petty, and Catherine Darin. Special thanks go to Joanne Fluegge for her endless hours of transcribing taped interviews under difficult circumstances. Thanks also to Roger Angell, Steve Bennett, Philip Bess, Brian Betzold, Bob Bluthardt, Dwight Cendrowski, Kathleen Conway, John Davids, Judy Davids, Tom Dietz, Judy Donlin, Irene Duranczyk, Bert Gordon, Holly Horning, Kelly Hurley, Max Lapides, Joe Lapointe, Bill McGraw, Eva Navarro, Marc Okkonen, John O'Neill, John Pastier, Rich Pickering, Marc-E. Pierre-Louis, Frank Rashid, Kathy Rashid, Don Shapiro, Walden Simper, Tim Slagle, Cindy Swift, Peggy Swift, Suzanne Thelan, Brian Tremain, Don Voelker, and the staff at the Burton Historical Collection of the Detroit Public Library.

We are grateful to Roger Angell for putting us in touch with Bert Gordon, Max Lapides, and Don Shapiro, the delightful trio of Tiger fans about whom he wrote an article for the *New Yorker* in 1973 called

xiii

"Three for the Tigers," and whose memories and thoughts are so valuable to this book.

We are honored that baseball's great historian, Dr. Harold Seymour, agreed to write a foreword. Dr. Seymour's most recent book is *Baseball: The People's Game* (1990).

Bob Mandel, Nick Altwerger, and Kyle Scott at Altwerger & Mandel Publishing Company deserve praise for seeing this book's potential and for following through despite the difficulties imposed by our tight timetable. Tom Seller deserves commendation for perceptive copy editing.

I am most grateful to my wife, Kathleen Conway, for her patience and understanding and for allowing me to realize my dream at the expense of an entire summer, and to my children, Patrick and Bridget, who put up with my absence.

We believe this book is the most definitive history yet written of the ballparks at Michigan and Trumbull, but it is far from complete. Tiger Stadium contains many, many more memories than we could possibly have gathered even with no time constraints, and more thoughts and feelings than any book could hold.

We are confident that this book tells the true story of Tiger Stadium, but it was impossible under the circumstances to research every anecdote told us or to verify every reference to the stadium's history. For any errors in the book, we are solely responsible.

Also, it is a daunting task to write a synopsis of a debate that continues to unfold. Events are moving fast, and some of what we have written may already be outdated by the time this book is published. In any event, the main arguments for and against a new stadium remain.

We look upon this book as only the beginning of a story. It has been only in very recent times that Tiger Stadium has begun to take its rightfully prominent place in the history of baseball and of Detroit. That history will remain alive as long as there are Detroiters and baseball. It cannot be obliterated by the actions of a few.

Beginning this project, I was keenly aware of the value of Tiger Stadium. Now I know even more deeply that this ballpark is an irreplaceable treasure. I am certain today that there is no place in the world like the corner of Michigan and Trumbull, and I am grateful for the hundreds of games I have seen there and the millions of fans with whom I have shared those wonderful days and nights of summer.

—Michael Betzold

INTRODUCTION:

THE TURNSTILE

A friend who likes to embarrass me in front of new acquaintances has two favorite stories about my clumsiness. The first involves the time in high school I dribbled a basketball off my foot during pregame introductions. The other is about the day I got stuck in the turnstile at Tiger Stadium.

It was in the early 1970s. The Tigers had won, and we were exuberant. Keeping with our tradition, we ran pell-mell down the ramps from the upper deck bleachers, careening through the crowd. At the bottom was a huge knot of people inching out Gate 8. To one side of the gate, I spotted a turnstile, with big iron bars from the cement floor to the top of the opening.

On impulse, I decided to go out through the turnstile. I ran up, pushed the bars, got halfway through, and found myself stuck. The bars wouldn't go forward or backward.

There I was, a long-haired gorilla in a cage. My friends taunted me and, doubled over laughing, pointed me out to passers-by, who joined in the ridicule. Ten minutes may have passed, or five — it seemed like an hour — before a stadium worker unlocked the door and let me out.

Goofy things happen at Michigan and Trumbull. After all, this is where Germany Schaefer played second base in a raincoat and Norm Cash took a table leg up to bat against Nolan Ryan. It's where grown-ups turn into children.

When I was a kid, I always brought my mitt to Ladies Day games. For fifty cents apiece, women and children could sit in the upper-deck reserved seats — prime foul ball territory. All game long, while keeping score with my right hand, I would keep my big, floppy first baseman's glove on my left. Game after game, year after year, no ball came near me. Finally, one day a batter hit a lazy foul pop-up right toward me. I

1

stood, glove outstretched, ready. Just then a man walked by carrying a tray with a Coke and a hot dog. Not missing a step, he reached up nonchalantly and snared the ball, then went on walking to his seat without spilling a drop of his drink.

Many years later, I was sitting in the right-field grandstands when a home run ball flew my way. It landed in my lap, but I was too shocked to catch it. A ball? Coming at me? Impossible. My friend, puzzled, picked it up off the ground and claimed it as his souvenir.

I grew up in a very provincial middle-class suburb. The ballpark was my first introduction to the varieties of city life.

I heard my first swear words at Michigan and Trumbull. I saw my first bag lady. I sat, mouth agape, as loud-mouthed drunks trained lethal insults on umpires. I saw women wearing brown-and-white striped Tiger leotards and men with beer bellies hanging over their belts. I heard vendors hawk "Harvey Kuenn's favorite ice cream" or urge "Getcher red hots!"

These days, a lot of ballparks have no-alcohol "family sections" to shield young eyes and ears. Luckily for my education, there has never been any such sanctuary at Tiger Stadium. A ballpark isn't supposed to be a church, though it can be a religious experience.

In high school I studied to be a priest, but I never really grasped the essence of communion until the summer of 1968 at Tiger Stadium, when thousands of strangers became one sacred body of worshipers at the altar of baseball. We found irrefutable proof of God's existence in the transcendent swing of Tommy Matchick, whose miraculous home run beat Baltimore and made believers out of the most seasoned skeptics. If Matchick, who hit .215 with four homers in his career, could slug a game-winning blast, anything was possible.

When the Tigers won the first pennant of my lifetime, I felt transformed. We were in the upper deck, beneath the scoreboard, but it was the work of an instant to scramble down the ramps, screaming, and clamber over the center-field fence. With thousands of other fanatics I danced on the green, green grass of home. For hours afterward, I drove my red Buick Special through the downtown street party, honking the horn while one of my friends sat on the hood and the other made a permanent impression on the roof.

A few weeks later, on a crystal autumn Monday afternoon, I sat in perhaps the worst seats in Tiger Stadium, in the far reaches of the lower grandstand behind two rows of posts. If I leaned hard to the left, I could see the pitcher. If I leaned hard to the right, I could see the batter. I was thrilled to be there. A lot of my friends who had sent in money in the mail-order ticket lottery hadn't gotten tickets at all. Some had seen the previous day's game, drenched in deep despair as the St. Louis Cardinals shellacked the Tigers in a pouring rain and moved within a game of taking the World Series.

I was there, behind those posts, when Willie Horton threw out Lou Brock at the plate. Like everyone in the park, I had a clear view of Brock's foot as it landed an inch off the plate, pushed off by Bill Freehan — well, at least a good enough view to roar approval at the umpire's call.

In May 1976 I was lucky enough to be lurking in seats behind home plate, upper deck, when Mark Fidrych made his debut, and I came back for all the Bird's wondrous flights, including a moonlit night when he dispatched the Yankees and became a national celebrity. I also witnessed all his sad comeback attempts.

Perhaps it is significant that I got married in May 1984 amid the Tigers' legendary 35–5 start. I had my bachelor party at the ballpark the night before the wedding and to this day can't understand why my bride, who has more baseball in her genes than I have in my heart, didn't want to get married in the bleachers.

Many of my best memories are recent ones. Most vivid still are the three gut-wrenching games with Toronto that put a resounding coda on the symphonic 1987 season. On a Friday night, with snow flurries flying on north winds, I watched from the bleachers as Doyle Alexander dispatched the Jays. The next afternoon, I sat chilled with autumn and nervous anticipation in the upper deck behind third base as Jack Morris hung tough and the Tigers won in extra innings on a grounder that went through shortstop Manny Lee's legs. And the next day, sunny and serene, I sat tense and hopeful behind the screen in the upper deck and hardly dared believe the miracle was happening until Frank Tanana took the final hopper and threw the ball — and then himself — into the big bear hug of Darrell Evans.

But the game I'll never forget from 1987 — and the game that remains one of my oddest and fondest memories at Tiger Stadium — was in May. The Tigers were in last place. There was a Red Wings playoff game downtown, and the crowd was small. After a few long rain delays it had dwindled to almost nothing.

As the clock passed midnight, my friends and I moved down into the lower deck and found some other people we knew. I met Peter

3

Dembski, a season-ticket holder who has been making the 360-mile round trip from his home in Waterloo, Ontario, since 1968. We saw Mike Henneman make his major league debut in the morning. By that time there were no more than 150 fans in the park.

The game went on, a private party for diehards. Every sound on the field reverberated in the empty stadium—the whip-crack of the ball hitting the catcher's mitt, the ping or thunder of a hit, the infield chatter. It was just a ball game, like a game on a Little League sandlot, just a bunch of guys playing baseball, and it didn't matter that the men playing were millionaires, that the home team was in last place, that the Tigers were going to lose.

It was just a game, just playing.

The next day, the Tigers started winning and began the most remarkable season-long comeback in the club's history. They were a savvy veteran team, pouncing on their opponents' mistakes, getting clutch hits and doing the little things that win ball games. They were mine, because I was there that night in May, because I hadn't given up.

The previous season, I had taken my first child to his first game at Michigan and Trumbull. We have gone to dozens of games together since. From infancy, he's watched the games intently, and something has clicked for him. From the beginning, for him, the stadium has been home, as it has been for me since my first glimpse of the great green panorama.

There's a place at the rail near the home dugout where my son likes to stand after a game. If he's lucky, a ball player might poke his head out of the dugout. If not, Patrick is content to stare at the bat boy putting away equipment or gaze at the grounds crew pulling the tarp over the close-cropped green grass. Fifty years ago, Patrick's great-grandfather pulled the tarp. At Michigan and Trumbull, the roots go deep.

Lots of cities have new ballparks with all the character and beauty of strip malls. Only a few have hallowed grounds where a young fan can be close enough to see spike marks in the base paths his great-grandfather groomed.

Tiger Stadium holds many great memories, but nostalgia is not the issue. Nostalgia is a sentimental attachment for things of the past. Tiger Stadium is still present. I am much less excited about what happened there in the past than I am about the prospect of going to see a game today. And I am concerned about the future.

4

INTRODUCTION

I don't want my son and my daughter to be shut out of baseball like the thousands of kids in Detroit who love basketball but can't go to Piston games because Pistons ownership has decided that wealthy fans are the only fans who count. I want my children to be able to go to Michigan and Trumbull and stand at the rail by the dugout with their children. I want them to hear the bat slap the ball, see red clay stick to flying spikes, and smell the sweat and the dirt and the hot dogs.

Tiger Stadium is their inheritance.

There are enough places in our world today that are climate-controlled, airtight, incapable of surprises and serendipity. Does Detroit need, does baseball need another new, deadly serious mega-bucks entertainment mecca where every moment is orchestrated, every need anticipated, every potential surprise captured before it has a chance to escape the web of the expertly packaged leisure commodity?

When I think of a new stadium for the Tigers, I think about Mark Fidrych and his goofy grin. Would there be any place in the manicured spectacle of a new ballpark for the Bird to act a little dopey? And would anyone notice if he did?

Could an impulsive adolescent get stuck in a turnstile at a new stadium? Not a chance. Some smiling guard would escort him to the right exit. That's where all of us who don't fit into the brave new world would be headed, and quick: right for the nearest exits.

Childhood, with its whims and its goofiness, doesn't fit in a place designed for commerce. Tradition? It too can be packaged and sold — maybe a little museum on the stadium grounds, maybe a little glass case with a piece of the old sod inside. Yes, at a new Tiger Stadium, nostalgia would be a top-selling item. The past would be preserved, dissected, and brazenly marketed.

The past is not what's at stake in the battle of Michigan and Trumbull. The past is gone. It's the present — this little space of spontaneity, this unpackaged moment that is ours and not the property of the corporation — that would be extinguished. This moment, when you can sit in a chair in the cool night air and see, up close, today's hero, today's scapegoat — this moment will be banished by a sales pitch, outlawed for being unmarketable, nonproductive, too whimsical, too playful, too goofy, too clownish, too clumsy.

Too much like a little kid.

Too much like Germany Schaefer.

Too much like the Bird.

— Michael Betzold

5

CHAPTER 1

DAY IN, DAY OUT

Ask the players or ask the fans.

The most beautiful park in baseball is Tiger Stadium. It's a baseball treasure. And fortunately for us, it's right here in Detroit.

Players love it because of the intimacy. Fans are close. Fences are cozy. And the atmosphere is electric.

Fans love it because they're smack in the middle of the action.

Tradition, charm and baseball lore. And modernization has made the great old park colorful, comfortable and safe.

Tiger Stadium is a state landmark. It's a focal point from which all else is measured.

> *—Detroit Tigers official score*
> *book and program for the*
> *1987 American League*
> *Championship Series*

For a century, the fine, true dirt on the old ball field at the corner of Michigan and Trumbull has been stirred by swift spikes and pounded by heavy feet; whipped by skipping throws from wild arms; stomped, kicked, poked, punched, smoothed, watered, raked, swept, chalked, pampered, and kissed. Ty Cobb pummeled this good, real earth; Mark Fidrych primped it; Lou Whitaker pirouettes on it. Baseball's best, from Ruth to Ryan, have used it as their dusty stage. In failure, in desperation, hundreds of heroes and hacks have inhaled its acrid clods. So when Darrell Evans got a mouthful of that dirt on the night of October 11, 1987, he was in good company.

Facedown, prostrate before the gaze of fifty thousand fans and the electronic stares of millions, Evans, a fallen star, gulped a long, vintage drink of ignominy. Stretched full length on his stomach on the ground, uniform striped with chalk, his outstretched right arm inches south of the third-base bag, cap askew, face contorted with self-directed rage, Evans lay: beaten, embarrassed, exposed, fooled, struck down, caught, taken, tagged, picked off. Out. Bonehead victim of the game's most embarrassing play, he had committed the unforgivable sin and killed the most crucial rally in years. The forty-year-old UFO-sighter, clubhouse philosopher, and overhang-banger was history, and so were the Tigers.

Fifty thousand people groaned in the dank autumn night, a two-tiered, half-mile-long headache pounding at the temples of the ancient stadium, the sharp wincing pain of sudden and utter defeat traveling a familiar, timeworn path. Evans clenched his right hand, fisted a few clods of the uncaring, immortal dirt, raised his arm, and pounded the diamond: once, twice, three times. The earth absorbed the gesture in an instant, swallowing the frustration as it had tens of thousands of times before. A second later, not a sign of his rage remained on the placid surface.

The besmirched veteran picked himself up and hobbled slowly, head down, mind raging, into the losers' dugout, and a splendid sun-kissed season trudged off with him into the cold, dim night.

Watching him from the owner's box was Tom Monaghan. As a boy, he had dreamed of playing shortstop for the Tigers. Instead, he had made millions selling pizzas. A few weeks after Monaghan bought the team in 1983 for a reported $53 million, the Tigers had spent a couple of million signing Evans. After Evans performed poorly in his first season, Monaghan had publicly questioned whether he was worth the money.

Monaghan had expressed no such doubts about his place of business. After becoming owner, he had gushed about his love for the club and the old ballpark and had made a vow to fans. "As long as I own this team, we will not build a new stadium," he had pledged.

Many fans were puzzled, then, when they left the ballpark the night of Evans's pratfall. Several people were passing out bumper stickers that read "Save Tiger Stadium." Save it? Was it in danger? Who would want to tear down this place? Hadn't Monaghan said he'd preserve it? Hadn't the city just spent millions fixing it up?

In fact, while Monaghan was still publicly proclaiming his love for his classic ballpark, his top employees were exploring ways to get the public to build him a new stadium. Earlier in 1987, club officials had secretly approached Wayne County officials to ask if the county would levy a hotel-motel tax to help finance a new stadium.

The afternoon following Evans's embarrassment, a brilliantly sunlit but cold and merciless day, there was another game to be played to close the ledger. The grizzled Tigers, proud and unlikely owners of the best record in the major leagues, were down three games to one to the lightly regarded Minnesota Twins. The Twins had won thirteen fewer games in the regular season but were poised to beat the weary Tigers and represent the American League in the World Series.

The quiet crowd filing perfunctorily into the venerable stadium harbored little hope. It wasn't just the odds; in 1968 the Tigers had trailed the magnificent St. Louis Cardinals and their ace Bob Gibson by the same three-games-to-one margin in the World Series, and had pulled it out. Michigan and Trumbull was the home address of never-say-die.

But this time it was clear that the aging Tigers were spent. Every ounce of effort had been drained by their protracted fight to the finish with the Toronto Blue Jays. The Tigers had vanquished them the previous weekend with three consecutive nail-biting one-run victories to cap the most unlikely come-from-nowhere title in the club's long history.

The Twins took the first two games of the play-offs indoors in the Hubert H. Humphrey Metrodome, a baseball traditionalist's nightmare. It had a roof and artificial turf. Pop-ups sometimes hit speakers suspended from the ceiling. In right field, instead of a wall, there was a tall dark blue curtain that looked like a garbage bag. When a line drive hit the garbage bag, the ball slid down among the folds. It was baseball in a rec room.

Minnesotans had been cool toward the Metrodome since its opening in 1982, but when the Twins slipped into postseason play, the yuppies of the Twin Cities discovered the place. During the play-offs and the subsequent World Series, well-dressed customers filled the dome. Their idea of cheering the team was to blow whistles and make as much noise as possible at every opportunity. The sunless, indoor din mimicked the atmosphere of a pop concert.

No place could have been more unlike Tiger Stadium. The ballpark at Michigan and Trumbull dated to 1912. There, the game and the fans were open to the expansive sky. The field bloomed with lush green grass. The seats were close, the fans attentive to the game. There were no distractions from baseball.

The Tigers, glad to be back at home, had shown signs of revival. In the third game, on Saturday, October 10, scrawny Pat Sheridan hit a startling game-winning home run, which settled softly into the welcoming arms of the right-field overhang. Detroit was poised for another winning rally Sunday night when Evans got himself picked off. So if the crowd that Monday afternoon was looking for someone to blame for this lame ending to the season's dramatic script, there was a scapegoat all dressed up in uniform number 41, with no place to go.

In the bottom of the first inning, Number 41, batting second for the Tigers, poked his head cautiously out of the dugout. He strode warily to the on-deck circle, ready to duck if need be. He rubbed his bat and looked around sheepishly. After Lou Whitaker took a called third strike, Evans began to trudge apprehensively toward the plate.

The public address announcer spoke his name: "Batting second for the Tigers, the first baseman, number forty-one, Darrell Evans."

At first there was an embarrassed silence, then a barely audible gasp, as if the crowd collectively had discovered a bug in its beer. Then it started: tentatively at first, out in a remote corner of the lower deck, picking up like an echo in an opposite corner, then filling in and closing the circle of sound.

The fans were applauding Evans! And not just politely, but with gusto. Soon they all were on their feet, clapping and cheering loudly. The embarrassment of the looming defeat and the missed opportunity of the previous night were melting away in a healing torrent of defiant town pride and a surge of unabashed love for the home team favorite. Evans, bewildered, stood transfixed at home plate as the applause hit him in waves like the first balmy breezes of a sudden spring day.

Evans smiled and drew a walk. The Tigers lost the game, 9–5. The miracles had run out. And the gates at Tiger Stadium clanged shut on another splendid season.

Detroit is not a coy town. It knows debasement and self-pity, but it could never develop a cult of defeatism, as Chicago has for the Cubs. It knows the cruelty of a season of hope dashed by a few days of failure, but it does not make a fetish of such disappointment, as New Englanders do for the Red Sox. And while Detroit has tasted victory and even on occasion the ultimate triumph of a championship, it is not a city of front-runners; its fans do not expect a pennant every season, like New Yorkers or Los Angelinos. Detroiters do not expect to lose or to win; they hope to win but understand that winning is a rare combination of a little luck and a lot of hard work.

Detroit, a city of laborers, admires dedication and craft. Its fans scorn the privileged and the overpaid; they disdain pretension; they prefer great effort to effortless talent. Its baseball heroes are the guys who go to work day in and day out, put in an honest and consistent effort, and do not try to hide their emotions beneath an air of self-importance. In the 1980s Tiger fans lionized Evans and Alan Trammell and Larry Herndon and Tom Brookens, but they were cool to Jack Morris, especially after he went shopping around the major leagues in a fur coat, selling himself to the highest bidder. The fans had violent mixed emotions about Kirk Gibson, the flashy and belligerent but oft-injured slugger. They liked his hustle—he seemed to be a hard worker—but they loathed his tendency toward self-aggrandizement.

Darrell Evans had no flash and no speed. He wasn't a handsome young box-office star like Gibson. He was more plodding than graceful. But every time at bat, he gave his best, methodically working his way on base with a walk, hitting a grounder to the right side to advance a runner, or unleashing his smooth, powerful home-run swing when it was most needed.

Evans was the kind of player best appreciated through careful observation day by day. He did the little things that win games. In two previous stops in his long big-league career, in Atlanta and in San Francisco, he had played in the shadows. When he came to Detroit, he seemed shocked to find himself the object of adulation, and when he eventually left town he expressed appreciation for the way the fans had treated him. He wasn't the first ball player to thank Tiger fans for their patience, their loyalty, and their love of the game.

People don't come to Michigan and Trumbull to see exploding scoreboards or cascading fountains. They don't come to play racing games with dots on giant video screens. They don't come to eat sushi. They don't come to watch ball girls in tight shorts field foul grounders. They don't come to shop for fashionable T-shirts, to go to a batting cage, or to work out at a health club.

They come to watch baseball.

For a century, they've come. They've perched on rickety wildcat bleachers in an alley behind the left-field fence at Bennett Park to get an unauthorized view of Ty Cobb stealing home. They've climbed trees on Cherry Street and sat on the roof of the Checker Cab Company on Trumbull to see Hank Greenberg belt homers over the fence. They've huddled in blankets on Opening Day and seen Frank Lary pull a leg muscle running out a triple in a snowstorm. They've baked in the bleachers while Mark Fidrych talked to the ball. They've stood in the left-field grandstands with mitts, game after game, hoping to catch Cecil Fielder's fiftieth home run.

11

In 1987 they watched closely, day after day, as Darrell Evans led his team to a division championship. They noticed him doing the little things.

And when he failed, they understood and applauded his effort. The ballpark at Michigan and Trumbull is common ground for millions of people, across a vast reach of space and time, who know what it's like to be down in the dirt and to have to pick yourself up the next day and go back to work.

CHAPTER 2

THE CHARLATAN

People who go to ball games are impressed with the well-kept scenery. The outfield is a velvet sheen of green. The infield is as smooth as a billiard table. People tell each other it's not possible after experiences they've had with their own lawns.

Well, it's possible because Neal Conway, in his own way, is both a geologist and a geometrician, who has an eye to loveliness.

— Sam Greene in the Detroit News*, 1934*

Neal Conway would get up every day before dawn, leave his tiny room above Trumbull Avenue, and go right to work. He'd walk through the empty, echoing concrete halls, up the ramp, through the stands, and onto the field.

At 6:00 A.M. the strongest men on the grounds crew would stagger bleary-eyed onto the diamond and begin pulling the heavy canvas cover off the infield. They would grab tight and start running. It was a dangerous job. Once a man broke his leg when he caught it beneath the rolling tarp.

Awakened by the removal of its quilt, the grass would sigh, stretch, and look through dewy eyes at another day. Sleep always made it brighter, especially when it had enjoyed its shampoo of vegetable dye the previous evening.

It was the brightest, lushest, most finely cropped, most beautifully manicured baseball field in the nation — thanks, thought everyone, to Neal Conway. From 1923 through 1951, Neal Conway was the head grounds keeper at Michigan and Trumbull, and he was as famous as almost any ball player. He knew all the important people in town. During the games, he would sit on his humble throne near the grounds

13

crew's entrance to the diamond, down the third-base line, and the chief of police would sit next to him and chew the fat.

Neal Conway had the Irish gift of gab and was a relentless self-promoter. Newspapermen loved him. When they needed a photo for their Opening Day editions, Neal would grab a hose and strike a pose. When they needed background on a ball player for a profile, Neal would oblige with an anecdote or two. When they needed a story to fill a dull news day, Neal would share his "secrets" about how he cared for the diamond.

It was mostly blarney. For three decades the charming, gregarious grounds keeper pulled the wool over everyone's eyes. For Cornelius Conway was something of a charlatan. He didn't know the secrets of caring for the field at Michigan and Trumbull. His older brother Jim did.

In the early 1920s Jim Conway took care of Sportsman's Park in St. Louis. It was the loveliest diamond in the nation. Frank Navin wrote to Jim Conway and asked him to come to Detroit. Jim excitedly told his sisters and brothers about the opportunity.

"At the time, my uncle Neal was a floorwalker in a department store," recalls Dorothy Rivard, Jim Conway's daughter. "He had a lawyer friend compose this official-looking letter. He acted as if he were the one they were contacting. My dad just worshiped his younger brother, so he'd go along with anything."

Neal Conway's only previous big league experience, says his niece, was a brief stint as an umpire. That career ended after a fan, angry at one of Neal's calls, stabbed him between the shoulder blades after a game.

"So they both came to Detroit," Rivard continues. "And Navin said, 'I understand you work together as a team.' My dad said yes. And Navin said, 'We can't have two head grounds keepers. Who would rather be the boss?' And they agreed it would be Neal."

Jim Conway didn't seem to mind.

"My father was very quiet," Rivard says. "Neal was much more outgoing. He really liked to be in the public eye."

Alice Conway, Jim's daughter-in-law, says, "Neal was sort of the phony-baloney one. When they came up here, he was such a talker, he was so charming, that he became the celebrity."

"Neal was the front man," agrees Ted Colias, who worked on the grounds crew after World War II. "He was the personality guy. He was always the guy out there with the hose watering the infield just before

14

the game started, when everybody could see. He was always in the spotlight."

Jim, working in the background, shunning publicity, turned Navin Field's stubborn grass to velvet. "He just really could grow grass on cement," his daughter says. "My dad loved it. He'd say people had weeds because they didn't water enough. You water in the morning but never in the afternoon, and then you water again late at night."

Jim Conway never used fertilizer or weedkiller, his daughter says. He had a more effective method. "Some of the guys on the crew who would drink their lunch, he'd put them out in the hot sun digging up the weeds as punishment," she recalls. "They'd take out the weeds by hand, with a basket and a knife."

Jim Conway would keep an eye out for everyone, making sure the neighborhood kids who entered the park after the seventh inning didn't get into too much trouble.

"He got a job for everyone in the neighborhood," Alice Conway says—even the ne'er-do-wells, even the guy who slept on the job at the ballpark. "Mr. Conway would always wake him up at the stadium, and say, 'C'mon, Eddie, wake up, they're going to catch you.' He was real soft-hearted."

Too soft-hearted, his wife might have said. German-born Ella Echternkamp was Jim Conway's long-suffering spouse. When they first arrived in Detroit, they had a home on Pine Street, just north of Navin Field. It soon became a boardinghouse for wayward ball players. Many young Tiger players just arrived from the minor leagues had no place to stay, so Jim Conway would bring them home. They needed a lot of taking care of, and Ella Conway was their den mother.

"She always said they had never had shoes on before they put their baseball shoes on," says Alice Conway. The Conways would find shoes for them. "She had all this work to do, cooking and laundry for all these players. She used to get up at four in the morning and get all her work done, and walk over to the game in the afternoon.

"She knew more about baseball than almost anyone," her daughter-in-law laughs. "She knew everything about the game, what they did wrong, what they didn't do wrong, what this player was doing, what that player was doing."

Ella Conway and her two sons, Lefty and Jimmy, talked constantly about baseball at home. They would argue about strategy and discuss trades. Lefty and Jimmy eventually joined the grounds crew.

"We had the rehash of the games at the table," recalls Dorothy

Rivard. "I got so sick of it. And I had to go to all the games. When you're four or five years old, you don't want to go to the game every day. And I didn't like sitting in the box seats because I was always afraid I'd get hit by the ball."

She did like eating the hot dogs, though.

At age twelve, Rivard recalls, she was trying to learn how to ride her bike, but "my mother didn't want me to ride in the street, and the sidewalks were too narrow, so my uncle said I could come over and ride in the ballpark."

Early in the morning, before the players arrived, Dorothy would ride her bike around the diamond.

Her uncle acted as if he owned the place, and in fact it was his home. He lived at the park in a tiny room above the main gate on Trumbull. He was a confirmed bachelor, and something of a ladies' man. Ted Colias says women would sometimes show up at the ballpark with boxes tied in ribbons — cakes or other presents for the famous Neal Conway.

When his brother got sick, Jim Conway would bring him home too, much to his wife's consternation.

"I liked my Uncle Neal, but my mother ranted and raved about him," says Rivard. "My dad always felt he had to take care of him and protect him."

For all her trouble, Ella Conway didn't get much in return from the Tigers.

"She would say all she ever got was a lifetime pass to the ballpark, and their old carpeting," Alice Conway recalls. "Every time they changed the office, that old carpeting would end up in her house. And towels, too. She always had tons of towels. They were just plain white and they'd have 'Banner Laundry' on them."

The Conways eventually moved to a big house on Twelfth Street. On the back porch of their house was a huge trunk filled with mitts, balls, and bats that Tiger players no longer wanted.

"I don't think anyone in the neighborhood ever played baseball with just normal bats," recalls Rivard. "They were all from Charlie Gehringer or Hank Greenberg. They supplied the neighborhood."

"That trunk was always on their back porch," says Alice Conway. "It wasn't locked or anything. It was just sitting there for anyone who wanted to play ball. The kids would always return the equipment. They never had any trouble with anyone taking things."

When the neighborhood kids grew up, Jim Conway would recommend them for jobs at the ballpark. After World War II, team owner Walter Briggs stocked his grounds crew with returning veterans like Ted Colias and Dan Gaule, Alice Conway's brother. They say they were paid ten dollars a day when the Tigers played at home, twenty dollars for doubleheaders, but nothing when the team was on the road. Union dues were fifty cents a day. And Ted Colias customarily would lose another twenty-five cents each day to Neal Conway, betting on the day's attendance.

"He knew every seat in the house," remembers Colias. "Hell, he lived there! He knew every section. And boy, every day he'd just about hit it on the nose."

Most of the crew would get to the park at 6:00 A.M. to get the tarp off the field so the grass could get a full morning of sunshine. Then the grounds keepers would sweep peanut shells, hot dog wrappers and beer cups in the stands until about eleven, sometimes finding a nickel or two on the floor. After the game they would put the tarp back on the field.

"It was a very, very heavy canvas cover," says Colias. "The guys would be running, running, running to get enough air under it so it would start to ride along pretty easily. You needed young guys to do that.

"After the war they came in with a nylon cover they got from one of the B-52 bomber planes they built out at Willow Run and we tried that. We started running and we're pulling along and pretty soon the air got under it and we thought half of us were going to go up in the air with this thing."

During the games, the grounds keepers would sit in their small room under the stands on the third base side. Some played cards. Some watched the game. Some watched the ladies. Some had other things on their minds.

"In those days, some people brought in their whiskey bottles," says Dan Gaule. Old Jockey, a crew member who was an alcoholic, "used to check the crowd to see who was drinking, where all the whiskey was. After the game he'd go up there and finish off the bottles that they left under the seats."

In earlier days, the grounds crew would collect other souvenirs. Well into the 1930s it was the custom for fans to hurl their straw hats onto the field after a home run, a great catch, or a game-ending strikeout. The grounds crew would run onto the field, gather up the hats, take them under the stands, try them on, and keep any they liked. Occasionally they would give away the hats to needy people, or cut holes in them for horses to wear.

Under Briggs, the grounds crew treated the field as if it were the Queen of England's front lawn. Briggs wanted the diamond immaculate at all times.

"We had a hundred acres out in Birmingham or Bloomfield Hills that grew grass for just one purpose," recalls Walter Briggs III, the original owner's grandson. "If there was ever any bad grass in Briggs Stadium, we went out and got that sod and changed it."

Football games were especially rough on the field.

"We had to rebuild the infield every spring because the Lions tore it up so much," says Ted Colias. "We'd have to start around the first of March."

Briggs hated the way the Lions chewed up his grass. He also loathed the damage from occasional boxing or wrestling matches. Walter Briggs III remembers his grandfather's response after one big fight: "The next day when the grass was in such bad shape, he said: 'There will never be another fight here.' And that was the last fight at the ballpark."

Briggs valued the grounds crew's performance so much that members were timed on how fast they could cover the infield when rain interrupted a game, and the Tigers would brag that they were the fastest in the league. Briggs was proud of his system of drains placed under patches of grass around the outfield and of how fast the grounds crew could sweep the water off the field after a downpour.

"When there was a torrential rainstorm, within forty minutes you could play a ball game," says Walter Briggs III. "There was no question at the time: It was the finest baseball field ever."

And the men who took care of the diamond got to be near the game's biggest stars.

"This guy Gordon and I used to take the batting cage out," Colias recalls. "That was terrific. When it was time to take the cage out to center field, you'd wait and watch these guys taking their last licks in batting practice. It was really an experience to be that close to hitters like Ted Williams. He had the fastest hands I'd ever seen. It was like he would wait until the last possible second before he'd swing."

Other players were not so revered by the crew. Colias and Gaule had little affection for ballyhooed bonus baby and matinee idol Dick Wakefield, whom they considered a lousy outfielder.

"We put the warning track in there in 1946," Gaule recalls. "Red crushed brick. When we saw Wakefield try to play left field, we knew why we'd put that track in."

Some players had exact specifications they wanted the grounds keepers to follow. "Greenberg would want the area around first base hosed down pretty heavily," Colias says. "But George Kell wanted third base as dry as a bone. It didn't much matter. Neal'd just go his own way anyway with that hose."

Neal Conway was friends with many players. Hank Greenberg trusted him so much that he gave him his billfold during games rather than keep it in his locker, says Dan Gaule. At the end of each season, Greenberg would give the grounds crew a party.

The Tigers voted Neal a half-share of their World Series money, says Dorothy Rivard. The Conways' youngest brother, Robert, was the clubhouse man, and even he got a quarter-share. Jim Conway got none, his daughter recalls.

"Neal shared his share with my dad," says Rivard. "They didn't make that much money to begin with, so it was kind of a big deal."

Jim Conway was passed over because he was so unobtrusive, even though he would sit in the dugout before every game. It was his job to press the buzzer in the dugout that signaled to the players when the game was starting, Rivard says.

During World War II, Briggs decided to cut expenses. He told Jim and Neal Conway that only one of them could remain to supervise the grounds crew. Jim volunteered to take the job of night watchman "because he didn't like the public eye," his daughter says.

"We hated that," she recalls. "Dad would work at night and help Uncle Neal during the day. He would tell my uncle what sod to order, when to plant this, how to take care of that. He would turn on all the sprinklers for him."

On March 27, 1949, Jim Conway died. It left his younger brother at sea, Rivard recalls: "The day my dad was buried, it was snowing, a real heavy, wet snow. And my uncle Neal told me: 'Your dad would be upset to know that I forgot to put the cover on the field last night.' "

With Jim Conway gone, the grass at Michigan and Trumbull was a little less green.

"I was so disappointed the first time I went into that ballpark after my dad died," Rivard recalls. "I couldn't stand to look at the grass. It used to look like velvet and now it looked so terrible. I told my uncle and he said, 'I know, I know.' But he didn't know what to do about it. He just didn't have that touch."

19

Neal Conway died in 1952 at the Tigers' spring training camp in Lakeland, Florida — just a few weeks after the death of Walter Briggs. Jim's son Lefty took over as chief of the grounds crew but resigned in May 1954 and went on to work with other major league teams. Soon after that, Briggs's son sold the team.

Dorothy Rivard now lives in Birmingham, Michigan, and says she no longer hates baseball. "I really like it now, but I don't go to any games," she says. "And today when I look back on growing up, I guess it was really a pretty good time."

CHAPTER 3

WOODBRIDGE GROVE

> The encouragement of these games will prove of incalculable benefit to young men in many ways; it will tend to occupy their leisure time in healthy exercise, counteracting the growing tendency to visit saloons and other places of resort with which the city abounds, thus saving them from early immorality . . .
>
> —Detroit Free Press, *reporting on the first organized baseball game in Detroit*

In the early 1700s, Huron Indians camped and hunted in a dense forest along the ancient Sauk Trail on the western outskirts of the tiny French settlement of Fort Pontchartrain. Fur traders, trappers and hunters walked the trail, which reached nearly three hundred miles west to the settlement that later became known as Chicago.

The first owner of the land where Tiger Stadium now stands was Robert Navarre, a descendant of France's King Henry IV. In 1730 Navarre was invited to Fort Pontchartrain to run its civic affairs, and in 1747 the governor-general of Canada rewarded him with a "ribbon farm," a long, narrow tract of land extending from the Detroit River past the Sauk Trail, three miles inland.

Navarre died in 1791. His son, Francis, inherited part of the farm. Francis sold his part six years later to his cousin, Joseph Beaubien, who grew wheat, oats, and corn and had apple and peach orchards. A century later, those orchards would become the stomping grounds for the Georgia Peach.

In 1810 a British merchant, James May, bought the farm from Beaubien. May had brought the first U.S. troops to Detroit in 1796 aboard his schooner the *Swan*, and in 1803 he had become the first licensed ferry operator on the Detroit River.

After nine years of indifferent ownership, May sold the farm to William Woodbridge, a former Ohio state senator. President James Monroe had sent Woodbridge to Detroit after the War of 1812 to be secretary of the Michigan treasury. Woodbridge went on to have a long political career as a judge, state senator, governor, and U.S. senator.

During Woodbridge's political ascendancy Detroit was growing rapidly, thanks to the opening of the Erie Canal, which provided a path for commerce and migration from New England to the Great Lakes. In the 1820s Woodbridge supervised the construction of the Chicago Road along the route of the old Sauk Trail; it was renamed Michigan Avenue in the 1830s. In 1836 the eastern boundary of the Woodbridge farm became the western city limits of Detroit. The boundary road was named Trumbull Avenue after Woodbridge's father-in-law, John Trumbull, whose "McFingal" was the most famous American poem of its time. Another street in the area, Leverette, was named after one of Woodbridge's sons.

By the 1830s Irish immigrants had settled into the neighborhood south of Michigan Avenue, leasing lots from Woodbridge and other landowners. After the Irish potato famine of the 1840s, there was a huge influx of immigrants from County Cork. The neighborhood became known as Corktown.

With Woodbridge's permission, a heavily wooded area on his property at the northwest corner of Michigan and Trumbull became a popular public picnic grounds. Woodbridge Grove was filled with stately hardwood trees, plenty of berries for picnic desserts, and hazel and hickory nuts in autumn. The spot became so popular that Woodbridge in the 1850s hired a man named Captain Quigly to schedule picnics and to supervise and maintain the grove. It isn't known whether Quigly sold hot dogs at the park.

In 1855 Woodbridge deeded the grove to his nine-year-old granddaughter, Juliana Philinda Abbott. Woodbridge died in 1860, and two years later his granddaughter was committed to an asylum and Woodbridge's son, Dudley, became administrator of the grove.

In 1875 Dudley Woodbridge leased most of Woodbridge Grove to the City of Detroit. The city needed a spot on the western edge of town for a wood and hay market and dog pound, and officials signed a twenty-year lease on the property for five hundred dollars a year. The big trees were chopped down and the land cleared and paved with cobblestones. For the next two decades, farmers brought their lumber and hay to Michigan and Trumbull to weigh and sell it under city supervision. The place became known as Western Market.

Dudley Woodbridge leased the remainder of the grove to the DeWitt-Spaulding Lumber Company in 1882, and the firm built a planing mill on the property. Dudley also donated land on Michigan Avenue, directly across from the grove, to the city for Detroit's first zoo. The zoo sheltered exotic animals abandoned by circuses, but it did not make money and closed in 1884.

It is not known if a baseball was ever thrown in Woodbridge Grove. The game was popular in Detroit before the Civil War, so perhaps some picnickers played a game of catch among the trees.

Legend has it that the national pastime is a Yankee country game invented in a cow pasture in upstate New York. In fact, the Abner Doubleday story is a myth concocted in the early 1900s by baseball officials eager to give the game an American pedigree.

The truth is that baseball is a melting-pot stew first played in America's big cities. The game's true inventor is a New York bank teller named Alexander Cartwright, who adapted the rules of popular British ball games into a sport with nine players, four bases in a diamond shape, and three outs to an inning. The first organized game was played under Cartwright's supervision in 1845 in the Elysian Fields of Hoboken, New Jersey. Soon after, Cartwright began a long trek westward across the middle of the nation, dropping the seeds of his game like Johnny Appleseed on his way to San Francisco and finally Hawaii, where he lived out his life. It is likely that baseball was played in Honolulu before it was played in upstate New York.

The game soon spread beyond the towns Cartwright visited and by the late 1850s baseball had made its way to Detroit. The earliest known reference to baseball in Michigan is an announcement in the October 4, 1858, *Detroit Daily Tribune*:

> BASE BALL CLUB. — We understand that a base ball club is about to be organized in this city. The game as played in accordance with the rules and regulations adopted by the National Association of base ball players is a great improvement on the ordinary play of base ball. There are over ten thousand members of clubs, who belong to the Association and adopt their rules of play in the city of New York and vicinity. Those who have signed the subscription papers, and also all who are desirous of belonging to such a club, are requested to be at the store of Edward Orr,

146 Jefferson Avenue, tomorrow evening the 5th inst. at 8 P.M. for the purpose of organizing and electing officers."

By the next summer, the club had more than sixty members and met to practice at 4:00 P.M. every Monday, Wednesday and Friday in King's fairgrounds on the Cass Farm. That same year, another club was formed. They called themselves the Early Risers, for good reason. Their practices were Monday, Wednesday, and Friday on Campus Martius at 4:00 A.M. This club had about twenty members, mostly young people.

The Early Risers and the Detroit Base Ball Club played the first organized game in Detroit on August 8, 1859. The game was played at 2:30 P.M. on King's fairgrounds. An announcement in the *Detroit Free Press* said: "Ladies and gentlemen are invited. Seats will be provided for those desiring to sit down during the game."

A story about the game and a primitive box score, listing outs made and runs scored for each player, were printed in the *Free Press* on August 9. The score of the game was 59 to 21. The Detroit Club jumped out to a 28–4 lead after three innings and coasted after that. The *Free Press* went to great lengths to endorse the activity:

The encouragement of these games will prove of incalculable benefit to young men in many ways; it will tend to occupy their leisure time in healthy exercise, counteracting the growing tendency to visit saloons and other places of resort with which the city abounds, thus saving them from early immorality; it affords them, with the sport, the most wholesome and effective exercise, bringing into violent use every muscle of the body, and creating, of the puny, enervated boy, a robust, muscular, active, hearty man. The more such games are patronized, and the greater zest and spirit with which they are entered into, the better it will be for the young men of the city. Those who hang around the billiard saloons and liquor shops, constantly complaining of a lack of exercise and consequent loss of appetite, would do well to join one of the base ball clubs, and take regular exercise with them.

With such a blessing from the newspapers, baseball continued to grow in popularity after the Civil War. But Detroit was still a small town, and disdained professional sports. According to an article in the 1868 *Detroit Post*:

> The Detroit Club is mainly composed of young men of honorable connections for whom aptitude for business is a greater desideratum than unequalled skill at handling ball and bat. . . . We have always condemned the practice of purchasing the service of professional players. . . . Such men are drones on the community. . . . Those without noble aim in life ought not be tolerated in a thrifty community.

With such an attitude, it was no surprise that the city was not invited to play in the nation's first professional baseball league, the National Association, which formed in New York on March 17, 1871.

It was just as well. During the Association's six-year life, baseball acquired an unsavory reputation. Betting took place openly at the ballparks, players often being in on the action. Liquor was sold openly at games. The National League was launched in 1876 to outlaw such abuses and rehabilitate the game's image. But Detroit again was spurned.

In 1881 the Cincinnati Red Stockings folded and the National League went looking for a new franchise. Detroit's mayor, William G. Thompson, formed a team and was its first president, running the club from the mayor's office when not attending to city business. Known as the Wolverines, the team played at Recreation Park on the far northeast side of town near Brush and Brady, in what is now Detroit's Medical Center.

The park had wooden grandstands behind the plate but no set outfield fences. Fans standing or parking their buggies defined the limits of the playing field. When balls were hit out of the park, a man on a white horse would chase them down. The baselines were simply ruts worn by the players. The pitcher's box was fifty feet from home plate. The players could use bats that were flat on one side. Most did not wear gloves until the mid-1880s, and even then they were unpadded.

Detroit and the nation were experiencing big changes in the 1880s. The country was trying to cope with rapid industrialization and hordes of immigrants. Detroit was becoming a muscular manufacturing city: Stove factories, iron foundries and railroad car plants were springing up along the river, and labor unions were forming along with them. In the 1880s the city's population nearly doubled, from 116,340 to 205,876. Baseball was a unifier during the turmoil, attracting great interest among all classes of people.

The rules of the game were changing rapidly too. The number of balls required for a walk declined from eight in 1880 to seven in 1881, six in 1884, went back to seven in 1886, down to five in 1887, and finally reached four in 1889. In 1887 a strikeout required four strikes. And until 1887 the batter could call for a high or low pitch and the pitcher had to comply.

During its first two National League seasons Detroit played .500 ball, but in 1884 the club dropped to last with a dismal record of 28–84, fifty-six games behind champion Providence. The team was the laughingstock of the town. On September 6, 1883, the Wolverines gave up eighteen runs in the seventh inning of a game against the Chicago White Stockings—the biggest inning in major league history. Detroit lost the game, 26 to 6.

During the next season, the directors discussed disbanding the team, but Frederick Stearns, a former second baseman at the University of Michigan and a prominent pharmacist, bought the club. Late that season, the troubled Buffalo franchise wanted to unload its four star infielders—Hardy Richardson, Jack Rowe, Deacon White, and Big Dan Brouthers, a slugging first baseman who wore gloves on both hands and confused base runners by chattering at them constantly. Stearns outbid the other owners and for eight thousand dollars landed the foursome. In all, he spent a reported twenty-five thousand dollars acquiring players for Detroit. The newcomers joined established stars like Sam Thompson, Ned Hanlon (later to become manager of the famous 1890s Baltimore Orioles), and Charlie Bennett, the town's premier sports hero. Bennett was the first catcher to wear an inside chest protector and to crouch close behind the batter. In 1886 the revamped Wolverines finished a close second to the Chicago Cubs.

To tout his team for the 1887 season, Stearns advertised a new reserved grandstand for ladies at Recreation Park. He sold six hundred season tickets for twenty-five dollars, or about forty cents per game, out of an advance box office in a sporting goods store on Woodward Avenue. Interest mushroomed when the club won all thirty of its games on a spring-training barnstorming tour. About thirty-five hundred fans attended the home opener on May 5 and were entertained by a military band playing the music of Strauss and Verdi. The Wolverines won and charged off to a 19–2 record. The club excited so much interest that fans traveled to Detroit from around Michigan to see games. Lithographs of the players were sold and displayed all around town.

Detroit won the pennant with the aid of Thompson, who led the league in batting. Thompson was one of eleven players to finish with a batting average over .400 with the aid of a unique rule, in effect only that year, that counted walks as hits. After the season Stearns challenged the St. Louis Browns, champions of the American Association, to a fifteen-game World Series to be played in ten different cities. After threatening a strike, the players accepted three hundred dollars for games played after October 15, when their contracts expired, plus a hundred-dollar bonus for each player on the winning team. For the series, Stearns raised prices at Recreation Park to $1.00 for general admission and $1.50 for reserved seats.

Detroit won the series by the eleventh game. But the team owners wanted to make more money, so the games continued. The Wolverines and Browns returned to Detroit for the fourteenth game. Thousands turned out for a parade and banquet for both teams. The game was interrupted in the fourth inning by fans who presented Bennett with a wheelbarrow filled with 520 silver dollars and made him push it around the bases.

The next year, 1888, the Wolverines became the first team in the major leagues to issue rain checks. But the team plummeted to fifth place and Stearns, saddled with a lot of high-priced and underachieving ball players, auctioned the stars one by one for a total of forty-five thousand dollars. The franchise was transferred to Cleveland for the 1889 season.

In 1889 and 1890 Detroit fielded a minor league team in the International League, winning the pennant the first year and finishing second the next. But after the world championship of 1887, Detroit fans couldn't get excited about minor league ball, and the franchise folded. Detroit had no professional team the next four years except during a twenty-nine-game stint in the Northwestern League.

In 1894 Ban Johnson awarded Detroit a franchise in his new Western League. The club played in tiny Boulevard Park at Helen and Champlain (later Lafayette), on the city's eastern edge. In six years in the Western League, the team never finished higher than third.

Detroit's ball teams were variously known in the early years as the Detroits, the Wolverines, and the Creams, but an anonymous headline writer at the *Free Press* changed all that on April 16, 1895, when the paper printed a story titled STROUTHERS' TIGERS SHOWED UP VERY NICELY. By May, *Sporting Life* began using "Tigers" in its dispatches. The next year, manager George Stallings added brown-and-yellow striped stockings to the team's uniforms. The name stuck; newspapers also frequently used "Bengals" and "Jungaleers."

After the 1895 season the team's owner, George Arthur Van der

27

Beck, decided he wanted a bigger ballpark. At Michigan and Trumbull, the city's lease with Woodbridge had run out, and the authorities decided that they could handle the farmers' business at the Eastern Market on Gratiot. Van der Beck worked out a deal with Woodbridge to turn the old hay market into a pro diamond.

The location had a pedigree well suited to baseball. It had been an orchard, a farm, a popular picnic grounds, and then a place where city and country met. On this plot of ground, people had taken respite from the bustle of city life; later, they had exchanged goods and services.

Organized baseball combined many aspects of the previous incarnations of Michigan and Trumbull: diversion, play, commerce, and social interaction. A ballpark continued the heritage of a location that joined a city's conviviality with a rural tranquility. By the time pro baseball solidified that connection between masses of people and a patch of earth, Michigan and Trumbull had long been for Detroiters a common ground.

CHAPTER 4

BENNETT PARK

The wildcat denizens are again facing trouble. Patrolman George Green has filed a complaint with Chief of Police Downey that the wildcat spectators have been making it a practice to expectorate tobacco on those who pass through the alley while taking a short cut to the grounds.

— Detroit Journal, 1906

The old hay market at Michigan and Trumbull became a ballpark over the winter of 1895–96. Henry Ford was tinkering with engines, and Detroit was a slowly growing city of about 250,000 people. The main industry was the manufacture of stoves.

Tiger owner Van der Beck spent ten thousand dollars on his ballpark. Crews covered the cobblestones of the old hay market with a few inches of dirt and sod and built a wooden grandstand and a set of bleachers to accommodate about five thousand fans. It was a rush job, and it showed.

On Tuesday, April 28, 1896, the new park was christened. It had rained hard the day before, and the field was wet. Opening Day was clear and cool. The Detroit squad and the visiting Columbus Senators returned to town by train after a three-game series in Columbus. About 10:00 A.M., players from both teams boarded gaudily decorated trolley cars and led a parade through the streets.

Fans started arriving at the park about 1:00 P.M. Eventually an overflow crowd of eight thousand sat and stood inside the fences. The visitors got to the park at 3:00 P.M. and started to practice. At 3:15, the Detroit team took the field in new gray uniforms with maroon trim, including an Old English "D" on the jerseys.

At 3:30, the teams lined up along the baselines. Cannons boomed as

Wayne County Treasurer Alex McLeod threw out the ceremonial first pitch to Charlie Bennett, the catcher for Detroit's old National League franchise. Bennett had lost his legs in a freak accident in 1894, when he fell off a platform and under a train. Until his death in 1927, Bennett would catch the ceremonial first pitch every year at Michigan and Trumbull.

Detroit pitcher Jack Fifield threw the first official pitch of the first game at Michigan and Trumbull to the leadoff man for the Senators, left fielder Campbell. It didn't take long to establish a tradition of fan participation. In the bottom of the first inning Butler, the Columbus center fielder, was chasing a long fly ball off the bat of George Stallings when he collided with a spectator who was crossing the field. Both lay stunned as Stallings circled the bases. Butler was unconscious for five minutes and left the game.

Detroit went on to rout the visitors 17 to 2. Fifield helped his own cause with a home run and would have had a second had the Columbus third baseman not tripped him rounding third.

The ballpark, at first called the Haymarket or Woodbridge Grove, soon came to be named for Bennett. Bennett Park was a ramshackle place with a playing field that resembled Abner Doubleday's cow pasture of legend. In his haste to build the park, Van der Beck had not brought in enough dirt to bury the old hay market pavement. Grounds keepers raked the infield only once a week. Infielders who muffed grounders could blame the cobblestones poking up through the dirt. The seam between the infield dirt and the grass was more like a ledge. The outfield grass was full of holes and soft spots. The drainage was so poor that the outfield turned marshy after even light rains.

Batters had reason to complain too. Home plate was near what is now Tiger Stadium's right-field corner. Games started at 3:30, and the late afternoon sun, sinking above the houses along National Avenue, glared in the batters' eyes.

Nor were the accommodations for the fans any great shakes. There was an L-shaped wooden grandstand with an unusual peaked roof behind the third-base line and home plate, and a set of bleachers along the first-base line. The ticket office and main entrance were at Michigan and Trumbull. There was a carriage yard between the left-field grandstand and the fence along Michigan.

The place was like wooden ballparks that had sprung up in many other cities. William Cammeyer invented the baseball park when he opened Brooklyn's Union Grounds in 1862; in the winter it was a skating rink. At these and other parks, dimensions were dictated by the location. Chicago's Lake Front Park, home of the White Stockings between 1878 and 1884, was so close to Lake Michigan that the left-field corner was only 180 feet from home plate and the center-field fence just 300 feet away. At Boston's Huntington Avenue Grounds, by contrast, it was 440 feet to left and 635 to center.

Bennett Park occupied roughly half the acreage of today's Tiger Stadium. A lumber mill stood beyond the right-field fence. The home team's clubhouse was in deep center field; the visitors had no clubhouse. The distances were about 300 feet down the left-field line, 400 feet to center, and 360 feet to the right-field corner.

Men wore black and dark gray suits to the games, and ladies wore full-length dresses and colorful bonnets. Baseball was trying to overcome its unsavory reputation, and Ladies Days were soon instituted to encourage women to attend.

Fire was the big worry at the old wooden parks. In 1894 a blaze broke out during a game in Boston and destroyed the South End Grounds. Other parks in Baltimore, Chicago, and Washington also burned, and in 1911 a fire destroyed almost all of New York's Polo Grounds.

Bennett Park managed to escape fire, but there were plenty of other dangers from weak floors and jury-rigged platforms — and those were in the stadium itself. Outside the park's walls, fans assumed even more precarious perches.

The left-field fence ran along an alley behind the houses on the east side of National. Property owners soon realized that their backyards offered a bird's-eye view of ball games, so they built tall, rickety wooden stands and sold seats for five to fifty cents. Other such stands sometimes were thrown up behind houses on Cherry Street near the lumber mill.

These "wildcat bleachers" attracted a rowdy element, or so the club argued. Fans making their way down the alley to seats inside the park often were subjected to verbal abuse or worse. Over the years, club officials tried various legal tactics to defeat the wildcatters. But the property owners always won in court and the stands would reappear.

The *Detroit Journal* in 1906 told a common tale:

> The wildcat denizens are again facing trouble. Patrolman George Green has filed a complaint with Chief of Police Downey that the wildcat

spectators have been making it a practice to expectorate tobacco on those who pass through the alley while taking a short cut to the grounds.

To substantiate his story, the officer exhibited his uniform, which was covered with tobacco spots and stains. Other people have also complained. It is also alleged that the stands are weakly constructed affairs and threaten life and limb.

From time to time, Tiger management strung strips of canvas atop the outfield fences, creating the first obstructed view seats at Michigan and Trumbull. From behind the canvas ribbons, the common folk in the cheap seats would hurl obscenities and vegetables at players.

Authorities considered baseball too disreputable for the Sabbath, in large part because many of the players and fans were Irish, the stigmatized ethnic group of the era. Until 1910 Sunday baseball was banned in Detroit, and the Tigers played Sunday games at Burns Park, just outside the western city limits in Springwells Township, near the stockyards on Dix Avenue between Livernois and Waterman. The park was named after James D. Burns, Wayne County sheriff and prominent hotel owner, who was the club's president at the turn of the century.

In 1900 Ban Johnson turned his Western League into the American League, and Detroit retained its franchise. On April 20 the Tigers made their American League debut. The players, wearing new white uniforms trimmed with black, rode to the park in a horse-drawn carriage. Then, before five thousand fans, they were held hitless by a Buffalo left-hander named Doc Amole, a former National Leaguer with a lifetime record of 4–10. The *Free Press* wailed that it was "impossible to imagine anything more harrowing than the calamity that befell the Tigers." Despite the awful start, the Tigers drew about 146,000 fans that season, third-best in the eight-team American League.

In 1901 Johnson's upstart league was admitted to the majors. To prepare for Detroit's reentry into the big leagues, Tiger management put up long, shallow bleachers in right and left field, expanding the capacity of Bennett Park to about eighty-five hundred. But the park was still the smallest in the major leagues. By Opening Day, the iron supports for the roof had not arrived, and the park remained unfinished.

It was a red-letter day nonetheless. After thirteen years without a major league ball club, Detroit finally was getting a chance to prove that it belonged back in the bigs. Its population was 285,704, smaller than nine of the other eleven big league cities.

Detroit went all out for the inaugural. Thousands of citizens lined up behind the mayor and other dignitaries, a marching band, and the players from both ball clubs and paraded through the streets to the ballpark. Although recently expanded, Bennett Park wasn't big enough to hold the crowd. Policemen spent all day trying to apprehend the many fans who tried to climb over or scramble under the wooden fences. The attendance was figured at 10,023. About a thousand patrons had to be placed in the outfield behind ropes. Balls landing behind the ropes were ruled doubles.

In the bottom of the ninth inning, the Tigers trailed Milwaukee, 13–4, thanks to seven Tiger errors. Fans were leaving on bicycles and in buggies. But the team wasn't about to give up.

Captain Doc Casey led off with a double into the standees. Jimmy Barrett beat out an infield hit. Kid Gleason lined a single to center. The standees grew excited and surged toward the infield. Ducky Holmes, Pop Dillon, and Kid Elberfeld all hit doubles into the crowd. The six consecutive hits brought in five runs to make the score 13–9 with no outs.

Along Michigan, people turned around their carriages and bicycles and streamed back toward the field. Milwaukee's manager, Hugh Duffy, playing center field, came in to pull his pitcher, Pete Dowling, and to complain to the umpire about crowd interference.

With the crowd screaming, reliever Bert Husting retired Doc Nance on a grounder to short. Fritz Buelow drew a walk, and Emil Frisk followed with a single, scoring Elberfeld. Casey then laid down a beautiful bunt, loading the bases. Barrett was called out on strikes. A hush fell. It was all up to Gleason.

Gleason bunted to third and reached base on an error, scoring another run. Holmes beat out an infield hit, scoring Frisk to make it 13–12. With the bases loaded, Dillon stepped up. The game was halted as policemen tried to push back the outfield throng. The din drowned out the umpire's voice.

With the count 2–2, Dillon lifted a fly ball down the left-field line. The ball fell in among the crowd, fair by just a few feet. The game was over. The Tigers had won, 14–13.

Pandemonium broke out. Men tossed their bowlers onto the field. The crowd mobbed the team and hoisted the players in the air. Thousands waved their hats and coats and tooted horns. Shopkeepers rang bells. The Tigers, in their first major league game at Michigan and

33

Trumbull, had staged the greatest rally in baseball history, with the help of their enthusiastic fans.

The next day the Tigers scored two runs in the eighth inning and two in the ninth to win 6–5. In the third game, they scored five in the eighth to win 13–9. In the series finale, the Tigers scored three in the eighth and four in the ninth to win 12–11, and again Milwaukee protested that the outfield crowd had interfered with the game, again to no avail.

The Tigers left town, having won every game in their last at-bat. The series drew 35,030 fans and propelled the team to a 14–4 start. When the Tigers returned on Decoration Day, 12,106 fans showed up, thousands more were turned away, and 1,500 watched from the wildcat stands.

Detroit eventually fell out of contention, but interest remained high. In the season's final game, played at Burns Park on September 15, Detroit won 21–0, and Cleveland fled town on a train after seven innings. The Tigers finished third, drawing 280,184 people. Burns made an estimated profit of thirty-five thousand dollars.

But Ban Johnson, tired of the constant bickering between Burns and manager George Stallings, banished both from the league and assigned the club to insurance agent Samuel Angus, who brought with him his bookkeeper, Frank Navin. Navin had attended law school but was more interested in horse racing and in shrewdly buying up stock in the franchise.

In 1902 a new clubhouse was built at Bennett Park and the reserved boxes were relocated to the back of the grandstand. The Tigers performed poorly and attendance declined so rapidly that Johnson wanted to shift the franchise to Pittsburgh. But a January 1903 peace pact between the American and National leagues specified that Johnson could place a team in New York only if he stayed out of Pittsburgh, which already had a National League team. So the Yankee franchise was born and the Tigers stayed in Detroit. But the team did not improve much in the standings or at the box office.

One of Angus's railroads was facing bankruptcy, so he sold his interest in the Tigers after the 1903 season for $50,000 to William H. Yawkey, who had just inherited $10 million from his father, lumber baron William Clyman Yawkey, the richest man in Michigan. According to historian Malcolm W. Bingay, Navin won $5,000 from Yawkey in an all-night poker game and the next day swung a deal that made him co-owner. Yawkey, who was a world traveler and something of a playboy, turned over day-to-day operations of the club to Navin.

Yawkey's nephew, Thomas A. Yawkey, later owned the Boston Red Sox.

Navin ordered some belt-tightening. He made players pay for their uniforms; too many had been stealing them. He took a hard line on player contracts and began to sell space on outfield fences for advertising billboards. Though some players claimed the ads distracted their batting eye, Navin sold more space as the years went by. The Stroh brewery sign got a prominent spot next to the scoreboard, and the Bull Durham sign in right center field became a popular target for sluggers.

Navin excelled as a business manager but was a poor judge of baseball talent. In an August 16, 1904, letter to manager Ed Barrow, Navin opined: "I have heard so many conflicting stories about Schaefer that I am somewhat dubious regarding him . . . so want to keep O'Leary for shortstop." Despite Navin's advice the Tigers did acquire Germany Schaefer, who became one of the club's most popular players. Navin later ignored the advice of a friend of Yawkey and declined to sign a pitcher named Walter Johnson. He also sold Carl Hubbell to the Giants after Hubbell spent three years in the Tigers' farm system. Johnson and Hubbell both went on to Hall of Fame careers.

In 1905 Navin almost made his biggest blunder. That year, the Tigers suffered their fourth straight losing season. Late in the season, the Tigers were to select a player off the roster of the Augusta, Georgia, minor league club as part of a previous deal. Navin wanted Clyde Engle to be the payoff player, but manager Bill Armour prevailed on him to draft a skinny eighteen-year-old named Ty Cobb. To justify his selection, Armour had to give Cobb regular playing time. Engle would go on to compile 748 hits in the major leagues, 3,443 fewer than Cobb.

Despite Cobb's arrival, the Tigers did so poorly at the gate that the Cleveland franchise waged a campaign to have Detroit thrown out of the league. The effort failed when it became clear that Cleveland's motives were to grab Detroit for a farm club.

The franchise hit bottom in 1906; it was another losing season and there were only 174,043 patrons, less than half the league average. The highlight of the season was a mammoth home run by Sam Crawford on April 29 that cleared the lumber mill in right field and bounded into a yard on the north side of Cherry Street. Estimated to be five hundred feet, it was the longest ball ever hit at Bennett Park.

It was time for drastic changes to keep the franchise afloat. In 1907 Yawkey and Navin bought property along Cherry Street, razed the lumber mill, and moved the fences back to create more room for fans.

The club also hired Hughie Jennings, a former star shortstop in the National League, to manage the team. Jennings had a law degree from Cornell, but on the field he acted like a yahoo. He jumped up and down in the third base coach's box and brayed "eee-yah!" like a mule. He also ate grass, mimicked the opposing pitchers' windups, and invented the two-fingers-in-the-mouth whistle when an umpire ruled that he couldn't use a tin whistle in the coach's box. Crowds loved Jennings, Crawford, and Cobb, but their favorite was Germany Schaefer.

Schaefer was baseball's first clown prince. He once stole second base at Bennett Park and then stole first on the next pitch to rattle the pitcher. His antics prompted a new rule against running the bases backward to make a travesty of the game. During a rain delay at Bennett Park, Schaefer trotted out to his position wearing hip boots, a raincoat, and a rubber hat borrowed from a grounds keeper. At another rainy game, he carried an umbrella to home plate.

The Tigers were contenders for the first time in 1907. With the team in a wild four-team pennant race, attendance soared. Detroit caught pennant fever. Stores sported colorful bunting. Citizens wore Hughie Jennings Fan Club buttons and blew tin whistles. Boys and girls paraded through the streets with torches. On August 12 a record crowd of 11,500 saw future Hall of Famer Rube Waddell and the Philadelphia Athletics beat the Tigers 7–3.

Cobb won his first batting title with a .350 average. The Tigers won the pennant over the Athletics by a game and a half, but were swept by the powerful Chicago Cubs in the World Series. Temporary bleachers set up around the outfield sat half-empty, to the club's embarrassment. Only 7,370 showed up to see the Tigers lose the last game.

Yawkey was discouraged by the paltry attendance and sat by as Navin gradually bought up stock. The owners enlarged Bennett Park for 1908 to a capacity of over 10,000. A new record crowd of 14,051 showed up for Opening Day. In another close race, the Tigers again prevailed. Attendance reached 436,199, a 250 percent increase in two years. Only Chicago and St. Louis drew more fans. Detroit at last was proving itself a big-league town.

The Tigers lost the World Series to the Cubs again, four games to one. The last game, played in Detroit, was the shortest in World Series history (an hour and twenty-five minutes) and drew the smallest crowd, only 6,210 fans.

In 1909 Ty Cobb won the only Triple Crown in Tiger history, and the Tigers won a third straight pennant. For the first time since 1901, Detroit's attendance exceeded the league average. This time, the Tigers faced Pittsburgh in the Series, which was billed as a battle between Cobb and National League batting champion Honus Wagner. A record crowd of 18,277 saw the third game, but Wagner and the Pirates won the series in seven games.

Navin again expanded Bennett Park for 1910, adding three thousand more seats. There were now three covered grandstands, one behind the infield and two smaller ones down the foul lines. A small set of uncovered bleachers nestled in the right-field corner near Trumbull and Cherry. Reserved seats at the renovated park cost one dollar.

In 1910 Navin built a tunnel under the grandstands from the dugout to the team clubhouse so that pitchers removed from the game would no longer have to walk in front of the fans on what had been known as the "path of sighs." Also that year, the Tigers started playing Sunday games at Michigan and Trumbull.

After the season, Navin announced plans to build grandstands in right field to increase the park's capacity to 15,000. But the plans were shelved because property owners along Cherry asked exorbitant prices for their land. There were now permanent bleacher sections in right and left field, but the park was still too small for big league ball.

Opening Day 1911 was postponed because of a blizzard. One local columnist wrote jokingly that someday the Tigers would play in a domed stadium to keep out the elements. The club started out with a 21–2 record but then slumped and fell out of first place in August. Jennings banned his players from seeing movies because he thought they were bad for the eyes and destroyed players' ability to judge a ball in motion.

There was no further way to expand Bennett Park. Detroit was ready for something grander. In a few years, Henry Ford's horseless carriage had transformed the city into the bustling hub of the booming automobile industry. Its baseball club also had been transformed, from a sorry also-ran to a perennial contender led by the game's biggest attraction, Cobb.

Around the majors, cities were replacing their nineteenth-century wooden ball yards with huge concrete-and-steel parks to accommodate a tremendous upsurge of interest in baseball. Philadelphia's $500,000 Shibe Park opened in 1909 and set an impressive new standard, with its French Renaissance dome at the entrance, grandstand seating for twenty thousand, and bleachers down both foul lines. Later that year, on June 30, Pittsburgh's luxurious Forbes Field opened. It had elevators, telephones, maids in the women's rest rooms, lighting in the grandstands, and ramps to the upper decks.

St. Louis's Sportsman's Park also opened in 1909. Comiskey Park opened in Chicago in 1910, and New York's new Polo Grounds in 1911. Cincinnati's Crosley Field and Boston's Fenway Park were set to open in 1912. Ebbets Field in Brooklyn would debut in 1913, and Wrigley Field in Chicago in 1914 as Weeghman Park.

After the 1911 season, Navin decided he could no longer tinker with Bennett Park. He decided to build a modern concrete-and-steel park like those being built in other cities.

CHAPTER 5

NAVIN FIELD

In those days they didn't have a phalanx of guards keeping you from going on the field. When the last out was made, everybody jumped over the box seats and walked across the field. You'd practice sliding into second base. Can you imagine that happening today? You put a foot on the field, you're thrown in the pokey.

— Tiger fan Don Shapiro

Navin hired Osborn Engineering Company of Cleveland, the foremost ballpark builders of the day. Over the winter of 1911–12 the general contractor, Hunkin and Conkey of Cleveland, erected a great horseshoe of concrete and steel extending about two hundred feet down each foul line. To create more room, the houses on the east side of National were leveled—the final defeat for the operators of the wildcat stands. Home plate was moved to the Michigan and National corner, leaving only the right fielder to battle the sun. Beyond the grandstand covered pavilions extended to the outfield corners.

The new park, which cost Navin $300,000, could hold more than 23,000 fans. The dimensions were 340 feet down the line in left, 400 to center, and 365 to the right-field corner.

The opener was scheduled for Thursday, April 18, but rain forced a postponement. Navin decided not to tempt bad luck by dedicating his new park on a Friday, so he waited until Saturday, April 20—the same day Boston was christening Fenway Park.

Saturday was sunny, hazy, and chilly. Civic dignitaries paraded to the park with the Tigers and the visiting Cleveland team, a marching band, and thousands of enthusiastic fans. A crowd estimated to be close to 26,000 jammed into the gleaming new stadium. Thousands stood in the outfield behind ropes. Others jammed into temporary "circus" bleachers beyond the right-field fence. The official paid attendance was 24,382.

According to sports writer E. A. Batchelor of the *Free Press*, "the assemblage was just as enthusiastic as it was big."

The crowd saw yellow grandstand seats and gray fences, a common color scheme for parks of the era. In left field loomed a big scoreboard with space for out-of-town scores. A large green panel in dead center field provided background for hitters, an innovation decades ahead of other parks. The other outfield walls sported the usual advertising billboards.

Paul Hale Bruske, in *Sporting Life* of April 27, described the dedication of Navin Field as a turning point in the history of Detroit:

> Detroit and its Tigers have just celebrated the most momentous occasion in the history of Michigan base ball. The opening of the new Navin Park [*sic*] can be described in no other way. For the first time in history, Detroit has a ballyard worthy of its rank among the cities. . . .
>
> Not one of the spectators, of all the thousands, failed to secure an excellent view of the entire game. The great horseshoe of cement and steel which forms the seating arrangement, was complete in every detail. Comfortable seats, with more than the usual allowance of room, were added sources of enjoyment. . . .
>
> All three of the outfields permit a wideness of range which is sure to result in some displays of ground-covering that will delight the crowds.

At 3:00 P.M. Charlie Bennett caught the ceremonial first pitch. In the bottom of the first inning, Ty Cobb stole home to score the first Tiger run in the new park. Later he stole another base and made two expert catches in center field as the Tigers won in eleven innings, 6–5. According to Batchelor, Cobb "put on the whole show" and besides his hits "failed by a very small margin in an attempt to perform his favorite stunt of scoring from second on an infield out."

The stadium was the real star, though. Bruske gushed:

> The most remarkable demonstration of all . . . occurred at the end of the game, when 25,000 persons walked, comfortably and without interruption, out of the elaborately planned series of exits, and the field was virtually emptied in ten minutes. . . .
>
> I believe the dominant impression we all carried away from the opening game was that of the majestic strength of the entire Navin Field

construction—an impression carried not only in the stands, but also in the solid cement and steel wall which surrounds the playing field.

Many fans wanted to keep the name Bennett Park, but the city council authorized the name to be changed to Navin Field. Its many good seats, large rest rooms, and concession stands quickly made Navin Field into a favorite of fans. The scoreboard was an instant hit. "Scores of all the American League games are posted in so conspicuous a manner that they can be read from any portion of the park," reported the *Free Press*.

The spacious field was a perfect showcase for the speedy Cobb, who was the game's biggest and most controversial star. The park was tailored to his talents. Grounds keepers kept the area in front of home plate well soaked to slow Cobb's bunts and make fielders slip. The quagmire became known as "Cobb's Lake."

The meanest man in baseball and the most feared base runner of his day, Cobb was hated by opposing players and even some teammates. He loved to play hard, and he cheated. On first base, he would kick the bag a few inches closer to second when the umpire wasn't looking. He always went in to a base with spikes high.

"He'd deliberately spike a man if at all possible," recalled Bill Stevens, a Tiger fan born in 1899, in a reminiscence recorded in 1988 at his home in Cheboygan, Michigan. "As a baseball player, he was the best that ever lived. As a human being, I have no respect for him at all."

Detroit fans loved Cobb's daring exploits on the basepaths. During Cobb's heyday, the local papers called the team the "Tygers."

Fans sometimes took after their hero. One of the wildest fan riots in history took place at Navin Field on a Sunday late in 1915 after Tiger third baseman George Moriarty was called out trying to steal home to end a game lost to Boston 3–2. As the umpire waved Moriarty out, Boston's catcher-manager, Bill Carrigan, spat a mouthful of tobacco juice in Moriarty's face. Moriarty jumped up and punched Carrigan in the face. The crowd spilled onto the field, and the players fought into the visitors' clubhouse. Carrigan got inside and locked the door.

For hours a lynch mob of Tiger fans waited outside, brandishing clubs, rocks, and ropes, deaf to the pleas of Navin to disperse. Finally a maintenance man dressed Carrigan in an old hat, rubber boots, and a raggedy coat, smeared his face with mud, and stuck a rake in his hand.

In this disguise, Carrigan walked out the clubhouse door and through the crowd.

World War I didn't diminish Detroit's growing interest in baseball. In those days, Stevens recalled, most people took streetcars to the park, and dozens of trolleys lined up on Trumbull after games. After the war, Detroit's auto industry went into high gear. Henry Ford's five-dollar day swelled the city's population from 466,000 in 1910 to 994,000 in 1920. Crowds at the park grew so large that many poor people on High Street (later Vernor Avenue) tore down their shacks, rented the empty lots for parking, and took rooms elsewhere. The lots charged fifty cents a car and seventy-five cents for doubleheaders, said Stevens.

The games were much quicker and looser than today. Batters didn't step out of the box and pitchers didn't walk around the mound between pitches.

At least, most pitchers didn't. The Washington Senators in 1919 had two pitchers, Al Schacht and Nick Altrock, who had learned baseball clowning from Germany Schaefer. Once, Stevens recalled, Altrock was pitching at Navin Field when an airplane flew overhead. Altrock stepped off the mound and, with exaggerated motions, followed the flight of the plane for several minutes. The umpires didn't interfere because the crowd was laughing.

Stevens also recalled a day at Navin Field when it rained so much that a pool developed on the tarp around the pitcher's mound. Altrock came out with a fishing pole and pretended to cast a line. Not to be outdone, Schacht charged out and dived into the water.

If legend is correct, in 1919 an automobile executive named Walter O. Briggs tried but failed to get a ticket to a sellout at Navin Field. As a young man, Briggs often sneaked into the grandstands at Bennett Park because he didn't have money for a ticket. Now he had the money, and he still couldn't get in.

According to Briggs's great-grandson, Walter O. Briggs IV, "He came to Navin the next year and said: 'You need some help because you need some ball players and I've got some money. And I want to guarantee that I can get into the game.' "

Detroit historian Malcolm W. Bingay told a different story. According to Bingay, Briggs couldn't get a ticket for the 1907 World Series and vowed then to buy the club when he made his first million.

Navin had become a baseball legend, the most astute owner in the game. Presidents of both leagues relied on him for advice, as did

Commissioner Kenesaw Mountain Landis, a thunderous foe of horse racing. Yet Navin remained an unreformed gambler who bet daily at least a thousand dollars on each race. Navin decided it would be good public policy to have co-owners, so in 1920 he sold twenty-five percent of the club's stock to Briggs and another twenty-five percent to John Kelsey, an automobile wheel manufacturer. Each new owner spent $250,000 on the deal. But Navin continued to run the show. Kelsey had business cards printed that read DON'T ASK ME, ASK NAVIN. HE'S RUNNING THE CLUB.

In 1921 Cobb took over from Jennings and continued as player-manager through 1926. The qualities that made Cobb a great player — his hell-bent drive, his perfectionism, his individualism — made him a poor manager. He pitilessly berated his teammates' shortcomings and destroyed their confidence. Stevens remembered a game when a Tiger player struck out and Cobb followed him all the way out to left field, gesturing to illustrate how high the last strike had been. Cobb once told a reporter that the hardest part of being a player-manager was "to stand out there in the outfield and watch my pitcher throw the wrong ball to the batter. I have coached him for that hitter over and over, but I can't throw it for him."

Outfielder Harry Heilmann supplanted Cobb as a perennial batting champion, winning titles in 1921, 1923, 1925, and 1927. But under Cobb, the talented Tigers were sullen and nervous and never in contention. The 1921 team had a .316 batting average but finished sixth.

As manager, Cobb continued to play every angle. When the Yankees or another slugging team came to town, he would have the grounds crew install temporary outfield bleachers to turn long drives into ground rule doubles.

In those days, fans threw straw hats onto the field after a victory. Cobb would order the grounds keepers to collect the hats and ship them to Augusta, Georgia, Cobb's home town, where the Tigers trained. The penny-pinching Cobb would use the hats the following spring to pay off laborers around the Augusta ballpark.

After the 1922 season Navin had the grandstand at Navin Field double-decked, swelling the capacity to about 30,000, and built a press box on the roof behind home plate. The press box was cramped and perilous and soon became hated by writers.

Ed Burns of the *Chicago Tribune* described it this way:

It is impossible to see the plate, batsman, catcher, or umpire-in-chief from the third-deck press box unless an author hangs out into space. The home scribblers have overcome acrophobia, but there are few steeple-jacks among the visiting scribes. As a result, many have to get news of what happens between the pitchers' mound and the screen by picking up rumors or looking at the text of the home steeplejacks.

The season opener in 1923 was delayed eight days for completion of the new stands. Fans camped out all night in snow and rain to get tickets. Temporary bleachers were put up around the outfield, and a record 36,000 fans turned out. Mayor James Couzens threw out the first ball to Charlie Bennett.

"Detroit is simply baseball crazy and if the team comes through, the newly enlarged stands . . . will not be adequate to care for the crowds on a big day," reported the *Sporting News* on April 19, 1923.

In 1924 the Tigers for the first time drew over a million fans. On May 13, over 40,000 crammed into Navin Field to see Hooks Dauss beat the Yankees. The city was exploding with people working in the auto plants, and baseball was their favorite recreation. The exploits of Babe Ruth had taken the game to new heights of popularity.

Ruth's rise and the introduction of a livelier ball meant the eclipse of Cobb's slap-and-run style. Cobb hated the Babe. When Ruth was at bat, Cobb would run in from center field to tell his pitcher what to throw him, then run back out, only to watch a long drive sail over his head.

In a game in June 1924 at Navin Field, the rivalry between the game's two greatest players exploded. When the Tigers' Bert "King" Cole hit the Yankees' Bob Meusel with a pitch, both benches emptied and Cobb and Ruth rolled in the dirt at home plate. Some of the fans tore seats from their concrete moorings and threw them on the field. About a thousand patrons joined in the brawl, which lasted thirty minutes. The game was forfeited to New York.

On August 3, the Tigers faced the Yankees again and another huge crowd came out. Just before game time, Navin entered to find the stands packed and fans all over the field. Policemen on foot and horse-back were summoned to get fans back far enough in the outfield to play the game. The attendance was a record 42,712.

Late in the 1924 season, a second baseman named Charlie Gehringer joined the club. Gehringer, known as "The Mechanical Man" for his smooth fielding, would play nineteen seasons for the Tigers and end up in the Hall of Fame.

On June 8, 1926, Ruth smacked a legendary home run over the twelve-foot wall in right center field. The ball landed on the other side of Trumbull, skimmed over several parked cars, and rolled down Cherry Street. A boy on a bicycle caught up to it at Brooklyn Avenue, two blocks from the ballpark. The New York papers the next day pegged the homer's distance at 626 feet. *Detroit News* baseball writer Harry G. Salsinger figured the ball rolled to a distance of 885 feet. Ruth's blast is generally regarded as the longest home run in major league history.

In stark contrast to Cobb, Ruth had a big heart. Bill Stevens told of taking his son, a big fan of Ruth, to a game at Navin Field. The bleachers sold out as they stood in line. The boy started to cry.

"I was kneeling down beside him and consoling him," said Stevens. "A gruff voice behind us said, 'What's the matter, Bub?'

"My son said, 'We can't get any tickets, because my daddy got here too late.'

"And the voice said, 'Who the hell says you need tickets?'

"And the boy looked up and said, 'Y-y-you're Babe Ruth!'

"He said, 'That's right, kid. You don't need any tickets. Your pop don't need a ticket. You come in with me.'

"He took us through the players' gate. Ruth carried a supply of Yankee uniforms in kids' sizes. And he told the clubhouse boy, 'Fit this boy with a suit.' I thought he was going to sit us in the grandstands somewhere, but we sat on the Yankee bench. And he gave my son a ball autographed by every member of the Yankee team. He treasured that for a long time.

"Ruth's first time up he said to my son: 'I'm gonna hit this one for you, Bub.' Ruth put the ball into the bleachers out in center field."

In 1927 Briggs bought Kelsey's stock and became half-owner of the team but remained in the background. With Cobb gone, the Tigers' decline deepened. In 1928 the team skidded to sixth place with a 68–86 record, thirty-three games out of first. Attendance fell to 434,056, the lowest since the war year of 1918. On September 24, the Tigers played before 404 fans at Navin Field — the smallest home crowd in team history.

That year was the first of six consecutive second-division finishes.

With the onset of the Great Depression, attendance plummeted from 869,318 in 1930 to 320,972 in 1933.

For fans the game and the players were much more accessible than today, even if then to a young boy they seemed larger than life.

"One thing I remember vividly," says Don Shapiro, a retired dentist now living in West Bloomfield Township, Michigan, "is getting on my bike — the gang I ran with only had one bike between us, so one of us was always sitting on the handlebars — and all the ball players, for some reason, lived mostly on Boston Boulevard and Chicago Boulevard, between Linwood and Dexter. They lived very modestly, in small apartments. They'd rent them for the summer, because they didn't live here during the winter. Some of them did. Charlie Gehringer had a gas station on Davison. I remember how many times I used to go by his gas station hoping to catch a glimpse of Gehringer.

"We would get on our bicycle, and we would go into each apartment house, and look up the names next to the bells. In those days, they didn't hide. Eldon Auker would have 'E. Auker.' We'd ring the bell, and we'd go up and knock on the door, and they'd answer the door, and we'd get their autograph. That was really exciting, to see them come to the door. Of course, without television in those days, the only image we had of them was newspaper images, and seeing them as small figures out on the field. To be next to them when they answered the door was a thrill that is indescribable. It was breathtaking!"

When Shapiro was twelve, he had an experience he cherishes to this day. "Jack Burns, who took over when Hank Greenberg hurt his wrist, had a son who was a little younger than we were, me and my friend," he says. "The day we knocked on his door it was six-thirty or seven o'clock, and he had just finished dinner. He asked if we wanted to go out and play catch with him and his son. God! Don't ask!

"I can see it vividly now. He took us out into the parking lot, and I remember there were overgrown weeds and stuff behind the apartment. And they began throwing a ball — they had an extra mitt for me — and he threw a ball to me, and of course I wanted to look real good. It was out of my reach, and I dove for it. Broken bottles, everything be damned. I dove for it, and I cut my thumb. I still have the little scar here.

"I began bleeding. He was so concerned — very nice man, as I remember. I waved him off; I didn't want a moment lost out of this magical moment. And I played, and I bled into the glove. It was just a wonderful, wonderful time."

Fans also could get close to the players at Navin Field. When big crowds were expected, circus bleachers were wheeled into place behind the outfield walls. During the 1933 season a twenty-foot-high screen, mounted on wheels, was placed atop the left field fence to thwart Philadelphia Athletics slugger Jimmy Foxx. Philadelphia writers called it the "Jimmy Foxx Spite Fence." It worked so well that Foxx hit only two homers that year in Navin Field.

After 1933 Navin went shopping for a new manager to replace Bucky Harris. Navin offered the job to Babe Ruth, who declined. Navin then turned to Philadelphia, where the Athletics' manager, Connie Mack, was selling off his three-time championship team. Mack wanted $100,000 for catcher Mickey Cochrane. Navin had lost a bundle in the stock market crash of 1929 and had to ask Briggs to back the deal. One of Cochrane's first acts as player-manager was to order the left-field screen removed so he could have a better shot at the seats.

Many Detroiters remember Navin Field affectionately.

"My fondest, earliest memories of the stadium," says Shapiro, "sustain me even today. I lived in a small apartment on Twelfth Street. The streetcar tracks ran right underneath my apartment window. It was a small apartment for a whole family— six or seven of us packed into a three-bedroom.

"I'd get up in the morning, play catch for a while. Around ten o'clock I'd get on the Trumbull streetcar, which ran right underneath me. I think the fare was a nickel at the time, and it would drop me off right in front of the stadium, on Trumbull. It must have taken about thirty-five minutes to get to the ballpark. My mother, of course, packed me the usual bologna sandwiches. This was the Depression; I couldn't afford to buy anything at the stadium.

"I would go around on Michigan Avenue, and they had these large grates, through which I guess they took equipment and stuff. At around ten-thirty, eleven o'clock, this curtain of steel would ring up, and there would be some guy there. He was like St. Peter at the gate, literally. He decided whether you would enter the kingdom of heaven or be consigned to going back home again. It's true; he decided who lived and who died.

"He would stand there and imperiously point his finger at you. Though I would go every day the Tigers played at home, I could never figure out on what basis he chose people. I never figured out why he chose me and not the guy standing next to me. It seemed to be totally at random, which made it more exciting, but also more devastating.

47

You'd think after so many times, that he would recognize and have favorites, but he didn't. Maybe he tried to be fair. Maybe it was an impartiality that a ten- or eleven-year-old couldn't fathom at the time. There was a whole bunch of us. There would be maybe twenty-five, thirty kids out there, and he would pick maybe a dozen. Most of the time I got in.

"They would assign us various places in the stadium to retrieve balls that were hit underneath the stands, and then when the customers began showing up, to show them to their seats. We hardly ever got tipped in those days.

"It wasn't exactly a rigidly controlled artisans' guild that I belonged to. It was a very loose kind of arrangement. Afterward, of course, we'd stand outside the dressing room, waiting for the players to come out.

"When I didn't get in, I had a backup card that I could play. This is inconceivable now, but in those days you could get in with an adult, free.

"I would go out, and I would stand in front of the ticket window. People would begin showing up, and I'd pick out an unaccompanied man, and I would say, 'Hey mister, will you take me in?' I remember the words, I spoke them so often! Some of them would say 'Go away, kid, you're bothering me.' But most of the time I was able to get in. The guy would say, 'Sure. Come on.' And he would just take me in, and tell the ticket taker, 'This is my kid.' I almost always managed to get in."

Max Lapides is a Chicago businessman who grew up in Detroit. "For a long, long time," he remembers, "the area from the left-field foul line was just a wall. When they had a particularly big crowd, like for a Sunday doubleheader, they would rope off the outfield, and they would sell standing room right on the field. And people used to stand out there in their straw hats and their shirt sleeves, and ties — because in those days you didn't go to a game very often without a tie on."

Shapiro says the kids used to walk through the fence to leave the stadium after a game. "In those days they didn't have a phalanx of guards keeping you from going on the field," he recalls. "When the last out was made, everybody jumped over the box seats and walked across the field. You'd practice sliding into second base. Can you imagine that happening today? You put a foot on the field, you're thrown in the pokey."

The ballpark also was a constant companion to kids in Corktown. Alice Conway grew up on Plum Street in the early 1930s. "My sister Katie and I played jacks on the sidewalks and the crowds would be

48

coming down the streets and we wouldn't get out of the way," she says. "We always used to park cars on the street. Everybody parked cars in the neighborhood. They'd pull up and park and we'd say, 'Watch your car, mister?' They'd say, 'Sure,' and we'd get a nickel or a dime. I was very good about it; I'd always watch my cars. Some other kids didn't, so if the people paid them before the game, they'd be in trouble."

Dan Gaule, Alice Conway's brother, says the children in Corktown were happier when the Tigers were on the road and they could use the vacant lots for playing ball.

Ted Colias also grew up around Navin Field and made money from parking cars. "We used to run down to Trumbull Avenue and jump on the running boards and steer the guy around to one of the neighbors' lots," he recalls. "We'd get paid a nickel or so for each car we brought into a lot. On Opening Day in our senior year we were excused from school for that reason. It's because they knew that parking cars was an extra income."

And most families in Corktown in those days needed the money.

"We always thought of anyone who went to the ball game as people with money," says Conway. "You know, the idea of people having cars and paying to go to the ball games, that was really something. We thought of them as being rich. They had *cars*. They dressed up, and they were always in a good mood. I can't remember anyone being nasty to you."

Neighborhood kids didn't pay to see games. After school the kids would just walk down to the stadium.

"At the seventh inning they would open up the gates in the back at Cherry and National," recalls Conway. "We'd always get in for free. We always used to run down there to look in and see what was going on. We roamed around and looked for money in the aisles."

Some kids would take a gunnysack as they entered the park, recalls Jack Swift, who also grew up in Corktown. If they returned the sack to the ushers full of discarded cans or bottles, they would get a free ticket to the next game.

There were other ways to see the action. Gaule recalls climbing trees on Cherry Street to watch ball games and other events, including a wrestling match between Orville Brown and Wrangler Lewis.

"When they put up Checker Cab on Trumbull, people used to go up on the roof and watch the game," Alice Conway says. "They didn't charge anyone for that. Anyone in the neighborhood could do that. We took the ballpark for granted. A lot of the people in the neighborhood worked there. Even during the Depression there was always a job at the ballpark. It was a place where you could always get a few dollars, though the Tigers were never known for being very generous. It was always like everything in the neighborhood revolved around the stadium."

Ted Colias recalls: "A lot of the ball players lived in the neighborhood and they walked to the ballpark. I'd see them at twelve o'clock mass at St. Boniface. You'd get kind of used to it."

Navin Field hosted much more than just baseball. Sometimes there were boxing matches at night. The ring was set up at second base with temporary bleachers around it and lights above it. Gaule remembers seeing the House of David—the famous sect of bearded barnstorming ball players—play donkey baseball at Navin Field. They would hit the ball and then get on a donkey to ride around the bases. For more culture, there was "Opera under the Stars."

In 1934 Cochrane led the Tigers to their first pennant in twenty-five years. The town, eager for an escape from the Depression, was crazy with pennant fever. Attendance nearly tripled, to 919,161, a third of the league's total.

It was the worst of times. Banks were closed, factories idle, markets deserted, office buildings empty. According to Bingay's history, *Detroit Is My Home Town*, Mickey Cochrane became a sustaining force: "Exhausted business leaders spent afternoons at the ballpark. Mickey was the only thing in all Detroit that seemed alive . . . a reincarnation of the old fighting spirit they had once possessed and which had made Detroit the talk of the world."

Bingay, who then was editor of the *Free Press* and had not been to a game in fourteen years, reinvented himself as a columnist named Iffy the Dopester. Cantankerous Iffy was the Tigers' biggest booster. The *Free Press* handed out half a million Iffy buttons, and Iffy clubs sprang up around town. Women made Iffy quilts. The Book-Cadillac Hotel served Iffy cocktails. If the Tigers lost, fans would castigate anyone who had forgotten to wear an Iffy button.

After Detroit clinched the American League pennant, Navin persuaded City Hall to tear down the few remaining houses on Cherry and reroute the street northward to make room for a 17,000-seat bleacher section. The left-field wall was torn down and the bleachers built in a few days.

The new left-field stands were the origin of the most famous fan incident in World Series history. In the seventh game, St. Louis was routing Detroit in the sixth inning. Cardinal outfielder Ducky Medwick slid hard into Tiger third baseman Marv Owen, spiking him. Medwick was angry because Owen had faked a tag without having the ball. Medwick kicked Owen, and the two stood nose to nose, but no punches were thrown.

When Medwick tried to take his position in left field to start the next inning, the fans pelted him with vegetables and fruit, paper, score-cards, pop bottles and shoes.

"The fans were just frustrated," recalls Ted Colias, who was sitting in the left-field stands that day. "They threw grapefruits and bananas. It was a fruit barrage that they threw at the guy. That is what was always amazing to me. Where did all that fruit come from? But then you remember everyone used to bring food in the ballpark. It was a picnic, especially at the World Series."

Medwick was twice forced off the field by the angry crowd before Commissioner Landis ordered St. Louis to replace him with another player to avoid an embarrassing forfeit. The Tigers lost, 11–0.

After the season Navin decided to keep his left-field pavilion, but Landis ordered it screened to prevent any recurrence of the Medwick incident. Back came the twenty-foot portable screen.

Bert Gordon, a longtime friend of Max Lapides and Don Shapiro, remembers: "Before the left-field stands were up, it was called a pavil-ion. They had one deck, and it'd be the same as in the bleachers—no roof, you know? And we had this wall out in center field.

"At the end of the game they would let everybody walk down from the stands across the field. The players would still be there and the coaches. One time I was there with my father, and Connie Mack was a hundred and seventy-two years old, whatever he was, he weighed about eleven pounds, and he was six feet tall. He walked so slowly, and he was holding his scorecard, and he had his white hair, you know.

"And my father said, 'You wanna meet Mr. Mack?' Like he knew him. He didn't know him. He said to Mr. Mack, 'This is my son.' We shook hands, we talked; everything was low-key, friendly, accessible."

In 1935, in the depths of the Depression, the Tigers again won the pennant and drew a club record 1,034,929 fans. They faced the Chi-cago Cubs in the World Series.

"In the old days," says Don Shapiro, "the National League was a distant land. It was a foreign country, populated by different kinds of savages. You could look at them statistically, but you never saw their pictures in the paper. They had their own warfare going, and we had our own warfare going in the American League. We didn't know much about the National League. Consequently, the World Series had a penumbra about it, an air of excitement. It was like two armies clashing in the night."

Alice Conway also remembers the World Series games in 1934 and 1935. "When we were in high school and the Tigers were in the World Series, the nuns would let the boys off to park cars — on the condition that they use the money to pay their tuition," she says. "But they never allowed the girls to park cars. We had a few friends who worked at lots, these boys, and they would come over and pick us up in these beautiful big cars and take us for joyrides while the men were at the games. We used to go for rides in these limousines and these great cars. They wanted to impress us. They'd always get the cars back just in time."

Crowds downtown followed the games on an electric diagram set up on the side of a building on Michigan Avenue. Lamps would light up at bases as players got hits.

The Tigers came home from Chicago leading in the Series three games to two. On October 7, in front of 48,420, the score was tied 3–3 in the ninth. The Cubs' Stan Hack led off with a triple, sending the huge crowd into deep despair. But Tiger pitcher Tommy Bridges got a strikeout, a grounder, and a fly ball to strand Hack at third. In the bottom of the inning, Cochrane singled with one out and took second on a grounder. With the crowd roaring, Goose Goslin lined a single to right, scoring Cochrane, who jumped on the plate, leaped in the air, ran to the backstop, whirled around, and was mobbed by his teammates.

The crowd exploded with a loud cry of euphoria, releasing the frustrations of the Depression and of almost half a century without a world championship. Legendary sportswriter Grantland Rice described it thus in the *New York Times*:

> That jungle-throated roar from 48,000 human throats as Goslin singled and Cochrane scored is one of the reverberations I won't forget. It was the pent-up vocal outbreak of nearly 50 years and it exploded with the suppressed power of nitroglycerine when the big moment came.

The fans stood and cheered themselves hoarse for an hour, then spilled into the streets. Ticker tape and confetti streamed from office windows. Pedestrians blew tin horns and motorists honked. Firecrackers, smoke bombs, even machine guns rigged up in office windows all added to the din. One fan climbed into the tower of City Hall and changed the timer on the town clock so that it rang every minute instead of every hour. Well after midnight, downtown was in gridlock. It was the wildest night in the city's history.

"The city went stark, raving mad," wrote Bingay. "The crowds swarmed through the streets until daybreak."

CHAPTER 6

THE BRIGGS ERA

Everybody was clean, friendly, and nice. It was a *happening*, you know, like in a square in Italy someplace. Nobody had any money; everybody had plenty of problems. But the ball game was a place to just shed your problems.

— *Tiger fan Bert Gordon*

A few weeks after the Tigers won the 1935 World Series, Frank Navin announced that the club's profits of $150,000 from the 1935 season would finance a major expansion of the ballpark. Navin and Briggs had decided that they needed more seats to accommodate the city's raging baseball fever. But on November 13, 1935, Navin fell off a horse and suffered a fatal heart attack at the age of sixty-four. Walter Briggs bought the rest of the team from Navin's heirs for $1 million and became at fifty-eight sole owner of the Tigers at the height of their popularity.

Briggs owned a factory that made automobile bodies for Ford Motor Company. He had started out working on the railroad; his father was an engineer. Then he rose from clerk to the head of Everitt Manufacturing Company, which he renamed Briggs Manufacturing. He eventually presided over a manufacturing empire, which included Briggs Beautyware, maker of bathroom fixtures; Briggs Commercial and Development Company (real estate); and Briggs Motor Bodies of England.

Briggs was a hard-nosed businessman with little tolerance for unions. In January 1933, after he reduced wages at his plant, nine thousand workers walked out, idling sixty thousand more at Ford. Briggs refused to negotiate with the walkout leaders, calling them "communists." Police arrested picketers, Briggs hired strikebreakers, and by mid-February he was back in production with reduced wages and a smaller work force.

As owner of the Tigers, Briggs was much more indulgent. Malcolm W. Bingay called him "America's No. 1 baseball devotee."

"He really loved the game and he had an absolute passion for his players," says his grandson, Walter Briggs III. "In the days when you were not allowed to give bonuses, my grandfather probably got slapped down more than anybody for breaking the rules. Hank Greenberg had cars and suits and stuff that just showed up."

As sole owner, Briggs could join his lifelong affection for baseball with his business acumen. He had a vision of a colossal stadium, completely enclosed and double-decked. He wanted to build the finest ballpark in the land.

Of course, business motives figured in his plan.

"It was done because he said: 'I know there are days when we can sell a lot more tickets than we can right now,'" explains Walter Briggs IV. "Some of it also was those guys sitting out there getting a free shot" —the people watching games from rooftops on Trumbull and backyards on Cherry Street.

Briggs in 1935 toured other stadiums to get ideas. His favorite park, says his grandson, was Wrigley Field. "Granddad was going to put ivy on the walls of Briggs Stadium, until he went to a World Series game in Chicago in 1935," says Briggs III. "They hit a line drive into the wall and it got stuck in the ivy and we lost the ball game. And that was the end of the ivy idea."

The expansion of Michigan and Trumbull got under way, sans ivy, over the winter of 1935–36. Osborn Engineering of Cleveland, the designer of Navin Field, was again hired. Briggs ordered the first-base pavilion demolished and replaced by a double-decked grandstand extending into right field.

In right field he had a problem. He wanted to maximize seating capacity, but Trumbull ran right behind the wall, which was 370 feet away from home. Briggs didn't want to move the fences in farther than 325 feet down the line.

His novel solution was to extend the upper deck about ten feet beyond the lower deck in both front and back. Along Trumbull the result is a bulge in the stadium's outer wall. Inside, the upper-deck "overhang" became the stadium's most distinctive feature. Originally, there was a 315-foot marker painted on the upper deck above the lower deck's "325" sign.

For more than half a century the overhang has been the midwife for hundreds of little fly balls that turn into strapping homers. The "porch" beckons left-handed sluggers and bedevils pitchers. High fly balls can hit the overhang as the right fielder camps out below, pounding his mitt. The overhang evokes memories of cheap home runs in backyard ball games.

Like Fenway Park's famous left-field wall, the overhang is a creature of urban geography. In old ball parks, street patterns imposed constraints that produced odd field dimensions. Baseball is the only major team sport influenced by the unique designs of its playing fields. At Ebbets Field, for instance, the left-field fence originally was 419 feet from home plate, but it was only 301 to right. The bathtub-shaped Polo Grounds was 260 feet down both lines but 500 to dead center.

New parks lack such irrational touches; most are standardized and symmetrical. The overhang in Detroit remains a touch of whimsy born of necessity and adds much to the crowd-pleasing reputation of the park as a slugger's paradise.

The first expansion of Navin Field increased the park's capacity to 36,000, but Briggs wanted more. Over the winter of 1937–38, he razed the third-base pavilion and built a double-decked grandstand that bent around the left-field foul pole and continued along Cherry Street. He then completed the center-field bleacher section, enclosing the field with two decks.

Briggs's new additions cost more than $1 million and nearly doubled the size of Navin Field, creating a superstadium of over 53,000. Only Yankee Stadium and Cleveland's cavernous Municipal Stadium were larger. It also was the first field in the majors to be completely enclosed and double-decked.

Pitchers warmed up in a tunnel beneath the center-field bleachers. In later years, relievers were driven to the mound in a car. Eventually the bull pens were moved to their present locations down the foul lines.

The distances to the fences were 340 to the left-field corner, 365 in left center, 440 to center, 370 to right center, and 325 to right. Those dimensions have remained essentially unchanged for over half a century. The center field today is the deepest in baseball. Near the old bull pen entrance is a 125-foot flagpole, the highest obstacle in play in baseball history. Originally, balls bouncing off the flagpole onto the field remained in play. Today, any ball hit above a line drawn on the pole at the level of the outfield fence is a home run.

Dale Alexander, a Tiger player in the 1930s, once hit a single off the flagpole, recalls Ted Colias. "He hit a ball on a line. I don't think that ball was twenty feet in the air, but it just kept going and going. It hit the flagpole, dead center, bounced back, and he got a single out of it. That was one of the hardest hit balls I've ever seen."

A giant hand-operated scoreboard topped the upper-deck bleachers. It was plainly readable from all over the park, and had space on each side for advertising. Two new electric scoreboards adorned the facing of the upper deck behind first and third base.

Bert Gordon remembers the center-field scoreboard. "The guy'd put the number up," he says, savoring the memory. "You know, like at Wrigley Field, one at a time. And then it'd be out a long time, and you'd say 'Boy, somebody's scoring!' And then they'd put up a big *four*. They got four runs, but it took you a half an hour to wait. The pace was infinitely slower, but it was *delicious*."

The dedication ceremonies on April 22, 1938, were an auspicious event. They included a reenactment of the 1901 Opening Day parade, replete with dignitaries in horse-drawn buggies. Unfortunately the Tigers lost to Cleveland, 4–3.

Fans loved the new stadium with its canoe green seats. The press was wowed by its accommodations in a new third deck hung below the grandstand roof from beyond third base to the overhang in right. It was the largest press area in baseball and reversed bad impressions left from Navin Field's cramped press box.

The experience of entering the stadium hasn't changed much since Don Shapiro was a boy. "The thing about Tiger Stadium," he says, "is when you enter the stadium, it's a cavernous place, inside. I think that's part of the attraction of the old stadiums. There's a certain aesthetic, in that you enter the stadium, and you're surrounded by concrete. You could be in the basement of a huge factory. It's just concrete, and pillars. There's nothing particularly attractive about it; it was dark, very dark. But part of the joy, and the thrill, and the ecstasy—the epiphany—was walking up the ramp and suddenly emerging to see the green prairie, and the sunlight. It was fantastic: from darkness to light. It was absolutely thrilling.

"It's like participatory theater. You go into a darkened basement, and then you're ejected into a gorgeous green space, with a diamond laid out, and the seats, and the sunlight. It was an experience, it really was. I never failed to be thrilled by it, ever. I was just a kid, but I'll never forget it."

The first year of Briggs Stadium was the end of the era of the old nineteenth-century wooden ballparks. The last wooden grandstands in the majors, at Philadelphia's Baker Bowl, closed in 1938.

It was a memorable year for Detroiters for another reason. Hank Greenberg made a run at Babe Ruth's record of sixty home runs in a season. Greenberg had been special to Max Lapides ever since the slugger visited Lapides at home when he was eight years old and confined to bed with a broken leg.

"That was a special time and a special place," says Lapides. "Greenberg was the first really big Jewish star. There was a lot going on at the time. There was the Depression; the Tigers won two pennants; World War II came. He was the first star that went into World War II. He was the first star to come back, in 1945, and he helped them win a pennant. And he became, during that whole era, a symbol and a rallying point for the Detroit Jewish community.

"In 1938 I was ten years old. I was awed by this thing, because it was bigger than life in my house. My father was a tremendous fan, and baseball was pretty much what we discussed in our house. The papers would track Greenberg day by day, by day, by day. That was the only thing alive in Detroit in 1938; we were in the middle of a Depression. It engulfed the whole town, and it became the focal point of everybody's daily activities. You had a team that had just recently won two pennants, in '34 and '35, and although the Yankees had come into their dominance, the Tigers were the next best team in those days."

Among Jewish people the excitement was "unbelievable. It was like if Thor came down into Sweden. A lot of it took on almost mythical proportions. Today it just wouldn't mean that much. But in those days a great number of the fans weren't even born in the United States, and baseball had become something that they learned after they came from Europe."

"Next to my father," says Don Shapiro, "Greenberg was probably the most important person to me. My parents were immigrants. He was our entry, for a lot of Jews, into American society."

Shapiro's parents both came from eastern Europe. His mother didn't even know what country she lived in. "Guaranteed," says Shapiro, "they didn't play baseball there!"

Greenberg, says Bert Gordon, "gave every one of the Jewish people a feeling of acceptability, of normalcy. He's really one of the guys, so aren't *we* one of the guys *too*? One of us is one of them. Now *we're* like *them*. A lot of my friends, their parents were foreign. They knew nothing of the game. But they would do things. My wife worked for a guy who owned a scrap-iron yard. He never went to a baseball game in his life. Old man. One time, he was going out the door, and he slammed the door, and Greenberg hit a home run. So he'd leave the game on, and every time Greenberg came up, he'd slam the door!"

Gordon's father was a rabbi and a religious Tiger fan. Walter Briggs was, he remembers, "a very staunch Catholic. He blocked out sixty or eighty seats every day, and he left free tickets for clergy at a place downtown called the Council of Churches, which is an ecumenical thing for all the religions. Whoever wanted would go down there and get them."

Most clergy who took the free tickets were Roman Catholic priests.

"They were in their early to middle twenties," recalls Gordon, "and they were mostly clean cut, good-looking guys, and they all wore the collar, you know."

Bert and his father "would sit there with them. He was in his forties, I guess, and I was ten or twelve, and he was a rabbi who was also a probation officer. He had as much in common with them as you got with that statue up there. But at the ballpark they had plenty in common.

"They would get into philosophical conversations having to do with religion and theology. They all read the same books, they were all educated guys, they all knew the same things. He got along well with them. And it was very invigorating to me.

"They, on the other hand, being priests, certainly had no children. So I was their kid too, you see? I was the only ten-year-old kid around. Those were wonderful times for me.

"The game used to be at three o'clock in the afternoon, and it was over in two hours. My father would come from the courts, and he'd arrange for me to get out of school early, because I was a good student. I would take the streetcar by myself, and I'd meet him at the ballpark. I'd go all the way downtown by myself. After the game, we'd take the streetcar home.

"Everybody was clean, friendly, and nice. It was a *happening*, you know, like in a square in Italy someplace. Nobody had any money; everybody had plenty of problems. But the ball game was a place to just shed your problems."

On September 9, 1938, the Detroit Lions of the National Football League played their first game in Briggs Stadium. Except 1940, the Lions would play every autumn at Michigan and Trumbull through

1974. The stadium wasn't built for football, but the Lions often would sell out in their glory days. The Lions won NFL championships in 1952, 1953, and 1957, and lost the championship game in 1954.

The football field stretched from the first-base line to left field. Many lower-deck seats were blocked by players and coaches standing along the sidelines. The best seats were in the upper decks. The upper-deck bleachers, overlooking a corner of one end zone, afforded great but chilly views.

"I haven't missed a play-off game that was played in this park, baseball or football, since 1952," says John Grindstaff, who grew up and still lives on Detroit's east side. "When I was a kid, I sat over in right field. In '53 the Lions played the Browns, and there were three or four minutes to play, and the Lions got the ball, and Bobby Layne went in the huddle, and he goes, 'Boys, just block, and I'll get you in that All-Star Game in Chicago.' And sure enough, he took them right down the field, and they won the championship. And we went ape, you know, ka-zinga. We went nuts. Of course, baseball was always king. Even though the Lions had those great teams, baseball was king."

On May 2, 1939, at Briggs Stadium, Yankee great Lou Gehrig ended his record streak of 2,130 consecutive games played with one final at bat.

"I happened to see the last game that Gehrig played," says Max Lapides. "Of course, we didn't know what it meant; it was just his last game. His last game ever. If memory serves me right—and it doesn't always—I believe he was listed as the shortstop, and he batted leadoff. He could barely move. There were probably a bunch of guys who thought he was drunk. He hit a ball weakly, and couldn't even run to first. He wanted to keep the streak alive, and they just took him out."

"According to some accounts," wrote Jack Saylor in the *Free Press* on May 3, 1989, "Gehrig . . . walked to Casey's on Michigan Avenue, then known as Shea's Bar, had a sandwich, and listened to the game on the radio."

Old-timer David Cutler of Southfield disputed that account. "No way," he told Saylor. "I sat in section 25 behind the Yankee dugout that day. Gehrig sat on the top step of the dugout and watched all during the ball game."

Gehrig soon after was diagnosed as having a fatal illness, amyotrophic lateral sclerosis. He died June 2, 1941, at the age of thirty-seven.

In 1939 baseball celebrated its centennial, based on the myth that

Abner Doubleday had invented the game in 1839 near Cooperstown, New York. To mark the anniversary, Briggs gave away seventy-five thousand souvenir books to Tiger fans. As always, he let kids in free, usually seating scout troops and church groups in the outfield grandstands. According to Bingay, a hundred thousand children saw Tiger games for free every year while Briggs was owner.

"By such gestures, he has raised the standard of baseballic culture in Detroit to a height undreamed of in other cities," Bingay wrote. "Even in the bleachers there would be almost as many cheers for a visiting player who had made a good play as there would be for one performed by a member of the home team."

By giving away tickets to children, Briggs hoped to create another generation of loyal Tiger fans. "It was the care and nurturing of the next year's fans and the next year's after that," says Walter Briggs III. "You took care of the kids."

Detroit fans were famous nationwide. The most notorious was Patsy O'Toole, whose real name was Sam Dzadowski. Known as "the all-American earache," he liked to yell from the roof of the dugout and was once clocked at thirty-five thousand words per game. His standard insult was "You're a faker!" and his standard compliment was "You're a great guy!"

In 1940 Dorothy Rivard worked as a concessionaire at Briggs Stadium. She recalls working at two Negro League games played there that summer. So fearful were Tiger officials and stadium workers of the huge crowds of black fans, she says, that police guarded the concession stands. Ted Colias also remembers a Negro League game at Michigan and Trumbull. "I saw Satchel Paige pitch" against the Detroit Stars, he says. "They had about fifty thousand people in there."

In other cities, Negro League games in major league ballparks were a frequent occurrence, but they were rare events at Briggs Stadium. From 1920 through 1931, the Detroit Stars played at Mack Park, on Mack and Fairview on Detroit's east side. The Stars played at Hamtramck Stadium, also called Keyworth Stadium, on Joseph Campau in Hamtramck, an enclave suburb of Detroit, in 1933, and at Dequindre Park on Dequindre near Davison in 1937. A Negro League team named the Wolves also played at Hamtramck Stadium in 1932.

The first night baseball game in Detroit was played June 17, 1930, at Hamtramck Stadium between the Stars and the Kansas City Monarchs. The Monarchs brought the lights, which were set up atop six high posts and on the grandstand roof.

In 1940 the Tigers moved Greenberg, an outstanding first baseman, to left field to make room at first base for another slugger, Rudy York, who had been a defensive liability at catcher. Greenberg was so determined to learn his new position that he hired Corktown boys to hit him fly balls every morning at the park. Ted Colias recalls another way Greenberg trained for the outfield.

"I can remember him running up and down the upper deck steps, building his legs," he says. "He would run up and down the concrete stairs so many times, it was a wonder he didn't kill himself."

While learning to play left field, Greenberg batted .340 with 41 homers and 150 runs batted in. The Tigers were in second place in mid-September, 5 1/2 games behind Cleveland, when the Indians went into a tailspin. The Cleveland players blamed manager Ossie Vitt for the collapse and tried to get him fired. Fans began taunting them as "cry babies."

The Indians came to Detroit for a showdown three-game series with the two clubs tied for first. Tiger fans met the Indians at the train station and pelted them with eggs, tomatoes, and fruit. Police had to sneak the visitors through the baggage room and onto mail trucks to take them to their hotel. The next day at the ballpark, fans hung diapers over the Indians' dugout, rolled baby carriages across the dugout roof, and waved diapers in the stands. The Tigers took two out of three games and went on to win the pennant. York, Gehringer, and pitchers Bobo Newsom (twenty-one wins) and Hal Newhouser were among the stars. The Tigers faced the Reds in the World Series.

In the four games at Cincinnati's Crosley Field, the attendance averaged 29,942 a game. The three games in Detroit drew 162,159, an average of 54,053. The largest World Series crowd in Tiger history — 55,189 — saw Newsom beat the Reds in the fifth game. But the Tigers lost the last two games in Cincinnati.

The next season, Briggs Stadium again was in the national spotlight. On July 8, 1941, the first All-Star Game at Michigan and Trumbull was played before a crowd of 54,674. The American League entered the bottom of the ninth trailing 5–3. With two out and two on, Ted Williams clouted a dramatic home run into the right-field upper deck to win the game, 7–5.

World War II took the nation's attention away from baseball. Many of the game's greatest stars enlisted, and the quality of play diminished. Newhouser was one of the Tigers' few remaining stalwarts. Prince Hal won twenty-nine games in 1944, twenty-five in 1945 and twenty-six in 1946.

Greenberg thrilled Detroit's Jews at a time when Father Charles Coughlin, the radio preacher, was spewing hate from his pulpit in Royal Oak.

"Hitler was wiping out the Jews in Europe," says Don Shapiro, "and you had Father Coughlin at the Shrine of the Little Flower going on the radio every Sunday, talking about international bankers, by which he meant international Jewish bankers. He was a dangerous political figure, with his anti-Semitism, right here in Detroit.

"And here was Hank Greenberg, the idol of millions, and he didn't change his name. He acknowledged he was Jewish. He did not play on Yom Kippur during the World Series, and he got a special dispensation to play on Rosh Hashanah. But he wasn't religious. He never said he was religious. Everybody loved Hank Greenberg. Even the people who hated him because he was Jewish admired him.

"He was a hero beyond heroes to the Jewish community in Detroit. The Jewish community was very homogeneous. And I think that one of the reasons why baseball has always been so popular in Detroit is that the Jewish community has been very supportive. Every one of us is a baseball fan. Because of Greenberg, essentially."

Greenberg's return from the service helped the Tigers win another pennant in 1945. It was a strange season of mistake-filled wartime baseball. The Washington Senators finished the season a week early so that their field could be used for football. They waited helplessly while the Tigers overtook them. Greenberg's grand slam on the last day of the season won the flag.

Detroit had won only eighty-eight games and in the World Series faced the Cubs, whose pitching staff included three starters over age thirty-five. The series was played with wartime travel restrictions. The teams opened with three games in Detroit; the Tigers won one and were shut out the other two. The two clubs rode trains to Chicago to play the final four games. The series went the distance; Newhouser won the finale, 9–3, to give the Tigers their second modern world championship.

Compared with the celebration ten years earlier, Detroit's 1945 victory party was tame. The war was still foremost on everyone's minds.

The year 1945, says Don Shapiro, "was the end of the magic. The war was over. Hitler was dead. I was already graduating from dental school, and Greenberg came back for one last heroic home run, with bases loaded, to win the game against the St. Louis Browns on the last day of the season. It was the loss of innocence, there's no question about it. It was never the same after that."

On January 18, 1947, Briggs sold Greenberg to Pittsburgh for $75,000.

The post-war era was one of unprecedented prosperity in the United States, the only industrial power not crippled by fighting on its own soil. Detroit played a big role in America's hegemony, turning out cars in record numbers. Detroiters spent some of their new leisure time at the ballpark. Baseball was still king in Detroit, and Briggs Stadium was the queen of diamonds.

It was the best kept ballpark in the country. Briggs supervised constant improvements to the field, the stands, and the concessions. Immaculate rest rooms featured attendants. Briggs Stadium was the first park to install an underground sprinkler system and the first to use a nylon tarp. Under Briggs, field managers and general managers came and went, but the club rarely changed its stadium manager or head grounds keeper. Walter Briggs III says the maintenance budget at the stadium approached $1 million a year in the postwar era. The green seats and gray exterior walls were painted annually; according to an article in the *Sporting News* of July 11, 1951, it was the only park in the majors to get a fresh paint job each year.

In September 1946 an Irish immigrant named Catherine Darin saw the first baseball game of her life at Briggs Stadium. She took to the game immediately. "I'd come to Detroit from Ireland that May and I had heard the word baseball, but I didn't know anything about it," she says. "But there was just something about the game. It was wonderful, and it was really a wonderful game that I saw. The Tigers trailed until the bottom of the ninth, one to nothing. Hank Greenberg tied it with a home run and the Tigers won it in the tenth, two to one.

"I had never seen a stadium like this before. In Ireland when you went to see hurling it was just a field and people sort of sat around. Hurling was my favorite game. I never cared for Irish football or soccer because they're like football here; they're kind of rough. And rugby is even worse. Baseball is like hurling because it has a ball and bat.

"The first thing that impressed me was the excitement of the home run. I could see that the score was tied, but I didn't really know what it meant. It was cool, it was sunny. The grass was a really pretty green. There were not an awful lot of fans in the stadium. And we talked about it and read about it in the paper the next day, and that was my first experience with baseball. I had the good sense to buy a banner, and I still have that banner today."

Darin was hooked. Over the years she went frequently to games with friends, neighbors and family. Sometimes she would take the bus from her home in northwest Detroit. Nearly half a century later, she is still a stalwart Tiger fan and has seen more than five hundred games.

In the postwar years, the Tigers' home attendance was consistently among the best in baseball. The club sold generous numbers of standing-room seats and occasionally opened the third deck to handle overflow crowds. All but one of the twenty biggest crowds in Tiger history occurred between 1940 and 1950.

On July 20, 1947, Darin saw the Tigers play a doubleheader against the Yankees. So did 58,368 other people. The crowd was so large that club officials resorted to the long-abandoned practice of putting stand-ees behind ropes in the outfield. It remains the biggest crowd in club history. The Tigers won the first game, 4–1, and took the nightcap 12–11 in eleven innings.

In 1948 the Tigers had the only American League park without lights. The first night game in the majors was played in 1935 at Cincinnati's Crosley Field. Briggs, a staunch traditionalist, believed that night baseball diminished the quality of the game. As usual, his philosophy was matched by an economic rationale: He had built a huge stadium, with more than ten thousand bleacher seats, with the working-class family in mind. The games started at 3:00 P.M. because that was when the day shift ended at the auto plants.

During the war Briggs had experimented with twilight games, starting at 5:00 or 6:00, but they were poorly attended and the late innings often were played in semidarkness. "My grandfather was absolutely dead set against night baseball," says Walter Briggs III. "He would have been just as happy to be another Wrigley Field and sit there with no lights on the thing forever."

After the war Briggs's son, Spike, became more active in club management. His biggest battle was persuading his father to put in lights. "It took my father and other people around my grandfather years" to change his mind, says Walter Briggs III. "It wasn't overnight. It had nothing to do with surveys or the cost or anything else. As far as he was concerned, baseball had started in the day and it should stay that way and that was the way it was."

But a growing segment of fans wanted to see night baseball. Finally, in 1948, the elder Briggs relented. As usual, when Briggs decided to do something, he did it in a big way. Eight state-of-the-art light towers were installed at Briggs Stadium. The towers held 1,458 light bulbs and required 2.75 million watts of electricity. On June 15, 1948, the first night game at Michigan and Trumbull was played.

The gates opened at 6:00 P.M. It was a chilly night; temperatures were in the high fifties and there was a north wind. The stands filled up quickly and the concessions sold a lot of coffee. The attendance was 54,480. The club didn't want to start the game until after dark, so the lights could have their full effect. The lights were turned on at 9:28.

Max Lapides was at that game. "I remember we all went to the game very early that night," he says. "We sat there, and we just waited. It was like waiting for a fireworks show. A lot of us had never been in a stadium for a night game before. At the last minute they turned on these lights. For a minute there was dead silence, because nobody could believe what they were seeing. And then all of a sudden there was a big 'Ooh!' "

Newspaper reports said that the field was illuminated with the equivalent of six hundred full moons.

The test in those days of a stadium's light system was whether a newspaper could be read on the field. The next day the *News* ran a picture of grounds keeper Neal Conway sitting in a chair at second base reading the paper under the lights.

The A's beat the Tigers and Hal Newhouser, 4–1, but that hardly mattered. *Free Press* sports editor Lyall Smith wrote in his column the next day: "For some reason I can't explain, all the action looks faster under the lights. Runners appear to rip down the base lines and every ball that starts out from the bat seems headed for the stands."

Detroit fans took immediately to night baseball. On August 9 the Tigers drew 56,586 fans for a night game; that would remain the club's attendance record under the lights. But Briggs still favored day baseball and kept night games to a minimum.

Former Tiger pitcher Jim Bunning, now a congressman from his home state of Kentucky, remembers that his years in Detroit spanned an important transition. His first year with the Tigers was 1955.

"When I started to play in Tiger Stadium," he says, "there were only seven night games a year. And then all of a sudden there were *fourteen* night games — My gosh, it was unbelievable. And then of course they moved it up where we played twenty-one, and then twenty-eight, until nowadays if they have a *day* game it's unusual. So I went through the transition from playing almost all day baseball to playing mostly night baseball."

In 1950 the club was in first place for 116 days before falling from contention late in September. The Tigers drew nearly two million fans, a club record. One of the greatest games in Briggs Stadium, according to Max Lapides, took place against the Yankees that year on June 23.

"That was the big home run game," he remembers, "that the Tigers won ten to nine. There's no greater advertisement for the stadium than that game, because you had fifty thousand people there, a huge crowd, a hot night. The whole focal point of everything was baseball — you had a lot of star players in that game. Mantle was playing. Trout pitched in that game."

In August 1967 Lapides wrote an article about the game in the *Free Press*, calling the game "the greatest slugfest in Tiger history." Summarizing the two teams' exploits, he wrote:

> The Tigers tied one record with their four home runs in the fourth. Both clubs hit a total of 11 homers to break the previous mark of 10 that had been set by the Phillies and Cardinals and had endured since 1923.
> The combined slugging average for the night was .827. And every run in the game was the direct result of a circuit clout.

"It was a wonderful game in a wonderful stadium," says Lapides, looking back. "And when there's fifty thousand people in Tiger Stadium, it's remarkable, because everybody is sitting right on the playing field. Even at its highest point, in the upper deck, you're just looking right down on the players, so it was wonderful. That was probably one of the great games of all time."

The next year, even more stars were at Briggs Stadium for another All-Star Game. The game originally had been scheduled for Shibe Park, but Philadelphia waited a year so baseball could help Detroit celebrate its 250th birthday. It turned out to be a characteristic game for the slugger's haven at Michigan and Trumbull. The two leagues combined for a record six homers, and the National League won 8–3. Both American League homers were hit by Tigers — Vic Wertz and George Kell.

Baseball remained extremely popular in Detroit in the 1950s despite a long series of second-division finishes by the Tigers. The city was vibrant and thriving, and the stadium was part of the excitement.

Until 1952 the Tigers were the only charter member of the major leagues never to finish in last place, but that year they lost 104 games, the most in franchise history. Yet Virgil Trucks pitched two no-hitters in 1952, the first on May 15. That gem was one of only two no-hitters ever hurled by a Tiger pitcher at Michigan and Trumbull. (The other was by George Mullin on July 4, 1912.)

Despite the Tigers' dismal 1952 season, over a million fans came to Briggs Stadium. From 1951 through 1960, the team never finished higher than fourth place, but the Tigers drew fewer than a million fans only once, in 1953, and were below the league's average in attendance only once, in 1952.

In June 1952 Detroit mayor Albert Cobo announced a plan to raze Corktown for an urban renewal project. For the next five years Corktown residents fought City Hall, eventually prevailing and preserving most of the neighborhood's historic homes.

Al Kaline was rapidly developing into one of the game's greatest right fielders, and the Tigers tailored the park to his talents. In the mid-1950s some box seats were removed from the right-field corner so the speedy Kaline could flag down more foul flies without crashing into the low wall. The area became known as Kaline's Corner.

Jim Bunning recalls having lost the first game he pitched in Briggs Stadium. "The first time I went into the park," he says, "I pitched and started, and so I have pleasant memories. I didn't win; I lost. But the second time I started I won.

"The memories I have of Tiger Stadium are all good. I won about seventy percent of my games that I started there, so that's obviously a reason I have good memories of the park." Briggs Stadium "was the biggest park that I had ever been in. Then, of course, I went to Yankee Stadium and to Municipal Stadium in Cleveland, and they were bigger. But they weren't as nice a park as Tiger Stadium. It was a great park to pitch in, it was a great town to play in."

Bunning remembers that he was "the only pitcher with the Tigers that threw home runs over both the left- and the right-field roof. Harmon Killebrew hit a home run off me over the left field roof that nobody believed, and I didn't either, and Mantle hit a home run that I'm not sure went over the roof in right field, but it hit on top and bounced into Trumbull Avenue."

Though outwardly the 1950s bespoke a tranquil America, a peaceful Detroit, and somewhat torpid Tiger teams, a cauldron of turmoil seethed just below the surface. For Tiger management, it was a decade of confusion and change. On January 7, 1952, Walter Briggs died. His son, Spike, became the team's president, but the stock went to Briggs's estate, touching off a long and complicated battle for control that involved assorted Briggs heirs, the federal government, and sundry suitors.

"The courts ruled that baseball was not a prudent investment and therefore shouldn't remain inside a trust," explains Walter Briggs III. "So the trustees said the team had to be put up for sale." The Internal Revenue Service also said there had to be an arm's-length transaction — a sale on the open market — and no special deal for Spike Briggs.

An appraisal of the club done for bidders in 1952 and published in 1956 showed that the Tigers made money every year from 1938 to 1951. At the end of 1952 — another money-making year, according to Briggs III — the franchise was valued at $2.1 million, but it would draw much higher offers than that.

By 1956 the team's sale was imminent. In January there were twenty prospective buyers. The Lions were set to put in an offer to buy the team and the stadium, but the National Football League forbade them. Eventually, eight syndicates put in bids. Among the bidders was Bill Veeck, the flamboyant populist owner of the St. Louis Browns and later the Chicago White Sox. In 1951 Veeck had pulled the most famous stunt in baseball history at St. Louis, sending in a midget named Eddie Gaedel to bat against the Tigers' Bob Cain. Veeck also put ivy in Wrigley Field, had fans vote on strategy and, during World War II, played games in the morning and served coffee and doughnuts.

In his book, *Veeck — As in Wreck*, Veeck claims he outbid the other syndicates but was shut out of the deal because major league baseball disapproved of him and because Spike Briggs preferred to sell the team to a business associate, Fred Knorr, a local radio-TV executive. A syndicate headed by Knorr bought the club for $5.5 million; Veeck later claimed he had bid $6 million. Knorr denied he got preferential treatment.

Knorr became team president and swept out some of Briggs's traditionalism. Attendance in 1956 at Briggs Stadium had averaged 29,146 at night and only 11,088 during the day, so Knorr increased night games from 14 to 21. He opened Tiger ticket offices in outstate towns and doubled the club's mail-order business. He hiked the price of box seats from $2.50 to $3.00 and the price of reserved seats from $1.75 to $2.00.

Knorr made Spike Briggs the general manager, but Briggs resigned a year later. In 1957 Knorr named Jack Tighe as manager. *Sports Illustrated* described Tighe as "a bald-headed vegetarian who once took a lie-detector test to prove he did not spit on an umpire while managing Buffalo in the International League." Tighe was fired after two losing seasons.

Knorr's changes seemed trifling compared to what Veeck bragged he would have done. Veeck wanted to sell the stadium to Jimmy Hoffa's Teamsters or Walter Reuther's United Auto Workers and lease it back.

Veeck claimed in his autobiography that "the Negro community of Detroit . . . was solidly and vocally behind me" because he would have made a clean break with the Briggs family. In Detroit's large and growing black community in the 1950s, the Briggs name was synonymous with racism. Though no definitive Briggs quote on the subject ever saw the light of print, many black Detroiters believed Walter Briggs had vowed never to have black players on the roster so long as he was in charge of the club.

Walter Briggs III vehemently denies the allegation. He said his father and grandfather were waiting for the right time and player and were afraid of fans' reactions to integration.

"They were just absolutely terrified that it would not work," he says.

Whatever the motivations for keeping the team segregated through most of the 1950s, the negative connotations that blacks attach to the Briggs name have persisted. In a 1980 interview in the *Free Press*, former Tiger player and then-Tiger coach Gates Brown was quoted on the subject.

"Briggs," he said. "The name doesn't set well in the black community. Say that name some places and you might get jumped on."

In 1947 Jackie Robinson had finally broken baseball's color bar by joining the Brooklyn Dodgers. By the time of Briggs's death five years later, the Tigers were the only major league team without a black player anywhere in their farm system.

Black Detroiters were passionate about baseball. They turned out in large numbers in the early 1950s to see the Cleveland Indians, the first American League team to integrate. At Briggs Stadium most black fans sat in the lower-deck bleachers. Jim Bell, a black Detroiter who worked for the Wayne County Road Commission, recalled those days in a 1980 *Free Press* article:

"My grandfather was an avid baseball fan and would take me out to Briggs Stadium. . . . We always sat in the bleachers. . . . It was a special treat to be at the ballpark when Larry Doby and Luke Easter came to town with the Cleveland Indians. I even saw Satchel Paige when he came to town with the St. Louis Browns. It was like a sea of happy black faces out there in the bleachers when the Indians came to bat. And even though the loyalist would be pulling for the home team, there was a special look of pride on everyone's face when the black players took the field. That rubbed off on me.

"As I grew, I also anticipated the day when as a Tiger fan, I would be both loyal to my home team and proud of my black brothers who I knew would be on the team. Someone in the Tiger organization let me down."

Jim "Mudcat" Grant, a black pitcher who was a rookie with the Cleveland Indians in 1958, recalled his first visit to Briggs Stadium this way:

"I remember walking out on the field with Larry Doby in 1958. The right-field bleachers were jammed with black people and half the center-field bleachers. And when we came out on the field, Larry and I, they just started screaming and hollering. I thought they had a party out there or maybe there was a special night or something. Larry said, 'They came to see you.' I said, 'Oh, come on, man, you're kidding.'

"When we walked out there, black people were shoving their fingers through the fence wire just to shake your hand and to let you know they were with you."

Dr. Edward Turner, a Southfield obstetrician and gynecologist, recalls: "I wanted to be a baseball player more than anything when I was young, but I realized when I became twelve—people would say, 'You can be like Satchel Paige, or Josh Gibson.' And I'd say, 'Who's that?' I knew Joe DiMaggio and Bob Feller. And I realized that I really could not become a major league ball player. Then I gave it up and went into medicine. Medicine," he says wistfully, "was my second choice."

Turner went to Briggs Stadium for the first time in 1940 with his father and sat in the bleachers. "Hank Greenberg hit a home run, and Bob Feller pitched," he remembers. "The second time I went to the ball game, I went by myself. I caught the streetcar going the wrong way, went downtown, and had to walk from downtown to Thirtieth Street, which is on the west side, to my aunt's home. I never made that mistake again. I've been going to Tiger Stadium ever since, alone or with other people, but alone in a minute, because I love baseball. I love a doubleheader. I'm almost like Ernie Banks, who said 'Let's play two.' I'd almost say let's play three. I was out there for batting practice, for the whole shebang." Turner's love of the game persists even though Tiger management throughout the 1980s spurned his efforts to have an African-American Night at Michigan and Trumbull.

The Tigers' black fans had to wait a long time before they had a team they could call their own. Not until 1958, eleven years after Jackie Robinson's debut, did the Detroit Tigers acquire Ozzie Virgil from the Giants. Virgil, a native of the Dominican Republic, was the first black player to appear in a Tiger uniform.

By then, every other team except the Boston Red Sox had integrated its roster. (The Red Sox followed in 1959 with Pumpsie Green.) Dozens of black players were competing in the majors. But the Tigers were cautious about integrating. They chose Virgil, a light-skinned Dominican, rather than a dark-skinned black American. They broke him in on the road. Finally, on June 17, 1958, Virgil made his debut at Briggs Stadium. An expectant crowd of 29,794, including a packed bleacher crowd composed mostly of black fans, gave him a rousing ovation after each hit. Virgil went 5-for-5.

But Virgil's fine performance was a fluke. He was a light-hitting utility player who ended up with a .231 career batting average. He could not crack the Tigers' starting lineup. Before the 1959 season, the Tigers acquired Doby, who was at the end of his career.

Carl Rollyson grew up in Detroit and is now a writer living in New York. "I lived on the east side of Detroit," he recalls, "on a street called Revere, not far from Pershing High School. In the 1950s it was a lower-middle-class neighborhood.

"On my side of Seven Mile Road," he remembers, "everyone was white. Maybe various varieties — Italians, a lot of Poles, and a few others. On the other side of Seven Mile Road there was a black neighborhood, which I had no contact with. My elementary school was solidly, completely white. That was my world, and not until I went to junior high school, not until I was about thirteen, did I go to school with blacks."

The stadium was where he first met black people. He says there was a "sense of community" at Briggs Stadium; at least "it felt that way to a kid. Even though I grew up in a neighborhood where there were no black people, I might be sitting next to blacks in the stands, or close to them. And that was no problem. Everyone was there to watch baseball, and that was great.

"I remember I went to one game with the Chicago White Sox. We were in the upper deck. What I remember most distinctly was a black woman, maybe in her mid-thirties, kept yelling, 'Mister Minoso! Mister Minoso!' " at Chicago's black outfielder Minnie Minoso. "It sounded so formal. It was almost an expression of pride, or respect. I don't think he could have heard her.

"There was something about going into the stadium, and mingling with other kinds of people, and feeling really close to the action, which certainly meant a lot to me later, as an adult, when I went to the more modern stadiums and really didn't feel much at all."

Rollyson remembers going to Briggs Stadium with his father, who died in 1961, when Carl was thirteen. "A lot of what I remember of going to Briggs Stadium is wrapped up with memories of him taking me to the park. I remember sitting next to my father. It would be the sixth or seventh inning, and maybe Harvey Kuenn hadn't gotten a hit yet. I can still hear my father saying, 'Well, he's about due.' And often he would get a hit, because you could sort of guarantee a hit out of him.

"To me, as a little kid, the stadium seemed real old. But I liked that. It wasn't like anything else. It was so distinct. And to an eight- or nine-year-old kid it seemed almost ancient. I would think of things when I came to the park: Ty Cobb played here, and Greenberg, and Cochrane.

"Going into the stadium, walking up the ramp, going up into the upper reaches of it made me feel, in a way, a part of that tradition. I associated the physical, concrete structure with the game that was being played.

"It was all of a piece. There was a kind of purity to it. There was something sort of classical about the fact that the Yankees were so dominant. And it seemed like such a struggle for any other team, including the Tigers.

"If I were writing a memoir about growing up in Detroit, I'd have to talk about baseball and the stadium. The distinctive quality of the stadium and how I felt about the sport really go hand in hand."

Briggs Stadium was a microcosm of Detroit, whose population peaked in the mid-1950s at nearly two million. The city was thriving and prosperous. Downtown was alive with cultural offerings, the city had an effective public transportation system, and tourists frequently visited on weekends from Toronto.

But just as the Tigers retained a color bar, the city held onto its segregated past. Black and white workers mingled in the factories but lived and played separately. Detroit's large, urbane black population had a separate entertainment district on Hastings Street, went to separate churches, and was confined to neighborhoods east of Woodward Avenue.

As the 1960s began, there was a new restlessness and sometimes an ugliness among the fans at Michigan and Trumbull. Their main target was troubled Cleveland outfielder Jimmy Piersall. Piersall, who had well-publicized emotional problems, used to taunt bleacher fans who razzed him. Soon it was open warfare.

In 1960 bleacher creatures peppered Piersall with bolts, ice cubes, and paper clips—and sometimes even giant firecrackers wrapped in hair pins and heavy wire. Piersall kept a collection of items donated to him by Detroit fans, including a hammer inscribed "To JP—Here's something you can use to knock some brains into your head."

The mayhem began to spread. Fans tossed ball bearings, marbles, paper clips, eggs, fruit, and money into all corners of the outfield. Tiger left fielder Charlie Maxwell told the press: "You can walk in left field and find a small fortune."

Just after the All-Star break in 1960, the Tigers were playing New York at Briggs Stadium and leading the Yankees 2-0 in the eighth inning when umpire Joe Paparella called a Bill Skowron drive down the line a home run. The next inning, fans in right field threw beer bottles and whiskey bottles at Roger Maris. A wooden slat torn from the back of a grandstand chair whizzed past Maris, who retreated. The umpires warned the fans, but the fracas continued. A fan dropped a bag of garbage and beer cans into the Yankee bull pen; the pitchers fled to the dugout. The Yankees could not warm up a reliever and lost the game.

Kuenn, who had been traded to the Indians before the 1960 season for Rocky Colavito, was the league's player representative. He demanded that the league restore order at Briggs Stadium and other ballparks. The Tigers stationed uniformed policemen around the park, and late in the 1960 season the Detroit City Council passed a law ordaining ninety days in jail and a five hundred-dollar fine for anyone caught throwing objects on the field at Briggs Stadium. It was called the DeWitt Law, after Tiger president Bill DeWitt.

DeWitt was the club's third president in three years. The front office seemed in almost as much chaos as the bleachers. Gradually, one man emerged from the confusing ownership group.

John E. Fetzer had amassed a fortune running radio and TV stations in Michigan and around the Midwest. In 1960 he showed his acumen by hiring Ernie Harwell to be the Tigers' radio broadcaster. That same year, Fetzer gained two-thirds control of the team. By 1961 he had bought up the remaining shares and become the sole owner.

The Briggs era, considered by many the heyday of Tiger baseball, was over. In twenty-three seasons at Briggs Stadium, the Tigers had drawn more fans than the league average twenty-two times.

CHAPTER 7

WE'RE ALL BEHIND
OUR BASEBALL TEAM

The Tigers in '68 were a really exciting team. It didn't hurt that we had a newspaper strike on that summer, so the media wasn't picking on them, or beating up on them. You listened to the game on the radio, and there was Ernie Harwell, and they were winning. Everybody was listening to the game, and everybody had heroes. It was really a great summer.

— Tiger fan Randy Westbrooks

On January 1, 1961, John Fetzer changed the name of the park at Michigan and Trumbull from Briggs Stadium to Tiger Stadium. The Tigers spent twenty thousand dollars to change the letters on the electric sign at Michigan and Cochrane and to reprint office stationery.

Breaking the connection between the Briggs name and the ballpark was important symbolically. Now the stadium was synonymous with the franchise, and the new name bespoke the solid half century of connection among the fans, the team and the park. Fetzer Stadium would have been a misnomer. Unlike the previous two owners, Fetzer made no important changes to the park. Unlike Navin and Briggs, Fetzer shunned publicity and moved behind the scenes to make gradual changes in the organization.

Under Fetzer the club started to move away from its mossbacked policies of the 1950s. Cynics might say that Fetzer really only moved the team *into* the 1950s. Fetzer was a traditionalist and made changes slowly. As most owners do, he gained a reputation among fans for tight-fistedness.

Opening Day 1961 was the first test of the DeWitt Law banning fans from throwing objects on the field. Jimmy Piersall was in town with the Cleveland Indians. Fans defying the ordinance threw a hair brush, a tape measure, golf balls, and other objects at Piersall, and a fifteen-year-old fan was arrested.

Jake Wood made his debut that day. Wood was the first regular black player the Tigers had developed. He batted leadoff in 1961, led the league in triples, and stole thirty bases—the highest single season total on the notoriously slow-footed team since Gee Walker had stolen thirty in 1932.

The stadium had a new name, the Tigers had their first regular black player, and the first Saturday night game was played on June 17 against the Yankees. Ladies Days were introduced on weekday afternoons. Women and boys and girls could sit in the upper deck for fifty cents.

"We went to almost every Ladies Day game for years," says Catherine Darin. "We would sometimes bring lunches and sometimes we would get hot dogs. One time we went with my neighbor across the street and her little boy, Mark, who was about four or five. Mark brought his favorite stuffed animal—a tattered old bear, I guess it was. Charlie Maxwell hit a home run, and everybody jumped up and got excited, and Mark got excited too and threw his bear down toward the field. Then he starting crying. We told him we would look for the bear after the game. Sure enough, we found it a few rows down."

Lots of Tiger fans got excited in 1961. Led by career years from Norm Cash (.361 average) and Rocky Colavito (45 home runs), the Tigers stayed in the race until September against the vaunted Yankees. Attendance, which had slumped a bit in the late 1950s, jumped to 1.6 million.

It was the beginning of a successful decade in which the Tigers finished under .500 only once, in 1963. The Tigers were assembling a team of young players, mostly groomed in their farm system, who would eventually mature into world champions.

The 1962 Tiger yearbook had a feature called "Watch for These Faces," picturing Mickey Lolich, Mickey Stanley, Jim Northrup, Tom Timmerman, Fred Gladding and Purnal Goldy. The 1963 yearbook listed as "Up & Coming" Lolich, Stanley, Don Wert, Gates Brown, and Willie Horton.

Horton and Brown joined the club in 1963. A talented athlete at Northwestern High School, Horton was the first black Tiger star to have grown up in Detroit and played in the city leagues. He played fifteen seasons for the Tigers. Brown, a premier pinch hitter, played thirteen seasons and later was a batting coach.

As the Tigers began their rise, the Detroit Lions prolonged their string of winning seasons. Tiger Stadium continued to host other events, including the annual Fireman's Field Day. It was the city's ball field, used by high schools, colleges, and sandlot teams as well as the pros. Each year, the stadium hosted the city's high school football and baseball championship games, pitting the top teams from the public schools against the Catholic League champs.

Doug Rutherford, a retired Detroit schoolteacher who now works as an usher at Tiger Stadium, recalls: "They used to play a lot of collegian football in here. I can remember seeing Notre Dame and the University of Detroit play in Tiger Stadium. For many years they packed this stadium. A lot of people don't realize all the football that's been played in there."

During the 1960s Fetzer accelerated the transition from day to night baseball. Scheduled night games doubled in three years, from twenty-one in 1963 to forty-two in 1966. Except for Ladies Days, midweek daytime baseball became a thing of the past.

In 1966 Don Shapiro and Max Lapides assaulted Tiger general manager Jim Campbell with letters protesting the advent of organ music in the stadium. "Now I see that one of the things they talk about nostalgically is the organ," laughs Shapiro. "For us, the organ was *breaking* with tradition. We didn't want anything. We wanted to be able to talk, to muse about what had happened the previous inning. The organ was a distraction; it was nonsense; it was dumb."

In 1966 the Tigers acquired another prominent black player, pitcher Earl Wilson, from the Red Sox. Horton, Brown, and Wilson joined veterans Kaline and Cash and a new crop of talented young white players—Denny McLain, Lolich, Bill Freehan, Dick McAuliffe, Northrup, and Stanley—to create a formidable ball club.

With a few black stars, the Tigers moved closer to fielding a team that reflected Detroit's population. During the decade between Ozzie Virgil's first game and the momentous events of 1967 and 1968, great changes were taking place around the nation and in the Motor City. A network of freeways chopped up city neighborhoods and opened the suburbs to white flight. Hastings Street, the longtime center of black culture, was demolished to make room for the Chrysler Freeway. The city began to lose population. Many whites left, and the city's black community expanded in area and numbers. Detroit, always a segregated city, was becoming a segregated metropolitan area.

At Michigan and Trumbull, more black fans were coming to games to see Horton, Brown, and Wilson. The three became extremely popular with white fans as well. Horton's powerful swing generated excitement, and Brown's clutch homers gave him a vocal following. At last, all Detroiters had a team they could be proud of.

In 1967 the Tigers were entangled in a wild four-team pennant race. Around the nation, inner-city neighborhoods were exploding in violence. In Detroit tense relations between the mostly white police force and the black population provided a potent trigger.

Early on the morning of July 23, a police raid on a "blind pig" — an illegal after-hours drinking establishment — sparked a riot. By the end of that Sunday the Twelfth Street area, not far from Tiger Stadium, was in flames. In the five-day riot that followed, forty-three people died, scores were injured, and hundreds of stores were burned and looted. On July 25 the National Guard was patrolling the streets of the city. The Tigers decided to cancel a night game against the Orioles and move the next two games to Baltimore.

The Tigers stayed in contention until the last day of the season. On October 1 at Tiger Stadium, Detroit won the first game of a doubleheader against the California Angels. A victory in the second game would give the Tigers the pennant. But they lost, 8–5, as McAuliffe grounded into a double play with two men on in the bottom of the ninth. Some fans spilled onto the field and ripped up sod. A pennant might have eased some of the pain of that terrible summer in Detroit, but at the very end it had slipped away.

The next season, the Tigers lost on Opening Day but won their next ten games and charged out to a big lead. The team captivated the town.

"The Tigers in '68 were a really exciting team," says Randy Westbrooks of Milan, Michigan. "It didn't hurt that we had a newspaper strike on that summer, so the media wasn't picking on them, or beating up on them. You listened to the game on the radio, and there was Ernie Harwell, and they were winning. Everybody was listening to the game, and everybody had heroes. It was really a great summer."

The team was a fascinating mix of personalities. Playboy McLain flew his own airplane and played the organ in gigs at night spots. Cash was a hard-drinking Texan, a good old boy. Many of the Tigers, black and white, were likely to show up at local bars after the games, and sometimes they stayed to close them down.

The Tigers led the league all season, but they managed to retain the mantle of underdogs by falling behind in many games and fashioning improbable comeback victories. Each day had a different hero. Gates

Brown often stepped off the bench to produce dramatic game-winning home runs, but even little-used reserves produced in the clutch.

The city was enthralled. Pulling up at stoplights, you could hear Harwell and radio sidekick Ray Lane from every car. On the beach, in the pool halls, at softball games and picnics, the voices of the Tigers were everywhere, and strangers would ask one another the score.

A corny song became the Tiger anthem:

> We're all behind our baseball team.
> Go get 'em, Tigers.
> World Series bound and pickin' up steam.
> Go get 'em, Tigers.

Tiger fan John Grindstaff was at the quintessential 1968 Tiger victory, against the second-place Orioles. "It was a Friday night against Baltimore," he relates, "and the bleachers were as packed as I've ever seen them. You could hardly get in here with a shoehorn. We were sitting in the aisle. We got here at six-thirty, and we couldn't get a seat.

"It was the bottom of the ninth, and two were out, one on, and we were one run back. The Tigers sent up a kid who hardly played at all that year, Tommy Matchick, and on a three-two pitch he hit a home run. That really was the most exciting moment I ever saw. I'll never forget that. The whole place just rose as one."

Tiger fan Bill Dow recalls that the '68 Tigers also had more subtle talents. "There was a game against Baltimore in 1968," he says, "where there was a runner on third, and a really deep fly to right field. The runner tagged and Kaline threw a ball on the line right into Freehan's mitt. No hop or anything. And the runner who was trying to come home stopped dead in his tracks half way and just slid back into third base. The whole stadium gave Kaline a standing ovation. It gives me chills thinking about it."

The integrated, never-say-die Tigers provided Detroit a badly needed image of achievement and equality. They were a team of strong-willed individuals, each contributing his share to collective success. Their victories produced a contagion of confidence no matter the score. In a city where people were arming themselves to the teeth, many were fleeing, and social divisions were widening, the Tigers embodied hope and unity.

Throughout that turbulent summer, Michigan and Trumbull was a common ground where people set aside their differences, where everything somehow turned out all right in the end. The Tigers were a team of destiny, and their ballpark was a mecca. For the first time, the club drew over two million fans.

Tiger Stadium witnessed the political drama of the controversial presidential campaign when Democratic candidate Eugene McCarthy came to Detroit for a rally focusing on opposition to the Vietnam War. Torrential rains hit the area all afternoon and evening, but tens of thousands of antiwar activists and McCarthy sympathizers converged on Michigan and Trumbull anyway.

"It was a big rally," McCarthy recalls. "It didn't mean much in terms of the campaign, because the Michigan delegation had been sewed up three years earlier. We let them know that they were being dishonest in not giving us any votes. We had a couple of big rallies. We had a big rally in Fenway Park, too. That was the only other ballpark. This was just about as big, probably thirty or forty thousand people."

On September 14 McLain won his thirtieth game before a national TV audience and a packed house that included Julie Nixon, David Eisenhower and Dizzy Dean, the last pitcher to win thirty games. Dean had performed the feat for St. Louis in 1934, the year the Cardinals beat the Tigers in the World Series and the fans at Michigan and Trumbull showered debris on Ducky Medwick. Now, thirty-four years later, the fans were showering McLain with love. Following the season's script, the Tigers rescued McLain from defeat with a psychedelic ninth-inning rally—bad bounces, good vibes—capped by a Horton base hit.

Three days later, the Tigers needed one win or a Baltimore defeat to clinch the pennant. Joe Sparma, a talented but erratic pitcher, took the mound against New York and turned in the performance of his life before a screaming packed house. The score was 1–1 in the ninth. As the Tigers came to bat, club officials learned that Boston had beaten Baltimore, making the outcome of the Tiger game irrelevant. But they feared that if they posted the Baltimore result on the scoreboard, the fans would swarm the field and cause a forfeit. So they held back the score, hoping the Tigers could win in the ninth. In a big game in 1968, that was a good bet.

Ernie Harwell's excited voice on the radio broadcast, describing the hit by Don Wert that ended the game, is etched in the memories of many Tiger fans: "There's the windup, and the pitch. Line shot, left field! Base hit! Wert singles, Kaline scores from third, the Tigers win it! The Tigers mob Don, the fans are streaming onto the field, and

Detroit has won its first pennant since nineteen hundred and forty-five. Let's listen to the bedlam at Tiger Stadium."

And bedlam it was. Fans poured onto the field from all directions. In the bleachers, they crushed the center-field fence and jumped by the hundreds onto the field. Strangers embraced and danced. Jubilant fans tore up the sod and held pieces aloft as trophies. They raced dizzily around the field, hardly believing they were touching the sacred ground where all the magic things had happened. It was a love-in.

A fireworks display in center field signaled a finale to the events in the stadium. But the celebration continued in the streets. As in 1935 downtown was jammed with cars blaring horns and snaking through the clogged streets. Bars threw open their doors.

Despite their domination of the American League, the Tigers were underdogs in the World Series. They were facing the Cardinals, who had the best pitcher in baseball, Bob Gibson, and the best runner, Lou Brock. To generate more offense, manager Mayo Smith moved Stanley, a brilliant center fielder, to shortstop, a position he had never played, making room in the outfield for Kaline. The gamble paid off; Stanley handled every chance at shortstop. In St. Louis, Gibson beat McLain in the first game, striking out seventeen batters, but Lolich won the second game. On October 5 the Tigers played their first World Series game at Michigan and Trumbull in twenty-three years but lost, 7–3. The next day, a rainy Sunday, McLain and the Tigers were humiliated by Gibson and the Cards, 10–1. It seemed the magic had run out.

The fifth game, played on Monday, October 7, opened in controversy. Irate callers flooded phone lines at radio and TV stations after rock singer Jose Feliciano, who had been recommended for the job by Harwell, sang a bluesy version of the national anthem.

In the fifth inning the Tigers were down, 3–2, with Brock on second base. The home team's cause seemed almost hopeless. Julian Javier lined a single to Horton in left, and Brock sped confidently around third. Horton's arm was ordinary at best. But he charged the ball and quickly unleashed a devastating throw. Brock, expecting to score easily, disdained a slide, and catcher Bill Freehan blocked him brilliantly and slapped down a quick tag. The umpire called Brock out, and the crowd roared.

A raging argument ensued. That tag at the plate is the most memorable and most debated play in the history of Michigan and Trumbull. Cardinal fans still insist Brock was safe. Photographs seem to show

Brock's left foot pushed just off a corner of the plate at the instant the tag was applied.

Horton's throw and Freehan's tag reversed the momentum of the Series. The Tigers had looked helpless against Brock; now they felt they could throttle the Cardinals' running game. It was the rebirth of hope. In the seventh inning the Tigers mounted their patented comeback, with a two-run single by Kaline winning the game, 5–3.

The Series went back to St. Louis and the Tigers won the sixth game with ease, 13–1. The deciding game, pitting Lolich against Gibson, was a scoreless tie until the Cardinals' usually brilliant center fielder Curt Flood stumbled and let a fly ball by Jim Northrup go over his head for a two-run triple that won the game and the Series for the Tigers.

Mike Ridley, now a local singer, grew up in rural Walled Lake and remembers that moment. "I was a junior in high school," he recalls. "I was running cross-country that year, and the seventh game of the World Series was on. Everybody wanted to hear the game, so they all went out to the football field, sat in the bleachers, and turned on the World Series. They listened to it over the football loudspeakers. I'm running the race, and the game ends just about the same time I'm crossing the finish line — twentieth, twenty-fifth in the cross-country race. And everybody's going nuts! I'm thinking: Hey, Mike Ridley just crosses the line, what's so big about that? But the Tigers had just won the World Series."

When Lolich secured the final out, pandemonium broke loose in Detroit. Work stopped and downtown streets grew thick with ticker tape. Delirious fans swarmed all over Metro Airport to welcome back their heroes; the Tigers landed at Willow Run Airport to avoid being crushed. Cars honked and people flashed victory signs all night. For a few hours, the entire Detroit area was united and happy.

The 1968 Tigers were the first championship team that really belonged to all Detroiters.

Lolich later recalled the triumph this way: "It was like a dream for people. The Tigers didn't win the pennant, the people won the pennant."

But the magic and hope of 1968 faded quickly. No mere baseball championship could stem the tide of decline in the city. And the sacred sod at Tiger Stadium soon came to be looked on as a quaint relic of the past.

84

CHAPTER 8

THE RIVERFRONT DOME SCAM

The so-called 'common man' will benefit more than big business from the stadium because it will provide a more attractive entertainment facility and more importantly create additional tax revenues for housing, education and other basic needs.

> — *Wayne County Stadium Authority Chairman Tom Adams*

They were threatening me. They said that if the stadium wasn't built, the Renaissance Center wouldn't be built and that the revitalization of downtown Detroit — that was the key word back then — would never come about.

They asked me, "Do you have kids?" I said I had five kids. They said, "Do you want your kids to remember you as the man who destroyed the city of Detroit?"

> — *Ron Prebenda*

The riots of 1967 and the world championship of 1968 dealt a one-two punch to the tradition at Michigan and Trumbull. In July 1967 business leaders in Detroit realized that the city and their investments in it were in jeopardy. By October 1968, noting how the Tigers' triumph had united the metropolitan area, many civic leaders had come to believe that baseball could save Detroit. A consensus began to form among opinion makers that a new downtown stadium would help reverse Detroit's decline.

This view was rooted in the theories of liberal social engineers who believed that large public works projects could stem urban blight.

85

Detroit's downtown area, with its aging buildings and declining tax base, could be revitalized with grand new projects that would compete with development in the suburbs, civic leaders thought.

Around the nation, many cities were tearing down their classic ballparks and building modern multipurpose sports arenas. The new stadiums of the 1960s and 1970s were vastly different from their predecessors:

(1) They were larger than most of the old parks. The classic ballparks generally had capacities of thirty to forty thousand. The new parks could hold fifty to sixty thousand.

(2) The new stadiums were multipurpose, which meant a circular design to accommodate football, concerts, and rallies as well as baseball. The oval shape meant most baseball fans had seats much farther away from the action than in the old parks.

(3) They were built on large parcels of cleared land without the constraints imposed by existing street patterns. They usually had symmetrical field dimensions for baseball, and were surrounded by an asphalt ring of parking spaces.

(4) With the sole exception of Dodger Stadium in Los Angeles, they were financed by the public rather than by private investors. The main impetus for this change was the plethora of franchise relocations in the 1950s and 1960s. Many cities felt they had to build new stadiums to keep their teams from leaving town.

The second modern era of stadium construction began in 1932, when the city of Cleveland built a monstrous lakefront stadium with a capacity of over 75,000. Like the modern stadiums built thirty-five and more years later, Municipal Stadium was a huge multipurpose oval on a large parcel of cleared land. Poorly designed and much too large for baseball, Municipal Stadium is a stark, wind-blown structure that quickly came to be known as the "Mistake by the Lake." The Indians were so uncomfortable with the municipally operated ballpark that they remained in old League Park, except for weekend games, until 1947.

In 1953 Milwaukee built a county-financed stadium to lure the Braves from Boston. In 1954 Baltimore built Memorial Stadium to grab the Browns from St. Louis. In 1955 Kansas City rebuilt its minor league park into Municipal Stadium and enticed the Athletics to move from Philadelphia. (The A's left Kansas City for Oakland in 1968.) In all three cases, the teams that moved left cities that had been support-ing two major league franchises.

In 1962 the last privately financed baseball stadium opened in Los Angeles. Dodger Stadium housed the team that had left Brooklyn's Ebbets Field in 1958 in the most wrenching franchise relocation in sports history.

One by one, the classic ballparks built between 1887 and 1923 met their demise. The oldest, Philadelphia's Baker Bowl, had been the first to go, in 1938. League Park in Cleveland closed for good in 1950. Braves Field in Boston was abandoned after 1952 and Brooklyn's Ebbets Field after 1957.

Between 1960 and 1973 six more classic ballparks were replaced by new stadiums, and eight other new parks were built for expansion teams or relocated franchises. Candlestick Park opened in 1960 in San Francisco. Griffith Stadium in Washington closed in 1961, replaced the next year by District of Columbia Stadium, later known as R.F.K. Stadium. Dodger Stadium was built in 1962. The legendary Polo Grounds in New York closed in 1963, replaced by Shea Stadium. In 1965 the first domed stadium was built in Houston. In 1966 new stadi-ums opened in Atlanta and Anaheim, California, and St. Louis replaced Sportsman's Park with Busch Stadium. In 1968 the Oakland-Alameda County Coliseum opened. The next year a new park was built in San Diego.

In 1970 Cincinnati substituted Riverfront Stadium for Crosley Field and Pittsburgh replaced Forbes Field with Three Rivers Stadium. In 1971 Philadelphia replaced Connie Mack Stadium (formerly known as Shibe Park) with Veterans Stadium. Kansas City built a new stadium for its expansion team in 1973.

Public financing changed the way ballparks looked. Cities generally had not bulldozed homes or moved streets to build or expand privately financed parks. The old parks had been molded to fit the space avail-able. When cities built new stadiums under the rubric of urban redevel-opment, vast spaces were cleared and homes and businesses demolished with the promise of new jobs and economic revitalization—a promise never delivered in most cases. On the cleared land rose huge dough-nuts, designed as neutral containers for any sport or entertainment.

Surrounding the new ovals were seas of controlled parking—an important source of revenue for the clubs. Displaced were the small businesses and homeowners who had earned money from parking cars on their lots or lawns. Left outside the ring of parking were the bars, restaurants, and souvenir shops that had flourished in the old stadium neighborhoods.

Each old ballpark had its own design and unique character, but the new stadiums had few distinguishing features. Almost all had symmetrical field dimensions. Much as malls and fast-food restaurants resemble one another, it is hard to tell when inside Three Rivers, Veterans, or Riverfront whether you are in Cincinnati, Pittsburgh, or Philadelphia.

"Until about 1960, visiting fans and players could unfailingly tell where they were from the shape of the stadium," writes John Pastier, a Los Angeles architecture critic and ballpark expert. "Today, they can't always be sure."

"There was a whole spate of new stadiums, and they all looked alike: the round, spaceship, flying-saucer kind of stadium," recalls Bob Buchta of Detroit. Twenty years later, Buchta would lead the fight to save Tiger Stadium, but in the late 1960s and early 1970s he was on the sidelines. "It was the tenor of the times," he says. "I think there was just the assumption that a new stadium is a good thing — that newer is better. There was little regard for history back then."

Houston brought two scourges to the game: the dome and the synthetic field. The Astrodome brought baseball in from the sun and fresh air to a controlled environment, where the summer game seemed stifled. Shifting winds, bright sun, rain and mud, even snow had long been factors in games; now the battle with the elements was eliminated. Artificial turf was ideal for multipurpose stadiums because it didn't get torn up by football teams or tractor pulls, and it was cheaper to maintain. It quickly became the rage, and within a few years half the teams in the National League were playing on carpets. The disadvantages of turf — more knee and leg injuries, ridiculous bounces — became apparent in time.

"I don't recall a lot of outcry about artificial turf when they put it in," says Buchta. "But after a while people saw how it was changing the game of baseball, and they didn't like those changes."

The symmetry of the new stadiums, the moving of the game indoors and the new playing surface profoundly affected baseball. The game's variety and its connection to sky and grass were smothered by the artificiality of the baseball mall.

But in the late 1960s the new stadium mania was unchecked. Even Boston formed a stadium authority to study replacing historic Fenway Park. Today's widespread recognition of the value of outdoor baseball, natural grass, and baseball-only stadiums came too late for many cities. It would have come too late for Detroit too, but for the arrogance and deceit of stadium promoters and the last-ditch efforts of a few outraged taxpayers.

As early as 1948 city fathers had proposed building a huge municipal stadium to lure the Olympics to Detroit. *Free Press* sports columnist Lyall Smith opposed the plan, arguing that the money should be spent on smaller high school stadiums:

> This is the city which is making a strong bid to become the site of the Olympic Games. It is talking of building a 100,000-seat stadium, and there seems little doubt that the money for such a tremendous project will be forthcoming.
> But this is the same city which is doing nothing for its kids in the manner they like best . . . a sports program with decent facilities.

Detroit failed to land the Olympics, and the stadium plan was shelved. But in 1956 City Councilman Edward Connor proposed a 100,000-seat stadium for the Lions, the Tigers, Wayne University, and the University of Detroit. "It should be somewhere in the outlying section of the city," said Connor. "Then we could get rid of Briggs Stadium, which doesn't belong in the heart of the city anyway."

Talk of a new multipurpose stadium in Detroit next arose in the early 1960s, when civic leaders made a bid for the 1968 Olympic Games. The state legislature increased taxes on parimutuel betting at race tracks to raise $25 million for a new open-air stadium to be built at the State Fairgrounds with seats for 110,000 fans. Lion owner William Ford backed the plan, but Detroit Mayor Jerome Cavanagh opposed it, saying: "We've got a lot of other unmet needs in this city." Also opposed was Councilman Billy Rogell, a former Tiger shortstop. "We haven't got enough money to pay our bills, much less build a stadium," said Rogell.

When Detroit again didn't get the Olympics, the plan for the gargantuan fairgrounds stadium was shelved.

But in 1966 Cavanagh formed a new committee to study stadiums. Within the next year stadium study groups were also formed by the Detroit Chamber of Commerce, the State Fairgrounds, and a state government group in Lansing. In July 1967 the mayor's committee recommended construction of a new 60,000-seat, $55 million domed fairgrounds stadium with parking for 10,500 cars. Construction was to begin late in 1968 and the target date for completion was the 1970 baseball season. The plan was released only a few days before the 1967 riots, and the vision of a new stadium was blotted out by the smoke and hate.

Detroit's 1967 turmoil may have prompted Ford to reconsider the wisdom of the lease he had signed a year earlier committing the Lions to play at Tiger Stadium for another ten years. Many Lion fans were moving to the suburbs. Ford, long unhappy with the Lions' secondary role at Michigan and Trumbull, began looking for a way out.

"He wanted his own stadium," says Walter Briggs III. "He didn't want to be a tenant. I think he felt that if he could get something with more than fifty-five thousand seats in it, the revenue would be all his."

In January 1968 the Lions published a glossy report, "The Detroit Stadium Story," gushing over new stadiums built or planned in other cities. The report called the Astrodome "the Taj Mahal of all stadia . . . shining like a precious jewel in southwest Houston, Texas."

Tiger Stadium's capacity of 54,082, the report said, "is wholly inadequate to meet the demands of pro football. Furthermore, after forty years [sic] of use, the present Tiger Stadium is badly deteriorated and its appointments are generally incompatible with the increasing size of the population of the Tri-County area."

The report called for a stadium authority to build a horseshoe-shaped stadium with Astroturf and luxury suites and said "The use of individual theatre-type contour moulded plastic seats with armrests is a 'must.' " The Lions wanted a stadium that would seat 50,000 for baseball and convert through the opening of electronic panels into a 70,000-seat football stadium. "A simple press of the button could provide additional capacity," claimed the report.

The report added: "Bleacher seats are fast becoming a thing of the past. There is the tendency for highest priced seats to sell out first."

In 1968 a group of prominent architects from the metropolitan area formed a stadium committee and studied eleven sites for a new stadium, only three of which were in Detroit.

Some officials looked at areas around Tiger Stadium as possible sites. The spread of blight was accelerated by the new Fisher Freeway, which had sliced between the stadium and the neighborhood to the north, sometimes called the Briggs Community. This working-class neighborhood had some of the city's oldest houses. Many residents supplemented their incomes by parking cars on their lawns, in their driveways, or in vacant lots. But over the years, more and more houses were demolished, and parking lot magnates took over larger parcels.

The increasingly depopulated neighborhood was considered prime stadium turf, but official opinion soon coalesced around a downtown site.

On February 5, 1969, the Chamber of Commerce endorsed Cavanagh's proposal for a domed stadium and a surrounding commercial development on an eighty-acre site along the Detroit River west of Cobo Hall, the city's convention center. Tom Adams, chairman of the board of Campbell-Ewald, an advertising firm, was named to head a stadium task force.

But there was fierce competition for the privilege of building a dome. In 1969 the Lions were considering moving to suburban Southfield, but residents there defeated the plan for a new stadium with a petition drive. In July the City of Pontiac proposed building side-by-side stadiums for the Tigers and Lions. In August a state task force recommended a 67,000-seat domed stadium at the fairgrounds.

The Pontiac proposal was attractive to Ford. At Michigan and Trumbull, he had little say in decisions about the ballpark. The Lions had to work their schedule around Tiger home games. The park was designed for baseball and was less than ideal for football.

"Football has grown to a stage where it no longer has to be a stepchild of baseball," Ford told the *Wall Street Journal*. "Our fans want a football-only stadium, and we're going to give them one."

In truth, opinion among Lion fans was far from unanimous. Though many welcomed a move to a new suburban stadium, many others cherished fond memories of games at Michigan and Trumbull and liked Tiger Stadium's central location.

But Ford was determined to get a new stadium, wherever he could get the best deal. Fetzer also was impatient for a modern ballpark. The pressure was on the City of Detroit to keep both teams.

Detroit attorney Charles Moon was heavily involved in plans for a new riverfront stadium. The original idea, he says, "was a desire to have a stadium that could handle basketball, hockey, baseball, and football. In other words, it was to be a four-way stadium. The principal supporters of it at the time, however, were the Tigers. . . . The rest of the entities . . . hadn't decided whether to come along or not. But it seemed pretty clear they would, because it was going to be the only action in town."

In February 1970 a working group appointed by Cavanagh and Governor William Milliken recommended a domed stadium on the Cobo Hall site. The dome would be about twenty-five stories high and would seat 70,000 for football and 55,000 for baseball. The cost was estimated at $150 million, including acquiring land and constructing parking structures, and it was to be financed through the sale of revenue bonds. Cavanagh favored calling the project "MegaSphere" but said he was also considering "River's Edge," "South Point," and "MetroSphere."

Like others around the nation, the downtown dome would have artificial turf, a closed-circuit color TV system with several large screens, a stadium club, luxury suites, and restaurants. It could be converted to a 20,000-seat concert arena. The plan included on-site parking for forty-six hundred cars, two adjacent structures to hold four thousand more, and an aerial cable car across the Detroit River to bring Canadians to the stadium.

"As envisioned by planners, the domed structure would rise as high as the Pontchartrain Hotel, and would be the hub of a gigantic downtown sports-shopping-dining complex that could surpass any other facility in North America," the *Free Press* reported on March 15, 1970. The stadium was "envisioned as a catalyst that would touch off a revitalization in a city plagued by racial problems, rising crime, and a loss of population, commerce, construction and spirit in recent years."

Civic leaders argued that the dome would spur downtown redevelopment and counter the flight of residents, jobs, and businesses to the suburbs. Soon, every major politician and business leader had lined up behind the stadium plan.

Hyperbole about the project's benefits flowed like wine. In a March 20, 1970, letter to Milliken and Detroit's new mayor, Roman Gribbs, stadium task force chairman Adams spelled out the rationale. "Our city needs revitalizing," he wrote, "to maintain its present business and resident population and to attract additional commercial revenue-producing interests which will help Detroit to grow and prosper. The stadium, with the opportunities it can provide for adjacent commercial development, can stand as a highly visible symbol of the determination of Detroit and its people to move forward with demonstrated confidence. It may be the most important thing we have ever done for the future of the city."

In July 1970 Governor Milliken signed a bill creating the Wayne County Stadium Authority. Adams was elected chairman.

The vision of the riverfront project continued to expand. The movers and shakers spoke of a pedestrian promenade near the stadium with shops, a convention hotel, high-rise apartments, and other ancillary developments. Backers argued that the project would generate new businesses, higher land values, a bigger tax base, more downtown residents, more police protection, and even better street lighting.

Robert Sweany, executive director of the downtown stadium working group, told Detroit's city council on October 9, 1970, that a recent Stanford Research Institute study showed that "greater Detroit would get an immediate boost of nearly $2 billion to its economy during the construction and first year of operation of the proposed stadium." Sweany added that the stadium "should lead to a complete turn-around in the central city area."

Actually, the Stanford study suggested that the stadium would generate $1 billion in new income, $2 billion in new retail sales, and more than $130 million in tax revenues by 1990. But it didn't matter what the numbers were. That a new stadium would revitalize the city was an article of faith.

Also a given was the idea that the stadium should be domed. For one thing, non-baseball events would be needed to pay off construction costs. And domes were the wave of the future; Detroit didn't want to be left behind. Adams put it simply in a *Free Press* interview: "Experts around the country have been consulted and they say that any stadium not domed would be outdated the moment it was built. We in the authority feel that a great city like Detroit should do at least as well as Houston or New Orleans."

As to the idea that the stadium would benefit only big business, Adams countered: "The so-called 'common man' will benefit more than big business from the stadium because it will provide a more attractive entertainment facility and more importantly create additional tax revenues for housing, education and other basic needs."

Detroit Renaissance, a new civic organization founded after the riots, came to see the stadium as the key to rebuilding the city. Detroit Renaissance raised $800,000 from the business community to hire an architect and operate the stadium authority. Every major business in town lent money, including $10,000 from the *Detroit News*, $7,500 from the *Free Press*, and $1,000 from WJBK, a leading television station. It was no wonder the media were filled with dubious claims about a new stadium's benefits.

Putting the land and financing together for the massive project was a slow process. In the fall of 1970 Milliken announced he would recommend that the state earmark horse racing revenues for the stadium. On November 20 Mayor Gribbs told a Detroit Renaissance meeting that the city had $3 million available for land acquisition. By the end of 1970 negotiations were nearly complete with two railroad companies that owned the land west of the riverfront.

Ford continued to apply pressure, setting deadlines and threatening to move to Pontiac. Fetzer said he would give Tiger Stadium to charity and move the Tigers to the new stadium if a satisfactory lease could be worked out.

Many fans didn't see a need to replace Tiger Stadium. "I don't see why everyone gets so excited about a domed stadium," Brenda Shuck of Findlay, Ohio, told the *Free Press*. "I like being outdoors watching people play on real grass. This is a good stadium."

But such sentiment wasn't about to get in the way of progress. A Chamber of Commerce staff report on January 26, 1971, outlined the history of the downtown stadium project in a triumphant tone. The report concluded confidently: "The new downtown stadium will soon be a reality."

During 1971 plans for the Pontiac dome progressed while the downtown stadium authority faced difficulties acquiring land and putting together the project. Ford expressed increasing doubts about the riverfront site, claiming it would have terrible traffic congestion and inadequate parking—concerns that appear to have been well founded. In a letter dated February 5, 1971, to James Wineman, a member of the stadium working group, Ford said he had given his "complete assent" to other Detroit locations, including the fairgrounds and a site near the existing Tiger Stadium, but he could not endorse a riverfront dome. Ford said the stadium authority had responded by insisting on the downtown site.

Ford's plans to desert the city despite his lease with Fetzer brought angry and bitter reaction. Black fans especially felt disenfranchised. For a time, there was even talk among Lion fans in Detroit about boycotting Ford cars.

Ford's position caused some doubts, but the project went ahead. Fetzer remained aboard the downtown bandwagon.

In a 1980 interview, Tiger general manager Jim Campbell said the Pontiac developers had tried and failed to woo Fetzer. "When the Pontiac Stadium was in the planning stage," said Campbell, "the group in Pontiac who were putting this plan together came to Mr. Fetzer first. We all sat in Mr. Fetzer's office next door and they offered us the chance to go to Pontiac" in a twin-stadium proposal. "Mr. Fetzer turned it down and I always admired him for the stand he took. He said he felt baseball belonged to the City of Detroit, to the central hub of the city. He didn't believe in going to the suburbs, although he had nothing against them. But he felt baseball could be a catalyst to the rebirth of downtown Detroit in a new stadium here."

Plans went ahead for both the Pontiac and Detroit projects. Civic leaders pressed Ford to stay in Detroit. They knew it would be difficult to sell the public on paying for two new stadiums twenty miles apart, especially given the pressing needs of the city. A few black leaders questioned the assumptions behind the downtown project.

"I don't see the stadium as a key to revitalizing the city," state senator David Holmes told reporters. "I'm more concerned that we have, ten miles from the Detroit stadium site, one of the highest infant mortality rates in the world. The taxes they want to subsidize the stadiums should go for housing, hospitals and schools. Let the businessmen use their own money if they want a stadium."

Such objections were drowned out in the general chorus of hosannahs for the stadium grail. On September 15, 1971, the stadium authority announced a financing scheme: a forty-year bond issue to raise $126 million, including $85 million for the stadium itself, $6 million for parking structures, and the rest for land and ancillary developments. Projected annual revenues were $9 million from stadium operations (including a planned fifty special events a year), $2 million from a five percent county hotel/motel tax, and $4.5 million from horse racing revenues.

Fetzer in early 1972 signed a forty-year lease to play in the dome and pay an annual rent of at least $450,000. The Tiger yearbook that season contained detailed sketches of a futuristic riverfront home.

With the media, business, and the team all lined up, the stadium steamroller was in high gear. But as the financial package finally came together, gadfly TV talk show host Lou Gordon started to raise some tough questions: Could the project really be built for $126 million? Would taxpayers be stuck with the bill if revenues fell short of projections?

The Wayne County Board of Auditors warned that the revenue projections were shaky and that citizens could be left holding the bag on the stadium bonds. Wall Street lowered the county's credit rating, meaning more costs to taxpayers for other bonds sold. It was calculated that the stadium project would commit governments to a total obligation of $370 million, including interest, over a forty-year period.

Gordon asked county officials to submit the project to a public vote. But officials did not want a vote at such a late date. Construction bids were taken. The bonds were approved for sale.

A few days before the bonds were to be sold, a financial analyst from Grosse Pointe named Marc Alan happened to meet an attorney named Ron Prebenda on an outstate business trip. They began complaining to each other about the riverfront stadium. According to Alan, Prebenda told him: "You're just like everybody else. You complain and don't do anything about it."

Months before, Alan had begun questioning the stadium deal. Alan says he was bothered when the stadium authority went to the Stanford Research Institute for a financial analysis instead of using local experts.

"I picked up the phone and called the Houston Astrodome," Alan recalls. "I was amazed at the findings. The data showed that you were not going to find the kind of surrounding development they were talking about in Detroit. Attendance was such that after a little of the novelty wore off, the revenue could not support the stadium."

Alan got a copy of the proposed lease with the Tigers. "It was a giveaway," he says.

"If you look at the lease it was so manifestly unfair that it staggered the imagination," Prebenda recalls. "They were trying to force Bill Ford into that facility downtown, but the facility was being built to satisfy John Fetzer. Fetzer had 340,000 feet of office space in there, which he got for nothing. We costed it out, and it was hundreds of millions of dollars' worth of free office space he was getting."

Within days of their meeting, Prebenda and Alan filed an eleventh-hour lawsuit to halt the sale of the bonds. Wayne County Circuit Court Judge Blair Moody scheduled a quick hearing on the case.

At the other end of Wayne County, in the small semirural suburb of Belleville, the proposed stadium deal was the topic of a stormy council meeting. Mayor Royce Smith was fuming at the idea of using public money for private enterprise. He wanted to sue.

"I remember Royce talking to me at the council meeting," says the city's attorney, B. Ward Smith. "I remember saying, 'Royce, we can't win this case. The entire power structure is against us. There is no way the people in power would let us win.' And he said, 'I don't care whether we lose or not. I want to do it.' He felt strongly that this should not be jammed down the Wayne County taxpayers' throats. They were trying to put through a revenue bond without a vote of the people. It was taking taxpayers' money for a private purpose."

At the mayor's insistence, the Belleville council authorized its attorney to file suit against the stadium deal. Royce Smith says that a few days after the suit was filed, checks started showing up in his mailbox. He started a legal fund, and several motel owners chipped in five hundred dollars apiece.

B. Ward Smith and Prebenda soon joined forces. Judge Moody held a preliminary hearing and issued a temporary injunction against the project. The ruling sent the city's power structure up the wall.

"There was a lot of power behind the deal," says Alan. "There was power like there was no tomorrow."

"It was two little guys down here in the trenches trying to fight our way to the top," is how Ward Smith characterizes the battle. The stadium backers enlisted Detroit's two largest and most prestigious law firms.

"I never really believed deep down we'd make it," says Ward Smith. "We went in on the idea something was wrong with this thing, that taxpayers shouldn't have to pay for it. Then we started looking at the documents and the case law and discovered some things. We found out we really did have a chance."

Officials had provided opponents with a huge legal opening by making confusing and contradictory claims about the bonds being sold. If they were revenue bonds, taxpayers would not be obligated to make up any shortfall if stadium revenues were not sufficient to pay off the debt to the bond buyers. If they were general obligation bonds, they were backed by "the full faith and credit" of the county — and county taxpayers would have to pick up the bill if the stadium failed to pay its own way.

Deception about the bonds could be found in the small print buried in the back of newspaper notices. "If you read in between the lines, it wasn't a pure revenue bond," says Alan, "because they could come after the citizens in Wayne County."

Prebenda says the stadium proponents quickly became aware that the fraudulent advertising could sink the project. "They knew as soon as I started a lawsuit that they were dead in the water," he says. "But they told the press that this suit was a bunch of bullshit, that we didn't know what we were doing."

Prebenda says he was invited to a meeting at the law firm Miller, Canfield, Paddock and Stone. "They said there were going to be maybe six people there," he recalls, "but when I showed up there were twenty people. They proceeded to give me a new asshole. They were threatening me. They said that if the stadium wasn't built, the Renaissance Center wouldn't be built and that the revitalization of downtown Detroit—that was the key word back then—would never come about.

"They asked me, 'Do you have kids?' I said I had five kids. They said, 'Do you want your kids to remember you as the man who destroyed the city of Detroit?'

"I couldn't believe it. I said, 'Screw you,' and I got up and left."

Alan says stadium backers tried a different tack with him. "They sat down with me at a luncheon table and said, 'What do you want?' " recalls Alan. "There were people who suggested I could have a box seat. I didn't want a box. That wasn't what I was after. I just wanted a fair shake for the people."

Alan refuses to name the people who he says made him these offers, saying only that "it was not a politician, not a lawyer" but simply "some emissaries."

On his TV show on April 30 Lou Gordon told Alan: "You're fighting for the taxpayers against the power structure and the newspapers and the politicians."

Alan argued that there were more important priorities than a new stadium.

As the stadium opponents studied the projected cost figures, they understood how much county taxpayers could be forced to pay if the deal went through. "The projections were ridiculous," recalls B. Ward Smith. "They were going to have rodeos and bring in a hundred thousand people. We asked their people where they had rodeos now in Detroit. They said at the State Fairgrounds. And how many people did the fairgrounds stadium hold? Eight thousand. And how many people came to see the rodeo? Four thousand. So how are you going to go from that number to a hundred thousand because you got a new stadium?"

"They were talking about tennis matches," Alan says, "and any other event they could throw in that stadium to justify their numbers. The figures were really cooked up."

The David versus Goliath battle proceeded quickly. Using a little-used state statute, Governor Milliken ruled that the case was of great public importance. Milliken ordered Judge Moody to issue only a factual finding and then to send the case immediately to the state Supreme Court.

"They wanted to get that shovel in the ground," Alan says.

After a nine-day trial, Judge Moody on June 1 ruled that the stadium authority's contract was too one-sided in favor of the Tigers.

On June 8 the Michigan Supreme Court heard the case. Alan described the project as "inflated figures and pie in the sky" and "the rape of the taxpayers of Wayne County." Charles Moon, attorney for the stadium authority, said the project would breathe new life into downtown Detroit.

Justice G. Mennen "Soapy" Williams, a former Michigan governor, questioned whether the authority had deceived taxpayers by telling the public that the stadium bonds to be sold were revenue bonds while advertising in the *Bond Buyer*, New York's official bond publication, that the bonds were general obligation bonds backed by the county. Moon said that recent legislative amendments allowed full faith and credit backing for stadium revenue bonds.

"To some extent, you're comparing apples and oranges," said Moon.

"Do you mean you were selling apples to the public and oranges to the *Bond Buyer*?" countered Williams.

Seven weeks after Alan's suit was first filed, the Supreme Court struck down the project, ruling six to one that stadium backers had misled the public about the nature of the bonds. Officials had told the public that they wouldn't be stuck if the stadium couldn't pay its way, when in fact taxpayers would have been left holding the bag.

Writing about the case later, Justice William Black said that the suit "prevented the sale and delivery of actually fraudulent Wayne County general obligation bonds aggregating $371 million in amount."

A few people had beaten the entire political establishment of the city, county, and state. The lawsuit sent bond buyers scurrying away, and all the bigwigs couldn't put Humpty Dumpty back together again.

"There never seemed to be a way to revive it after that," says Moon.

Royce Smith says the state legislature passed a bill and reimbursed the City of Belleville for its legal fees. Alan says he paid a "handsome legal fee" but was never reimbursed. Was it worth it?

"I'm not against baseball, and I'm not against the city of Detroit," Alan concludes. "I'm just interested in the principle. It was a self-rewarding thing. I proved that all of these so-called professionals didn't do their homework. I proved that one man can make a difference if he's willing to step forward."

Prebenda says he got quite a different reward. "It gets you called a lot of names," he says. "I suffered terribly because of that with the establishment. I was kind of a rebellious guy, but I learned my lesson. I learned you don't mess with the establishment."

Two decades later, Prebenda is still amazed at the magnitude of the riverfront scam. "These men, including some of the most prestigious and influential people in the state, had actually perpetrated what amounted to almost a half-billion-dollar fraud. That was done in a totally calculating fashion, and no one was ever brought to task for that."

CHAPTER 9

BILLY AND THE BIRD

This franchise belongs to the inner city of Detroit. I'm just the caretaker.

— John Fetzer

At the corner of Michigan and Trumbull, the magic of 1968 soon gave way to frustration. Playing in what was portrayed as a doomed stadium, the Tigers sank below .500 in 1970.

In 1971 the All-Star Game returned to Detroit, and once again the stadium provided some excitement. With the wind blowing out, six future Hall of Famers hit home runs—Hank Aaron, Johnny Bench, Roberto Clemente, Harmon Killebrew, Frank Robinson and Reggie Jackson. Jackson's clout rattled off the light tower atop the right-field roof.

Eva Navarro of Dearborn was a young Tiger fan who attended that game. "I climbed on top of the visitors' dugout because I wanted to get some autographs," she remembers. "I had a pair of glasses in my purse, and I accidentally put my purse underneath my knee. Crash! I cracked my glasses. But it was worth it: I got Rusty Staub's autograph, Joe Torre's autograph, and I got a picture of Sparky Anderson's head peering up above the dugout."

In 1971 the Tigers replaced their lackadaisical manager, Mayo Smith, with battling Billy Martin. It was the perfect jump start for a team that had been sinking slowly into senility. Bert Gordon and Don Shapiro told the writer Roger Angell in 1973 that they thought Martin was the best Tiger manager since Mickey Cochrane. "He's winning ball games," Shapiro told Angell, "and that's absolutely all that counts." "Plus he's exciting," said Gordon. "This is the first time since I was eleven years old that you see a Tiger base runner go from second to third on a fly ball." Martin's usual script was to ignite a veteran team into one great season, then crash in a tailspin of bar fights, tantrums and defeats.

"That's not the way it happened in Detroit," claims Shapiro today. "He was a winner up to the end. He took an aging ball club, and made them winners. He was a fine manager."

Shapiro notes that the Tigers finished second with 91 wins in 1971, won the division title in 1972, and had a winning record when Martin was fired in 1973.

The town was so excited by Martin that a record Opening Day crowd of 54,089 turned out to welcome him in 1971. It took only a year for Martin to produce his miracle. In 1972, brash Billy goaded his veterans through a tight pennant battle. The nucleus of the 1968 squad remained, minus McLain, who had run into trouble with gamblers and baseball's commissioner and had been traded to Washington.

The 1972 season climaxed in a three-game series at Tiger Stadium against the Red Sox. The Tigers had to win two games to take the eastern division crown, and suddenly the whole city, which had most of the summer seemed disdainful of the team's chances, turned baseball crazy. Fans stormed the ballpark for tickets to the first game, which the Tigers won. The second game was a sellout, with many fans turned away. Behind pitcher Woody Fryman and a key hit from Al Kaline, the Tigers won the division title. When the game was over the crowd went berserk, flattening the outfield fences and rushing the field.

Navarro was there with her dad. She remembers it this way: "Everybody just went nuts. It was just great. Everybody was just running around, screaming, people running onto the field. We were sitting in the grandstand section. We started walking downwards, towards the field. We obviously had different ideas of which direction to go, because I darted out onto the field. I didn't think of it consciously, make a decision, should I or shouldn't I? I just did it because everybody else was doing it. I didn't have any idea of destruction in mind, but I just wanted a little souvenir. I climbed over the railing and grabbed a little handful of dirt, which I still have.

"Everybody was just celebrating, and people didn't want to leave. We got caught up in a little bit of a traffic jam. Everybody was honking their horns, and hanging out their windows, and celebrating. For some reason I started to feel sick; it just came on me.

"We made it home, I went to bed. And next thing I know I'm in the hospital. I had some sort of gastrointestinal problem, and they had to rush me to the hospital. After that my dad started saying that was it, he couldn't take me to any more Tiger games, because I got too excited. I'd get so excited I'd make myself sick."

Expansion in 1969 had changed the format of baseball's postseason play. Both leagues had been split into divisions, and the Tigers had to face the American League West champion Oakland Athletics to get to the World Series. The A's were fashioning a dynasty built around Reggie Jackson and pitcher Vida Blue.

The Tigers lost the first two games of the five-game series in Oakland, but battled back to take the next two at Tiger Stadium. In the fourth game the Tigers faced elimination, trailing 3-1 in the bottom of the tenth inning, but rallied to win the game with the help of an error, a wild pitch and a bases-loaded walk.

But the sense remained that an Oakland win was inevitable. The boundless optimism of 1968 had faded. In the final game Oakland scored in the fourth inning to take a 2-1 lead. Despite the close score, many fans didn't seem to believe the Tigers could win. The bleacher crowd started throwing toilet paper, pop cans, wine bottles, smoke bombs, and firecrackers onto the field. Several times the game had to be stopped to clear away the debris, and the national TV announcers had a field day trashing Detroit fans. No more runs were scored. The final out of the game was a fly ball to Oakland center fielder George Hendrick, who waded in a sea of bottles and garbage and somehow caught the ball without tripping.

It was a sad last hurrah for a team that only four years earlier had captivated Detroit. Martin was fired late in 1973.

With the riverfront stadium dead, the State of Michigan spearheaded a new plan to build a multipurpose dome in Pontiac for the Lions and the Tigers. Construction began in September 1973 using $55.7 million in public revenue bonds and city millage taxes.

But Fetzer stuck to his decision not to move the team. "This franchise belongs to the inner city of Detroit," he said. "I'm just the caretaker."

The Lions moved to Pontiac in 1975, leaving the Tigers alone at Michigan and Trumbull.

Management had stuck too long with its veterans and shortchanged its farm system, and the club hit bottom. The Tigers lost 102 games in 1975, including 19 in a row. Still, the team managed to draw more than a million fans.

The franchise needed a shot in the arm. Many Tiger fans were fleeing the city, and the club was making little effort to replace them. The Tigers had no programs to reach out to city youth. The club remained a staid organization, to which marketing was an alien concept.

Through sheer luck, a public relations bonanza landed in the Tigers' lap in 1976. On May 15, a drizzly Saturday afternoon at Michigan and Trumbull, a gangling, frizzy-haired rookie pitcher named Mark Fidrych got his first major league start. For five innings, he held the Cleveland Indians hitless. He eventually emerged with a 2-1 win.

Fidrych did not have blazing speed, but he had tremendous concentration and control. He could keep his pitches low in the strike zone, and opposing batters would beat them into the ground. Ground-ball pitchers like Fidrych often have great success in the tall grass at Tiger Stadium.

Fidrych had other qualities suited for his environment. On the field, he displayed youthful enthusiasm and concentration with a weird set of endearing mannerisms. He would get down on his hands and knees and smooth out the dirt on the mound. He would hold the ball in his hand and appear to be talking to it. He would hop around the mound after a strikeout. He would shake hands with an infielder who made a good play on a grounder.

Writer Thomas Boswell has called Fidrych "the first rock-and-roll pitcher," but his antics were not an act. Fidrych was a natural showman, not a showboat. His enthusiasm was genuine. His routine helped him keep his concentration, and his display of emotion helped release his excess energy. This combination of intense concentration and unbridled joy captivated Tiger fans.

Nicknamed "The Bird" after the "Sesame Street" TV character Big Bird, Fidrych was an instant phenomenon in Detroit. Since the days of Germany Schaefer at Bennett Park, Tiger fans always have been attracted to comic characters. Free spirits such as Denny McLain have spoken to Detroiters' desire, held barely in check during the long hours on the assembly line, to break free of convention and tedium.

Michigan and Trumbull is where fans let loose, unleashing verbal torrents of abuse or encouragement, erupting in glee at victory or in anger at defeat — ordinary people displaying emotions and doing and saying crazy things that they couldn't elsewhere. The Bird was just as playful and spontaneous as the fans, and the fans loved him for it.

Tiger Stadium also is a place where magic can happen, and the Bird seemed magical. Strange transformations occurred when Fidrych took the mound. Mediocre players such as shortstop Tom Veryzer and catcher Bruce Kimm, who became the Bird's personal good-luck battery mate, suddenly became world-beaters. The Tigers were a last-place team, but when Fidrych took the mound, they played like champions.

Could Fidrych have flourished in other surroundings? Possibly. But in the new multipurpose stadiums, seats were far from the field. Not as many people could have seen his expressions, followed his gestures, or heard his constant, wacky chatter. And in the new ballparks, there were plenty of other distractions: giant electronic scoreboards with video games, waterfalls, batting cages, a cornucopia of concessions. In Tiger Stadium there was only the game, and Fidrych playing it.

The Bird brought out the little kid in everyone. Like a child, he was naive, ingenuous, unself-conscious, and lived completely in the present.

His powers of attraction were incredible. Not in decades had the game seen such a sudden box-office star. Fidrych on the mound meant an extra thirty or forty thousand fans in the seats.

On June 28, before a sellout crowd and a national TV audience, Fidrych dispatched the Yankees, 5–1, in a quick, two-hour masterpiece. America discovered the Bird. An All-Star Game appearance soon followed, and Fidrych was named Rookie of the Year after a 19–9 season. He completed twenty-four of his twenty-nine starts and led the league with a 2.34 earned run average.

But the Bird never pitched another full season. He suffered a series of injuries and his arm went dead. The Bird tried several comebacks but won only ten games after 1976. It is fitting that he retired well before he reached the age of thirty. He remains in memory the eternal child.

CHAPTER 10

THE THIRTY-YEAR COMMITMENT

The Tigers will remain in the city for an entire generation.
— *Detroit Mayor Coleman Young, 1977*

In 1973 Detroit elected its first black mayor, a onetime radical named Coleman Young. Young reformed the police department and put more black people in power in city government. He also presided over a series of new riverfront developments, topped by downtown's gleaming fortress, the Renaissance Center, which had been launched under his predecessor, Roman Gribbs.

The continuing flight of residents and businesses to the suburbs was chief among the obstacles to Young's renaissance. The city's sports teams were a minor employer, but symbolically their presence meant a lot. Young could do nothing about the Lions' move to Pontiac, which had been decided before he took office. He had three other teams to worry about: the Tigers, the National Hockey League's Red Wings, and the Pistons of the National Basketball Association.

The Red Wings had threatened to move from venerable Olympia Stadium to suburban Oakland County as early as 1971. The team was courted for the new riverfront stadium, but when that project fell through, Young began negotiations. In October 1976 Young told Red Wings owner Mike Ilitch that the city would build a $20 million, 17,000-seat arena on city-owned riverfront land to keep the Red Wings from moving to a rumored new arena near the Pontiac Silverdome. Many hockey fans and Detroiters opposed plans to raze Olympia, but they did not prevail. After nearly a year of negotiations, the Red Wings agreed to the deal. Detroit used federal and city loans to finance public revenue bonds for the new Joe Louis Arena, which ended up costing $57.8 million, nearly three times Young's original projection. The Wings played their first game in Joe Louis on December 27, 1979.

The Tigers were issuing no public threats to leave town, but they wanted Tiger Stadium repaired. In 1976 John Fetzer claimed the park would last only ten more years if no improvements were made. Fetzer complained of maintenance costs of $500,000 a year—less than the team's maintenance budget had been twenty-five years previously, according to Walter Briggs III.

On September 28, 1976, Fetzer announced a $15-$26 million renovation program. A month later, the City of Detroit tentatively offered to buy the stadium for one dollar, secure $5 million of federal money to make repairs, and lease it back to the Tigers. But the plan was rejected initially by the federal government. In February 1977 a fire destroyed the wooden press box at Tiger Stadium and damaged part of the third-deck seating area. The cause of the fire was never determined. The blaze made renovation even more urgent.

On July 13, 1977, Young announced that the city had finalized the deal to buy the stadium. The federal grant of $5 million had been approved and the city, Young said, would sell additional bonds to repair the ballpark. Young bragged that the deal "ensures the Tigers will remain in the city for an entire generation."

On August 6, 1977, the *Sporting News* estimated Tiger Stadium's value at $8 million. In October Fetzer sold the park to the city for a dollar and agreed to a thirty-year lease with three optional ten-year renewals. The city issued bonds for $8.5 million. The bonds would be repaid with a surcharge of fifty cents per ticket. The lease was finalized and signed in 1978.

It was the first time any public body had taken ownership of the land at Michigan and Trumbull.

In May 1978 the Detroit architectural firm Rossetti Associates presented the city with a master plan for a $23 million renovation. The plan included a new mezzanine level with a press box and thirty-seven private luxury boxes, glass-enclosed exterior escalators, parking decks over nearby freeways and other parking structures near the stadium, and expansion and modernization of the club's concessions, storage, maintenance, and office facilities. Under the Rossetti plan, the renowned seats in the front rows of Tiger Stadium's upper deck would have been replaced by luxury suites.

The plan was never carried out. Repairs to the stadium's concrete and steel foundations ate up much of the budget. In a 1986 interview Charles B. Davis, general manager of the Detroit Building Authority, said that the concrete and steel at the park had been in worse shape than planners originally had thought. Davis blamed the condition of the park's foundation on rock salt spread in the aisles "like butter" to melt snow and ice during Lion games.

But Ralph Snyder, Tiger director of stadium operations since 1970, said in 1986 that snow and ice and the extremes of winter temperatures in Detroit had done a lot more damage to the concrete and steel than had salt.

Whatever the cause, the structural repairs were extensive. But there was still enough money to make many major changes. A new press box was built on the third deck to replace the one destroyed by fire, and the remainder of the damaged deck was reinforced and the roof repaired. Major repairs were done to the concrete and steel decking, the plumbing, the electricity, and the rest rooms. The 1948 light towers were replaced by new, smaller light towers with 550 high-intensity multi-vapor lamps.

Behind home plate, new broadcast facilities and two luxury boxes — one for the owner and one for the media — were hung from the facing of the upper deck. The boxes ruined the view of fans who sat in the back rows of the lower deck. Instead of being able to follow the flight of foul balls, fans now watched pop-ups disappear behind the owner's box and then reappear in the mitts of the fielders.

At the top of the upper-deck bleachers in center field, the old hand-operated scoreboard was replaced with a modern, computer-controlled scoreboard. Inside the old board a worker had provided out-of-town scores by changing numbered blocks. The new board no longer displayed all out-of-town scores at the same time, but could display pictures of the players, more statistics, and other graphics.

Traditionalists mourned the passing of the old scoreboard and the replacement of the old green wooden chairs with new blue and orange plastic seats. The old seats quickly became collector's items. Within a few years, many a diehard Tiger fan had an old green stadium seat at home.

The team wanted more renovations, so the city decided to float a second bond issue. But Detroit was in terrible financial straits. A recession had blown out another engine in the chugging automobile industry. The city's bond rating was too poor for investors. Not until 1982 was the city able to sell $3.6 million in bonds to finance a second phase of renovations. To pay off the additional bonds, the ticket surcharge was hiked to ninety cents.

In the second phase of renovation, completed in time for the 1984 season, the old painted brick walls of the stadium, which for years had been left to peel and chip, were covered with beige metal siding and graffiti-proof blue-glazed masonry at ground level. The stadium's forty-eight rolling gates were repaired or replaced. Team clubhouses were modernized, and two new bathrooms were built.

The total cost of the two-phase renovation was $18 million. With the renovation, the capacity of Tiger Stadium shrunk slightly to 52,806.

While Young had managed to keep both the Tigers and the Red Wings in town, he lost the Pistons, who moved to Pontiac in 1978 to join the Lions as tenants of the Silverdome. Ten years later, the Pistons moved into a privately financed arena in nearby Auburn Hills. But the Tigers' commitment to stay in the city and the city's willingness to buy and manage the stadium seemed to signal a secure future. The renovations were guaranteed for thirty years.

During the renovations, the team rebounded on the field. Starting in 1978 the club enjoyed an unprecedented eleven consecutive winning seasons. Sparky Anderson, who had won two world championships in Cincinnati, took over as manager in 1979 and became a fixture.

The revival centered on the team's young double-play combination. In 1978 second baseman Lou Whitaker and shortstop Alan Trammell both became regulars at the age of twenty. Playing together in the minors, they already had perfected a graceful, synchronized ballet in the middle of the diamond. They were a smooth duo who knew each other's every move and played to each other's strengths. Whitaker, a black kid from Brooklyn, and Trammell, a white kid from southern California, united around second base as an inseparable and nearly impenetrable barrier to ground balls. They would become the longest-playing and most successful double-play combination in major league history.

The Detroit farm system also produced catcher Lance Parrish, pitchers Jack Morris and Dan Petry, and outfielder Kirk Gibson. They eventually were joined by key players acquired in trades — outfielders Chet Lemon and Larry Herndon, reliever Willie Hernandez and first

110

baseman Darrell Evans—to form what would become another world championship team.

While waiting for Anderson to deliver on his promise of a pennant within five years, fans sometimes got too rowdy. On June 16, 1980, bleacher patrons pelted Milwaukee center fielder Gorman Thomas with bottles and debris. The next day Tiger general manager Jim Campbell announced that the bleachers would be closed indefinitely. They reopened on June 30 under tighter security and with new restrictions on beer sales.

In the 1980s major league baseball experienced a tremendous increase in popularity. Attendance boomed. Television contracts grew lucrative, and baseball discovered product marketing. Players' salaries skyrocketed, reflecting the owners' growing profits. The Tiger franchise appeared more stable and profitable than ever.

The Fetzer years had brought the Tigers only one world championship. But through a quarter century of change and turmoil in the nation, the city and the sport, the team had stayed at Michigan and Trumbull and expanded its huge loyal following. The franchise that Fetzer and Knorr had bought for $5.5 million in 1956 was worth almost ten times that much by the mid-1980s.

CHAPTER 11

TOM, KIRK, AND BUBBA

As long as I own this team, we will not build a new stadium.
> — *Tom Monaghan, after buying the Tigers in 1983*

I would go along with Jim.
> — *Monaghan on Opening Day 1986, asked whether he had plans to replace Tiger Stadium, referring to Tiger president Jim Campbell*

John Fetzer had built a broadcasting empire and bought a major league team. He had helped put baseball on national TV, opening a vault that made owners and players rich. His ball club had won a world championship. He had kept the Tigers in Detroit.

As he grew older, he became fascinated with Eastern religions and less interested in worldly affairs. He turned over operation of the Tigers to Jim Campbell, lessened his involvement with major league executive committees, and made sure the old stadium got the renovation it needed. Most of the important things were in order. It was time to turn over his baseball club to a successor.

On October 10, 1983, the eighty-two-year-old Fetzer sold the Tigers to forty-six-year-old multimillionaire Tom Monaghan, founder and owner of Domino's Pizza. Fetzer reportedly had turned down offers from several others, including Monaghan's rival, pizza magnate and Red Wings owner Mike Ilitch. The reported sale price of the franchise was $53 million.

Fetzer's choice was a surprise. Though Monaghan was one of the richest men in Michigan, he was not well known. He was not a part of

Detroit's sports circles or civic leadership. He was not used to being in the public eye. In front of cameras, he looked at his shoes and stammered.

Monaghan's childlike mannerisms and lack of smooth social graces may have appealed to Fetzer. They seemed to bespeak a humility unusual for a multimillionaire. Fetzer himself had never been a publicity hound or a big talker; lately he had become something of a hermit. Monaghan was a devout Catholic who spoke frequently of his religious convictions, and Fetzer was increasingly preoccupied with the spiritual realm.

Above all, Fetzer wanted someone who would continue to honor his trinity of team, town, and ballpark. By refusing to take his team to the suburbs, Fetzer had staked the Tigers' future on his conviction that major league baseball belonged in downtown Detroit. Any successor would have to uphold the deal with the city to have the Tigers play at Michigan and Trumbull into the next century.

Nothing in Monaghan's background suggested any commitment to Detroit. His headquarters were in Ann Arbor. But Monaghan was an architecture buff and a collector of antique cars. Perhaps those interests, coupled with his boyish adulation of the Tigers, were enough to convince Fetzer that he would keep the faith.

Monaghan told the press of his boyhood ambition to play shortstop for the Tigers. He said he'd give anything to be in Alan Trammell's shoes. Monaghan's interest in the team appeared genuine. He seemed as interested in the team's heritage as in its profit margin. He expressed awe at becoming owner and exuded respect for the franchise. "When I grew up in an orphanage, the only fun we had was listening to the Tigers on the radio," he explained. "That's why I can't believe I own the team."

He also publicly vowed that he would never tear down Tiger Stadium. "As long as I own this team, we will not build a new stadium," he said. "I like the old stadium, and we'll do all we can to keep it. We'll keep fixing it up and making it look as good as possible."

Monaghan also said he wanted to undo some of the recent changes and restore the park's old-time charm: "I'm thinking about putting the green seats back in Tiger Stadium. I don't know why they took them out of there in the first place."

About the park's shiny new exterior, Monaghan demurred: "People tell me the outside of our stadium looks good. It's a joke. All they've done is cover it up with a lot of tin. I'd like to strip it right down to its natural concrete base and grow ivy on the walls. That would look beautiful."

The initial response from fans and the media to the change in ownership was generally positive. John and Judy Davids, who spent a year living as architects-in-residence in a Frank Lloyd Wright house owned by Monaghan, recall liking him on first meeting. "We knew Monaghan as this guy that was very approachable, very easy to get to, very open-minded," says Judy Davids. "He seemed like a nice, caring, sensitive person, who was trying to help out two poor kids."

To Tiger fans, Fetzer often had seemed distant and uncaring. Many regarded him as a skinflint who skimped on player salaries and ballpark maintenance. Though he had brought baseball big bucks through TV contracts, Fetzer had refused to compete in the free-agent market those dollars had created, explaining in 1978: "We are constitutionally opposed to the creation of young sports millionaires."

Monaghan shared Fetzer's antipathy toward free agency, but shortly after he bought the team the Tigers plunged into the market and signed Darrell Evans.

Monaghan did fit one pattern. Since the 1930s, each major Tiger owner had represented the cutting edge of the economy. Briggs had made his fortune in the automobile industry when the car was king. Fetzer grew rich in broadcasting as the media revolution reshaped the nation's life and culture. Monaghan made his bucks in America's most recent emblematic growth industry: fast food. He presided over an empire of low-overhead carry-out pizza joints, employing tens of thousands of low-wage workers. Domino's drivers sometimes had to go at breakneck speeds to deliver on the company's pledge of getting a cheap pizza to the customer's door in thirty minutes or less.

Monaghan took Domino's to the top with a simple formula for giving a broad mass of customers instant gratification. Taking over the Tigers, he again found himself in the right place at the right time. The Tigers had a product in 1984 that brought everyone instant pleasure, and Monaghan was blessed with overnight success. The club won thirty-five of its first forty games and practically clinched the division by Mother's Day.

Tiger tickets quickly became the hottest items in town. The club shattered its old attendance record, drawing 2.7 million fans. The newly renovated stadium was shiny, bright and popular. Vendors and souvenir stands did record business; bars along Michigan Avenue prospered; parking lot owners had their best years ever.

115

Monaghan prospered as well. In his first year as owner, the club made an estimated $8 million. Monaghan had a helicopter landing pad constructed on top of the Brooks Lumber Company on Trumbull Avenue and frequently flew in from Ann Arbor for games.

With the outcome of the season never in doubt, Michigan and Trumbull became a carnival. Thousands normally indifferent to baseball showed up for the scene. Fans giddy with winning turned into grandstanders. The "wave" became an everyday standard; the bleacher creatures served as orchestra leaders. The waves went clockwise, then changed directions; sometimes they were conducted in slow motion, sometimes double-time. In the bleachers, fans would jingle keys in unison and clap outstretched hands like snapping alligators. Games often were halted to retrieve beach balls batted over the fence.

Some of the mischief spilled over the ballpark's loose boundaries of decorum. Parodying a beer commercial, half the bleachers would shout "Tastes great!" and the other half would reply "Less filling!" The two cheering sections would then change the words to obscene taunts. Campbell eventually closed the bleachers again for a few games. When they reopened, there were signs posted banning profanity.

As the season went on, Tiger mania took on a defiant edge. Detroit had seen hard times. The automobile industry, devastated by foreign competition, was reeling in a recession from which Detroit would never fully recover. The Big Three auto companies were taking jobs to cheaper labor markets. Plants were closing and jobs disappearing. Thousands of unemployed Michiganders migrated to the Sun Belt in search of work.

As the triumphant Tigers traveled around the league, hordes of transplanted Detroit fans showed up to raise a ruckus. At some games, especially in Texas and California, the home team's rooters were drowned out by fans of the visitors. The 1984 Tigers became the era's answer to the patrician New York Yankees of the 1950s. The Tigers were America's team of the laid-off, its players the heroes of the new downwardly mobile middle class.

Beneath the team's easy success was an undercurrent of belligerence reflected in the cocky grimace of outfielder Kirk Gibson. Gibson had grown up in suburban Detroit and was an All-American flanker at Michigan State University, turning to baseball only in his senior year. He brought his football style to the diamond.

Gibson played baseball like a bull in a china shop. He slammed home runs and charged into walls or opposing players with fierce

116

abandon. Gibson never grasped that baseball was an everyday sport and that it was risky to court injury on every play. The only way he knew to play was all out.

Like some of the newly dispossessed fans who loved him, Gibson wore a chip on his shoulder, turning a surly face to the media, autograph seekers, and the general public. Like the bleacher creatures chanting profanity, his attitude seemed to be: "The hell with the rest of the world. I'm gonna do it my way, so buzz off." With Gibson leading the charge, the Tigers rolled toward the pennant, clinching it on September 18 at Tiger Stadium against the Brewers.

After the game, the field was cordoned off by armed Detroit police officers and security guards. Still, a few fans managed to wreak a little havoc. As was the custom, the crowd took to the streets to slap hands, drink, and honk horns. But it was only the beginning.

Fans camped overnight around the ballpark to get tickets for postseason play. The first step was easy. The Tigers swept the Kansas City Royals in the American League Championship Series. The final game was a spare, taut 1–0 victory at Tiger Stadium. The key play was an unlikely one: The lumbering Evans dived to his right for a grounder, then to his left to the first-base bag, and his outstretched hand reached the base a split-second before the speedy Willie Wilson.

The capture of the American League flag touched off a second raucous celebration. Again guards protected the field, again without complete success. Again crowds paraded through the streets, a noisy motorcade tied up the downtown area, bars were filled with boozy celebrants, and the party grew louder and more outrageous.

Many were hoping the Chicago Cubs would be the Tigers' World Series opponents, providing a matchup between the two best teams in baseball, two charter franchises playing in two classic ballparks. But the Cubs blew the National League play-offs to the San Diego Padres, a team without tradition or much hope of beating the Tigers.

The Tigers split the first two games of the Series in San Diego and then took the next two at home. Needing one more win to clinch the title, Detroit was poised for an explosion that had been building all year.

On a misty, gloomy Sunday afternoon, October 14, Tiger Stadium filled early with a boiling crowd, pumped for a victory. The season's climactic moment was a fitting one. In the eighth inning, the Tigers were clinging to a precarious lead when Gibson strode to the mound to face veteran fastballer Goose Gossage. Runners were on second and third and Padres manager Dick Williams went to the mound. Fans were on their feet and screaming. In the bleachers, stadium vendors did an impromptu snake dance up and down the aisles, holding aloft their empty containers. Stadium loudspeakers blared the hit song "Ghostbusters" and, on cue at the chorus, everyone yelled, "Goose-busters!"

At the mound, Gossage shook his head. With first base open, Williams wanted to walk Gibson. Gossage wanted to pitch to him. The Goose prevailed, and he and Gibby drew their guns for an old-fashioned duel: heat against heat. On the second pitch, Gibson gleefully turned and blistered a fastball into the upper deck in right. Gibson pranced around the bases like a boxer who had delivered a knockout punch, raising his clenched fist aloft and screaming. The image of the conquering wild man summed up the season and drove berserk the crowd at the park, as well as those watching TV at home, in the bars, and on a giant screen set up at Hart Plaza downtown.

Outside the stadium, on the streets and around the bars and souvenir shops, a crowd had been milling all afternoon. Now hundreds of slap-happy fans were driving to the stadium area to join the celebration. By the time the game ended, thousands inside and outside the park were drunk with euphoria and alcohol. When Larry Herndon squeezed the final fly ball, hundreds spilled over the outfield fences and started tearing up the grass.

"We didn't have tickets for the fifth game," recalls Tiger fan Dave Osinski of Warren. "My cousins and I came down here during the fifth game, and as everybody else was pouring out of the stadium, we were sort of pouring in. We saw the center-field fence down, and we said, This is our chance. If we don't go out there now, we'll never get a chance. So we went over the fence with everybody else. They had just laid new turf in center field, because it was all torn up from when they won the pennant. So we were picking up pieces of turf and slinging them over our shoulders like they were togas."

It quickly became clear that this was not a reprise of the 1968 love-in. The Tigers did not want their field torn up. Quickly, a phalanx of police, linked arm in arm, swept the crowd out of the stadium via the old center field bull pen under the bleachers.

Outside was a crushing, curb-to-curb mass of happy people. Along Michigan Avenue, radio stations had set up giant speakers blaring Motown tunes, and soon hundreds were dancing in the streets.

"We were outside the stadium," says Osinski. "We were like heroes, handing pieces of grass to everybody. It was just mass joy."

Observing from ramps near the top of the stadium were baseball officials and the national media. Police tried in vain to keep things under control, but the crowd swallowed vehicles that tried to move. Then, in an instant, the mood changed from joy to panic. Flames shot up from the corner of Michigan and Trumbull. A police car was burning. People fled in all directions and the police moved in with gas masks and batons to restore order.

"Some idiot started throwing some bottles and glasses at the police horses," says Osinski. "When we saw that, we got the hell out of there. It was getting a little crazy."

The next day, a picture of a fan waving a Tiger pennant and standing next to the burning police car blazed across the world's newspapers and TV screens. "A photographer working for Associated Press snapped the picture," reported the *Free Press* in a follow-up story on October 24, "and 'it was used virtually across the board,' said Brian Horton, photo enterprise editor at the wire service's New York headquarters. 'It seemed to be the picture that was used of events happening outside the stadium.' "

"It got wide usage in Europe and Asia," Horton told the *Free Press*.

The media had a field day with the photo and the news that a man had been shot to death late that night in a holdup at a downtown Coney Island restaurant. Police said the shooting was not linked to the Series celebration, but the story across the country was: Detroit wins the Series, Detroiters celebrate by torching cop cars and shooting one another. It was a bad rap. Other cities, including San Francisco, turned ugly and violent in the 1980s after sports triumphs. They didn't get Detroit's bad press.

"In '84 when the Tigers won," says fan Randy Westbrooks, "people made a big deal about car burnings, and stuff that happened downtown, that have happened in other cities since then, but have not been publicized like in Detroit." Like many other metro Detroiters, Westbrooks nurses a resentment against the national media. "They've never been here, they don't know what we're about, and I just think that we've become the whipping city of America. People in Detroit don't do anything any worse than people in other cities."

Most Detroiters celebrated the Series triumph peacefully and legally. But a volatile chemistry was at work: economic frustration, a defiant season of front-running, the icon of the raging Gibson, and the equation of sports with alcohol, cemented by endless beer ads on TV. Added to all that was the unusual circumstance that the Tigers had won

119

the division, the pennant, and then the Series at home, all within a month's time. Each party had to top the last.

Detroit suffered a public relations disaster instead of reaping the rewards of a national sports championship. The national media portrayed the Series aftermath as more evidence that Detroit was violent and crazy. Those who blamed the citizens of Detroit or its mayor for the city's problems found more ammunition for their stereotypes. To many, the burning police car was a dramatic affirmation that downtown Detroit was a dangerous place.

There was plenty of irony in that perception. The "fan" in the famous photo turned out to be a teenager from suburban Lincoln Park named Bubba Helms. Tracked down and interviewed by the *Free Press*, Helms admitted that he had "watched the first seven or eight innings of the game at home and then drove with three friends to the stadium." Helms had not torched the car, but he had enjoyed being there. He didn't mind revealing his identity, he told the paper, because "I didn't do nothing. I just got my picture taken." Helms was not a Detroiter. Like some suburbanites, Helms seemed to believe that Detroit was a place to run wild. "It was one big party," he told the *Free Press*. "It was great."

Helms and his friends joined the festivities by molesting a parked armored truck. "Me and my friend went up there, and we jumped on top of it," he recounted. "We was up there screaming and dancing and stuff."

Helms also tried to grab one of the stadium's steel doors as it was closing, and then climbed a pole, when he was hit on the head with a club by "security or somebody."

The *Free Press* story continued:

> Then, Helms said, he heard a "whoosh" and saw a car on fire. "I just ran right over there," he said.
>
> Helms said one of his friends, who had been picking up returnable cans and bottles, tried to dissuade him.
>
> "I gotta get my picture taken!" Helms said he told the friend.
>
> Helms said about nine photographers were taking pictures of the burning car, and he "just jumped right in front of them and stood as still as I could." One of the photographers told him to get out of the way, he said, but Helms only made an obscene gesture and yelled, "F— — — you!"
>
> "I was just having a good time," he said. "It was the best time in my whole life. Serious."

Helms and his friends returned to Lincoln Park, where he passed out "face down in the mud" on a neighbor's lawn.

Corktown and the Briggs Community had been dealing with the likes of Helms for some time. Some fans dumped their prejudices on the neighborhood when they attended Tiger games. Homeowners in the stadium area had to contend with fans throwing beer cans on their front yards and urinating in their backyards. Such incidents reached a peak in 1984.

White flight, and the change in attitude toward the city that resulted from it, put distance between some fans and the neighborhood around the stadium. Years before, Corktown and the Briggs Community had looked much like the areas most fans lived in. No longer. Now most fans at Tiger Stadium were suburbanites, and the area around the stadium was alien to them, even though Corktown was rebounding as urban pioneers renovated its historic houses.

The relationship between stadium fans and the neighborhood could have been smoother had the Tigers been skilled at community relations. But Tiger management continued to act as if all it needed to do were to open the stadium gates. That was hardly enough in the 1980s.

At Michigan and Trumbull, sixty-three seasons passed before a black player joined the Tigers. And long after Ozzie Virgil arrived on the field, the Tigers continued to be indifferent to the many potential black fans living in Detroit.

In other cities, forward-thinking ballclubs have bridged the old gaps between baseball and the black community. In Oakland, California, the Athletics are heavily involved in community programs. The team has featured many black or Hispanic stars such as Reggie Jackson, Rickey Henderson, Jose Canseco, and Dave Stewart. Almost every big-city club instituted special programs in the 1960s, 1970s, or 1980s to reach out to city youth — but not the Tigers.

Black kids, says Dr. Edward Turner, a Southfield physician who grew up in Detroit, "are being lost to baseball." Turner cites the many black and white major leaguers who have come out of Detroit in years past — players such as Willie Horton, John Mayberry, Billy Pierce and Hal Newhouser. "Bill Freehan told me he came to Detroit to play because that's where the best competition was. He didn't want to play in Royal Oak or Ferndale. He wanted to play where it was tough.

"I have five sons, three of whom played Little League ball," says Turner. "I used to be a coach, and sometimes an umpire. The league that my sons grew up in, which was a wonderful, wonderful league, has died. The problem is from the top. There is not enough input from the top—and I'm speaking of the Tigers, primarily—who can inspire and make young men want to become ball players. They should be feeding into these leagues, to help them. Sandlot ball in general in Detroit has gone way down. When I was a kid at Northwestern High School, Class A ball in Detroit in the sandlots was comparable to the minor leagues. There's nothing like that going on now."

In Detroit, old attitudes on both sides persist. Black baseball fans have not forgotten the Briggs era. The Tigers, for their part, have done little to change the perception that the club cares little about black fans. In the 1980s black attendance at Tiger Stadium continued to erode even as the city's black majority grew larger. The old-timers sat in the lower-deck bleachers, as they had since the days of segregated ball. They were the remnants of the huge crowds that had jammed the outfield seats when Larry Doby came to town.

The Tigers integrated very late, and it was a long time before it was more than tokenism. Under Fetzer, the limit seemed to be four black players on the roster. In 1980 a *Free Press* survey found only 21 black players among the Tigers' organization of 147 active players—a far cry from the proportion of black players in baseball as a whole.

During the 1980s a black grounds keeper named Herbie Redmond provided stadium entertainment. Redmond, says Turner, "would dance a jig while he swept. He was a clown, a first-class clown, an Uncle Tom. It was an insult to black people."

To erase the past, the Tigers needed aggressive community programs. But management continued its long-standing disdain for public relations and marketing strategies that had become standard fare in most other cities. And even when offered a chance to make amends, the team resisted.

Turner and others tried off and on for a decade, beginning in 1979, to get the Tigers to hold an African-American Day at the ballpark. Their efforts were ignored and rebuffed, even while the Tigers continued to hold Polish-American Night, Lutheran Night, and other long-standing events geared to other segments of the fan base. It was not until 1991 that African-American Night was added to the Tiger calendar.

Throughout the 1980s the club gradually added more black players. But unlike Horton and Brown in the 1960s, the most prominent black players on the team in the 1980s, Lou Whitaker and Chet Lemon, did

122

little in the community. Neither had grown up in Detroit, and they did not take visible leadership roles.

Under Monaghan, the Tigers did increase the number of black personnel. In the front office, Michael Wilson made a rapid rise to the rank of vice president/controller. And the Tigers eventually entered the modern era of promotions by hiring Jeff Odenwald as marketing director in 1987. His arrival, says Odenwald, "was a start from scratch. There had been no emphasis on marketing activities. Promotional activity was minimal at best. There was basically no advertisement per se in radio or television. Very, very little community involvement. Very few outreach programs in the community as well."

But giveaway days and affirmative action fell far short of redeeming the Tigers' image among many city residents. The Tigers after the 1984 World Series did nothing to counter the Bubba Helms effect—the perception by many fans that the stadium neighborhood was a dangerous place. Management did not release crime figures showing that the area was one of the safest in the city. Club officials did not join with area businesses and residents to support neighborhood revitalization projects. Rather than counter the fears of some Tiger fans, club management clung to many of the same unfounded fears.

Tiger vice president Bill Haase, asked whether the club has given thought to marketing among Detroit's black population, replies: "That's an issue that's aside from the stadium, and I don't think that I want to get into that at this point in time. I think that's something that the commissioner's office is addressing on their own."

Odenwald, who came to the Tigers from the Chicago Cubs, calls Wrigley Field "a great place. A great ballpark." Asked to compare the neighborhood around Wrigley with the Tiger Stadium area, he says: "The mystique of Wrigley sitting right in the middle of a huge revitalized area just helps enhance the image of that franchise. We don't have all of that around here. We don't have thousands and thousands and thousands of people taking and revitalizing the area." Corktown, he says, is "not a real large community, by comparison with what you've got in Chicago on the near north side."

Monaghan is no Detroit booster. His expressed affection for Tiger Stadium has never been accompanied by kind words for the neighborhood or the city. Even after taking over the Tigers, he has remained an outsider to Detroit's movers and shakers.

If there were people within the Tiger organization or Monaghan's inner circle who saw the Tigers' location as a liability, Bubba Helms and the burning police car gave them ammunition. The 1984 World Series aftermath may have been a turning point in the stadium's history. While Monaghan continued to present a public posture favoring preservation, after 1984 club officials started talking about a new stadium.

In 1985 Campbell was quoted as saying the Tigers would need a new ballpark by the end of the century, even though the Tigers had a lease obligating them to play at Tiger Stadium until 2008.

By 1986 Monaghan was waffling on his pledge made just two years earlier. On Opening Day, he was quoted as saying: "I would go along with Jim" on any decision about the stadium. Contrarily, a month later, the *Detroit News* reported that Monaghan wanted to preserve Tiger Stadium into the next century. "It is a shrine," he said in the *News* of May 23. "The Chicago White Sox are building a new stadium now to replace Comiskey Park, and that will make this the oldest stadium in baseball. I think that means something."

When he was asked how long Tiger Stadium could last, Monaghan said: "I don't know. I hope forever, but I don't know. I'll have to be a little realistic at some point, I'm sure, but I just want to gather all the facts. I want more information than someone just telling me it won't last. I want to see why."

About a new stadium, he said: "I'm kind of resistant because I like old Tiger Stadium, although Tiger President Jim Campbell keeps telling me that I'm dreaming because it won't last forever like I think it will."

In 1986 Campbell sent Monaghan a report recommending that the park either be replaced or renovated using elements of the 1978 Rossetti plan that had not been carried out. Both Campbell and the city dismissed as costly and impractical a new Rossetti proposal: to install a removable Teflon dome atop the ballpark. Revenues from a stadium used only for baseball would not support the expense of such a dome, Campbell's report said.

Campbell said late in 1986 that any decision on the stadium was up to Monaghan. But Monaghan acted as if the decision were not his to make. As long as he could, he acted like a stadium lover whose heart was being overruled by the bean counters—and by his landlord, Coleman Young.

The mayor was the man with the most power to enforce the lease and keep the Tigers playing in Tiger Stadium until 2008. Yet Young didn't even wait until the city's stadium renovations were finished before he started talking about how Detroit needed a new domed stadium like the one Toronto was building. Instead of acting like a proud landlord who had just spent millions to fix up his property and keep his tenants happy, Young was the most outspoken proponent of a new stadium.

Young's strategy of rebuilding Detroit favored grand new developments over renovation of existing buildings. He fervently argued that Detroiters needed jobs and that big projects were worth the cost if they brought those jobs. Young's opponents said rebuilding the city's neighborhoods and saving existing homes and small businesses should take precedence over the showcase downtown and riverfront projects the mayor espoused.

Young habitually has decried preservationists as standing in the way of progress. Perhaps it is because much of Detroit's past is infected with the cancer of racism. Old Detroit was segregated Detroit, run by whites. Why preserve symbols of that painful, unjust past? Tiger Stadium, particularly, has a segregated past so recent that it still hurts some black Detroiters just to look at it. Tearing it down might blot out some of the pain.

Others suggested another motive for Mayor Young's advocacy of a new stadium. If the city built a new ballpark, it could be named after its mayor. City Councilman Mel Ravitz told *Detroit Monthly* magazine in 1988: "I think from the mayor's standpoint, the more things in motion that he can have, tearing down and building up, the greater he believes the public's image of a successful operation. I think what Coleman Young is looking for is a stadium named Coleman A. Young Stadium."

While talk of a new stadium increased after 1984, the euphoria of that championship season subsided quickly. The Tigers continued to be contenders, but many fans who had become used to all the winning in 1984 turned elsewhere when the Tigers failed to deliver another championship in thirty minutes or less.

By 1987 the wave of '84 had long been beached. Other Detroit sports teams, long dormant, had revived. Red Wing and Piston games gave the Tigers new competition in April, May, and June. The Tigers, a hodgepodge of fading veterans, started out badly and were in last place in mid-May. Then they started winning, beginning a steady, season-long climb into contention.

In August the Tigers drew even with the first-place Toronto Blue Jays. The teams battled neck and neck for eight weeks. Using brains,

125

guts and heart, the Tiger veterans pushed their abilities to the limit. Four games behind Toronto with seven games to play, the Tigers fought back and the Blue Jays choked.

The inspired schedule put Toronto in Detroit for three games to end the season. The Tigers were one game behind going into the series. They won all three games by one run, with the pennant clincher on Sunday, October 4, a 1–0 nail-biter decided by a Larry Herndon home run that barely cleared the fence in left field and would have been an out in almost any other park.

When Darrell Evans squeezed the last out, the fans stood and cheered in their seats. A well-behaved celebration followed. There was none of the frenzy of a few years earlier. If 1984 was a season for front-runners, 1987 was a far more satisfying campaign for true baseball fans, despite the Tigers' loss to the Minnesota Twins in the play-offs. The pennant chase against the Blue Jays and the culminating series at Tiger Stadium provided pure baseball, and the Tigers' home-field advantage in the final series provided the winning edge.

But the ballpark, such a perfect setting for the Tigers' classic come-back, was in danger. While Monaghan continued to say publicly how much he loved Tiger Stadium, the Tigers already were secretly seeking public money for a new stadium. Mayor Young made no secret of his desire for a dome. It was clear that if Tiger Stadium were to be saved, neither the owner of the ballpark nor the owner of the team would lead the campaign.

Only the fans could.

CHAPTER 12

THE GRAND OLD LADY

It's obvious the damned thing is falling down.
> — *Detroit Mayor Coleman*
> *Young, January 21, 1988.*

There is not a structural problem with the stadium. There is no risk that it is going to fall down. . . . The stadium will stand there for a hundred years if nobody touches it.
> — *Deputy Wayne County*
> *executive Michael Duggan,*
> *testimony to the Detroit City*
> *Council, June 17, 1991*

"Save Tiger Stadium" urged the red-white-and-blue bumper stickers that members of the Tiger Stadium Fan Club passed out to fans leaving the ballpark the night Darrell Evans got picked off first base to all but finish the 1987 season. No one had made that plea fifteen years earlier, when Detroit almost got a dome. But a lot had changed. Then, almost everyone considered an old stadium an impediment to a city's progress. Now, many viewed it as a rare civic treasure.

By 1987 the ballpark Frank Navin had built over the winter of 1911–12 had lasted seventy-six baseball seasons. Expanded by Navin and Walter Briggs, and newly strengthened by the renovations of the late 1970s and early 1980s, the stadium had outlasted twenty-five managers and nearly a thousand Tiger players. It had embraced the exploits of over a hundred Hall of Famers and hosted three All-Star games and five World Series. Nearly six thousand major league baseball games had been played there in front of over 85 million fans. The Lions had played 185 football games there over thirty-seven seasons, including two world championship games. Countless high school, sandlot, and college games had been played there, and the park had hosted boxing, wrestling, opera, concerts, and political rallies. Combining all the events, the turnstiles at Michigan and Trumbull had clicked over 100 million times.

Frank Navin's field had survived the ice and snow of Michigan winters, the pounding of millions of feet and thousands of souvenir bats, and the fraudulent scheme of Detroit's most powerful people to replace it with a dome. Through strength, grace, and luck, it had endured.

Generation after generation, fans had come, shivering in the chill of Opening Day, baking in the bleachers in the blazing sun, huddling in desperate hope against the onslaught of autumn: kids and parents, husbands and wives, friends and neighbors, bosses and workers. Since 1945 the Tigers had fallen short of drawing a million fans in only three seasons — 1953, 1963, and 1964.

For all those years, Detroiters had pretty much taken Tiger Stadium for granted, and so had most baseball fans around the country. Lacking grand architectural flourishes or fancy frills, it didn't look like a very special place. It didn't have ivy like Wrigley Field, a Green Monster like Fenway Park, an exploding scoreboard like Comiskey, fountains like Royals Stadium, or a roof like the Astrodome. It didn't even have a catchy nickname: It wasn't the House That Ruth Built, the Mistake by the Lake, the Big A, the 'Stick or the Hump.

It was just a great old place to watch a ball game.

In the 1960s most old parks were considered unappealing relics and the new stadiums tremendous advancements. But the initial euphoria for the modern ovals soon gave way to widespread disdain. Attendance in many cities with new stadiums, after a short-term initial spurt, leveled off or dropped.

Baseball analyst Bill James calls the new stadiums "sterile ashtrays." The seats are far away. Domes divorce the game from the influences of weather and diminish its variety and authenticity. Artificial turf makes baseballs bounce like ping-pong balls and hurts players' knees and backs.

John Pastier, former architecture critic for the *Los Angeles Times* and a consultant on ballparks to several major league teams, wrote in a 1989 article that the new stadiums are "discrete objects divorced from any context."

"Their uniform dimensions do little to favor specific players or styles of play, and this has diminished the sport," he wrote in *Inland*

Architect magazine. "Surprises are rare, as are chances for fans to ponder how a particular player's hitting or pitching might vary if the configuration of the home park were different."

Many fans in cities such as Pittsburgh, Cincinnati, St. Louis, and Philadelphia came to regret that their old parks had been replaced by multipurpose stadiums.

"At the time, everybody was interested in progress," Steve Morris of Pittsburgh told the *Detroit News* in 1988, mourning the demise of Forbes Field. "But now that it's gone, everybody's sad about it. If we had to do it again here, they'd renovate it."

"By now," Pastier wrote, "most observers of the game agree that the best parks are the earliest 'fireproof' stadiums built in a heady seven-year period just before World War I. This realization took hold only after wrecking balls battered Ebbets Field, Sportsman's Park, the Polo Grounds, Crosley Field, Griffith Stadium, Forbes Field, Shibe Park, Braves Field, and League Park. . . ."

"Those parks had unmatched character and priceless histories," Pastier wrote in a 1991 article for *Inland Architect*.

> They offered a quality of experience, a type of action, and a view of the game that current stadia cannot match. They were better citizens, economical of land and gentler to their neighborhood. . . . Their unique geometries . . . gave a strong flavor to the games they hosted. Some were so large as to be pitchers' dreams; others were small enough to make batters salivate . . . Their size allowed sluggers to hit balls onto, or over, the roof on rare occasions, an exciting feat that cannot occur in today's huge ballparks.
>
> Outfield walls and fences often had odd angles and corners . . . that would lend unpredictability to well-hit balls.
>
> If baseball stadia were music, these would resemble complex and inventive improvisations, while today's versions would be repetitious finger exercises.

Roger Angell of the *New Yorker* also likes unusual outfield dimensions. "I think an eccentric design is always interesting," he says. "It gives fans more to think about and talk about and poses a challenge to the manager and general manager about what kind of players to get."

The pressures of modern life may be a factor in the recent resurgence of affection for older ballparks, says Dale Swearingen, vice president of Osborn Engineering Company of Cleveland, foremost builder of ballparks since the turn of the century. "People once looked on old ballparks as dinosaurs," he says. "It's a whole different mind set today. It's respecting the old. We're constantly being blitzed by a lot of technology that people can't handle, like computers that constantly need new programs. In your mind, it just seems that baseball in the old parks was life in its simplicity. We kind of yearn for those days when you just took some time off and went to the ballpark."

Several modern stadiums were built in the 1970s and 1980s, though not at the breakneck pace of the 1960s and early 1970s. In 1977 the Kingdome opened in Seattle and the Expos began playing in Montreal's garish and hastily built Olympic Stadium. In 1982, after a long political battle, the Minnesota Twins moved into the Hubert H. Humphrey Metrodome. None of these replaced a classic ballpark.

Hallowed Yankee Stadium, which dated to 1923, fell victim in the mid-1970s to a radical change. The park's tradition was virtually destroyed by an expensive renovation that amounted to building a new stadium within the shell of the old. The old roof, with its distinctive facade, was removed, and an imitative frieze was placed atop the outfield walls. The park's famous monuments in deep center were removed from the field of play. Exposed exterior ramps made the outside of the park resemble San Diego's Jack Murphy Stadium.

The rape of Yankee Stadium left the major leagues with only four classic ballparks. Two of them — Chicago's Wrigley, built in 1914, and Boston's Fenway, built in 1912 — had long enjoyed the status of national shrines. Ivied Wrigley was the last bastion of day baseball, and Fenway had the Green Monster and Bostonian tradition. Writers and commentators frequently lauded them; thousands of tourists visited them. They enjoyed a secure status among the elite. The other two old parks — Tiger Stadium and Chicago's Comiskey, built in 1910 — were bigger, more proletarian parks, with a smaller though growing national following.

By 1987 three of the four classic parks were in danger. In Chicago the addition of luxury sky boxes financed through tax-exempt city industrial revenue bonds wasn't enough for the owners of the White Sox, Eddie Einhorn and Jerry Reinsdorf. They vetoed a plan by a fan group called Save Our Sox to designate Comiskey a national park. Instead, they threatened to move their team to Florida if the public didn't build them a new stadium. They claimed that Comiskey, once known as the Baseball Palace of the World, was too decrepit to renovate.

Wrigley Field was threatened for a different reason. Major league moguls had tolerated a quaint ballpark without lights as long as the hapless Cubs remained perennial losers, but when the Cubs reached the National League play-offs in 1987, all hell broke loose. National television networks now control the scheduling of important games. Post-season games at Wrigley couldn't be aired in prime time, and that meant big advertising money down the drain. The owners of the Cubs insisted that lights be installed at Wrigley. Efforts by a group of neighborhood residents and Cub fans to keep lights out withered in the face of the team's threats to leave, and the first night game was played there in August 1988.

Like the parks in Chicago, Tiger Stadium was old. The team was owned by an architecture buff with a fondness for antiques, but those passions didn't motivate him to act to preserve his historic ballpark. The stadium was owned by a city whose powerful mayor equated progress with massive new monuments. Mayor Young looked enviously at Toronto, a city that every weekend attracted thousands of tourists from Detroit. In Toronto, the Ontario government had committed to huge public support for a colossal new stadium, to be called the Sky-Dome, with a retractable roof, an attached hotel, and shops like those in an upscale suburban mall. Mayor Young insisted that Detroit needed its own dome.

Spurred by the growing talk of replacing Tiger Stadium, a few staunch Tiger fans, all Detroiters, met one night in September 1987 and formed the Tiger Stadium Fan Club. The club's members strongly believed that replacing Tiger Stadium would be a tragedy not only for baseball but for their city, which could better spend its limited resources fighting crime, poverty, homelessness, and blight.

One of the club's founders, Frank Rashid, an English professor at Marygrove College in Detroit, told a reporter: "Here we are, a city with the kind of problems we have, and they want to spend money on an entertainment palace. If the mayor really wants to build a baseball field, there are lots of rundown city parks that could use a good one."

The Tiger Stadium Fan Club's initial plans were not ambitious. The organizers pooled a few hundred dollars of their own money, printed up some bumper stickers and T-shirts, and started to gather names for a mailing list.

Late in October 1987, Rashid wrote a letter to Tom Monaghan asking where he stood on the stadium issue. Rashid received a reply in late November from a Domino's Pizza publicist. The letter referred to an ongoing feasibility study on the ballpark and said, in part:

131

> Ideally, we'd love to preserve Tiger Stadium. It's an institution that has been a strong part of baseball, locally and nationally, and it contains a lot of fond memories for the majority of us. We will keep you informed of the feasibility study results and any other information concerning the future of the Stadium.

It was the last letter the fan club ever received from Monaghan.

On November 12 the *Free Press* reported that Monaghan was "awaiting an engineering study" on Tiger Stadium that "will determine the costs of shoring up its long-neglected foundation and superstructure." The "long-neglected" foundation had just been repaired within the last decade.

The rumors about new stadium plans soon became reality. On January 5, 1988, the City of Detroit announced it would take proposals from architectural firms for plans to renovate Tiger Stadium or build a replacement.

The next day, the *Free Press* reported that John McDevitt, chief stadium aide for Monaghan, had said an engineering study of the ballpark — presumably the same study referred to on November 12 — had shown renovation would cost $45 million to $100 million. McDevitt said the figure surprised Tiger officials. "That's a lot of money to put into a very old structure," he said.

On January 7 the first measure of public sentiment about Tiger Stadium's future was a resounding victory for the fan club's preservationist stance. Readers responding to a *Detroit News* question favored renovation over replacement of the stadium by a 2-to-1 margin.

Monaghan assumed the stance of a helpless tenant, not revealing that Tiger officials had approached county officials a year earlier about paying for a new ballpark. Asked on January 14 by the *Free Press* where he stood regarding a new ballpark, Monaghan replied: "I stand back. I love the old stadium, but I'll let the mayor and the engineers figure out what to do. I won't butt into it. I'll let them build a new stadium, then I'll cry."

In an interview a few months later, Monaghan said he had offered, shortly after buying the team in 1983, to buy the park from the city, but had been turned down. He said that he would prefer to stay in the old stadium but would go along with Young's plans for a dome so long as the Tigers didn't have to pay for it.

Young, for his part, was openly antagonistic to preservation. Approached by reporters on January 21 about his views on Tiger

Stadium, Young growled: "It's obvious the damned thing is falling down."

Alarmed at the city's plans and Monaghan's inaction, Tiger fans rallied to support the stadium. On January 24, nearly three hundred people showed up at the Gaelic League Irish-American Club near the ballpark for a Tiger Stadium Fan Club meeting. Fans signed an open letter to Monaghan challenging him to back up his stated sentiments with action. The letter asked the Tiger owner to make public all engineering and feasibility studies on the stadium and the costs of renovating it.

A few days after the meeting, McDevitt called Rashid asking for a meeting to talk things over. On February 2, at the Tiger office annex on Michigan Avenue near the stadium, Rashid, Bob Buchta and Mike Gruber of the fan club met with McDevitt and two Tiger publicists. Buchta remembers that the meeting was cordial and that McDevitt's intent seemed to be to deflect the heat away from Monaghan and the Tigers and onto the city. "He took the line that, 'Aw, shucks, we're just the tenants. It's the landlord who makes the decision,' " Buchta says.

The fan club leaders asked McDevitt to show them the study that he had cited to reporters in January claiming a renovation cost of $45-$100 million. "He said there was no study, there was nothing published," Buchta says. "He said it was just a 'conversational estimate,' and that's where the $45-$100 million figure came from."

According to Buchta, McDevitt said repair costs would be high because salt spread on the concourses to melt snow and ice during Lion games had caused the decking to deteriorate badly. "He talked about the deterioration, the salt damage, the structural integrity, and the maintenance costs," recalls Buchta. "What he didn't say to the press and what the press didn't ask him apparently is what the $100 million price tag would buy. We asked him that, and he said it would buy a fabric roof." McDevitt's estimates, widely reported in the press as authoritative figures for repairing structural defects in Tiger Stadium, were really undocumented estimates for extensive renovation projects.

"The newspaper reports left the impression that it would take up to $100 million just to keep the place standing and functional," says Buchta, "and all the while McDevitt knew that the $100 million was really for a radical and absurd renovation, namely, putting a dome on Tiger Stadium. He came about as close to lying as you could come without actually doing it."

(McDevitt declined to be interviewed for this book to respond to these charges. A spokesperson said McDevitt was "comfortable with how his position was represented in the media in past years.")

After the meeting, Buchta says, fan club leaders tried to point out to the media that the reported price tag for fixing Tiger Stadium was really an estimate for radical changes. But Buchta says the media didn't seem interested, and local newspapers, radio, and TV continued to give the McDevitt figures as the cost of saving Tiger Stadium.

McDevitt never explained the inconsistencies in his statements. After the meeting with fan club leaders, he told reporters that the issue was one of economics versus sentiment: "The real question is going to be, is it really economically feasible to save the old stadium, no matter how much we all love it? Our perspective is that the stadium isn't going to fall down tomorrow, but this grand old lady is getting old."

At a news conference the same day, Mayor Young said he wouldn't let affection for Tiger Stadium get in the way of what he defined as progress: "We're rebuilding a new city and there comes a time when we need a new stadium. And the only question before us is whether it's now, five years from now or ten years from now. Nobody in their wildest dreams expects that stadium to last beyond ten years. Most people say it will fall down in five." Young said the city was investigating building a park like Toronto's—a multipurpose stadium with a retractable dome and an attached hotel. The mayor also wondered aloud if the members of the Tiger Stadium Fan Club were just a bunch of suburbanites trying to meddle in the affairs of Detroit.

Responding to Young's charges, Rashid and Buchta held a press conference on February 5 outside the mayor's office. Young was gone, but they left him a more cost-effective "retractable dome" —an umbrella. Their public statement read, in part:

> Tiger Stadium is more than nostalgia. For both residents and visitors to Detroit, it is a living, vital connection to our past and a superb place to play and watch baseball. To baseball fans everywhere, it is a national landmark—a treasure to be respected and preserved. Old Tiger Stadium adds far more distinction to Detroit's image than would another predictably faceless modern stadium.
>
> We speak as an organization founded in Detroit by Detroiters. We are proud of our city, but we recognize that Tiger Stadium belongs in a very real sense to the people of this entire region, and that we as Detroiters are only its stewards.
>
> We represent the large majority of Tiger fans who, by any available

measure, prefer this great urban ballpark to an antiseptic entertainment facility.

Tiger Stadium is a public building. Both renovation and replacement would almost certainly involve public money. Even the highest cost estimates of renovation are far less than the cost of a new stadium. And thus far no studies have been released about the structural integrity of Tiger Stadium. The public has a right to this information before any decision is made about the future of the ballpark.

The battle for the future of Michigan and Trumbull had begun. On one side were arrayed some very influential people. Monaghan was one of Michigan's wealthiest citizens. Young was the most powerful mayor in modern Detroit history and one of the state's most important politicians. As the battle progressed, they would be joined by wealthy developers, business leaders, opinion shapers, and political bosses — and a famous collegiate football coach who became, with one crass personnel decision, one of the most despised men in Michigan.

The proponents of a new stadium eventually would include many members of the state's power structure. The faces were different, but the titles were like those aligned with the riverfront dome in the early 1970s. This time, though, there was far less unanimity among the establishment — and a large popular movement for preserving Tiger Stadium.

Polls showed the opposition, led by the Tiger Stadium Fan Club, had the support of most of the people of Detroit and Michigan. With so much popular support, the fan club soon grew from a small group of friends into the largest and most effective stadium preservation organization ever. The fan club would eventually count among its allies some government officials, famous national baseball writers and commentators, prominent architects and attorneys, a broad mass of disgruntled taxpayers, and many of baseball's most passionate fans.

But the fan club's most important ally would be the stadium itself — its unmatched intimacy, its proud character, its prominent ghosts, its vivid and persistent memories.

The debate about Tiger Stadium centers on the value of an old ballpark to the nation, the city, the franchise, and the sport. Is its age a liability or an asset? Is its past a crucial part of a city's present and a sport's future? Or is it merely an unproductive impediment to progress? Is there something important in Tiger Stadium that would be forever lost if it were replaced? Or is the ballpark just another expendable and outdated building?

Tiger Stadium, long ignored and taken for granted, within a few years would become an important national symbol of sports heritage. Through the efforts of the fan club, it was placed in 1989 on the National Register of Historic Places. Cleveland's Municipal Stadium is the only other ballpark ever to earn that recognition. The listing on the register prevents federal money from being used to tear down Tiger Stadium, to build a replacement, or to build any other structure at Michigan and Trumbull.

In June 1991 Tiger Stadium gained another impressive honor. The National Trust for Historical Preservation included Tiger Stadium on its fourth annual list of the nation's most important endangered historic sites. Also on the list were Walden Pond, Antietam National Battlefield, and Philadelphia's Independence Hall.

The National Trust, a nonprofit organization, was chartered by Congress in 1949 and has 250,000 members nationwide. It is supported in part by the National Park Service. Peter Brink, an official with the trust, says Tiger Stadium deserves to be preserved as one of the few remaining examples of the classic era of ballpark construction. "But equally important is the way ordinary folks have viewed it as a very special place," says Brink. "If the fans thought that it had no meaning, I doubt we would have included it."

Brink contends that preservation isn't just for relics from the past. "A lot of the things that deserve preservation are right in our cities and have importance in our lives, like Tiger Stadium," he says. Brink believes that Tiger Stadium will be a strong candidate for landmark status when the National Park Service turns its attention to sports facilities.

The importance of classic ballparks is gaining more recognition as the years pass. "No building type demands more allegiance than the early 20th-century ballpark," wrote Paul Sachner in the *Architectural Record* of June 1991.

But fans don't own ballparks. "Knowledgeable fans may show strong loyalty," wrote John Pastier, "but people who decide the fate of these unique landmarks can usually find reasons to destroy them."

Those reasons deserve close scrutiny, especially because public money is always involved in the building of new stadiums.

The arguments for replacing Tiger Stadium aren't novel. The proponents of a new stadium have sought to minimize the park's value by focusing on what they consider the defects of its age and location. Their case has been built largely on shibboleths borrowed from the idiom of other sports franchise owners. These include the following: (1) The old place is a classic, but it's falling apart, and it's too expensive to repair; (2) renovation won't work; (3) it doesn't have enough good seats; (4) not enough fans come any more; (5) the club can't make enough money to compete in an old facility; (6) the club will skip town if no new stadium is built; and (7) a new stadium is inevitable because the people in power want it.

The success of these arguments in most cities has depended on the ability of team owners and their political apologists to dominate the media and define the terms of the debate. In most cases, might makes right.

In Detroit unique circumstances would make the stadium scam more difficult to pull off than in other cities. These circumstances would include the untimely gaffes of Tom Monaghan and his underlings, the internecine warfare among the big egos involved in the decision, the dogged professionalism and headline-grabbing tactics of the Tiger Stadium Fan Club, the national historic recognition, and the deep skepticism of Michigan taxpayers.

But chief among the impediments would be the stadium's great popularity. The first strong proof of that overwhelming sentiment came on February 7, 1988, when the *Free Press* released the results of a scientific survey. The poll showed sixty-five percent of metropolitan Detroit residents favored keeping Tiger Stadium. Subsequent polls confirmed that finding, and even in August 1991, after six months of virtually unmitigated official propaganda for a new stadium, Detroiters still favored saving their ballpark.

What if all those people are foolish sentimentalists who don't know the facts? What if Young is right and the stadium is going to collapse?

Tiger Tale No. 1:
The stadium is going to fall down.

The first argument for a new stadium was enough to end the discussion in Chicago. White Sox owners Einhorn and Reinsdorf breezily claimed that Comiskey Park was crumbling despite publicly financed renovations in the early 1980s. This assertion provided a rationale underpinning the owners' threat to move to St. Petersburg, whose good citizens had built a domed stadium just to try to attract a major league team. The threat was so effective that Einhorn and Reinsdorf never had to prove their contention that Comiskey had dire structural problems — luckily for them.

Pastier characterized Chicago in the late 1980s as "bent on fixing something that isn't broken." Public officials "hired a structural engineering firm with no experience with stadiums or preservation issues," he says. The firm, Bob D. Campbell & Company of Kansas City, was given a mandate by the Illinois Sports Facilities Authority to study Comiskey to "evaluate the feasibility of renovating . . . and converting it into a modern, state-of-the-art baseball facility."

That mandate, Pastier wrote in 1989, was "just a way of canonizing the absurd opinion that new parks are better in every respect than old ones." Pastier says Campbell & Company "came up with a report sort of condemning the building to death. But they did do structural tests, and the building passed every one of them!"

In one test, Pastier says, engineers made a pyramid of fifty-five-gallon drums, filled them with water, and set them in the middle of one of Comiskey's concourses. "When they filled all the drums up, it didn't move a fraction of an inch," Pastier recalls. "They couldn't give an explanation; they were almost complaining in the report. The worst things they could find were visual evidence of minor things here and there. They tested the steel: It was okay. They tested the concrete: It was okay. So if one read their report open-mindedly, they were giving it a clean bill of health, but their conclusion that renovation was hopeless was at odds with all the particular evidence they came up with."

The Campbell report estimated the chances of significant structural failure as one in ten or twenty thousand. Yet the report abounds, Pastier wrote, "with photos of worst-case conditions that are presented, either implicitly or explicitly, as typical."

The Campbell team estimated that it would cost $86-$129 million to meet the mandate of converting Comiskey into a stadium "competitive in all respects with professional stadiums recently constructed or under construction." In the report, Pastier wrote, the proposed renovation "was left virtually undescribed" and the cost estimates had no documentation. "Since this proposal was given less space than an analysis of lightning protection, one wonders if it wasn't a quickly devised straw man abetting the case for a new stadium," he wrote.

When Edward DeBartolo, a prospective buyer for the White Sox, had his own engineers inspect the park, they could find no important defects. The charade that Comiskey was falling down seemed merely an effort to justify the Sox owners' threats to leave town.

Why would it take anything more to convince Detroiters that Tiger Stadium was crumbling? After all, Detroit is the city that invented planned obsolescence. Detroiters are used to replacing their cars every few years. And Detroit has an abysmal record on preserving historic buildings.

But the city had just spent $5 million of federal money and $13 million of public bonds to renovate the ballpark. Fans were still paying ninety-cents-per-ticket surcharges to retire those bonds.

It fell to longtime Tiger official Jim Campbell to start raising questions about the effectiveness of the repairs to Tiger Stadium. In January 1986 Campbell told reporters in Grand Rapids that "it's an old, old edifice; it's old underneath," and he complained about rust and plumbing problems. In May of that year he clarified, saying: "This stadium is in good, sound condition right now, but near the end of the century it more than likely will have to be replaced."

Campbell cited no evidence for his assertion that the stadium would last only another decade. The man most familiar with the stadium didn't seem to agree. In August 1986 Ralph Snyder, director of stadium operations for the Tigers, told a reporter: "There's no question but that the stadium is sound and safe. It's just a matter of maintaining it."

Early in 1988 McDevitt surfaced as the new ersatz expert on the stadium's condition. In February he told *Detroit News* reporters that the decking eventually would need to be replaced. "The superstructure has corroded," he said. "We have determined that an extensive amount of steel has to be replaced."

Soon after, he told Lowell Cauffiel, a reporter from *Detroit Monthly*: "There is a deterioration that is occurring to the superstructure. Slowly, steel is corroding. There's a replacement program going on, but even that doesn't get in and rebuild the heart of it." McDevitt told Cauffiel that his $45-$100 million cost estimate was not based on any engineering study, but was "really a number we developed internally. It's based upon different remodeling concepts. The outside figure is kind of putting a canvas dome on the old stadium. The inside figure is a kind of a steel-replacement, further-restroom, concession-enhancement type of thing."

McDevitt refused to give Cauffiel the name of any expert who could confirm his statements about the stadium's condition, but he offered to let the magazine bring a structural engineer in to inspect the stadium. *Detroit Monthly* took him up on the offer.

On March 22 Lev Zetlin, a top investigator of structural problems in buildings and bridges with forty-seven years of experience, conducted a thorough visual inspection of Tiger Stadium. His conclusion: The stadium is an example of "landmark construction — a classic." If properly maintained, Zetlin said, it can last indefinitely.

Zetlin said the park showed no signs of structural weakness and that he could find no evidence — no deflections in trusses or floors or beams, no bending of columns, no very large cracks in concrete — to indicate underlying problems. He said there was no evidence of salt damage and that the concrete and decking were solid, except for a section near the visitors' bull pen that apparently had been missed in the recent repairs. He compared that to a loose brick on a building: "If you have a loose brick, you fix the brick. You don't tear the whole building down."

Zetlin asked why the stadium had not been properly maintained. "Why don't they paint it? This is below-normal maintenance. That's why some areas look like hell. It doesn't mean anything structurally, but aesthetically it looks bad and could scare a lot of people."

Zetlin's opinion on the stadium's condition was echoed by two other experts hired by local television stations: structural engineers Constancio Miranda and Horst Berger.

Cauffiel's *Detroit Monthly* story on the official deception about Tiger Stadium's condition was released on April 20, 1988 — the seventy-sixth anniversary of the dedication of Navin Field.

That evening, in rainy, windy, forty-five-degree weather, over twelve hundred supporters of Tiger Stadium came out to surround the ballpark in a unique and unprecedented demonstration of affection. No stadium — not Ebbets Field, not Fenway, not Wrigley — had ever gotten a hug before.

The attention-grabbing protest was the culmination of several months of popular agitation in defense of the ballpark. A local radio station circulated petitions for saving Tiger Stadium and collected over a hundred thousand signatures in a few weeks. The Tiger Stadium Fan Club was in high gear, printing T-shirts and bumper stickers and buttons, publishing newsletters, lobbying the media, and organizing the hug. The hug got national publicity for the fan club and for the issue of Tiger Stadium's fate.

The stadium's landlord did not join in the birthday party. When told by a WDIV-TV reporter that day about the *Detroit Monthly* story, Young dismissed Zetlin and his forty-seven years of professional experience, saying: "Well, I gather this guy spent two hours in the stadium. He didn't go into any of the key rooms. He didn't look at any of the blueprints. So he doesn't know what the hell he's talking about."

The stadium's tenant, Monaghan, had told Cauffiel that he didn't want to "get near" the notion of sharing the cost of a new stadium, as the mayor had proposed. "It's an incredible amount of money," he said. "It kind of blows my mind. With the cost of a new stadium, it seems like you can do an awful lot of improvement on the existing stadium for that kind of money. I think big, but I don't think that big."

Cauffiel's story did not change the local media's penchant for misstating the cost of repairing Tiger Stadium as $45-$100 million. As the summer progressed, the Young administration stonewalled all requests by reporters for information on stadium renovation.

Finally, on July 31, 1988, the results of the engineering study mentioned in the November 12, 1987, *Free Press* story saw the light of day. Using documents obtained under a Freedom of Information Act request, the *News* reported that Turner Construction Company had submitted its study on the stadium to the city in November, but the city had never released the results. No wonder: The Turner study put the lie to Young's claims that Tiger Stadium was falling down and to McDevitt's contentions that salt had seriously damaged the concrete and steel at the ballpark.

The study, conducted for the city in the fall of 1987, recommended just under $6 million in improvements to the stadium. Turner said it would cost $1.4 million to repair decking and patch concourses, with most of the money going to replace a section of the lower deck in right field that had been missed in the 1977–84 renovations. Needed repairs to the plumbing and electricity would cost another $1.3 million, the report said. The rest of the money would be used for new toilets and concessions, an upgraded public address system, motorized doors, and exit signs.

News reporter Scott Faust noted that the Turner study, a "row-by-row" inspection, identified no irreparable problems threatening the stadium's foundations. McDevitt and Bob Berg, Young's press secretary, insisted that the Turner study addressed only the stopgap measures needed to keep the stadium going.

The release of the study raised questions about the veracity of earlier statements by Young and McDevitt. "McDevitt certainly had to know the Turner study existed" when he met with the fan club in February, Buchta says. "We asked about a study, and he didn't mention it. He gave us the impression there was only one study to be discussed. He never acknowledged the existence of the Turner documents. This was certainly misleading, and it was very close to being simply a lie."

In his interview with *Detroit Monthly*, Lev Zetlin argued that no proof would ever be offered that Tiger Stadium was structurally unsound. "You will never be able to prove that it has to be taken down from an engineering standpoint, that I guarantee," he told Cauffiel.

Zetlin's guarantee was sound. Over the following years, two other firms, HOK Sports Facilities Group of Kansas City and BEI Associates Inc. of Detroit, would study the stadium and issue reports on renovation. Though each firm had clear incentives to dismiss renovation, neither could document any serious structural deficiencies at Tiger Stadium. Neither the city nor the team has ever produced one bit of evidence to prove their contention that the stadium has major structural flaws.

The absolute lack of evidence didn't stop proponents of a new stadium from continuing to claim structural problems. Usually the statements were vague references to mysterious problems "deep inside" the "bowels" or the "heart" of the stadium. Often they were linked to claims that the 1977–84 renovations had not gotten to the real problems lurking within the ballpark.

"The way they're dealing with structural integrity now," says Buchta, "is not to say that the place is falling down, but to say we don't know what might happen, to raise the specter of this mysterious unforeseen malady that will inevitably afflict the stadium in the next fifteen or twenty years."

Tiger vice president Bill Haase was the club's point man on the stadium after McDevitt disappeared from the public eye in 1988 and before Bo Schembechler dived into the stadium controversy late in 1990. Haase described the 1977–84 renovations to *Free Press* columnist Bob Talbert this way: "When we opened it up and looked inside, it was like opening up someone and discovering a body full of cancer. All we did was seal up the visible holes and seal up the outside. You can't see the infrastructure decay — but it's there."

Talbert picked up the medical analogy in his June 3, 1990, column advocating a new stadium: "Rust and decay inside the bowels of Tiger Stadium is [*sic*] an inoperable ulcer, an internal bleeder no renovation suture can stop," he wrote. Talbert said the renovations had amounted to "nothing more than a facelift on a very old face," while inside, "the arteries and veins were clogged and bleeding. Still are."

Over two years after the Turner report said Tiger Stadium needed only a few million dollars of structural repairs, club officials continued to misrepresent the costs of fixing up the ballpark as being close to the price of a new stadium. In his April 22, 1991 speech to the Economic Club of Detroit, Schembechler put a price tag on the mysterious internal disease that only certain club officials could see: "A renovation with cost overruns when you find out what's in the bowels of that stadium will cost you $100 million. As I'm standing here, I promise you it will cost that much."

A few weeks later, BEI, a firm hand-picked by Wayne County to swat down renovation proposals, released its report saying it had found no structural defects in the stadium. The report said the Cochrane Plan, which would add luxury suites and other amenities to the ballpark and expand concessions, rest rooms, offices, and other facilities, would cost $50 million, twice the original documented cost estimate but half what Schembechler had promised.

After nearly four years of quack diagnoses that Tiger Stadium was suffering from an incurable internal disease, the patient was still alive and well as the 1991 season ended. "Given their public relations efforts to sell a new stadium, if the Tigers or the city or the county had any evidence whatsoever of structural problems inside Tiger Stadium, it would have been all over page one long before now," says Buchta. "All they've been able to come up with is unsubstantiated allegations. Their silence on this issue is damning."

Though they lacked evidence of structural defects, officials still could get mileage with claims that the age of the ballpark made the cost of routine maintenance prohibitive. It seems a logical argument: The older the building, the more it costs to maintain. But it is not necessarily true.

Twelve years after it opened, Montreal's Olympic Stadium "had stained and eroded concrete, with dozens of roof leaks apparent on the field, in the seats, and behind the stands," wrote Pastier in 1989. On Friday, September 13, 1991, a fifty-five-ton chunk of concrete fell onto a walkway at the stadium. No one was injured, but the Expos had to play the rest of their season on the road. By 1990, twenty-year-old Veterans Stadium in Philadelphia needed more than $30 million in repairs.

Many of the older ballparks such as Tiger Stadium were overbuilt, says Swearingen of Osborn Engineering. Today, computers can calculate exactly how much support is needed for grandstands and concourses. In the old days, Swearingen points out, such precise figures were impossible to get, so engineers erred on the side of caution. Steel columns and concrete supports in old stadiums are thus stronger than those in many new stadiums and can withstand more deterioration without affecting safety.

Over the years, officials have made wildly conflicting claims about maintenance costs at Tiger Stadium. In a *Free Press* article of January 6, 1988, Monaghan claimed Tiger Stadium maintenance costs were $4-$5 million per year. Officials a few months later told Cauffiel that the costs were $1 million a year. Haase said in June 1990 that maintenance costs escalate every year and that the club was spending $1 million annually. In fact, documented maintenance costs for Tiger Stadium don't match official claims and compare favorably with much newer ballparks. The evidence shows that the Tigers were spending no more on maintenance in the 1980s than the $1 million Walter Briggs III says was spent annually in the 1950s.

"I don't see any evidence to back up their claims that maintenance is excessive," Buchta says.

Under the Tigers' lease with the city, the club must maintain the park in good condition and is to be repaid by the city for its expenses. Official summaries of expenses submitted by the Tigers to the City of Detroit showed total maintenance costs of $1,158,461.22 for the period from February 12, 1985 through February 25, 1987 — about $580,000 a year.

During 1987 the Pontiac Silverdome had structural maintenance costs of $772,774, according to Bob Haney, director of Silverdome operations. "We could have spent a lot more," Haney told Cauffiel. "But there just isn't the money."

If maintenance on a classic ballpark is reasonable, it's worth it, says Swearingen. "I think the heritage justifies the costs of maintaining the old parks," he says. "You can't really weigh the dollar amount of history and tradition."

Wayne County officials, dismissing renovation plans in 1991, echoed McDevitt's 1988 claims that it would be too expensive to keep history alive at Tiger Stadium. In its report released in May 1991, BEI dismissed the Birkerts-O'Neal renovation plan as impractical because of "the high maintenance costs of the existing concrete and steel." But

BEI had no experience in evaluating ballparks, and BEI president Christopher Kittides can cite no evidence that maintenance costs on Tiger Stadium are higher than at a new ballpark.

"The only two things we think are old and really need to be replaced is the steel and the concrete on the first level," Kittides says. "If you talk to Haase, he'll tell you that concrete chips away every year, and they have to go and patch it, this and that. And the steel, because it's old, you have to paint it at some point. You have to watch the cross section of the steel to make sure that it hasn't gotten to the point where you need to reinforce it."

Asked if BEI studied maintenance costs on new stadiums, Kittides replies: "We don't have that. We didn't develop that cost. All we're saying is that the statement is made that because you're dealing with two existing elements that are not being changed, the concrete and the steel, you will have higher than new stadium maintenance costs. We didn't attempt to get all those numbers."

To proponents of a new stadium, data don't seem to matter. The argument on Tiger Stadium is self-evident: It's old, so get rid of it. Mayor Young has never wavered from this view. "I think we need a new stadium," he told reporters in May 1991. "The old one, for all its nostalgic reminiscence, is about to fall down."

Lack of sound evidence often leads people to speak in metaphors. An analogy suited to Detroiters became a favorite adage of stadium proponents: Just as you change models on the road, so you change buildings.

"When Tiger Stadium was built, people were driving Model T's," said Bob Berg to the *News* in July 1988. "And there aren't many model T's out on the road now."

Talbert agreed: "A 1938 Packard is a classic, but I wouldn't want to drive it every day anymore," he wrote. "The '38 Packard should be in a museum, certainly not on the road. Tiger Stadium should be a museum, not a major league stadium. Tiger Stadium is an antiquated, dying facility at Michigan and Trumbull — a major detriment and expensive handicap to the future of the Detroit Tigers."

CHAPTER 13

RENOVATION: STOP MAKING SENSE

> With the cost of a new stadium, it seems like you can do an awful lot of improvement on the existing stadium for that kind of money.
> *— Tom Monaghan, quoted in* Detroit Monthly, *May 1988*

> To me it's vandalism to take down something like Tiger Stadium.
> *— George F. Will*

Tiger Tale No. 2: Tiger Stadium can't be renovated.

THE CHARADE

On January 5, 1988, the City of Detroit announced it would hold a contest. Architectural and engineering firms were asked to submit design proposals for renovating Tiger Stadium or replacing it.

Three months later, on April 1, Mayor Young announced two groups of finalists, each headed by an established ballpark construction company based in Kansas City and a prominent Detroit architectural firm. The group submitting the winning proposal would get the contract to proceed with the plan. The losing team would get paid less than eighty thousand dollars.

Who would judge the contest? The stadium's landlord, Mayor Young, perhaps with help from his tenant, Tom Monaghan. Young and Monaghan had met late in March with Governor James Blanchard and the city's development director, Emmett Moten, Jr. Monaghan told reporter Lowell Cauffiel that the parties had agreed not to decide on a new stadium until the two teams of experts had finished. Monaghan said that he had sought and received assurances that the studies would be impartial.

Leaders of the Tiger Stadium Fan Club doubted that. "Any suggestion that this was an objective competition is ludicrous," argues Bob Buchta. "The same firm that was being asked to propose options for the stadium would be automatically awarded the contract to build a new stadium. So there was a built-in incentive for a firm to argue a new stadium is better." A contract for a $150-$200 million new stadium is a bigger plum than a contract for a $40 million or $50 million renovation. Besides, critics said, the contest's judge would be Young, and his position was clear. The competition was more like the start of the bidding for a new stadium than an objective study.

In August 1988 one team dropped out. The winner by default was the team headed by HOK Sports Facilities Group of Kansas City. It included Detroit architects Albert Kahn Associates and the structural engineering firm Charles S. Davis Associates, which had been part of Turner Construction Company's 1987 Tiger Stadium study.

When HOK finally released its report on March 16, 1989, it contained not a word about any structural problems at the stadium. The study outlined two renovation plans for Tiger Stadium and two plans for new multipurpose stadiums, one with a fixed roof and the other with a retractable dome. By far the most attention was given to a plan for a new open-air, baseball-only stadium that HOK estimated would cost $117.9 million.

Four hours after the HOK announcement, Monaghan endorsed the open-air stadium, giving the cost as $180 million. It hadn't taken the helpless tenant long to decide. No longer now could Monaghan claim he was being dragged by Young into a new stadium he didn't want.

HOK's study was based on criteria provided by representatives of the city and the Tigers. Fans, community leaders, and neighborhood business people had no input.

The criteria included:

(1) A capacity of no more than 55,000, with 40,000 seats located in foul territory, and 24,000 seats that could be sold as season tickets.

(2) A total of 150 luxury suites to accommodate 1,800 patrons.

At Recreation Park in the 1880s, there were no outfield fences. Fans on foot or in buggies defined the limits of the playing field. *(B)*

Homeowners along National erected tall, rickety wooden "wildcat" bleachers beyond Bennett Park's left field fence and charged from five cents to fifty cents a seat. *(B)*

To block the view of fans in the wildcat stands, Tiger officials hung strips of canvas, creating the first obstructed view seats at Michigan and Trumbull. *(B)*

Fans in the wildcat stands generally behaved with less decorum than the Tigers' paying patrons. *(B)*

The outfield walls at Bennett Park were painted with elaborate billboards advertising soda pop, clothing, shoes, cigars, taxi service and even dandruff treatment. *(B)*

The Bull Durham sign in right center field was a popular target for sluggers at Bennett Park. *(B)*

The Opening Day parade in 1907 at Bennett Park. *(B)*

Fans among an overflow crowd on a warm spring Sunday in May 1908 at Bennett Park find their own perches in right center field. *(B)*

Enthusiastic crowds often filled Bennett Park as the Tigers won American League pennants in 1907, 1908, and 1909. *(B)*

A guard keeps an overflow bleacher crowd at Bennett Park from encroaching on the field. *(B)*

Fans ring the outfield as a capacity crowd watches the Tigers play the Philadelphia Athletics on May 21, 1911 at Bennett Park. *(B)*

To test the newly erected upper deck at Navin Field, tons of sandbags were placed on the decking in February 1923. *(M)*

Aerial shot of Navin Field in 1928 from the Michigan Central depot a few blocks to the west. *(M)*

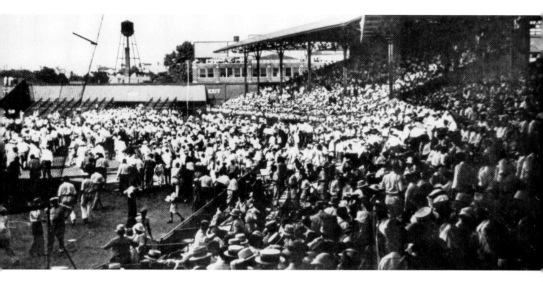

Fans leave stands at Navin Field and exit through main gates on Trumbull. Roof of Checker Cab Company is visible beyond right field wall. *(B)*

Navin Field in the late 1920s and early 1930s had a double-decked grandstand behind home plate, circus bleachers in the outfield, and a high wall in left field along Cherry Street. *(B)*

In September 1934 huge crowds packed Navin Field as the Tigers eased the pain of the Depression by capturing their first pennant in 25 years. *(FP)*

A photo from 1934 shows a run scoring on a bases-loaded walk. Note the dirt path between home plate and the pitcher's mound. *(FP)*

Again in 1935, the Tigers fought for a pennant. This capacity crowd of August 23 is composed mostly of men in shirt sleeves and hats. Note photographers kneeling beside the third-base coach. *(FP)*

The Tigers won their first modern World Series in 1935 in front of capacity crowds that filled the old Navin Field grandstands and the mammoth left-field bleacher section added in 1934. Note the screen in front of the bleachers in left. *(M)*

After the 1935 season, Walter Briggs began his park expansion by extending the double-decked stands into right field. The famous right field overhang is shown here under construction in early 1936. *(M)*

On Opening Day in 1936, fans crowded all three decks to watch the traditional flag-raising ceremonies. *(FP)*

In 1936, the third deck in the right-field corner was not yet completed. *(M)*

On April 21, 1937, a capacity crowd on Opening Day much resembles Opening Day crowds a half-century later—except for all the hats. Press photographers kneel on field, others jam photographers' box on facing of second deck. *(FP)*

Flag-raising at the 1937 opener. Note upper bleachers have no scoreboard above them; that would be in place for the 1938 season. *(FP)*

The Briggs Stadium bleachers gave working families great views of the action for affordable prices. You have to search hard in this 1940 crowd to find the Tigers' female fans. *(M)*

On June 15, 1948, Walter Briggs finally dropped his crusade against night baseball and the Tigers joined the rest of the American League under the lights. *(M)*

By 1953, the Tigers had a new office building behind the stadium walls at the famous corner of Michigan and Trumbull. *(B)*

In 1968, the Tigers united a city torn apart by racial and economic strife. This aerial photo from that year looks east along Michigan Avenue toward downtown and the Detroit River. *(B)*

The Cochrane Plan would include additions along Michigan and Trumbull that expand stadium concessions and team office facilities. (*Photo by Bartush Photography*)

Engineers studying renovation for Wayne County officials claimed this view from the third deck at Tiger Stadium would be a poor one for luxury suites.

On June 10, 1990, Tiger fans encircled the stadium for a second ball park "hug."

The little kid in all of us awaits the coming of another season at Michigan and Trumbull. (*Photo by Michelle Andonian/Detroit Monthly*)

(3) Expanded restrooms, concessions, commissaries, clubhouses, press facilities, team offices and other support spaces.
(4) New restaurants, clubs, shops and other amenities.
(5) A new scoreboard.
(6) Advertising panels throughout the stadium.
(7) Fewer obstructed seats while keeping seats as close as possible to the field.

Luxury suites had first been proposed for the Tigers in 1978, but were dropped from the renovations for lack of money. A decade later they were considered so essential that in every new stadium they take up many of the best views.

Could the Tigers find a corporate market for 150 luxury suites? Analysts were doubtful. Charles Child of *Crain's Detroit Business* wrote in 1989 that corporate suites, "a boon for Detroit Pistons owner William Davidson at the Palace in Auburn Hills, probably won't hold the same financial magic for Detroit Tigers owner Tom Monaghan. . . . It is possible that 150 new Tiger suites would saturate the market in Detroit."

The Tigers also wanted a stadium with 40,000 "infield" seats, almost twice the existing total. That made renovation a tall order. To try to fill it, HOK proposed lowering the field and moving home plate toward Trumbull to squeeze in 5,000 to 10,000 more box seats. The right-field stands and the park's famous overhang would come down, replaced by a thin sandwich of club seating between the outfield fence and the stadium's outer wall, topped by a new gizmo-filled scoreboard.

HOK offered a pick of costly and crude renovations. For $57 million, you could lose 3,500 bleacher seats, put in a couple of tiers of luxury suites and a new press box, and take out a few posts. For $82 million, you would get no posts, a new upper deck, two rows of loges on a mezzanine level, and 8,000 fewer bleacher seats, but you'd have to find somewhere to play for two seasons, and the Tigers already had made clear that they wouldn't do that. As in Chicago, the renovation plans looked like straw men in the path of the new stadium tornado.

HOK's report "looks very cursory to me," says ballpark consultant John Pastier. "They would have been foolish to put a lot of money into it. They were basically just spelling out a direction and trying to make it look good."

How about a new stadium? For a mere $157 million, HOK offered one with a roof. For $245 million, the roof moves, just like Toronto's.

Clearly, the centerpiece of the study was the proposal for a 56,000-

149

seat natural-grass, open-air, baseball-only stadium with no bleacher seats, a fancy picnic lawn and terrace, a huge stadium club topped by four large party suites, 150 corporate boxes, a helipad, a Hall of Fame plaza, a novelty store, a Domino's Pizza outlet, a six-hundred-square-foot players' spa and purse holders in the women's rest rooms.

Normally, when team owners and their municipal backers announce such fancy plans, they get great press, with sketches and charts in the papers. But the front pages after Monaghan's announcement were filled with the Tiger Stadium Fan Club's charges that the pizza king was pitching a shutout of the average fan.

At a press conference on March 17, 1989, Buchta shot back on behalf of the fan club. "We as taxpayers are being asked to subsidize the further enrichment of Tom Monaghan," he said. "We as Detroiters are being asked to divert precious resources from the critical needs of our city to build a yuppie pleasure palace. . . . It is an insult to destroy a treasured baseball landmark in the name of luxury boxes and more expensive tickets. It is a double insult to ask us as taxpayers to pay for the privilege."

The populist heat about a park without bleachers singed politicians as far away as Lansing. Blanchard said no way would the state government ante up for any stadium that didn't have plenty of affordable seats.

The fan club announced a boycott of Domino's Pizza. On March 19, about 250 fans marched around Tiger Stadium, carrying placards with the names of all the Hall of Famers who had played at Michigan and Trumbull. Some then picketed a Domino's outlet across the street.

Many fans were surprised by the turn of events. Some thought the fan club had won the battle a few months earlier when Tiger Stadium had been put on the National Register of Historic Places. The listing did not prevent the park from being replaced — and it obviously hadn't settled the issue.

Neither had public opinion. The latest scientific poll, by Lansing's Marketing Resource Group a few weeks after the HOK announcement, showed fans statewide favored renovation 61 percent to 16 percent. In Detroit, the margin was 75 percent to 16 percent. The poll also found that people opposed state money for a new stadium, 71 percent to 20 percent.

The city had conducted its rigged contest, HOK had issued its foregone conclusion, and Monaghan had signed on. But there was one catch. On April 6, 1989, Monaghan said he needed tax breaks and land from the city to help him build a new stadium, and he wasn't sure he could get it. "It seems to be politically impossible for them," the Tiger boss told interviewer Jeff DeFran on WPZA, a radio station Monaghan owns. "It sounds like the only way that a new stadium is going to be built is I'm going to have to build it. And I don't know how I'm going to do it. I'm going to need a lot of help."

In 1988 Monaghan was listed by *Forbes* as the 124th wealthiest person in America; his estimated worth was $480 million. In 1990 his estimated worth was above the billion-dollar mark, according to *Fortune* magazine. But he told DeFran he couldn't afford a stadium. "I'm not all that liquid," he complained. "People talk about the billions of dollars I have. Well, I'm scratching every day to get by."

THE COCHRANE PLAN

Through an architecture professor at the University of Michigan, John Davids had met Monaghan late in 1983, just after the pizza king had bought the Tigers. "We seemed to hit it off pretty good," Davids remembers. "He told me how much he loved the stadium, but that the one thing that he didn't like was his private box. It was real nondescript and just kind of a crummy little box. I was a student at the time, and I said, 'I'd like to redesign it for you. I love Tiger Stadium, and I love the Tigers, and it'd really be a great honor.' I was really surprised. He goes, 'Yeah. That sounds good.'"

Doing the box didn't advance Davids's career, but it gave him free rein of Tiger Stadium. "He was like Mr. Monaghan's architect," recalls his wife, Judy, an interior designer. "It was so bizarre. He was twenty-four years old, and every time he'd come to the stadium, people would say, 'Mr. Monaghan's architect is here.'"

The Davidses sat in Monaghan's newly designed box on Opening Day, 1984. "Before the game, we were sitting in there by ourselves, and in walks Al Kaline and his wife," John Davids remembers. "Kaline was talking about how great the stadium was. He goes, 'Yeah, I wish they'd put the green seats back in. Such a beautiful stadium.' He was really fired up about the stadium."

So were John and Judy Davids, but they preferred the bleachers. About fifty times a year, they would drive in from Ann Arbor to hang out with their friends in the lower deck in right field. "We just got so nuts about going to games there, and about the stadium too," John Davids says. "We met all these great people."

Those people included John Sinclair, Detroit's most famous 1960s radical and still a hip guy on the city cultural scene. Sinclair's bleacher friends, says John Davids, included people from "the cool fringe of Detroit society."

John Davids spent so much time in the bleachers that he started giving friends the number at the pay phone there. "It was just a great place to sit," he says. "That's where we really got connected with the stadium, I'd say."

In August 1988, leaving the bleachers after a game, John and Judy Davids saw a small gray-haired woman passing out flyers. It was Catherine Darin, the Irish immigrant who had gone to her first game at Briggs Stadium in 1946 and who had become a key member of the Tiger Stadium Fan Club.

John and Judy Davids went to their first fan club meeting in 1989, after the release of the HOK study. "The fan club talked about how they were going to do their own study on the stadium," remembers Judy Davids. "I don't really know what they were calling for. I don't really think they were expecting to do a Cochrane Plan."

The fan club announced in June 1989 that it wanted to do a study on renovation. At the time, there seemed to be room for a compromise. Plans for a new stadium appeared to be stalled. Monaghan reportedly was talking to various famous architects from England, France, and Japan. The only politician talking about a new stadium was Mayor Young, and his city was broke. The public wanted the stadium saved. With a little creativity, perhaps the park could be renovated in a way that would appeal to the Tigers.

The fan club offered its own criteria: (1) Preserve Tiger Stadium, its historic character, its outfield dimensions and its distinctive features; (2) keep as many seats as possible as close as possible to the playing field and improve existing sight lines; (3) retain good, affordable seats in all price ranges; (4) improve concessions, rest rooms and handicapped facilities; and (5) protect the existing neighborhood and consider the city's social priorities.

Who better than John and Judy Davids, bleacher creatures and ex-Monaghan architects, to reconcile what the fans wanted and what the Tigers wanted? The fan club wasn't entirely sure, at first.

"I think they were a little leery of us," says Judy Davids. "I sensed that there was a fear that we were going to come in, and we were going to advise them that the way to go was to rip out the upper deck or something, and that we were really going to screw up the stadium."

Those fears were soon allayed. John Davids remembers the first presentation of his plan to the fan club, in August 1989. "We walked in, we started flipping through boards," he recalls, "and you could see people shaking their heads: 'Yeah, yeah, this is looking good. This is going to be something.' "

Helped by an associate, Harijs Krauklis, the Davidses say they "really played off the energy in the fan club" and within a few months produced, on a volunteer basis, the most thorough Tiger Stadium renovation proposal ever done. "People were really excited that this could be the thing that wins the battle," John Davids remembers. "A plan that works, that's been done by a professional architect, that addresses the needs of the Tigers, but that still doesn't ruin the intimacy or the essential character of the stadium."

There was not total unanimity, he recalls: "Some people in the fan club, understandably, did not want to see luxury boxes as part of this project at all. But the opinion of the majority was that we don't like the idea of having this exclusive part of the stadium, but it's going to be a reality. The Tigers are going to insist on these luxury boxes, because it's modern baseball. And we thought that the location we had was an excellent location. It was a great view of the field. Plus, it didn't mess up everybody else's seat. It didn't put the upper deck twice as far away, so you could slide some boxes in underneath the upper deck."

If you have a beautiful house but you need more room, you knock out a wall or two and build an addition. John and Judy Davids's Cochrane Plan proposes the same solution for Tiger Stadium.

To fit in more concessions, rest rooms, clubhouses and offices, new dining facilities, and other amenities, the plan would add three additions to the outside of the stadium. The largest would require closing little-used Cochrane Avenue, formerly National, where the wildcatters fought the team owners to a draw. Another along Michigan would provide more wide concourses to serve the prime seating areas behind home plate. Together, they would double the stadium's concessions and rest rooms, triple the area for food storage, triple the size of the cramped visitors' clubhouse, and more than double the size of the home clubhouse.

A third addition would more than double the space for the Tigers' offices and ticket department. Along Michigan, a new building would house a museum and marketing department, and on a pedestrian plaza

153

John Davids envisions statues of the Tigers' great double-play combination, Lou Whitaker and Alan Trammell. New elevators would rise to a new third deck housing seventy-three luxury suites for about twelve hundred patrons and punctuated with glassed-in lounges that would shine like beacons atop the stadium at night. Nearly half of the upper deck posts would go, but nothing would disturb the park's intimate seating arrangement or field dimensions.

The plan's beauty is all the more impressive given how quickly it was created. In the fall of 1989, John Davids recalls, "we heard that Monaghan was talking to James Sterling, a very prominent architect from England, about a stadium. We all panicked; in the fan club we tend to panic. The fan club all agreed that we had to get this thing done by the end of the year."

The group hired a reputable local firm, Jeffsan Inc., to do a professional cost estimate, and the news was good: Including a fifteen percent contingency fee, the Cochrane Plan came in at $26.1 million, about an eighth of the cost of a new stadium.

The architects and the fan club believed they had a plan that made good business and good baseball sense. What better investment for Monaghan than a low-risk renovation plan that would make him a hero with the fans? Rental of the luxury suites alone could raise enough money to finance the Cochrane Plan.

The Davidses were confident that Monaghan would be receptive. "We were telling people at this meeting, 'No problem, Monaghan's cool. We'll just call him, and we'll tell him who we are,'" recalls Judy Davids. After designing Monaghan's private box, the Davidses had lived as "architects-in-residence" at Snowflake House, a Frank Lloyd Wright house he owned near Ann Arbor. Judy says she remembers thinking: "If he can decide in a matter of five minutes that we're okay to live in a house worth a quarter of a million dollars, certainly he can spend five minutes looking at the Cochrane Plan."

The fan club planned to present the plan to Monaghan in early January 1990. "We started making contacts with the Tigers in December," says John Davids. "We were totally rebuffed. We wrote letters; I made lots of phone calls. I was really angry, because they wouldn't even entertain the idea of meeting with us. I remember Bill Haase was really quite threatening on the phone with me. I called him up and said, 'Mr. Haase, this is John Davids. I worked on Mr. Monaghan's box back in '83 and '84. My wife and I have developed this plan to renovate Tiger

Stadium.' He had already gotten some calls and letters from Frank Rashid and Bob Buchta."

According to John Davids, Haase asked: "Is this that same plan with the Tiger Stadium Fan Club?"

"Yeah, it is," said Davids.

"We're not going to look at renovation," replied Haase, according to Davids. "We're going to build a new stadium. We have no time to do that. We've made the decision. It's just too late; we're not going to look at renovation."

"You haven't even seen it," said Davids. "How can you just dismiss it out of hand?"

"We've made the decision," said Haase, according to Davids. "We're building a new stadium; that's all there is to it."

Davids says he called him again, "one more time, and the same thing. He wouldn't meet with us."

Davids then called Tom Monaghan's daughter, Susan. "I gave her my number at work and said, 'We'll be there all weekend, working on the plan. Please have your father give me a call.' I never heard from him. So I called her again the next week. She said, 'Yeah, I mentioned it to him, and he didn't make any commitment to call you.'

"We had put in hundreds of hours on this thing, and we had spent all the time going around getting it endorsed by many prominent architects in the Detroit area. We decided we were not just going to let it die. We decided what we had to do was have a press conference; it was the only thing we could do.

"We had the press conference on a Monday. The Friday before, I told Bill Haase, 'Since you haven't agreed to meet with us at all on this thing, we're going to have a press conference Monday to unveil this plan. But we still would like to meet with you. We'll be available any time this weekend for Mr. Monaghan to meet with us.' It never happened."

The Cochrane Plan was unveiled on January 22, 1990. The fan club distributed a handsome seventy-page booklet describing the plan and its rationale and including detailed architectural drawings and the twenty-five-page cost estimate. Formal endorsements included ten prominent local architects and ballpark consultant Pastier. Broadcaster Ernie Harwell contributed a pat on the back. The plan was convincing. Editorials in the *Free Press*, the *News*, and *Crain's Detroit Business* lauded its creativity.

Tiger officials ran for cover. Haase told the press that the team was committed to a new stadium and would not consider renovation. The fan club delivered copies of the proposal to Monaghan and to Tiger officials, but no one responded. The team's strategy was to ignore the Cochrane Plan and hope it would go away. The Tigers appeared to believe that commenting would confer on the proposal a dignity that they hoped to avoid. But the strategy backfired badly. With no counter-attack, the plan gained in legitimacy, and the club's refusal to discuss it was viewed widely as intransigence.

"We continued to try to show it to the Tigers," recalls John Davids. "And we had people trying for us, friends of Tom Monaghan and Bo Schembechler, trying to get a meeting with these guys to show them the plan. And they steadfastly refused to look at it. At that point, it just became more and more confrontational. And very honestly, not from our side at all. We didn't have a confrontational attitude. We just wanted them at least to give us the courtesy of meeting with us. We had a plan that was endorsed by a blue-ribbon list of people, and they just would not even meet with us."

Walter Briggs IV, great-grandson of the man who expanded Navin Field into Briggs Stadium, believes Tiger management made a serious error in ignoring the Cochrane Plan. Even if the Tigers were going to reject the plan, it would have been politic to meet with the fan club and at least give the appearance of goodwill, says Briggs.

Fan club co-founder Bob Buchta agrees. "From their point of view," he says, "the wisest thing to do would have been to meet with us before the plan was even made public, as we tried to do, and come out with a press conference the same day as ours saying that they have met with us, they've examined the plan, but they've already decided that it unfortunately doesn't meet their needs; they very much appreciate the sincere efforts that we've done on their behalf but they unfortunately have to come to the conclusion that the Cochrane Plan is unfeasible. If they had done that, it would have been a lot harder for us to counter.

"I think they probably felt that to give a hearing to renovation would open up the process to the public and would put pressure on them to continue their deliberations in a way that was responsive to the wishes of the fans and the ideas of the public. They didn't want to do that. They've never wanted to do that.

"I also think there are very strong egos involved here. The fan club had boycotted Domino's. The fan club had been very critical of the Tigers."

In an interview in February 1991 Haase admitted that he had

"glanced through" the Cochrane Plan but had never read it. When asked if Tom Monaghan had seen it, he replied: "Not to my knowledge, no."

"For people to come out and make strong statements that we're addressing this situation with utter contempt for their feelings is totally wrong," Haase said. "We understand that the fans are our supporters. . . . But you do reach a point in time where you do have to make a decision and you have to go on. And we've done that.

"We haven't ignored the stadium fan club people in the sense that they may feel. But their plan came along way after the decision had been made, and after we had studied several different renovation plans. To go back and open up the renovation prospect again, when we already had crossed that bridge, would just add to public confusion, and then people would have no idea where we're headed or what we're doing. We don't feel that there's anything out there that would lend itself to changing that direction that we've decided is the best to go."

The Cochrane Plan was displayed all over town in 1990. John and Judy Davids and fan club leaders presented it to many civic groups. The City Planning Commission reviewed the plan and recommended that it be seriously considered.

The success of the Cochrane Plan cemented the fan club's reputation as a serious opposition group. Meanwhile, the club continued to demonstrate its grass-roots appeal. During 1990 the club's membership grew to over ten thousand. On June 10 the club led a second hug of Tiger Stadium. Once again, over a thousand fans linked hands and surrounded the ballpark. This time, the mood was more determined.

At the ballpark that summer, the fan club distributed over 120,000 postcards asking Monaghan to change his mind and save Tiger Stadium. But Monaghan was not listening to his customers. In an interview on WPZA, he said: "The way I feel about it, I'd rather have the old stadium. But everybody that knows better wants a new one, and I'm going with that."

In Detroit for a book signing during the summer, columnist George F. Will lauded the Cochrane Plan. In an interview in December 1990, Will said: "I understand that baseball is a money-making business. I can understand the desire to have sky boxes. I also believe, from what the [Tiger Stadium Fan Club] has shown me, that it's possible to add sky boxes to Tiger Stadium without destroying the integrity of the place. To me it's vandalism to take down something like Tiger Stadium."

157

Asked to assess the character of Monaghan, Will said: "I don't know the gentleman; he's a very successful American entrepreneur. There are always those who suspect — and I can't judge this, but it's a suspicion you have to entertain in a case like this — that the man wants to build a monument to himself. I don't know if it's true or not. I hope not."

Despite its great popularity and many endorsements, the Cochrane Plan proved to be dangerous for John Sinclair. In December 1990 he was fired from his job as editor of *City Arts Quarterly*, a magazine funded by the City of Detroit. The subsequent issue of the magazine appeared with two missing pages, which Sinclair said had been devoted to the Cochrane Plan. He sued the city, claiming that his immediate supervisor, Council of the Arts director Shahida Mausi, had been approached by her mother, a friend of Mayor Young, who "suggested to Ms. Mausi that the article on the Cochrane Plan be deleted from the magazine." Mausi denied the charge, saying the story had been pulled because it didn't fit the issue's theme of "cultural diversity." She said her decision "was an editorial prerogative."

BO IN A CHINA SHOP

While fleeing the Cochrane Plan, Tiger officials hid behind problems real and exaggerated at Tiger Stadium. Despite expert evidence to the contrary, club spokesmen kept alluding to terrible structural problems lurking deep in its bowels. They cited cramped clubhouses, long lines at concession stands, small offices, and a host of other deficiencies that the Cochrane Plan remedied. In the club's mind, the Cochrane Plan didn't exist.

Bob Talbert's *Free Press* column of June 3, 1990, used Haase's comments to revive an army of phantoms.

> Players' facilities such as dugouts, locker rooms and clubhouses are so far out of date they are laughable. The bullpens are virtual prisons. There is no fitness center and year-round rehabilitation area for the players to use, as there is in modern parks. 'And there is no room for us to create these areas to keep up with the rest of the teams and stay competitive,' Haase said.

Manager Sparky Anderson chimed in, saying the Tigers needed a new stadium because his office was too small.

Figures seem to indicate that the Tigers inflated their space require-
ments to make renovation seem less feasible and more costly. Following the Tigers' criteria, both the Cochrane Plan and the HOK renovation proposals provide 30,000 square feet of administrative facilities.
But design criteria for three proposed new stadiums — two in San Francisco that were never built and the Orioles' new park in Baltimore —
allow for an average of 23,000 square feet of administrative facilities.
Tiger Stadium renovations allow 19,360 square feet of clubhouse
space, the new stadium plans average 10,375 square feet. Team facilities average 23,160 square feet in the Detroit renovation plans, more
than double the average (10,613 square feet) in the new stadium plans.
And concession space is 30,000 square feet, compared to an average
15,500 square feet for the new stadium designs.

All reasoned arguments to the contrary, the Tigers appeared to have
their minds made up. Stop making sense, they told those favoring
renovation, and let us get on with the new stadium. But the man hired
to sell fans on a new stadium had a rough first year.

Before the 1990 season, Monaghan hired his close friend from Ann
Arbor, Bo Schembechler, as club president. His main task, Tiger officials told the press, was to get the public behind a new stadium.
Monaghan passed over general manager Bill Lajoie, widely respected
in baseball circles as savvy, professional, and successful. Lajoie's smart
trades and wise scouting had kept the Tigers in contention in the
1980s.

Schembechler had been the winningest football coach in the history
of the University of Michigan. His teams were perennial champions
that almost always failed to win bowl games. He was famous for his
tirades against referees and a win-at-all-costs attitude.

Bringing in a college football coach to run a professional baseball
team was an unorthodox move. Schembechler admitted he didn't know
much about the baseball business, but claimed he was a quick study.

In his autobiography, *Bo*, he seemed less sure about life after coach-
ing: "I was never a desk guy," he wrote. "Maybe I should just disappear
when I take the black sneakers off." Within a few months many Tiger
fans — even University of Michigan alumni who had admired Schembechler's achievements on the gridiron — had reason to agree with his
assessment.

Midway through his first year, Schembechler defended pitcher Jack
Morris after Morris harassed a female *Free Press* reporting intern who
had approached the pitcher for a clubhouse interview. When *Free*

159

Press publisher Neal Shine complained, Schembechler penned a reply which Shine published in full in a Sunday column.

> Dear Mr. Shine:
>
> Jack Morris' remarks were out of line but predictable.
>
> Dan Ewald called your sports editor, Dave Robinson, just prior to the incident to caution him of a potentially volatile situation. After your intern watched men from 20 to 65 years of age undress and dress for more than half an hour without asking questions, Dan was concerned.
>
> Your sports editor's lack of common sense in sending a female college intern in a men's clubhouse caused the problem.
>
> I really wouldn't doubt that the whole thing was a scam orchestrated by you people to create a story.
>
> I can't speak for Tom Monaghan, but rest assured no female member of my family would be inside a men's locker room regardless of their job description. Since you most likely never competed in the athletic arena, understanding the sanctity and privacy of the locker room is impossible.

The new Tiger boss made other startling statements. Once, he reportedly said that he didn't understand why the manager wasn't called the head coach and that he was thinking of changing Sparky Anderson's title. Fans grew suspicious of Schembechler's qualifications and ill at ease about the direction he would take the Tigers. And he apparently was making little progress in advancing the team's demands for a new stadium. Talks with the City of Detroit had broken off, for reasons not entirely clear.

On October 2, 1990, Schembechler appeared on David Letterman's late-night TV talk show. Expecting to be assailed for his comments on women in the locker room, Schembechler barely had time to grab a chair before Letterman laid into him: "Are you gonna tear Tiger Stadium down?" Letterman asked. Schembechler hesitated. Letterman screamed: "Uh-oh! It's gone! It's gone! It's a cloud of smoke now! C'mon, don't tear it down."

"We do feel that something has to be done," Schembechler replied, but Letterman cut him off.

"Oh, my God! These are the great old baseball fields, this is where the sport became the national pastime, and you guys are just putting up malls now." Before Schembechler could formulate a reply, time ran out.

On December 20 things went from bad to worse for Bo. Ernie

Harwell, the Tigers' much-loved longtime broadcaster, called a press conference at Tiger Stadium to announce that Schembechler and executives of radio station WJR had decided not to renew his contract beyond the 1991 season.

It was akin to Santa Claus announcing he had been terminated by executives of Toys R Us. Harwell was a member of the broadcasters' wing of the Baseball Hall of Fame and had been a fixture in the Tigers' radio booth for thirty years. Most of the team's fans, from the most loyal to the most casual, had grown up listening to his gentle Georgia voice. For half a lifetime, Harwell had been the Tigers' best public relations asset, and his honest, straightforward, unassuming professionalism had gone a long way toward easing fans' discontents.

Harwell's announcement was so shocking that reporters present gasped and shook their heads. Harwell had no known enemies in baseball. Fans, players, club officials, and members of the media all counted him as their friend. Fire Ernie Harwell? Schembechler had done the absolutely unthinkable.

Tiger officials seemed to be taken by surprise by Harwell's announcement. The only Tiger representative at the press conference was marketing director Jeff Odenwald, who tried to explain the decision by saying that the Tigers were going in "a new direction."

Harwell told the unbelieving press that Schembechler had suggested he announce on the winter press tour in January that he had decided to retire at the end of 1991. Harwell said he had rejected that proposal because it would have been a lie. He didn't want to retire. The same day Harwell announced his departure, his longtime sidekick Paul Carey also said he had decided on his own to retire after the 1991 season.

Angry fans deluged the Tiger offices, Domino's headquarters in Ann Arbor, and the media with calls and letters. Many linked the decision to can Harwell with the Tigers' desire to replace Tiger Stadium. Both were a bald repudiation of the franchise's long and proud heritage. The Harwell decision made it clear to many fans that the Tigers under Schembechler cared little about tradition or about them.

"Bo Schembechler and the Tigers organization took everything that was decent about what I felt about Detroit and its ball club and threw it on the ground and stepped on it," Larry J. Koch of Ypsilanti wrote the *Free Press*. "Somehow Schembechler's accomplishments in Ann Arbor are not in my memory anymore. What remains is a deep hurt for what he has done to Ernie Harwell, millions of fans, and me."

Ruth Kaufman of Southfield asked in another letter published in the

Free Press: "What is the cure for the mean-spirited forces that are taking away the symbols of the things we should cherish? Is it really only the bottom line that counts? Some of us don't think so."

Some fans believed Harwell's firing was linked to his support for saving Tiger Stadium. Harwell had given a mild vote of approval to the Cochrane Plan after fan club leaders had shown it to him the previous winter. And days before his startling announcement, he had appeared at a comedy benefit for the fan club. He had collaborated with singer Mike Ridley on a baseball song, included on a cassette with comedian Thom Sharp's new song about saving Tiger Stadium, "Don't Tear It Down." The cassette was being sold to raise money for the fan club. Harwell insisted, though, that the decision had been made in October and was not linked to his feelings about the stadium.

Haase also denied any link. "The stadium decision has nothing to do with the Harwell thing," he said in February 1991.

After Harwell's announcement, the Tigers' stock with the public sank to an all-time low. *Crain's Detroit Business* wrote that it was time for Monaghan to sell the team. Former Tiger pitcher Hank Aguirre, president of a local automotive supply company, went public with an offer to buy the club, but Monaghan rejected it.

"They fired Harwell," says Aguirre, "and then the Detroit Tigers sort of started to disintegrate. As much as I love Tom Monaghan, I thought he had made a serious mistake when he hired Bo Schembechler. That's when everything started to happen, seemed like. Whether it was Bo's fault or not, you know, it just started to disintegrate. Bo's a wonderful football coach, and probably a wonderful friend of Monaghan's, and that's all fine and dandy. I thought if he wanted to hire Bo, he could hire him and put him in some position other than running the baseball team. I still think strongly that was a mistake."

The *Detroit News* editorialized on December 23, 1990, that Monaghan should not expect the public to help him build a new stadium. "If the Tigers want to toss tradition aside so casually, let them pay for it all by themselves," wrote the *News*, adding that "communities tempted to cut deals of their own with the Tigers should remember how management treated Ernie when it tired of him."

The Harwell firing was a public relations disaster for the Tigers. It was followed by the resignation of Lajoie, whose departure was linked to disputes with Schembechler over authority. Schembechler also failed to sign longtime Tiger pitching ace Jack Morris after insisting on handling the negotiations himself, and Morris jumped to the Minnesota Twins.

Angry Tiger fans boycotted the 1991 Opening Day, protesting the team's "new direction." Harwell urged fans to forget their antagonism, but the game, usually sold out weeks in advance, drew only 47,382. Outside the stadium, hundreds sat in makeshift bleachers set up along Michigan Avenue by the Tiger Stadium Fan Club and listened to Harwell broadcast the game on WJR.

Monaghan and Schembechler had become two of the least popular people in Michigan.

THE PHANTOM TAG

As 1991 began, it had been five years since club officials had started talking about a new stadium and two years since Monaghan had endorsed HOK's proposal. But no architect had been selected and no site chosen.

Rumors had the Tigers headed to various suburbs west of the city. But residents of Dearborn overwhelmingly opposed a new stadium, and the Novi city council unanimously rejected rumored Tiger overtures and urged the club to stay in Tiger Stadium for the good of the entire metropolitan area. Similar council resolutions followed in several other suburbs.

In the wake of the Harwell fiasco, public financing for any possible new stadium seemed a real longshot. Michigan's new governor, Republican John Engler, said shortly after his surprise November 1990 election that no state money would be used to build a new stadium for the Tigers.

Legal mechanisms remained from the failed 1970s riverfront dome project that might allow Wayne County to help finance a new stadium. Since 1987 the Tigers had been approaching county officials about financing, but had been spurned. In late 1990 the county's leaders came to the Tigers.

County Executive Ed McNamara was reportedly eyeing the governorship after fellow Democrat Blanchard's defeat. There also were rumors that he wanted to run for the U.S. Senate. McNamara's assistant, Michael Duggan, reportedly wanted to succeed his boss.

Blanchard had failed to turn out voters in heavily Democratic Wayne County. His frequent snubs of Mayor Young had cost him the support of many Detroiters. McNamara needed an issue that would increase his name recognition statewide and portray him as a strong backer of Detroit. Duggan needed to become better known.

Duggan, a tireless self-promoter, would spend much of 1991 billing himself and his boss as the politicians who went all out to save the Tigers for Detroit. According to a chronology Duggan released in June 1991, he and McNamara met with Schembechler, Haase, and Jim Campbell twice in December 1990. Duggan said that the county initiated the meeting because of reports that the Tigers were ready to abandon Detroit.

The Tiger officials told the county, according to Duggan, that Tiger Stadium could not be saved and that they wanted a new stadium at whatever location would be most profitable. Duggan says that McNamara told the Tigers that the county would be willing to float bonds for a new stadium and levy a hotel-motel tax, but only if the team stayed in the city.

On January 8 county officials met with members of the Tiger Stadium Fan Club to review the Cochrane Plan. Present was Christopher Kittides, president of BEI Associates. Duggan told fan club members that BEI would evaluate the plan for the county and issue a public report on its findings. According to the fan club, Duggan said that he personally favored renovation and hoped to persuade the Tigers to change their minds.

"He told us they would not give a proposal to the Tigers for a new stadium until they were satisfied that the Tigers had given renovation a serious hearing," says Bob Buchta. "He presented himself as this heroic figure who was championing renovation against tough opposition from the Tigers."

Fan club leaders were cautiously optimistic. For the first time, public officials had pledged to present the Cochrane Plan to the Tigers. And for the first time the plan would get a serious and detailed evaluation open to public scrutiny.

Such hopes proved unfounded. By April, Duggan had made it clear to the press that he considered the Cochrane Plan dead, even before BEI had released its report. "The Cochrane Plan doesn't come close to what the Tigers need," Duggan told *Crain's Detroit Business*.

In May the county released BEI's report. It said the Cochrane Plan was feasible but would cost twice as much as estimated, wouldn't remove enough posts to give the Tigers enough prime seats, and offered poor views from the proposed luxury suites.

Just as the Chicago media had allowed the Campbell team's suspect study on Comiskey Park to pass muster, the Detroit media took the BEI report on the Cochrane Plan as gospel. On WJR, the Tigers' flagship station, reporter Pat Vitale commented that it was a relief that renovation had "finally" been laid to rest.

But was the BEI report fair? Did it make sense? Had Wayne County officials fairly evaluated renovation? Ballpark consultant John Pastier thinks not. "It's not a report," he sneers. "It's a bunch of conclusions without substantiation in most cases. It's very amateurish. There's been no methodology to this thing, and there are these totally unfounded opinions."

Several key points about the process remain unresolved. The refusal of Michael Duggan and Ed McNamara to discuss these points for this book leaves several important questions unanswered:

Was BEI qualified to evaluate the Cochrane Plan? BEI had never done any work on baseball stadiums. Pastier says a top BEI employee working on the project called him for help on calculating ballpark distances and was ignorant of the most basic facts about stadium design. The employee, says Pastier, pronounced "loges" as "low-geeze."

Did BEI have a stake in the outcome? Though it had no stadium experience BEI was selected, said Wayne County official Patricia Kukula, for its "independence and reputation." The firm agreed to do the work gratis.

"We didn't charge anything," confirms Kittides.

BEI was then being considered for lucrative county projects, including the expansion of Metro Airport. And Kittides was at meetings in the spring of 1991 concerning plans for development around a stadium. Kittides says he came to an April 15 meeting with major land developers, including Wayne Doran of Ford Land Development Corporation, because "I was asked to make a presentation."

"At the time, we were looking at some parking possibilities around Tiger Stadium," Kittides explains. "We were still looking at Tiger Stadium as a renovation option. What Wayne Doran had come up with was a generic development scheme around a stadium. It could be Tiger Stadium, it could be a new stadium, it could be a stadium in Detroit, or it could be a stadium in Dearborn, or anywhere else."

The BEI report on the Cochrane Plan has a cover letter that says the firm "looks forward to our continued participation in the county's efforts to provide a state of the art baseball stadium for the Detroit

Tigers." With that letter, says Pastier, "they were admitting that their own report was a mechanism for getting a new stadium rather than settling the issue through a genuine report."

As with HOK two years earlier, BEI's clear interest in getting a piece of the new stadium action mitigated against any favorable report on renovation. As Pastier noted in his September 1991 *Inland Architect* article, "Hoping to work on a new stadium inevitably compromises BEI's 'independence' in assessing plans to save the old one."

Asked if he hopes to take part in designing a new stadium, Kittides says, "Oh, hope, yeah. Everybody hopes. Every architectural firm in town would like to participate."

Kittides denies that there was any understanding regarding a stadium project. He says doing the work for free was a matter of "client relations."

"We do favors for General Motors sometimes," he says. "We do favors for the City of Detroit. These are things that are give and take. There's no agreement or prearrangement or anything. But naturally, you ask me, would I like to be involved? Sure."

An article in *Crain's Detroit Business* on July 29, 1991, quoted Jerry Shea, president of the local chapter of the American Institute of Architects, as saying that BEI's free work for the county "might give them the inside track" for a contract to work on a new stadium. Asked if it was customary for architectural and engineering firms to do free work for governments, Shea said it was "hardly ever" done.

Tiger fan Mike Ridley, a Detroit area singer, has an analogy for BEI's situation: "It's as if I, as a car salesman, and part-time car mechanic, were to take your car, look at it, and say, 'You need a new car.' Whether you do or not, it's a conflict of interest. And then I tell you, 'Well, I have this car for sale.' "

Pastier wrote that BEI's report reads "more like a brief for a new stadium than a balanced analysis."

Kittides claims that there also was "a little bit of civic duty" in his firm's motivation. "We just kind of felt that it was part of a team that would help keep the Tigers in Detroit." The Tigers have a lease binding them to the current stadium until 2008. Might civic duty involve helping the city enforce that lease? Why should BEI accept the rationale that the Tigers need a new stadium?

"Because leases," says Kittides, "are meant to, uh, sometimes change."

Did county officials dismiss the Cochrane Plan out of hand? In his

June 5 report, Duggan writes that Kittides told him "shortly thereafter" the January 8 meeting with the fan club that "the preliminary opinion of himself and his staff was that the plan had little merit."

According to Duggan's report, this "preliminary opinion" encompassed the three major arguments against the plan delineated in the final report released in May. Sometime in January, Duggan writes, Kittides "indicated the costs had been significantly understated, that the great majority of obstructed view seats were unimproved and that the proposed location of the suites on the roof of the stadium would provide such a poor view of the game that the suites would be very difficult to lease."

The opinion on cost contradicted a documented professional evaluation. The opinion on the luxury suites contradicted a yearlong study conducted by stadium design experts who previously had proposed luxury suites in the same location. BEI, writes Duggan, arrived at these evaluations within a few weeks. Duggan writes in his report: "Had the Cochrane Plan been the only alternative, we would have ruled out renovation in January."

But Kittides says it was much later than the end of January before BEI made up its mind. "We issued the Cochrane Plan [report] in May," Kittides recalls. "I would say maybe a month before that we were beginning to formulate that opinion. . . . I think 'shortly' is too short. I would say well into the evaluation. . . . We wouldn't have been able to conclude in January."

Buchta recalls that Duggan made up his mind quickly. "Relatively early in the process he told us he didn't think the Cochrane Plan was feasible," Buchta says. He says Duggan told the fan club that the Tigers were not interested in looking at the Cochrane Plan. "He said it was all he could do to get Bo Schembechler to look at the Birkerts-O'Neal plan [another renovation proposal] and it would have been pointless and fruitless to try to present the Cochrane Plan to him."

Buchta and other fan club leaders believe Duggan folded his hand quickly when faced with opposition from the Tigers, if indeed he had any intention of playing poker at all.

"They laid down their cards. They gave up on renovation," says attorney Bill Dow, a member of the fan club's executive committee. "Then they had to convince the public that renovation would not work, that it was too expensive and impractical, so that they could sell them on the idea of a new stadium. And so they have this BEI report; it's quite a conflict of interest. Duggan's the minister of propaganda for Schembechler. It's just ridiculous."

"The bottom line for Duggan was pleasing the Tigers," says Buchta. "Duggan treated the Tigers as a client, and he was interested in renovation only to the extent the Tigers were."

At one point, Duggan even weighed in on the engineering merits of the Cochrane Plan. In *Crain's Detroit Business* of April 9, 1991, Duggan questioned whether the upper deck posts could be removed. "I really don't believe you can take out 40 percent of the posts in the upper deck and put suites on the roof and have it hold up," he said. But he cited no evidence, and the final BEI report does not raise such questions.

Duggan canceled a scheduled interview to discuss these issues and did not respond to several attempts to reschedule it.

Was BEI's cost figure of $50 million — almost double Jeffsan's documented estimate — justified? The Cochrane Plan's reasonable price tag of $26 million is a major problem for the Tigers because it shows renovation can be done for a fraction of the cost of a new stadium.

BEI's report contained little evidence for its conclusion that the Cochrane Plan would cost $50 million. Jeffsan, the original estimator, listed five hundred twenty-three cost items; BEI listed forty-six.

"A few of the added costs appeared justified," wrote Pastier, "but many were dubious. For example, BEI added $1 million to replace all toilet fixtures even though it estimated their useful life at 25–35 more years, $1.25 million for kitchen and concession fixtures that should be the concessionaire's responsibility, and $5.6 million for suite construction that was already covered in the original estimate, or was finish work normally paid for by tenants."

Kittides says the plumbing costs were added because "even though plumbing appears to be okay, ten years from now it may not be. That's why we decided to put in all new."

The Cochrane Plan proposed seventy-three suites to hold twelve hundred customers, meeting the Tigers' original criterion for seats. But because the Tigers had specified one hundred loges of a smaller size, BEI added twenty-seven suites to its cost estimates. BEI also added fifty dollars a square foot to suite costs, for no stated reason.

Kittides says "we're putting ourselves in a position where we may be a buyer or a lessor of the suite someday. What sort of amenities do you need, to make it truly a luxury suite? It's an opinion, it's a judgment.

. . . We're not saying they're wrong. We're saying we're using a different number."

Customarily, lessors furnish suites. Concessionaires usually equip their own stands, too, but BEI included $675,000 for that. And it tripled the costs of demolition, adding $588,000.

About demolition costs, Kittides explains: "That's the number we came up with. We just didn't dream it up. We just calculated a number. It happened to be different from theirs."

Kittides says BEI added costs to reinforce structural steel and foundations based on its assessment that the lower-deck columns would have to bear more load if forty percent of the upper-deck columns were removed. The assessment is undocumented.

"Some of the costs we added were not in the Jeffsan plan because they did not consider these things," Kittides explains. "Some were adjustments where we felt they were, in our opinion, light. It was a combination of those two things. It wasn't just that the Jeffsan estimates were off the wall."

Michael Ferber, president of Jeffsan, says his firm stands by its estimate. "We tried to be as realistic as possible," he says, citing his twenty years of experience as a conceptual cost estimator and his firm's track record of eight years. Ferber says his firm is impartial on the stadium question and judged the Cochrane Plan on its merits.

"I wasn't playing politics," he says, adding: "The whole thing is a political football, and facts do get lost in a situation like that."

Despite the questionable cost inflation, BEI found that the Cochrane Plan met all other important Tiger criteria. The report concurred that the plan would give the Tigers the space they desired for concessions, rest rooms, offices, and support facilities.

"If you can fix up a great old ballpark for $50 million or you can abandon it and build a new one for $150 million, it would seem to be very imprudent to take the second course," John Pastier argues. "So even if the BEI figures were accurate, I would not say that they made the case for not going ahead with remodeling."

On what basis did BEI claim the views from the proposed luxury suites would be poor? No one had ever claimed the third deck was a bad location for loges. HOK, a firm that has designed luxury suites in many stadiums, put luxury suites on the third deck in one of its Tiger Stadium renovation plans. Duggan writes that he became convinced by the end of January that BEI, a firm with no experience with baseball

169

stadiums, had found viewing problems that one of the nation's foremost stadium designers hadn't considered.

The Cochrane Plan would place a new third deck about sixteen feet farther from the field than the present third deck. The seats in the existing third deck offer a panoramic view of the field and the downtown Detroit skyline. For decades, the Tigers used the third deck to handle overflow crowds. During postseason play, the national press corps sits there. The press box is in the third deck, and so is the scoreboard operator. For years the official scorer sat in the press box. And in 1991 the Tigers opened a "fantasy play-by-play booth" on the third deck where fans pay thirty-five dollars an inning to announce the game and get a videotape of their broadcast. The woman selling the fantasy booth at the Tigers' new fan relations center in Tiger Stadium says the views from there are splendid.

Duggan explained the supposed problem this way in his report: "As far as the suites are concerned, by building them on the roof of the third deck, they are put in the worst possible location in the stadium. They are at the furthest distance from the field and at the location they are proposed [*sic*] there appears to be a depth perception problem (i.e., the average fan will have difficulty telling a line drive from a pop up). The sight lines are such that a spectator in the suite would have to sit on a 30-inch stool with his nose against the window in order to see the playing field."

Pastier says the depth perception problem is "nonsense." "I have never heard anyone," he says, "in reading almost every piece of literature on the subject, and talking to quite a few baseball people, stadium operations directors, clients — no one has ever talked about depth perception. It's a total red herring. They don't define it or explain it anywhere. . . . They just declare that there would be bad depth perception from that location.

"If there's bad depth perception from that location, about eighty feet above the field, what happens at a hundred and thirty feet when you're in a new ballpark? Since that's such a big problem at eighty feet, shouldn't that preclude building a new ballpark? Or are they only concerned about so-called depth perception for the people who are paying fifty thousand dollars a year for their seat?

"If depth perception is a problem as defined by pop-ups and line drives, it doesn't matter how close you are to the edge of the field, because the pop-up or line drive is not occurring at home plate. It's not occurring straight down from you. It's going out away from you."

Pastier says there are no perfect seats in a ballpark, that every location involves a trade-off. "The question is, what does one want in a loge seat?" he asks, adding that many people in luxury suites don't watch the game anyway. "They're there to do business. They're either entertaining clients or doing office politicking."

As for the assertion that luxury suite patrons would have to press their noses to the glass and sit on a thirty-inch stool, Pastier replies: "If there was something inherent in the angle involved that would make that statement plausible, I think it would be very easy to just adjust the sill of the glass line. The glass could go right down to your feet if that's an issue. That's pure balderdash. It's a cheap shot. That automatically disqualifies Mike Duggan as a serious observer of the problem. It immediately makes him a partisan who has very little respect for the truth and is just looking for something to get him through a particular phase in a foregone process. . . . It's just a big lie."

Kittides downplays the problem of sight lines in the luxury suites. "It's not that you can't have them there," he says. "You can have anything you want. Our conclusion was that they were less than ideal."

Asked how his firm evaluated the sight lines, Kittides says: "We made studies. We drew cross sections where we drew out the luxury suites and put a person seated there, and we drew lines to see whether you could see home plate or how much of the field you could see. We actually made a lot of drawings, study drawings, nothing that was published."

Astoundingly, local newspapers dutifully reported Duggan's contentions about poor sight lines from the third deck without checking with their baseball beat reporters to confirm whether they could tell a line drive from a pop up while sitting in the press box. If they couldn't, it would be difficult to write an accurate account of the game.

"Once people start behaving like this, you know everything's on a greased rail," observes Pastier. "It's sort of like what you have in a poorly run corporation or a really heavy-handed dictatorship, that once the word comes out what the party line is, everybody just repeats it."

Duggan's conclusion about the Cochrane Plan was: "Too much money for too little benefit." And so the Tigers, who had tried without success for more than a year to scuttle the Cochrane Plan by ignoring it, seemed to have found a way to get the devil of low-cost renovation behind them, with some help from Wayne County's top officials.

In July 1991 the Cochrane Plan received another fake tag when a committee of the Detroit chapter of the American Institute of Architects issued a press release recommending that a new stadium be built. The chapter president, Jerry Shea, called Tiger Stadium "functionally obsolete" and said that renovation was "a less than acceptable solution."

"Coming to this conclusion was not easy for us," Shea told the *News*. "There's no place like Tiger Stadium. It's tough to have to say that this wonderful place has outlived its usefulness."

Shea was quoted in the press release as having said that "as architects, we look forward to the opportunity of working with all interested parties to develop facilities and areas that will satisfy the needs of the Tiger organization, while at the same time safe-guard the interests of the public."

In the same article, Duggan told the *News*: "Nobody tried to save this stadium harder than we did, but anybody who approaches this professionally and objectively will come to the same conclusion — the Tigers need a new stadium."

Some objective professionals questioned how "professionally and objectively" Shea's committee had looked at the question. *Crain's Detroit Business* wrote that Gino Rossetti, the prominent local architect whose firm had done the 1977–84 renovations of Tiger Stadium and designed the Palace of Auburn Hills, "said he will ask the local chapter of the American Institute of Architects why none of the four members of its subcommittee . . . had stadium experience."

Crain's also asked: "Why didn't Jerry Shea, president of the local AIA chapter and an ex-officio member of its subcommittee, reveal that he works for developer-entrepreneur Richard Kughn, who is a member of the city-county site-selection panel for a new ballpark?"

Shea is vice president of Kughn Enterprises, a Southfield-based development firm. Both Shea and his employer denied that there was any conflict of interest. "Shea happens to be president of the AIA, and he happens to work for me," Kughn told *Crain's*. "He has responsibilities in both arenas. He and I have not discussed stadium sites. We have done that deliberately."

A provision in the AIA's Code of Ethics and Professional Conduct states: "Members making public statements on architectural issues shall disclose when they are being compensated for making such statements or when they have an economic interest in the issue."

172

BIRKERTS-O'NEAL:
ANOTHER WAVE OF THE HAND

There was yet one more renovation hurdle to surmount. According to Duggan's scenario, county officials got a phone call late in January from Joe O'Neal, an Ann Arbor contractor who had developed a renovation proposal with Birmingham architect Gunnar Birkerts and structural engineer Robert Darvas. Birkerts, Darvas, and O'Neal had all worked closely with Monaghan in the past. Birkerts's firm designed Domino's Farms, Monaghan's corporate headquarters, and the "Leaning Tower of Pizza," Monaghan's dream conference center, which was never built. Darvas was a design consultant on Domino's Farms. O'Neal spent time building Monaghan's uncompleted $5 million dream house in Ann Arbor Township.

Despite all these connections, the trio had not reached first base with the Tiger owner on their stadium renovation plan. "I thought Tom Monaghan wanted to save the old stadium," says O'Neal. "We thought we were doing something that Monaghan wanted to do."

O'Neal and his associates had first shown Monaghan their idea in the summer of 1988. But O'Neal says Monaghan told him the Tigers were "pinching pennies" and could not pay for a thorough renovation study.

Their plan got a mention in the press late in 1988, but since then O'Neal and associates had sat on the sidelines, waiting for the right moment. When the news was out that Wayne County officials were evaluating the Cochrane Plan, they jumped back into the game.

Birkerts and O'Neal presented their renovation proposal to Duggan and Kittides in late January. The plan centered on a difficult, somewhat exotic engineering feat: sliding the upper deck back and up from the field, removing all the posts, and hanging the deck from a new superstructure built like a shell around the stadium's exterior. This was radical surgery, and prompted plenty of questions: Was it feasible? Was it affordable? Would the added structure around the stadium interfere with traffic along Michigan Avenue? Could the work really be done in the off-seasons without the Tigers having to find a temporary site for home games?

Duggan says he was impressed enough with the plan to set up presentations with Mayor Young, Schembechler, and other business leaders.

Buchta says Duggan told fan club leaders that Schembechler was so

173

opposed to renovation that he kept O'Neal and Birkerts waiting in an office for twenty or thirty minutes before consenting to see the plan. Then, after seeing the plan that had been rejected by his boss more than two years earlier, Schembechler expressed interest, or so Duggan reports. Young, the earliest and most vociferous advocate of a new stadium, was so intrigued with the radical renovation plan, according to Duggan, that he directed his staff to study whether parking could be provided around a renovated stadium.

According to Duggan's report, Schembechler derailed the renovation scheme. At Schembechler's urging, Duggan wrote, the county sent a staff person to New York in May to investigate the Yankee Stadium renovation project of the mid-1970s. The rationale, as Duggan reports it: "Yankee Stadium is the one place where renovation of the extent we are discussing here has actually been done." The Yankee Stadium renovation had involved extensive demolition and rebuilding in the face of threats by the team to move out of the city. The cost, at first estimated at $24 million, reached $100 million. Many considered the result a travesty.

"The comparison is crazy," says John Pastier. "That was almost a clean slate rebuilding."

O'Neal and others point out that many of the current problems at Yankee Stadium are a result of poor rainproofing on the roof of the luxury boxes. Darvas says that failing concrete at Yankee Stadium is new, not original, and that new loads were placed on old structural footings—something the Birkerts-O'Neal plan would not do. About the Yankee Stadium fiasco Darvas contends: "They could have the same problems in a brand-new stadium." Darvas also says that widespread, endemic bribery and corruption in the building trades in New York caused much of the project's cost overruns.

"That near-total rebuilding," wrote Pastier, "the most expensive in history, was marked by massive irregularities that no city would tolerate today."

But, following Schembechler's suggestion, Yankee Stadium was used as a yardstick. In its report BEI concludes that the ambitious Birkerts-O'Neal project is feasible from an engineering standpoint. It concurs with the plan's claimed costs of about $85 million. But BEI frets over the possibility of massive cost overruns, citing Yankee Stadium.

O'Neal points out that although BEI inflated the cost of the Cochrane Plan by raising the number of sky boxes to a hundred, it did not save costs by reducing the 198 suites provided under his plan. O'Neal says the cost of his plan with only a hundred sky boxes would be closer to $70 million.

In the end, Duggan and McNamara argued, the Tigers could do the Birkerts-O'Neal renovation, but they would be left with a stadium with "old concrete and steel." Better to spend a few million more and get a new stadium, they said.

The contention about "old concrete and steel" is ludicrous, claims O'Neal. Concrete often gets stronger with age, he says. It is usually sound if it has no problems during the first five years. He adds that the current stadium's steel "is probably overdesigned by today's standards," and that the stadium would be eighty percent new and set on new footings under his plan.

Wayne County did not send anyone to visit Wrigley Field or Fenway Park to study recent examples of successful remodeling projects in old parks. In each case, it was possible to install luxury boxes, expand concessions and rest rooms, and make other improvements with low-cost renovations that continued the tradition as well as the profitability of both franchises.

Many modern touches were added to Fenway in the 1980s, including new suites atop the left- and right-field stands, a new color video board, a new restaurant facility, a new souvenir outlet and, most recently, six hundred club seats in an air-conditioned bubble on the grandstand behind home plate, and a broadcast booth and press box above it. The Red Sox also made massive renovations to the ticket office and built a new weight room and multipurpose room near the home clubhouse.

Chicago Cubs president Don Grenesko is quoted in the April 15, 1991, issue of *Sports Illustrated*, gushing about the improvements made in recent years to his park. Over the last eight years, the Cubs spent $31 million installing lights, sixty-six luxury boxes, new rest rooms and concessions, and new seats, and renovating the clubhouses. Grenesko scoffed at "the idea that Wrigley is not economically viable" and said that "the renovations will enable the Cubs to keep playing at Wrigley Field indefinitely."

"These old parks are all products of remodeling," points out Pastier. "It's not as though remodeling is some novel idea. Remodeling is the essence of all these parks, and every one of those remodelings worked out economically until Yankee Stadium."

Kittides claims that estimating renovation costs "is a risky business no matter how well" you do it. For a new stadium, says Kittides, "the chance of overruns is much less." But O'Neal asserts that "you can estimate this thing just as accurately as you can a new stadium." Darvas notes that "public projects are sold to the public using low figures" and wonders, citing Detroit's downtown monorail: "How did the People Mover end up at $220 million, if estimates for new projects are so accurate?"

The arguments on cost overruns and cost comparisons seem self-serving. Duggan writes that the cost of a new stadium would be $115-$135 million, but few new stadiums are being built for that figure. The Texas Rangers, who are at a later stage in their quest for a new stadium than the Tigers and thus less subject to cost inflation, estimate that their new stadium will cost $170 million.

Darvas calls Duggan's estimate of a new stadium's cost "a lot of baloney." He and O'Neal point out several costs a new stadium would involve.

Land acquisition. With the Tigers' demand for twelve to fifteen thousand parking spaces in a cleared location, a new stadium could require a hundred acres of land, Darvas calculates.

Using a figure of $10 to $20 an acre, Pastier estimates that land costs for a new stadium in the Briggs Community, the site favored by the Tigers, would range from $32-$64 million for a 71-acre site to $52-$105 million for a 120-acre site.

There is also the human and financial cost of displacing people from their homes. O'Neal says no one is considering "the number of people you're going to displace, who have no vote" on whether they want a new stadium in their neighborhood.

Demolition of the current stadium. O'Neal says that this would cost a minimum of $10 million.

New utilities. New lines for plumbing, electricity, and other utilities would cost $15 million, O'Neal says.

Pastier estimates total costs of a new stadium in downtown Detroit at $200 to $225 million.

"Even if one accepts BEI's questionable renovation price" of $50 million for the Cochrane Plan, Pastier wrote, BEI's reports implicitly recommend added costs to build a new stadium of about $150 to $175 million over the Cochrane Plan or $115 to $140 million over the Birkerts-O'Neal plan. "Taxpayers will supply most, or all, of this sum," he pointed out. "Surely the issue demands a full scale cost-benefit analysis, rather than an unpaid effort by inexperienced consultants who hope to work on a new stadium."

To strike out the Birkerts-O'Neal plan, the county and BEI also argued that there was no place to put parking for twelve thousand cars. O'Neal shows a visitor a poster of Tiger Stadium, an aerial photograph taken during a sold-out 1984 World Series game. "See these empty lots?" he asks, pointing to empty parking lots within walking distance from the park. He contends that there is plenty of adequate parking around Tiger Stadium. He also cites the easy ingress and egress from the area. "What better parking system could you develop," contends O'Neal, "than in this area, with the existing freeways right there?"

Responding to rumors that BEI was planning to release a report favoring the Birkerts-O'Neal plan, until a county official prevailed on BEI to change its recommendation, O'Neal says: "They had concluded that it was feasible. You couldn't have any closer numbers" than O'Neal's and BEI's separate estimates of the plan's cost. "Had they been opposed to it, their easiest way out would have been to say $106 million" or some other arbitrary figure higher than O'Neal's estimate.

While Duggan and BEI labored mightily to shoot down the two prominent renovation plans, club officials continued to bring up their litany of complaints about the stadium. In his speech at the Economic Club of Detroit on April 22 — the first time Tiger management had made a strong, detailed public criticism of renovation — Schembechler acted as if there had never been a Cochrane Plan proposal, two HOK proposals, or a Birkerts-O'Neal plan. "You have narrow concourses that make it very difficult for people to move when we have a large crowd," lectured Schembechler. "That is fundamental. We have inadequate rest rooms. We have limited concession stands. We cannot even give the full menu that other ballparks have, because we do not have the space in order to do it. We are the only club that has no sky boxes."

The last contention was not true; Dodger Stadium in Los Angeles has no sky boxes, and the Tigers in 1991 opened several luxury suites in Tiger Stadium's third deck, the very location BEI and Duggan ruled inadequate for sky boxes. And Schembechler's marketing director, Jeff Odenwald, notes that the club's 1990 fan survey showed that fans don't want croissant sandwiches and DoveBars. "We thought that our food menu was not as attractive to fans as it would be somewhere else," says Odenwald. "We thought that maybe our limited menu had an adverse effect. It didn't. They like popcorn, and hot dogs, and Italian sausage, and pizza."

Schembechler also told the Economic Club: "Our clubhouse facilities, our facilities for training are too small and inadequate. We have no office space. We have to split our staff so that half of them work out of the stadium and half of them in an annex across the street." The ex-coach continued to raise the phantoms at Tiger Stadium because they sounded convincing to many people who had not studied the renovation proposals.

Many members of the media also continued to run interference for the Tigers. On June 6, 1991, the day after Duggan's report was released, George Cantor of the *News* wrote: "The forces of necessity have driven the final shaft through the heart of Detroit's best loved landmark. . . . When all the appeals to nostalgia and sentiment and urban values are exhausted, the equation comes out the same. You can sometimes fight progress, but you can't stop necessity."

The "necessity" of replacing Tiger Stadium remained very much in doubt in many people's minds. "Anybody but an imbecile has to know that there are ways to enlarge a clubhouse, ways to enlarge a rest room," says Bob Buchta. "That's not the real issue. That's public relations fluff. It may very well be true that the Tigers have believed at least since 1987 and maybe much earlier that they wanted a new stadium, and it was only a question of how to present it in terms of public relations. I don't think that at any time since the early 1980s have the Tigers given renovation the hearing it really deserves."

Crain's Detroit Business reported on July 29, 1991, that Gino Rossetti "said that despite studies of the feasibility of renovating Tiger Stadium, he thinks it was 'a done deal' all along to build a new stadium."

Had the people's representatives given renovation a fair hearing? At a meeting of the Detroit City Council on June 17, 1991, Michael Duggan admitted: "We have a rule with Bo Schembechler that if he doesn't bring up suburban sites anymore, we won't bring up renovation anymore."

CHAPTER 14

OBSTRUCTED VIEWS

No better spectator park exists. By actual measurement, its seating proximity to the field surpasses all other parks, old or new. This is the prime gauge of the ballpark quality. It creates intimacy and involvement that are lacking in newer stadiums, and will surely be missing in any replacement. As design, it is a rare specimen of the Golden Age of ballparks, full of character and complexity, and miraculously combining both monumentality and human scale.

> — *Stadium expert John Pastier,*
> *in a letter to Tiger owner Tom*
> *Monaghan, December 6, 1989*

You've got to understand more than half the seats at Tiger Stadium have an obstructed view. It's fundamental. It's there. There's no denying it. Half the seats in that stadium are in the outfield. They are not down the lines. They are not close to the action. Did you know that Tiger Stadium has the fewest box seats of any major-league club? Nine thousand, that's all we have. If you're not one of those who gets the 9,000 seats you may have an obstructed view.

> — *Tiger president Bo*
> *Schembechler, at the Economic*
> *Club of Detroit, April 22, 1991*

Tiger Tale Number 3: Tiger Stadium doesn't have enough good seats.

Who is right about Tiger Stadium? Is it the best fans' ballpark in the major leagues, or the worst? Does Tiger Stadium have the fewest or the most good seats in baseball?

179

The answer depends on the definition of a good seat. Walter Briggs believed the long-term stability of his franchise depended on a large, loyal fan base, so he constructed a stadium with the most seats as close to the field as possible and the most outfield seats in baseball.

Today's Tiger management disdains affordable outfield seats as unprofitable. Its definition of good seats includes only infield seats with completely unobstructed views that can be sold as season tickets to corporations and well-heeled fans for fifteen dollars a game or more. It doesn't matter to team officials if some of those seats are two hundred feet or more away from the playing field. They just sell the seats; they don't have to sit in them.

Dale Swearingen of Osborn Engineering Company says club owners promote "the fictitious Nirvana of columnless viewing." In a 1989 interview in the *New Yorker*, he said new stadiums don't deliver on their promise of tens of thousands of great seats:

"We'll build you a stadium without columns, they say. Well, without columns, you need a cantilever, and the expense of that really intimate angle is too great. And so you get these huge stadiums where the upper decks are miles from the field, and the fans are so far away from the action that you need a huge television screen to keep them interested."

In Toronto's SkyDome, there are so many seats in nosebleed territory that concessionaires rent binoculars for seven dollars a pair. In 1991 seats in the top deck of the SkyDome started at ten dollars, except for a few four-dollar seats in the far reaches of the outfield. Fans sometimes use the binoculars to watch the game; other times they train them on rooms in the attached hotel. During a game in 1990, a couple in one of the hotel rooms made love with the blinds open.

"It's a glorified shopping center," says Bill Craven, a Tiger fan from Guelph, Ontario, who went to one game at the SkyDome and vows never to return. "It's great for the millionaires and for the people who like to look around at people in hotels and huge scoreboards. If there's forty thousand people at a game, at any one time only about ten thousand are watching the game."

The SkyDome is a far cry from the ballparks built in the first quarter of the century. The view of the game in older parks is far superior to views in the SkyDome or Three Rivers or the new Comiskey, Pastier contends.

"In an old ballpark, fans could not only see a better game, but could also see it better," he wrote in the September 1991 *Inland Architect*:

Moderate seating capacities and tighter space standards put seats close to the field, and upper decks situated above lower decks (rather than behind them) gave top-level patrons much better vantages than they would have in modern stadia. That gain grew out of deep cantilevers and columns within the seating areas. The posts blocked some views, but the bad seats were the last to be sold, and normally only for a few big games each year.

The classics' top decks were also closer than today's because they weren't on top of club and luxury suite levels, and because they extended further into the outfield and thus could be shallower. . . .

Upper deck distance is important since lower-deck field proximity is almost a given. The critical issue is what occurs above the first bank of seats. Newer parks are notoriously poor in this regard. . . . Even disregarding the modern blights of artificial grass and indoor stadiums, older parks provided a baseball experience that today's stadia inherently cannot deliver.

Many knowledgeable baseball fans prefer upper-deck seats. But only upper decks supported by posts can be placed right on top of the action, as at Tiger Stadium.

New ballparks built without posts have no obstructed views. But unimpeded sight lines don't always translate into good seats. The new Comiskey Park was heralded as a faithful modern replica of its venerable namesake. The two parks' capacities were virtually identical. But according to Pastier's precise measurements, *the best seat at the front of the upper deck behind home plate at the new Comiskey is farther from the field than the worst seat at the very back of the upper deck in the old Comiskey or in Tiger Stadium.*

The new Comiskey's designers tried to compensate for the remoteness of the upper deck by making it steeper. But it is so steep that fans complain of vertigo. "Fans approach the stairs and wail," wrote reporter Ann Sweeney of the *Detroit News* in August 1991. "Some turn back."

People lower themselves down the aisles by pulling themselves along from step to step in a sitting or squatting position. "This is way too steep for the average civilian," White Sox fan Ron Allgaier told *News* reporter Jon Pepper. "The reason you come to the ballpark is to relax, not to be a nervous wreck."

Making the upper deck steep didn't solve the distance problem at the new Comiskey. A Livonia resident, Tony Amadori, in July 1991 compared a box seat he had in the new Comiskey's upper deck with the upper deck boxes at Tiger Stadium. "Now, imagine this," he wrote in a letter to the *News*. "Move your 'box seat' away from the field by 45 feet, and raise it approximately 50 feet (five stories). Can you now picture your new view in your new stadium 'box seat'? Even the White Sox fans in the row behind us were grousing about this new long-range view. If this is what Tiger management wants for Detroit, there are going to be a lot of disappointed fans, particularly if you get an upper deck box."

The new stadium in Baltimore is widely heralded as the first modern stadium to duplicate the character of a classic ballpark. But its seats are as far from the field as those at the new Comiskey. A front-row seat in the upper deck behind home plate is about 160 feet away from the plate, the same as at the new Comiskey. The same seat at Tiger Stadium is 85 feet from home.

How good are Tiger Stadium's upper-deck seats? Wonderful enough to inspire baseball's keenest and most respected observers to great rhetorical heights.

Roger Angell, dean of American baseball writers, says that the upper deck at Tiger Stadium "has this wonderful sort of tenement feeling, like you're sitting in the window and watching the street below you. I grew up in parks that had that feel, like Ebbets Field and the Polo Grounds."

Thomas Boswell described in his book *Why Time Begins on Opening Day* how a visit to Tiger Stadium's upper deck gave him a new understanding of the fundamentals of the game he had been covering for years:

> In Detroit there's a cozy seat at the railing in the second deck where you can lean forward and hear the swish of the bat when the on-deck hitter swings. When there's an argument at the plate, you don't have to ask the players afterward what was said. This is the best spot I've found to grasp the central aspect of the sport, the tense business being conducted between the pitcher and the hitter. It was here that I suddenly said to myself, "So *that's* changing speeds."

In an April 1991 *Time* article, Walter Shapiro marveled: "The cantilevered, closed-in upper deck gives you the impression of sitting in a cherry picker over the umpire's shoulder."

Out-of-town broadcasters often gush at the view from the radio and TV booths on the facing of the second deck above the backstop. Tiger announcer Paul Carey rates this location as by far the best in baseball. It's so close to the field that foul balls imperil broadcasters and sometimes even batters. On July 23, 1991, Rob Deer was almost hit by his own foul ball, which had caromed off the broadcast booth.

Praise for Tiger Stadium's upper-deck chairs is based on feet and inches, not sentiment. Figures show that Tiger Stadium has the closest seats in baseball.

Old Comiskey's distance of 101 feet from home plate to the front of the upper deck was second-best to Tiger Stadium's 85 feet. At Dodger Stadium, it's 203 feet.

The distance from home plate to the last row of the lower deck behind home plate is shorter at Tiger Stadium (147 feet) than anywhere in the majors. Wrigley Field, by comparison, is 199 feet. (This calculation does not include circular stadiums, which have few rows of seats behind home plate.)

Averaging viewing distances behind home plate, Pastier found that Tiger Stadium's 113 feet is unmatched among all multidecked stadiums. The three most widely acclaimed modern open-air stadiums cannot compare. The average distance at Anaheim Stadium is 156 feet, at Dodger Stadium 161 feet, and at Royals Stadium 162 feet.

"Fans don't realize what they have at Tiger Stadium," contends Buchta. "Most fans who go to games at the ballpark don't have a lot of experience going to games in other cities. When they hear about a stadium with unobstructed views everywhere, they think, 'Wouldn't that be great?' And yes, it would be great if those unobstructed views were as close to the action as they are at Tiger Stadium. But if they were to go to the new Comiskey Park, for example, and find out that those unobstructed views are the equivalent of being on the fifteenth floor of a building, then the unobstructed seats would lose a lot of their appeal.

"When you know something well and you don't have a lot to compare it with, you tend to focus on what's wrong and not really recognize the positive things you've got. Tiger Stadium is a trade-off. It has posts and a lot of seats in the outfield, but what you get in return is the closest seats in baseball.

"Since the average major league ball game draws far less than capacity, you have to ask: What will be the best situation for the most number of fans in most games? All you have to do is look at Shea Stadium or the new Comiskey Park and ask whether seats in foul territory way down the foul line at the top of the highest deck are as good as seats in the right-field porch at Tiger Stadium. No way are they as good."

Given that comparison, it's wrong to contend that all infield seats are better than any outfield seats, says Buchta.

"There is an inevitable trade-off between the goals of intimacy and fully unobstructed seats," wrote John Pastier in 1989. "The fierce loyalty of fans to old parks indicates that they prefer the former, and also prefer age and history to newness."

The men who built Tiger Stadium valued intimacy and accessibility above all other attributes in a ballpark. Both Frank Navin, who added the upper deck behind home plate in 1923, and Walter Briggs, who extended the upper deck around the ballpark between 1935 and 1938, decided that the posts were a worthwhile trade-off for abundant seating close to the action.

Until recently, the wisdom of that design rarely was questioned. Fans for decades put up with the minor annoyances caused by the posts. Today, Tiger officials argue that what fans accepted in the past is no longer tolerable. But the contention comes from a club bent on convincing fans that a new stadium would be better for them. And it rings hollow, says Buchta, considering how Tiger management has only exacerbated the post problem at Tiger Stadium.

For years, local journalists urged the Tigers to mark clearly all obstructed view seats before selling them, as other clubs long had done. Yet the Tigers continued to sell customers unmarked tickets for seats blocked by posts, even when better seats went unfilled.

Knowledgeable fans realize that they usually can change seats if they find their view obstructed. But fans who attend games infrequently may fear being reprimanded if they move. So they sit behind a post and stew. Taking their cue from Tiger management, many blame the stadium.

When Monaghan first took over the team, he expressed affection for the posts. "I even like the way the posts look," he said. "It gives a good feeling to the ballpark. It reminds me of the stadium in Cooperstown. I'll probably take the posts out one day, but I don't want to."

In 1984 Monaghan commissioned structural engineer Robert Darvas to study whether some posts could be removed. Darvas reported that half the upper-deck columns could be taken out cheaply and safely. Darvas even offered to have his University of Michigan students remove a post during a team road trip as a demonstration. The project was never carried out. Reportedly the City of Detroit scuttled the idea, and Monaghan never again raised the possibility of post removal.

Under Monaghan the Tigers finally did start marking some seats as obstructed. But fans still complained of being sold unmarked seats with obstructions when better seats sat empty.

Buchta says Tiger management is to blame. "I think there is a lot of concern among fans who buy tickets, especially from outstate Michigan, about whether they'll be behind a post," he says. "The problem is that the Tigers' ticket selling policies have been abysmal. In the age of computers, there is no reason they can't publish an accurate and detailed guide of the location of each one of their tickets and make all their tickets available to any ticket seller in the state. Instead, their practice has been to send only certain seats to their outstate ticket agencies. Outstate ticket sellers have told fans that if they really want the good seats they have to come to Detroit and buy them at the box office here. Why do they do that? They're shooting themselves in the foot. Is it calculated or is it just stupid? I don't know. But they have turned off many fans."

No one should have to sit behind a post, says Buchta, except during the few games a year when crowds exceed 40,000. Many argue that is a small price to pay for the intimacy that most fans enjoy at Tiger Stadium at every game. "Why shouldn't thousands of fans in the upper deck rejoice in an intimate view?" asks Swearingen of Osborn Engineering. "Just because several hundred would be blocked by pillars?"

Interestingly, as the Tigers turned up the volume on their demands for a new stadium, the number of obstructed view seats at Tiger Stadium rose dramatically.

For years the Tigers had been saying that there were about three thousand seats they mark and sell as obstructed. But in his speech at the Economic Club of Detroit on April 22, 1991, Bo Schembechler made an amazing new claim. He said that more than half the seats at Tiger Stadium have obstructed views—about 23,000 more than the club's previous figure. Incredibly, no one in the media asked for an explanation.

It was left to Michael Duggan to elucidate Schembechler's statement. In his June 5 report to Ed McNamara, Duggan wrote:

> The Tigers have only 11,700 box seats, the fewest in baseball. They have 24,000 reserved seats, but virtually all of those seats are from the posts back and have some obstructed view.

Being in a reserved seat does not necessarily mean you miss a large share of the game. What it does mean is that at some point in the game the action will be such that your head will be turned staring straight into a post. You might miss the catch in right field, or the plays at shortstop, but there will likely be some obstruction to your enjoyment of the game from the reserved seats.

Duggan's definition of obstructed view includes all seats where an obstruction might occur at some time during the game in any direction fans might turn their heads, including the direction of the concession stands.

He is contending that all fans sitting in the two dozen or so seats in every row between the posts at Tiger Stadium have a post interfering with their view of the game — even though they are facing the field and the posts are in their peripheral vision, if visible at all. In most of these seats the columns do not obstruct any part of the playing field.

Astonishingly, the man charged with marketing Tiger Stadium to the public says he's not sure how many seats are obstructed. "I don't even fool with that," says Jeff Odenwald, the club's vice president for marketing and communications. "That's a ticket operation, and they've got their charts and all of that. I know that it's a substantial number. I know that it's a topic of discussion. That's the bad news. The good news is, you get into a new facility, and that discussion isn't even there any more. It gets into a definition of what's an obstructed view. . . . I don't really know, to be honest with you."

The inflation of the number of obstructed view seats bolsters Tiger management's constant complaint that there are not enough good seats — meaning only those seats that can be made into boxes and sold as season tickets. "This is a business, and your high-priced tickets are going to have to be from foul pole to foul pole, low, with unencumbered view," says Odenwald. "And we just don't have a large quantity. It's around ten thousand or less. And that's a tough number to work with."

Most knowledgeable fans would dispute Odenwald's contention that the best locations in a stadium are "low." And in many new stadiums, "prime" upper-deck seats are hundreds of feet from the infield.

Schembechler claims 9,000, Odenwald less than 10,000, and Duggan 11,700, but whatever the accurate number of box seats, team officials argue that Tiger Stadium doesn't give them enough prime season ticket locations. Yet the Tigers in 1991 had to mount an advertising campaign to try to sell the boxes they have. And if demand for season tickets were to rise, there are thousands of seats that could qualify — namely, the seats in the rows between the posts in the upper and lower decks that Duggan and Schembechler now claim are obstructed, but which in fact are among the best and closest seats in baseball.

And there would be thousands more such seats if Tiger Stadium were renovated. Under the Cochrane Plan, nearly half the posts in the upper deck could be eliminated. The Birkerts-O'Neal proposal would take out almost all the stadium's posts in both decks.

In his report to McNamara, Duggan said the Cochrane Plan was unacceptable because it would leave "the most serious obstructed view problems untouched" in the lower deck and because removing posts from the upper deck "benefits the view only from a portion of the seats at the rear of the upper deck — the least desirable seats in the stadium."

These claims illustrate serious misconceptions about Tiger Stadium. The seats in the rear of the upper deck are far from the least desirable seats in the stadium, especially if half the upper deck posts were removed. Much worse are the seats in the back of the lower deck behind home plate, ruined in the 1978–84 renovations when engineers hung broadcast booths and luxury boxes for the owner and the media from the facing of the third deck.

The Birkerts-O'Neal plan would eliminate the lower-deck posts by pulling the upper deck back from the field. Observers disagree on whether such a drastic renovation would on balance improve fans' view of the action. In his 1991 article, Pastier called the Birkerts-O'Neal proposal an "ingenious scheme" that creates "an artifact rather different from Tiger Stadium." Pastier calculated that the plan would increase upper-deck viewing distances by thirty-four feet and the height of the stadium by twenty-five feet, and create a forty-foot-wide bulge in the outer wall along Michigan Avenue. "The result," he wrote, would be "neither a preserved old park nor an unencumbered new one, but instead a structure with some of the advantages and disadvantages of each."

The current stadium's biggest advantage is in its remarkable marriage of size and intimacy. Tiger Stadium's capacity and its many outfield seats allow tens of thousands of fans to get their money's worth.

In Tiger Stadium, most fans are close enough to the field to see the players' faces, to observe their mannerisms, to eavesdrop on infield chatter, or even to contribute to the conversation themselves. The closeness creates in fans a feeling of belonging. Fans do not keep a respectful distance from their heroes. In a society where entertainment has become a mass spectacle, a seat at Tiger Stadium is the equivalent of seeing a musical superstar in Carnegie Hall.

Author Carl Rollyson compares the recently restored Orchestra Hall, home of the Detroit Symphony, with Tiger Stadium. "I've been to Ford Auditorium," he says of the symphony's more modern home, before it returned to Orchestra Hall, "and that's terrible. It's just a big auditorium. In Orchestra Hall you feel much, much closer to the musicians. In Orchestra Hall you can feel a part of the music, and in Tiger Stadium you can really feel a part of the game."

Walter Briggs recognized that the backbone of his franchise was the average fan, so he created a stadium with over 25,000 outfield seats. If a lot of working people had access to decent seats for an affordable price, reasoned Briggs, the franchise could prosper over the long term. His calculations proved correct. His affordable outfield seats often were filled, and entire generations of loyal Tiger fans nurtured their love for the game in the bleachers and grandstands.

No other stadium builder has duplicated Briggs's feat. The other classic parks had intimacy but not Tiger Stadium's capacity. Many modern stadiums are large but lack intimacy.

In other classic ballparks, outfield seating is limited. At Wrigley Field there is only a small single-decked bleacher section in center field. At Fenway Park, the Green Monster occupies all of left field. Wrigley has a capacity of 37,741; Fenway holds only 34,142. These two parks are nationally known symbols of baseball's heritage. Yet it can be hard to get a good seat in either without buying far in advance.

Most modern owners disdain outfield seats. They can't charge top dollar for them, and cheap seats no longer go very far toward paying the salaries of multimillionaire players. The main target now is no longer the broad mass of fans, but the smaller, pricier market of season ticket holders. The prime attribute desired in new ballparks is exclusivity — not intimacy or accessibility.

That exclusivity is often a chimera. In the SkyDome, many people pay big bucks to sit far from the field. Trappings of privilege make fans in remote regions feel it's worth the price. When it was time for Toronto's grounds crew to sweep the infield during the 1991 All-Star Game, they stepped out of limousines wearing tuxedos.

At most stadiums, the outfield seats are too distant to attract many fans. But the seats in the upper deck in left field and right field at Tiger Stadium are so good that the Tigers sell the front rows as box seats. In right field the upper-deck boxes hang over the playing field, offering a commanding view.

Tiger Stadium has the only double-decked bleachers in the majors. There are more than 10,000 bleacher seats; in 1991 they were priced at four dollars apiece. They always go on sale two hours before game time. The upper-deck bleachers, directly above the center-field wall, offer a panoramic view of the field. The lower-deck bleachers are smaller and extend well into right center field, "so close to the field," wrote Walter Shapiro in *Time*, "that you can nurture the illusion that you are not a spectator but the Tigers' right fielder."

The lower deck grandstands in right and left field sold for seven dollars in 1991. Fans there get a close view of outfield catches and a good shot at catching home runs.

Tiger Stadium has in abundance what is rare in modern sports arenas: accessibility. Good seats are available to the average family. You don't need connections or a corporate portfolio to see a ball game, nor a lot of money. Free street parking is available, if you don't mind walking a few blocks.

Gary and Vicki Dutton of Petaluma, California, and their two children visited Tiger Stadium in July 1991 on a tour of Midwestern ballparks. "In Cincinnati and St. Louis, it's almost a surreal outlook on the game, if you get way far away, like out in left center field where we were in St. Louis, or right down the right-field foul line in Cincinnati," says Gary Dutton.

"The thing I like about this stadium," says Vicki Dutton, "is that it doesn't have luxury boxes. It's more of a stadium for the people." In other stadiums, she says, "it's very difficult to get tickets. If you can get them, they're not necessarily the best seats. Those are always saved for companies."

On August 7, 1991, a *Detroit News* story refuted the "Bo-inspired legend" that there are no bad seats in Comiskey, and few good ones in Tiger Stadium. "The reality," wrote reporter Ann Sweeney, "is that fans in the cheap seats have a better view of the game at Detroit's ballpark than at Comiskey, which gives the store away to those lucky enough to have luxury suites or box seats. The lesson for Detroit: A new stadium doesn't necessarily mean a better view of the action." Sweeney concluded: "Overall, especially in the cheaper bleacher seats, Comiskey lacks the intimacy of Tiger Stadium." Photographs showed that the cheapest and most remote seats in Tiger Stadium are far closer to the action than in the new Comiskey.

A fan named Ed Murphy, sitting in Comiskey's upper deck, told Sweeney: "I sit up here for the night air. I just wish they'd run more replays."

"In Chicago," wrote Sweeney, "the best views are reserved for those who can pay":

> Well-heeled fans get a fine view from $90,000 glass boxes with built-in bars. Or they watch the game over dinner from the windows of a club that costs season ticketholders $500 a year to join. Or they cheer the action from premium box seats that ring the lower deck infield.
>
> Everybody else has a clear view — but not necessarily an intimate one.
>
> They're cut off from the game by height, distance and an extra warning track behind the outfield wall.

"Tiger fans sitting in the counterparts of the Comiskey seats talked differently than the Chicago fans," concluded Sweeney. "They said they felt part of the game."

"What obstructed view? This seat's perfect," fan John Meade told the reporter in the lower-deck right-field grandstands at Tiger Stadium. "I sat in the same seat in left field last week and caught Fielder's 26th home run."

EUGENE V. DEBS MEMORIAL KAZOO NIGHT

On July 11, 1991, a large, rowdy crowd filled Tiger Stadium's upper-deck bleachers for the tenth annual Eugene V. Debs Memorial Kazoo Night. Every year T-shirts are sold, kazoos are passed out, and tunes are played in unison between innings: "This Land Is Your Land," "Look for the Union Label," "We Shall Overcome" and, at the seventh-inning stretch, "Take Me Out to the Ball Game." Before the game starts all rise and reverently intone the national anthem. All the kazoos sound, in the apt phrase of Scott Martelle of the *Detroit News*, like "six million killer bees in heat."

"It just started out as a celebration with my brother Scott and a bunch of his friends," says Detroiter David Brooks. "They started to make jokes about people they'd see in the stands. Like: 'Oh! He looks like so-and-so!' And one of them was Eugene V. Debs."

"We were just trying to think of obscure people from history that one of us could say we saw at a ball game," says Jeff Ellison, Scott Brooks's friend and law partner and another Debs Night founder.

"And Debs turned out to be one of them. After we discovered him, and we read up on him a little bit, we thought it would be neat to see him at more ball games. And so he became our imaginary friend at the ball game, and we decided to have a Kazoo Night to honor him."

Debs is a suitable icon for this crowd. The fiery labor leader and five-time Socialist Party candidate for president was an uncompromising champion of working people. And though Ellison acknowledges that "we have never, never uncovered any evidence that he watched a baseball game or played baseball," they feel the Tiger Stadium bleachers are just the place to celebrate him.

Every year, the organizers invite famous people to be guest conductors. In ten years of Debs Nights, the only indisputably famous person ever to accept their invitation was former U.S. Senator Eugene McCarthy, who came in 1991.

"We're very pleased" at McCarthy's acceptance, says Scott Brooks. "We're also very amazed, and somewhat shocked. We usually send out a hundred, two hundred blind letters to famous people—anyone we can get an address on. It says we'd like them to come, we can't afford to pay their air fare, we can't afford to pay their expenses, we'll give them a free T-shirt and a kazoo. And we get some pretty funny letters back. I think some of the other celebrities that have come may question your definition of national stature. But in terms of ex-presidential candidates, or former U.S. senators, or anyone anyone ever heard of, McCarthy is the first."

On the flyer they send out to their mailing list, under the heading "Here's what they're saying about DEBS NIGHT," Ellison and Brooks print some of the rejections they've received:

> It sounds like fun! Unfortunately . . . I will be out of the country at that time. —DICK CLARK
>
> Unfortunately, I will be unable to attend. However, we would like to donate some Chiquita bananas to help energize your volunteers. — CARL LINDER, President, Chiquita Bananas.

"If they don't show up, we can play 'Yes, We Have No Bananas,' " Ellison told the *News*. They did show up, though.

"There are five cases of bananas in my foyer right now," says Brooks. "I've been eating them, but there's just so many you can eat. There are approximately a thousand bananas there. They're good bananas."

During batting practice, about half an hour before game time, Scott and David Brooks and Jeff Ellison and several of their associates arrive carrying large garbage bags full of T-shirts and trinkets for sale and cardboard boxes of complimentary kazoos. They pause as they come out of the tunnel, and Ellison introduces an elderly gentleman, dressed casually in a light blue windbreaker and gray slacks, to a woman. "I'm Eugene McCarthy," says the gent, offering his hand.

The masses begin tuning their kazoos as a vendor climbs the aisles, yelling, "Programs here!" No one pays him any heed. Of greater appeal to these southpaws are the Debs doodads being hawked from the garbage bag, such as T-shirts and tote bags reading "10th Annual Eugene V. Debs Memorial Kazoo Night," sponges emblazoned with the exhortation to "Wipe Up Capitalistic Scum," and refrigerator magnets that say "Stick It to Capitalistic Tools."

The crowd seems to be made up of young families, middle- to upper-middle-class young people, and a sprinkling of older radicals with memories of the sixties. One young man carries on his head, attached to a bicycle helmet, a Sony video camera. "I feel bad," says another. "I haven't been able to make it in two years." He pulls out a wooden noisemaker that makes a sound like a mournful train whistle.

Just before game time, Eugene McCarthy reminisces about baseball and politics. The kind of coercion employed by the owners of the White Sox against Chicago for a taxpayer-financed stadium is not remarkable, he says, and is not confined to sports teams. "All these corporate guys do it," he says. "They're like independent countries, you know."

McCarthy's well-known populist leanings are in fine form this fine evening. "The whole thing of baseball players making three million dollars a year is unbelievable," he says. "It's all a projection of television. It's like these damn television newscasters. Hell, they couldn't make a hundred thousand dollars a year as honest newspaper men. Eight million dollars for Dan Rather—what the hell? He couldn't even write a sentence, you know.

"Any business or institution like baseball or television that exists because of a government monopoly ought to be subject to the salary schedule of the federal government."

A gray-haired woman introduces herself to the senator. "I'm Maryann Mahaffey," she says. Mahaffey is the president of the Detroit

192

City Council. "This is the first time I've been this close to him. I want my picture!"

Mahaffey volunteers that it would be "ridiculous" to replace Tiger Stadium. "It's a good stadium. Where else can you get this close to the field?" she says. "And it's in good condition. I was on the council when we did the deal that they would stay until 2008. And now they turn around and say, 'Well, it's not in that good condition.' And they want to use taxpayers' dollars, and we can't afford it."

"It's just like the corporations," notes McCarthy. "They won't come to the state until you give them the capital and . . ."

"The tax abatements, and all that stuff," adds Mahaffey.

"The corporations," says McCarthy, warming to his theme, "they're like separate countries now. They have their own foreign policy, their own military policy, their own welfare programs. You've got to negotiate with them. They're not subject to the law."

Tom Monaghan is "one of those Irishmen that rocks on his heels," says McCarthy, himself an Irishman. "You ever know those Irishmen that do that? Look out for that guy."

As they talk, the national anthem begins, and the Debs Nighters rise to accompany it on the kazoo.

Jim Bristah, a retired United Methodist minister, is not a veteran of Debs Night. "But back in the 1930s I was a democratic socialist," he says, "and Debs was still around in memory. He's been part of my tradition. I just think it's neat that you can have fun with something like this. We don't have enough opportunities to have fun, and even make fun of Debs Night, you know?"

And how about the stadium?

"We live in a society that is so wasteful," he says. "We're always knocking down and rebuilding. And they're not doing it for the sake of the fans. This kind of an experience in the stadium, when people can come together and have a good time, and good fellowship, and be out here in the bleachers, where the common people tend to be, is to my mind the city at its best."

"This is the only real ballpark left, this and Fenway Park," says John Grindstaff, a Tiger fan for four decades and a veteran of "three or four" Debs Nights. "You don't hear them talking about tearing Fenway Park down. It's a money deal, obviously. A lot of it is parking. All of these mom-and-pop lots all around this ballpark, none of those hundreds of thousands of dollars go into the Tiger coffers. They want a controlled environment. If you come to their game, they want you to pay them for parking."

Randy Westbrooks of Milan, at his first Debs Night, has come because "I'm a UAW member. And it's fun!" Though he's here for a good time, not politics, he says: "I definitely wouldn't show up for Joe McCarthy Night."

There are over 10,000 bleacher seats in Tiger Stadium, all with great, close views of the field for four dollars. What would become of Eugene V. Debs Memorial Kazoo Night should the Tigers get a new stadium?

"Frankly, an event like this would not work in a place where you have reserved seating only," says Ellison. "That issue, aside from the cost of getting into the stadium, would very much hamper an event like this. It may come to an end if they build a new stadium."

The Tigers' expressed desire for fewer cheap seats is "a lousy idea," says Ellison. "The cheap seats are for working people. They're for families who can't afford the more expensive seats."

"With a new stadium," says Scott Brooks, "the way they build these sports complexes nowadays, is the common man or woman going to be able to go? They presell fifty percent of them, with the boxes, and the superboxes, and they presell the season tickets. Like the Red Wings, where ninety percent are season tickets. The common person just is not going to be able to afford to go to a sporting event any more. By the year 2000, it's just not going to be available."

194

CHAPTER 15

EMPTY SEATS AND SCAPEGOATS

Detroit all of a sudden has become one of the worst baseball cities in the United States, when it used to be one of the best. I blame it on the location. We're probably a million less fans than we would be if we were in a perceived-safe location.

— Tom Monaghan, February 1991

I like to think of what would happen if Monaghan decided to buy the Catholic Church, of which he's a big proponent. He might put a bid in for it. First thing he would do is fire the pope, and hire Bo. He'd be the bope.

The first thing Bo would do, I think, would be to fire Mother Theresa. Yeah, sure, she holds a lot of respect in the Catholic Church. But she's just too old.

Second would be to get rid of all the organists in every church, and replace them with tapes.

Number three would be to get rid of the pews, and put in nice, comfortable plastic seats.

— comedian Tim Slagle

Tiger Tale No. 4: Fans don't come to Tiger Stadium anymore because they don't like the park or the neighborhood.

Tom Monaghan took over one of the most stable and successful sports franchises in North America. In 1984, his first season as owner, the Tigers were world champions and drew over 2.7 million fans. It was the second-highest single-season attendance in American League history.

Monaghan had a classic, popular, newly renovated ballpark with the closest seats in baseball, at the oldest address in professional sports. He had a large core of loyal fans; the best team in baseball; an announcer, Ernie Harwell, who was probably the most popular man in Michigan as well as the most respected announcer in baseball; and a general manager, Bill Lajoie, widely regarded as one of the game's most astute judges of talent.

By early 1991 Monaghan had squandered all these assets. The team was rebuilding from a total collapse. Harwell had been fired. Lajoie had resigned. And Monaghan was vowing to move out of Tiger Stadium.

At the corner of Michigan and Trumbull, the club had been profitable for generations. The Tigers attracted at least a million fans every season from 1965 through 1991 — the longest such streak in the American League. Attendance was respectable even in the worst years. In 1975 the Tigers lost 102 games, more than any team, yet outdrew four American League clubs. The Tigers drew a million fans from 1954 through 1960, though the team never finished higher than fourth. In 1952, when the Tigers lost 104 games and had the worst winning percentage in club history (.325), attendance was just barely below the league average.

Fans continued to come to the park despite the massive depopulation of Detroit. Detroit's population fell from two million in the mid-1950s to one million in 1990, yet attendance at Tiger games continued to increase.

Between 1934 and 1988 the Tigers drew fewer people than the league average only six times: in 1952, 1963, 1964, 1975, 1977, and 1982. The team's average winning percentage in those six years was .444. Between 1912 and 1990, the Tigers drew 18.4 million more fans to Michigan and Trumbull than the league average for that period.

Yet Tiger management argues that the club needs a new stadium because attendance isn't good enough. The Tigers say fans aren't coming in sufficient numbers because of too few good seats, cramped concessions, and inadequate rest rooms — but most of all because they think the neighborhood is unsafe and the parking is inadequate.

To many, these arguments seem like a way to blame the victim for problems created by Tiger management. "To me, it's a classic false-cause argument," says Frank Rashid of the Tiger Stadium Fan Club.

"They want to zero in on one thing, instead of the many reasons, particularly the richly deserved disgust that people have with Monaghan. People aren't so stupid that they don't recognize the hypocrisy in all this, in the Harwell firing, in the way the team has been run. And people realize too that this is the man under whose leadership the team went from world champions, with a phenomenal record, to last place and worst in baseball in five years."

The Tigers, and Wayne County's Michael Duggan, point to the 1987 season as evidence that attendance is not what it should be. That year, the first-place Tigers drew 2,061,830 fans — the third-highest total in club history. But six other teams attracted more fans.

Though the Tigers finished 1987 with the best record in the league, the team got off to a poor start, and until June Detroit's sports attention was focused on the Pistons and Red Wings. Many fans wrote off the aging Tigers early and didn't believe they would remain in contention against the powerful Toronto Blue Jays.

The Tiger Stadium Fan Club's counter-argument focuses on 1989. That year, the Tigers had baseball's worst record and fielded perhaps the most boring team in club history. Yet attendance was 1,543,656, better than five other teams. Were all those people coming to see Ken Williams (.205 batting average), Doug Strange (.214), Rick Schu (.214), and Jack Morris (6 wins, 14 losses, 4.86 ERA)? Or did they come for the familiar and pleasant experience of a day at the corner?

In 1990 the Tigers drew just under 1.5 million. It is well known that a team's performance in one year affects attendance the following season. The 1990 figure likely was due in part to the team's dismal 1989 record.

Attendance in 1989 and 1990 was the lowest for the Tigers since 1977. The two-year average of about 1.5 million represents the Tigers' hard core of diehard fans. Most other clubs have a much smaller fan base. Sixteen other major league franchises have drawn substantially fewer fans in recent years. Only two of those sixteen clubs compiled worse records in their low-water season or the previous season than the Tigers did in 1989. (See Table 2–5 in Appendix 2.)

In 1984 the Tigers drew 1,069,658 more people than the league average. In 1990 the club drew 722,405 below the league average. This is a huge drop — but it is a drop from the highest peak in club history to the worst team in memory. Could the stadium, the neighborhood, and the parking, which were good enough to draw 2.7 million in 1984, have deteriorated enough in six years to account for such a free fall? Or does the explanation lie in the club's policies and attitudes?

Many in Tiger management long have been displeased with the stadium's inner-city location. Monaghan has no ties to the city and the Tiger organization has few community programs. In an April 6, 1989, interview on WPZA, Monaghan suggested that the city would have to "clean up" the Tiger Stadium neighborhood if it wanted the team to play in a new stadium there. Monaghan said people were afraid to go to games because of the neighborhood.

Monaghan spoke even less guardedly two years later to a *Free Press* reporter who he mistakenly believed was an out-of-town writer. In an interview published February 22, 1991, Monaghan told Jack Kresnak: "Detroit all of a sudden has become one of the worst baseball cities in the United States, when it used to be one of the best. I blame it on the location. We're probably a million less fans than we would be if we were in a perceived-safe location. I don't think it is that bad. I think it's the perception."

Detroit City Councilman Clyde Cleveland responded angrily: "It's got to do with the quality of the club. He's got Domino's Pizzas all over the city of Detroit. He wouldn't be putting those there if they weren't safe."

Prominent Detroit minister Jim Holley reacts just as strongly to Monaghan's disdain for the city. "A lot of black folk," he says, "eat Domino's Pizza. Have eaten it, they're eating it, and will eat it. His success has been because of the masses. Rich people don't eat a lot of pizza. And now that the poor people have made you, then you turn around and take your wealth, and provide it for the rich and the elite. That to me is an insult, not only to race relations, but to human relations."

Bo Schembechler apparently has a much different view of corporate responsibility. "Despite the fact Mr. Schembechler felt the neighborhood was safe, he did not see any prospect for changing the perceptions of the public," wrote Michael Duggan in his June 5, 1991, report to Ed McNamara, summarizing an early meeting between the county and the club. "He pointed out that the Lions and Pistons had both left town and that the Red Wings had committed to leave before Mayor Young stepped in and not only built Joe Louis Arena, but gave the team control of Cobo Arena. He further pointed to Hudson's and hundreds of other businesses that left Detroit and indicated that he thought it was unfair for one business—the Detroit Baseball Club—to be saddled with the burden of having to save the City of Detroit by staying in town after so many others had left."

Neither Monaghan nor Schembechler nor Duggan says publicly that he personally believes the Tiger Stadium neighborhood to be unsafe. But they all contend that "the fans" perceive the area as dangerous.

That perception is at odds with the facts. Tiger officials, though, don't let facts get in the way of perceptions. When told that the area around Tiger Stadium is one of the safest in the city, Tiger vice president Bill Haase said in an interview in February 1991: "Well, those people who say that, I think, are talking from their own point of view, and I'm not going to get into addressing that issue."

The "people who say that" about the neighborhood's safety include the Detroit police department. Police statistics show a dramatic decline in crime in Corktown from 1984 to 1990. The number of incidents of all serious crimes — homicide, rape, robbery, assault, burglary, larceny, and auto theft — in the three census tracts that surround Tiger Stadium dropped from 1,832 in 1984 to 834 in 1990.

"I'm not saying it's totally crime free, but this is one of the safest areas in the city," said police inspector Ronald Vasiloff in an interview published in the *Detroit News* August 11, 1991. About auto thefts Vasiloff said: "If people park in the approved lots, we have no problems at all. I don't know why people have the perception they have. Maybe people just think there ought to be crime there. But it's one of the safest areas in the city."

Tiger fan Dave Osinski of Warren has been coming to games since the 1970s. "I've never had trouble in terms of crime," he says. "You take your normal precautions, like you would in any major city. It's no big problem."

Catherine Darin has been coming to the park since 1946. She can't understand why the neighborhood has become an issue. "There is no problem with parking, and there's also no problem with crime," she contends. "In all the years I've been coming here I've never had anybody bother me, nor my family nor my friends."

Comedian Thom Sharp says the perception of fear is something the Tigers are fostering. "I don't think people are afraid to come to the ball game," says Sharp, who grew up in Detroit. "I've been going there since 1955. I've never once had anyone approach me nor have I felt threatened — ever. The fact that the Tigers keep hammering on this thing that people are afraid to come down there makes people afraid to come down there."

The only evidence officials can muster to back up their "perception of crime" assertion is a single result from a Market Opinion Research poll of May 1990. In the survey, thirty-one percent of residents of Wayne, Oakland, and Macomb counties said the neighborhood around Tiger Stadium kept them from attending games. But sixty-five percent said it didn't.

The poll didn't ask any follow-up questions to determine why the thirty-one percent felt that way, but Tiger officials and Duggan have been quick to offer explanations. Duggan asserts in his report, without citing any evidence, that the thirty-one percent are kept away by "the lack of secure, lighted parking."

In fact, there is plenty of secure, lighted parking around the stadium, as Inspector Vasiloff points out. It's just not controlled by the Tigers—though Monaghan does now own a major parking lot at St. Boniface Church. Parking around the stadium has always been a quilt of lots, alleys, lawns, and street spaces. In the old days, nearly every homeowner in the area got some revenue from parking. In recent years parking ventures have been consolidated, but stadium parking remains a business that provides jobs and incomes for many area residents.

So it seemed more than a bit self-serving for Schembechler to argue on April 22, 1991: "The stadium has some definite limitations. One of them is parking. You can say there's enough parking around the stadium, but in order for you to be sure that parking is safe and convenient, it should be run by the ball club itself. I believe that strongly."

There is no evidence that crime is lower when a parking lot is run by a baseball club than when it is run by anyone else. But the argument suits the Tigers' hunger for parking revenues.

"The reason they want to surround it with a parking lot is so they can get the revenues instead of giving it to the citizens," says Walter Briggs III. "There's a whole cottage industry there around Tiger Stadium that has been there since time immemorial, and those people survive off that."

Asked in February 1991 if neighborhood safety was a factor in the team's desire for a new stadium, Haase offered the company line. "I think it's a consideration," he said. "I think anywhere you locate you have to provide a safe and secure area for people to feel comfortable in, or they won't come. I think that can be addressed by adequate, safe, and secure parking."

Asked if parking was inadequate around the current stadium, Haase replied: "Oh, without a doubt. Everything around Tiger

Stadium at this present time is these individual lots that are scattered hither, thither, and yon — I mean, they're all over the place." Fans, says Haase, "can find parking, wherever that may be. But we don't control any of that parking, and whether it's clear, or whether it's well-lit and that, we have no disquisition over that."

For the Tigers to blame the parking around Tiger Stadium for the recent drop in attendance helps their cause in several ways, critics say. It deflects blame for the attendance decline away from the club. It twists some suburbanites' fear of the city — a complicated issue tangled up in race, history, politics, economics, and media propaganda — into a purported desire for a huge parking lot. That image may be reassuring to some suburbanites. And it dovetails nicely with club officials' desire for a lucrative source of revenue that many other teams enjoy.

Duggan has used the Tigers' demand for twelve to fifteen thousand "controlled" parking spaces as a way to dismiss renovation, saying no site near the present stadium is big enough to meet the Tigers' "needs."

Regarding team revenue from parking, Haase is careful to claim that "parking revenue isn't as important as providing secure, well-lit parking for the fans, making it easy for them to attend the ball game and to feel secure about where they're at, and enjoy themselves. Revenue obviously comes with that. But that's not the paramount reason, that's not what we're concerned about."

But Philip Bess, a Chicago architect and ballpark expert, says "the revenue is the primary concern" of the Tigers, not safety. "I wouldn't think that the people who own the lots in which people are parking would be cavalier about the safety of the cars," says Bess.

If some fans fret about the safety of independent parking lots, there are ways to alleviate their concerns without building a new stadium or leveling a neighborhood, says the Tiger Stadium Fan Club. "You could put up new lights," points out Bob Buchta. "Would it help to dress up the parking lot attendants in blazers and nice uniforms? Would it help to put a few more security guards around? If that's what they're looking for, why do you have to spend $200 million on a new stadium? If there are some fans who want that sort of thing, there is plenty of land close to the stadium where they could give them that parking atmosphere and where they could allay their fears, misplaced as those fears may be. The real issue is that the Tigers want a monopoly, and the problem with Tiger Stadium is that it gives people so many other options. I happen to think that's a good thing."

Buchta is not alone. The same Market Opinion Research poll that

Duggan cites frequently to illustrate the contention that some fans fear the neighborhood also showed that twenty-eight percent of those surveyed approved of the parking around the stadium, twenty-nine percent disapproved, and thirty percent were neutral. That's hardly a mandate for a huge asphalt apron for the grand old lady.

Fans who prefer the existing parking arrangement at Tiger Stadium cite these reasons: (1) There is a choice of prices and locations, ranging from free street parking to six-dollar lots next to the stadium; (2) there is the option of spending your money with local small business owners rather than giving it to Tom Monaghan; and (3) there is easy ingress and egress. Within twenty minutes after a game, the area is cleared. If fans need a quick getaway, they can find spots on the street or pay extra to lot owners for the privilege.

Parking is a red herring, say Buchta and other Tiger critics. Some suburbanites don't come anywhere downtown, whether there's lighted parking or not. They don't really care what the crime statistics are or what neighborhood the stadium is in.

But for many others, Michigan and Trumbull offers many assets: tradition, familiarity, a wide range of parking options, easy access, a central location, and a low-crime neighborhood with a variety of bars, restaurants, and shops.

The Market Opinion Research poll shows that Tiger fans like the stadium's location. Asked what location they would prefer if a new stadium were built, a third identified the existing neighborhood and another nineteen percent said elsewhere in Detroit, with the remainder split among various suburban locations.

No suburban location would be as central to fans from Detroit and surrounding suburbs and to the many Tiger fans from outstate Michigan, southern Ontario, and northern Ohio. "In the city," says Stewart Selis of Farmington Hills, stating the obvious about the park's location, "you've got people from all sides of town who come to a ball game."

Blaming low attendance on the stadium neighborhood is self-serving, argues Buchta, given the Tigers' campaign for a new stadium. "If you can solve the perception of fear in coming to a new stadium in the city," he points out, "then why couldn't you solve the problem by keeping Tiger Stadium and taking the same steps as at a new stadium?"

Critics say that the drop in attendance at Tiger Stadium since 1984 is largely a result of the team's poor performance and the misguided policies of club management. They cite these main reasons for fewer fans:

1. Lousy teams. After 1984 the Tigers fell from the sublime to the ridiculous. By 1989 they had become the worst team in baseball. The drop in attendance was commensurate with the decline in performance on the field.

In 1984 the club won 104 games and drew 2,704,794 fans — an average of 26,008 fans per team victory. In 1989 the Tigers won 59 games and drew 1,543,656 fans — an average of 26,164 fans per win.

"Give us an A-1 ball club, and the park will be so crowded you won't be able to get in there," said councilman Clyde Cleveland in February 1991. It didn't take long to prove Cleveland right. In mid-August 1991 the Tigers were suddenly back in contention, and the club drew near-sellout crowds for a three-game weekend series with the first-place Toronto Blue Jays. The August 18 attendance of 48,724 was the largest non-Opening Day crowd since October 4, 1987, the day the Tigers beat the Blue Jays to clinch the division flag.

Economists Robert Baade and Laura Tiehen, who studied major league baseball attendance for 1969 to 1987, concluded that team standings and the previous year's attendance are the most significant variables affecting the number of fans a club draws.

"Fans are discriminating; poor teams simply do not enjoy the following which quality teams do regardless of the size of the city," Baade and Tiehen wrote in the *Journal of Sports and Social Issues*. "There is less tolerance for losing teams in the largest cities," they added.

2. Too much TV. Before Monaghan bought the team, the Tigers televised few home games, and never any home night games. Then PASS cable, owned by Monaghan, began airing almost every night game at home. By 1986, sixty-nine of the eighty-one scheduled Tiger home games were available on PASS or WDIV-TV. Since the onset of saturation coverage by PASS, attendance at Tiger night games has declined dramatically.

"The function of the stadium has changed," asserts longtime Tiger fan Max Lapides. "The stadium is nothing more than a stage. The revenue that comes from the fans is almost incidental. In a major television market like New York, you could truly play the game without any paying customers."

3. Too many night games. The Tigers came late to night baseball and even into the early 1960s played few night games. But by the 1970s they had virtually eliminated day baseball during the week and played half of their Saturday games at night.

Since 1984 day games have drawn consistently bigger crowds than night games. In 1991, excluding the first week of the season, the Tigers played five midweek day games. Attendance at those games averaged 19,338. Attendance at the five games against the same opponents on the nights before those day games averaged 13,839.

In 1991 there were twenty-five day games on the home schedule and fifty-six night games. The Tigers' refusal to schedule more day games makes it clear that Monaghan is more interested in revenue from PASS than in attendance.

"Ability to generate revenue is enhanced with an evening game," acknowledges marketing boss Jeff Odenwald. "And you have to make a decision. If you're getting a ten thousand extra hit at the gate, and the average ticket price is eight dollars, let's say that's eighty thousand dollars. Where are you going to make more money? It's television. Television is the driving force."

Odenwald also asserts that Tiger management has "got to put cheeks in the seats. We've got to have live, warm bodies sitting there." But with Monaghan's blessing, thousands of those live, warm bodies are sitting at home watching the Tigers on PASS.

4. More competition. For decades, Detroit's other professional teams lured few fans from the Tigers. The Red Wings and the Pistons were rarely in the play-offs. But both teams revived in the 1980s, especially the Pistons, who with back-to-back national championships and several other seasons of long play-off battles dominated the sports page well into May and even June. The Tigers had several slow starts in the late 1980s, even in 1987 when they won the division title, and had a hard time recapturing the interest of the casual sports fans who had come out in 1984.

5. Poor customer relations. Increased competition from other teams and other leisure options made it imperative that the Tigers improve their customer relations. But changes were slow in coming.

Fans long had complained about archaic or seemingly corrupt ticket-selling practices. Getting good seats often seemed to depend on whom you knew. Fans were sold seats behind posts. Until late in the 1980s fans couldn't charge tickets to their credit cards.

The Tigers refused to institute policies that had long been common practice in other stadiums. There were no TVs or radios at concession stands or in the rest rooms; management said they would cause congestion.

Club officials and fans often were at odds. Surly ushers and security guards were a Tiger Stadium tradition, though many employees believed the actions of a few were giving most of the stadium workers a bad rap. The bleachers had taken on the trappings of a detention camp. Entering fans were subjected to body searches. Armed security guards and city police officers patrolled the aisles. Barbed wire topped the fences between the bleachers and the upper-deck grandstands.

Monaghan made changes slowly. He replaced the hired rent-a-cops with well-trained, clean-cut college students. Older ushers and ticker sellers were gradually weeded out. Monaghan's corporate officials moved against longtime Tiger personnel to make a show of disciplining some ticket sellers suspected of scalping.

Finally, in 1990 and 1991, as the club intensified its pitch for a new stadium, the Tigers got around to making the park friendlier. Radios were installed in rest rooms. Cup holders were placed on the backs of stadium seats. Televisions were installed at concession areas and hung on posts.

Odenwald says that the TVs were put in at his insistence, and that Tiger CEO Jim Campbell was leery at first. "We've not had the congestion problems that people thought we'd get," explains Odenwald.

But other steps were less friendly. Monaghan ended the tradition of opening the gates after the seventh inning. Now every gate is closely guarded until the end of the game.

6. Indifferent marketing. It wasn't until November 1987 that the hidebound Tigers hired a bona fide marketing director to promote the club. Odenwald, who formerly had promoted the Chicago Cubs, went to work filling the Tigers' schedule with giveaway days—a promotional device other clubs had used for years.

Odenwald even reinstituted Bat Days, suspended years before when club officials had said the pounding of thousands of bats could endanger the concrete decking.

But still the Tigers did not market the attractions of their ballpark. For the Cubs, Odenwald had pitched the Wrigley Field tradition of ivy and day baseball. But the Tigers do not promote their stadium's history, its intimacy, its bleachers, the wide choice of parking, and the statistics that show that the neighborhood is safe.

Club officials don't even know the park's history. Tiger publications date baseball at Michigan and Trumbull only to 1900, not to 1896.

205

It is news to Odenwald that Michigan and Trumbull is the oldest address in professional sports. "Oldest address?" he says, puzzled. "I don't know how long Fenway has been there. Wrigley is 1912. So it's got to be a couple of years somewhere in there."

Wrigley Field, the park Odenwald promoted before the Tigers hired him, opened in 1914 as Weeghman Park. Navin Field and Fenway Park opened on April 20, 1912.

On why he doesn't promote Tiger Stadium's close seats, Odenwald is similarly confused. "But the average fan has a tough time buying that seat," he says, "because of our season-ticket base. I'm leery of doing that, because if I tell you, 'You can sit almost on top of the field,' and then when you ask me where are those tickets, and I show you, but I can't sell them to you because they belong to season-ticket holders, then I leave myself vulnerable."

But the back row in the upper deck at Tiger Stadium is closer to the field than the front row at the new Comiskey.

"Oh, yeah," replies Odenwald.

On the park's accessibility and its many bleacher seats, Odenwald says that "as a business person I have a tough time promoting the low-end seats."

About parking he can only comment: "Parking. Where are you going to park?"

Isn't there a wide range of parking options around Tiger Stadium?

"Oh yeah," he scoffs, rolling his eyes. "It runs the gamut."

Odenwald is caught in a bind. The Tigers don't want to attract too many fans and ruin their case for a new stadium.

"During the protracted brouhaha over a new stadium," wrote *Free Press* columnist James Ricci in August 1991, "it's been possible to wonder if Messrs. Monaghan and Schembechler almost hoped for a mediocre team and resultant mediocre attendance this season to buttress their case for new surroundings to be built, in part, with public funds."

"The stadium situation is so volatile that I have to be careful," says Odenwald. "If you've got one side of the organization saying we're moving to a new building, and the other saying there's no place like it, you just can't live without it, I think it'll pretty soon hit you internally: What are we talking about here?"

Odenwald, then, needs to toe the company line, perhaps reluctantly. "Oh, sure," he says. "Sure. And I *believe* in the company line."

Club officials' constant denigration of the stadium, the neighborhood, and the parking doesn't help sell the experience of baseball at Michigan and Trumbull. The poor maintenance at the park — the peeling paint, the spalling concrete — makes some fans fear that the stadium is unsafe. The Tigers' campaign against their own ballpark doesn't boost attendance.

"That's a good question," acknowledges Odenwald a little wistfully, when asked why a fan should bother to come to the old stadium when so many Tiger officials knock the place. "And that's part of my task. I can't control what's going on with the new park. I can't control the rhetoric that's bandied about."

7. New directions. Firing Ernie Harwell didn't put many live, warm bodies in the seats in 1991. Thousands of fans turned hostile to the Tigers' "new direction" — a phrase Odenwald coined to explain the decision to ax the popular announcer. That decision, and the club's determination to discard its historic ballpark, led to a boycott of Opening Day and continued to affect attendance all season. Many former fans turned indifferent or hostile to the club. Many vowed never to attend another game unless Harwell was reinstated. Others stayed away because of Schembechler's bullying.

"I never saw a town become so enraged" as Detroit became over the Harwell firing, says Don Shapiro, who has lived in the Detroit area and been a fervent Tiger fan for nearly seventy years. "It dominated the papers for weeks. Front-page stuff every day. Ernie's an extraordinarily likeable man. People sense that, and they really felt as if they were being personally insulted. How could they do this to us? The firing of Ernie really ignited this city. I've lived in Detroit all my life, and I've never seen anything like the outpouring of indignation and anger."

Peter Rosen, who sells peanuts outside the ballpark, says fans' resentment has affected attendance. "This is the worst attendance I've ever seen relative to how the team's doing," he said in July 1991, when the second-place Tigers were averaging about 19,000 fans per game. "People aren't going to the games this year because people can't stand Monaghan and Schembechler. It's a boycott. Who wants to go to a game for an owner who calls the people of Detroit criminals?"

Tiger officials' complaints about low attendance grew louder and more frequent in 1991. In some respects it became their most fervent argument for a new stadium.

It is the phoniest issue of all, say critics. Club officials virtually assured low attendance by firing Ernie Harwell, mistreating their fans, badmouthing their ballpark, and refusing to schedule more day games.

"How do you attribute a decline in attendance to a ballpark," asks Bob Buchta, "when you have all those other things?" He says one of the biggest reasons for the Tigers' current attendance problems is "the hostility people have over the Tigers' crassness in wanting a new publicly funded stadium and ignoring the fans' wishes."

"The firing of Ernie, Bill Lajoie leaving, the new stadium: It's all of a piece," says Don Shapiro. "Fetzer and Briggs were people who left the organization to baseball men: Jim Campbell, Bill Lajoie, Ernie Harwell. These folks ran the club. Fetzer was only an occasional visitor; he hardly ever interfered. Walter Briggs was the same way. Frank Navin. They always had a history of disinterested baseball lovers. But then it all changed, when Monaghan came in. He even alienated me."

CHAPTER 16

SHACKLED TO
A RUSTED GIRDER

Whether we like it or not, to them it is a business. There's nothing else to it. The bottom line is that they have to at least break even, and they don't believe they ought to be losing money operating a baseball team.

> — *Michael Duggan to the Detroit*
> *City Council, June 17, 1991*

In the Middle Ages all you had to do was say "The Church says," or "God says," and that was it. Now all you have to do is appeal to business. You say, it's business. You can ask no questions further.

It has its own theology. You can't say, "Yes, but the poor are starving." "Yes," they say, "but we have to make a profit."

> — *Tiger Stadium Fan Club*
> *co-founder Frank Rashid*

Tiger Tale Number 5:
Without a new stadium, we can't compete.

The great lawyer William Jennings Bryan was well known in days gone by for his "cross of gold" speech. The intrepid Glenn E. Schembechler likely will be immortalized for what became known around metropolitan Detroit in 1991 as his "rusty girder" speech.

Bo's boss, Tom Monaghan, had called the play: Get me a new stadium. In football you take the ball and you run with it. If people try to stop you, you push them out of the way.

"It's unfair," whined Schembechler at the Economic Club of Detroit on April 22, 1991, "for you to think that you can shackle us to a rusted girder in Tiger Stadium and expect us to compete and win, because it's not going to happen."

If we keep playing in Tiger Stadium, Schembechler told the Economic Club, someday the unthinkable might happen: The Detroit Baseball Club might lose money. And it's your responsibility, he told the assembled big shots, to make sure we never get red ink on our hands.

Frank Rashid chews on a corned-beef sandwich and on some thoughts on the lawn of Detroit's Marygrove College, where he teaches English. "People in baseball," he says, "think it's only a baseball issue, not realizing that the sports establishment has been profiting out of the public trough for a long time, and that the scam has been going on ever since the first publicly funded stadium was built. We are taking money away from really important things that are the proper business of the state and the city, and investing in private businesses."

Commentators for decades have bemoaned that baseball has become big business. Money has corrupted the game, they say. Fans hate paying high prices to see millionaire ball players loaf.

"Whether we like it or not," Michael Duggan told the Detroit City Council, "to them it is a business. There's nothing else to it. The bottom line is that they have to at least break even, and they don't believe they ought to be losing money operating a baseball team."

Baseball is a business, but one unlike any other. No other business is the national pastime.

"The cliche that baseball is a business," says Rashid, "is only that, it's a cliche. Major league baseball in particular, of all the major sports, has become a system of public subsidies for the owners." Government pays for clubs' physical plants. Fans pay players' salaries. And owners get millions of dollars' worth of publicity in the media. What business wouldn't love to have an entire section of the newspaper and ten minutes of the nightly news devoted to its product?

"Teams get tons of free advertising in the papers every day," says Thomas Shull, Michigan director of the Heartland Institute, a Midwestern think tank. "Sports has accumulated a kind of mythology about it. It carries a lot of positive images that are very hard to tarnish."

Baseball clubs get all that attention largely because of the sentimental fiction that the team belongs to the people of the town. That hasn't been true since the dawn of professional baseball.

Major league baseball operates a monopoly that would be illegal were it not for an exemption to federal antitrust laws. That loophole — illogical and often challenged, but never overturned — is based on the notion that baseball does not engage in interstate commerce. The exemption allows owners to restrict competition to whatever number of teams they want in whatever cities they sanction.

Jim Gray, manager of the National Sports Law Institute at Marquette University Law School, says the Supreme Court has never overturned the exemption because Congress has let it stand. Citing the most recent Court challenge in 1972 he says: "If the *Flood v. Kuhn* case had been heard for the first time," with no precedents in the case law, "major league baseball would be subject to the antitrust laws."

With the exemption, major league owners have sustained a contrived scarcity, limiting the number of cities that compete in the big leagues. "This artificial limitation on the number of teams is what creates the demand for teams in cities that don't have franchises," wrote Mark Kozlowski in the *Free Press* in August 1991, "allowing existing franchises to blackmail cities into providing taxpayer-subsidized stadiums below market rents."

"Team owners want capitalism when it comes to profits and socialism when it comes to risks," says Rashid. "To me, the idea that we should be investing in a pleasure palace for Monaghan is unconscionable. The big money people can play tricks and games with financing, and make it look like the people aren't getting screwed, but the people are getting screwed."

Shull notes that there is a tension between the purposes of government and of business, and business usually wins. "A businessman is going to look at the bottom line," he says. "That's not the kind of person you want to get involved in business deals with as a city. He's looking at the bottom line, and you're looking at civic pride. The two don't always coincide."

Sports teams have used fan loyalty and civic pride as bargaining chips to get new stadiums, higher ticket prices, and other business advantages. For a century, the Tigers have benefited from metro Detroiters' identification with the team, daily free publicity in the media, and the goodwill that has accumulated through the exploits of players, the memories of fans, and the tradition of the game and the ballpark.

Past owners took the risks of running a major league franchise. The

Tigers rarely lost money, but when the team performed poorly and attendance fell, the owners never asked the city to bail them out.

Now, apparently, the rules of the game are different.

Schembechler claimed in his rusty girder speech that the Tigers had barely broken even in the last few years and were facing financial losses of about $3 million in 1992 and $4 million to $7 million in 1993. The current lucrative CBS-TV contract expires after the 1993 season, and Schembechler estimated the club would lose $11–17 million in 1994.

But under Monaghan, the Tigers have made a profit every year— even in 1989, when the team was the worst in baseball. According to the July 1991 *Financial World*, the Tigers' profit in 1990 was $5.1 million.

"The Tigers have always been profitable," says Walter Briggs IV. "They continue to be profitable. They will always be profitable."

Analysts say that baseball soon could face an economic downturn when the next TV contract is negotiated. "CBS overpaid" on the current contract, says columnist George Will. "They knew going in they had overpaid. It's nonsense."

Impending financial disaster helps team owners justify higher ticket prices or taxpayer-financed new stadiums. But if there is economic trouble ahead, it is of the owners' making. No one held a gun to their head and made them squander the $10-$14 million that each club makes annually on the current CBS contract. No one forced them to make journeymen such as Franklin Stubbs, Matt Young and Rob Deer millionaires.

"There'll be a cold shower at the end of this four-year contract, I think," says Will.

Despite the gloomy forecasts, baseball remains enormously profitable. The proof is the breathtaking increase in the value of franchises. Monaghan bought the Tigers in 1983 for $53 million. In 1991 ownership groups in Denver and Miami paid $95 million for the right to field National League expansion teams. *Forbes* estimated the Tigers' worth in June 1991 at $100 million. Many experts believe the Tigers could sell for more than that.

Certain franchises could be in jeopardy because of the growing disparity in local media revenues. The Yankees can turn a profit before they even open their gates, with $40-$50 million in local broadcast money. The Seattle Mariners, on the other hand, struggled even as attendance rose in 1991 because they play in a much smaller market.

There "has to be revenue sharing sooner or later," says Will. "The idea that Pittsburgh and Milwaukee and Minnesota and Kansas City can compete, when their local revenues are less than a tenth of, say, the Yankees and Dodgers, is absurd. There is a built-in imbalance there that sooner or later will overwhelm competitive balance."

Other sports have found ways to address the same problem. The National Basketball Association and the National Football League negotiated salary caps. But baseball owners so far have stonewalled any salary limitation or revenue sharing.

Because millionaire owners won't police themselves, fans pay for their fiscal irresponsibility. Fans pay more for tickets, for parking, for concessions, for cable channels and pay-per-view TV, and for new stadiums. The fans underwrite the salaries of the millionaires on the field and the profits of the multimillionaires in the owners' boxes.

If there is a financial shakeout in the mid-1990s, Detroit would weather it better than teams in smaller cities. The Tigers have very loyal fans and solid local broadcast revenues.

Frank Rashid insists that the Tigers demonstrate a need for any public subsidy. "What Schembechler was saying when he made his rusty girder speech was: 'We're in bad shape; we're in trouble,' " says Rashid. " 'We have labor problems. We have these expenses. We need you to do this for us.' To me, that's just like Lee Iacocca going to the Senate. But he didn't expect the U.S. government to take it on his say-so. If their cause is just, and if they really are in trouble, then they have to be willing to open their books — and open all their books, not just the immediate books of the Detroit Tigers. These people really do benefit tremendously from team ownership."

Even if Schembechler's predictions are correct, and the Tigers face losses in the mid-1990s, should taxpayers subsidize a new stadium for an owner who has made tens of millions of dollars from their loyalty?

Whoever would pay for a new stadium would lose money.

According to an August 13, 1991, story in the *Free Press*, stadium operators say that "a private corporation cannot make money on an open-air stadium used for eighty-one home games a season and little else the rest of the year. This is especially true in a cold winter climate like Detroit's, they say."

A few weeks later, Monaghan told the Associated Press that he couldn't afford to build a new stadium himself. "I wouldn't be in a position financially to do that," he said. "I don't think you could attract partners because the investment is a losing proposition."

Public financing of baseball stadiums puts dollars from fans' and

213

taxpayers' pockets into team coffers. This transfer of wealth is most dramatic in Toronto where, despite record attendance, the publicly financed SkyDome lost $39 million in 1990, while the team made a profit of $13.9 million, according to *Financial World*.

In his rusty girder speech, Schembechler cast the issue as winning. Don't you want a winning team, Detroit? How can we win without a new stadium? How can we make enough money to buy or develop the players we need to win? "We have to make enough money so that we can compete," he said. "That's what we want to do, compete."

And if we can't compete, Detroit will suffer, because Detroit will be identified with a losing team.

There are several assumptions in the rusty girder speech that merit scrutiny.

A winning ball club requires a new stadium. "Do you think the Boston Red Sox are not competitive because of Fenway Park?" scoffs Walter Briggs III. The Red Sox, according to *Financial World*, made $12.3 million in 1990.

If a new stadium leads to a winning ball club, why did the Seattle Mariners have fifteen years of nothing but losing seasons at the Kingdome?

If an old stadium is a handicap, why did the Tigers enjoy winning seasons from 1977 to 1988?

You need modern facilities to compete. Other clubs have big club-houses, weight-training rooms, video equipment and the like. The Tigers don't. There is no correlation between clubhouse size or training equipment and on-field performance. If there were, the Tigers would finish last every year and the Twins and Blue Jays would be perennial champions. And no visiting team would ever win after getting dressed in the tiny visitors' clubhouse at Tiger Stadium.

Tiger Stadium can have expanded team facilities through renovation. You don't need to build a new stadium to have a place for the players to lift weights.

The more money teams make, the more competitive they will be on the field. Even this claim, which appears logical in the era of high-priced free agents, is not supported by the record.

Since the dawn of free agency in the mid-1970s, doomsayers have predicted that richer teams like the Yankees and Dodgers would buy all the best players and dominate their leagues. It hasn't happened. In the last fifteen years there has been more parity than ever.

Success on the field clearly depends less on revenues than on how well club officials judge talent and assemble cohesive teams. The Oakland Athletics have become the American League's flagship franchise in recent years through exemplary management by professionals such as manager Tony La Russa and general manager Sandy Alderson, and the Haas family's benevolent ownership. The league's former flagship plays in New York, the nation's largest media market, yet managed to self-destruct through owner George Steinbrenner's intrusive and chaotic reign of error and rotating-door policy for field managers.

A new stadium will bring more fans out to the ballpark. Does a new baseball stadium attract more patrons? The evidence is inconclusive. Monaghan is counting on a million more fans a year in a "perceived-safe" location. If the experience of other cities is a guide, he may be right — for a few years. Attendance rises when a new stadium replaces a cramped or unpopular facility, as in Toronto and Minnesota. But when owners abandon a treasured classic for a modern stadium, they are gambling with fan loyalty.

Nine major league ballparks built between 1909 and 1923 remained in the 1960s. Of those classic yards, four — in St. Louis, Pittsburgh, Philadelphia, and Cincinnati — were replaced between 1966 and 1971.

The other five parks — in Chicago, New York, Detroit, and Boston — remained in use through the 1980s. Yankee Stadium had extensive renovation between 1974 and 1976, and Comiskey was replaced in 1991.

The accompanying chart (next page) shows average annual attendance figures for those nine parks for the period 1960 through 1989 (excluding the strike season of 1981).

Franchises that replaced their classic parks had an attendance increase of 73.3 percent between the 1960s and the 1980s; attendance in old parks jumped by 65.8 percent. But almost all the increase at the new parks occurred in the first decade after they were built. In the 1980s attendance at the classic parks soared; attendance at the new stadiums leveled off. Comparing the 1980s to the 1970s, franchises that kept their parks had a 28.5 percent attendance increase; teams that replaced their old parks increased attendance by only 5.4 percent.

In each of the last three decades, attendance at the classic parks has exceeded the major league average. The five old parks outdrew the four new stadiums in the 1980s even though the average capacity of the old parks is more than 12,000 seats smaller. Philip Bess, in *City Baseball Magic*, notes that the "Red Sox, playing in Fenway Park, the

Franchises That Replaced Classic Ballparks

	1960s	1970s	1980s	Current Capacity
St. Louis	1,395,775	1,530,987	2,200,752	56,227
Philadelphia	883,500	1,929,529	2,103,880	62,382
Cincinnati	895,488	2,145,247	1,731,054	52,952
Pittsburgh	1,001,453	1,263,385	1,201,015	58,729
Average	1,044,054	1,717,287	1,809,175	57,572

Franchises That Kept Classic Ballparks

	1960s	1970s	1980s	Current Capacity
New York	1,333,458	1,598,637	2,273,656	57,545
Boston	1,150,469	1,814,588	1,965,188	34,142
Detroit	1,282,476	1,518,351	1,908,942	52,416
Chicago NL	879,671	1,356,673	1,853,352	37,741
Chicago AL	1,083,043	1,105,387	1,500,180	44,492
Average	1,145,823	1,478,727	1,900,264	45,267
Majors Average	1,133,626	1,331,647	1,847,860	

smallest park in baseball, have over the past 20 years drawn more fans than any other team" in the American League.

These figures suggest that a new stadium that replaces a classic often sparks only a temporary attendance increase. When the novelty wears off, crowds diminish. In contrast, the value of old ballparks seems to increase with age. As these old parks become rarer, they gain more power to attract fans.

Economists Robert Baade and Laura Tiehen, in their study on major league attendance, concluded that "the newness of a park does not impart any discernible advantage in attracting fans."

The Tigers would make more money in a new stadium. An attendance rise is not the only way the Tigers believe they would make more money in a new stadium. Ticket sales are no longer any team's major source of income. Much more important are revenues from broadcast rights, merchandising, parking, and concessions. At the park, it's not

216

how many fans come, but what kind of fans. The Tigers and other teams seek patrons with plenty of discretionary income.

"We need a new stadium," general manager Tom Grieve of the Texas Rangers told the *Sporting News* in an article of August 5, 1991, "to offer more quality seating and allow the team to make more money per capita."

The Tigers believe they could prosper in a new stadium because: (1) They could control parking revenues; (2) they could get money from advertising billboards, concessions, a stadium club and sky boxes; (3) the average seat would be more expensive.

Parking is a reliable source of income in a new stadium surrounded by acres of club-controlled asphalt. When fans no longer can choose where to park and how much to pay, owners profit.

Income from luxury suites, concessions, and advertising would also be available in a renovated Tiger Stadium. According to *Financial World*, the Tigers had "stadium revenue" of $1.1 million in 1990. Using a conservative estimate of $50,000 per luxury box, and the Cochrane Plan's seventy-three suites, a renovated Tiger Stadium could provide an additional $3.65 million annually in suite rental alone.

Financial World estimated that 1990 stadium revenue for the Red Sox was $6.9 million and for the Cubs $4.2 million. Clearly, the same or greater potential exists for the Tigers in their larger classic stadium.

In a new stadium ticket prices would rise, just as they did in the new Comiskey Park. The White Sox decided during their first season there to raise ticket prices by two dollars for 1992, bringing the price of a bleacher seat to eight dollars.

Modern parks have few good cheap seats. The Tigers now have a park with over 10,000 bleacher seats and about 10,000 box seats; they want a new stadium with 24,000 box seats and few or no bleacher seats.

But, after the uproar in 1989 over HOK's plans for a new stadium with no bleachers, Tiger officials are sensitive to the charge that a new park would cater only to the rich. "We're going to have some luxury suites," says Haase. "There's going to be club seating. . . . There'll be box seating, and reserved seating, and some general-admission seating. The idea is to build a stadium that will generate revenues, but still keep it very affordable for the working person." When pressed he says: "We haven't put any designs on costs for seating at this point in time."

Odenwald says when asked about where the cheap seats would be in a new stadium: "I'm not real sure what the design's going to be. Personally, I don't think that the person that can't afford the good seats should be penalized some place where you've got to phone your part in. That'll be all taken into consideration when the facility is designed."

Would Odenwald push for outfield seats, then? "I don't even know. I haven't even sat down to think about that yet."

Clearly, many outfield seats are not in the Tigers' plans. The new strategy in marketing is to limit seats to high price ranges, and even limit the number of seats, to create an artificial demand that pumps up ticket prices.

The local masters of that art are the Detroit Pistons. At the new Palace of Auburn Hills, they charge twenty to fifty dollars a ticket in a 20,000-seat arena, and sell out nearly every game.

"The Tigers won't sell out even if they do build a new ballpark, because watching baseball is not an elitist thing to do," says Rosemary Hogan, a Tiger Stadium Fan Club leader from Livonia. "Baseball in Detroit is a blue-collar sport. Basketball has been turned into a white-collar sport. The same people that go to Pistons games don't go to Tiger games."

The Reverend Jim Holley stirred a controversy in the late 1980s when he coined the phrase "plantation basketball," suggesting that Piston basketball was the exploitation of black performers for the amusement of upscale white spectators. "Here is a team that carries your name — Detroit Pistons — that basically had no real relationship to the city," he explains. "At that time the ownership, to my research, had only given five thousand dollars" to charity in the Detroit area. Anyone who cannot afford the Pistons' steep ticket prices is excluded. "There was no way that senior citizens could see the game, because of the ticket price," notes Holley. "There was no way that the kids could see the game."

The Pistons have been a championship team while playing at the Palace. What will happen when they take a nosedive? "If the Pistons, God forbid, should stop being contenders, I think they will stop selling out," says Hogan. "A lot of people who are Pistons fans now were not Pistons fans five years ago. Now, it's the place to be seen."

When Piston games stop being the place to be seen, how will they fill all those high-priced seats? The club's natural fan base in the city of Detroit has been shut out.

With their good, affordable grandstand and bleacher seats, the Tigers have for years had a place to recruit and nurture young fans. Many season ticket holders grew up in the bleachers, at Ladies Day games in the upper deck or with scout troops in the outfield grandstands.

In their quest for a new stadium, the Tigers "are alienating their real fans, who support them through thick and thin," says Joe O'Neal, the contractor. Without a place for those fans baseball could become, like basketball, entertainment for the trendy. In 1984 it was trendy to see the Tigers. They were front-runners, so 2.7 million fans turned out. Five years later 1.5 million came to see the dregs of baseball.

How far would attendance fall if the Tigers went from first place to last in a new stadium? Though many casual fans enjoy the amenities of modern stadiums, serious baseball fans often are turned off by the glitz, the hoopla, and the remote seats. If the Tigers alienate their most loyal fans, what happens to the franchise when the novelty wears off, the new stadium is no longer trendy, and the casual fan stops coming?

Max Lapides is not casual about the Tigers. "Did you read Schembechler's statement?" he asks in disbelief. "He said that he does not want fans, he wants customers. That is a very incisive statement; it's very meaningful. He doesn't want the person that wants to see a ball game. He wants people who want to come to an event, not fifty times a year, but even half a dozen times a year, and who'll spend a lot of money. He doesn't care about people who really like baseball. He doesn't really care about the person who doesn't have a lot of money. And the person who can't afford a six-dollar seat is not going to come to the park with a great deal of money anyway. He's not going to build a stadium for that person."

The White Sox have perfected the art of revenue enhancement. According to an article by Jon Pepper in the *Detroit News* of June 30, 1991, fans at the new Comiskey Park can buy DoveBars, cheesecake, carrot cake, quesadillas, cinnamon rolls, White Sox trash cans, White Sox shot glasses, White Sox Christmas ornaments, White Sox inflatable baseball bats, bricks from the old Comiskey Park ($12.95 each), eighteen-ounce Porterhouse steaks ($25.95) and bottles of Dom Perignon ($130).

"Comiskey is a baseball emporium for the '90s," observes Pepper, "a baseball mall, a place where you can root, root, root for the home team while the home team roots through your pockets, searching for the treasure it needs to pay $5 million for a pitcher."

By learning the trick pitches of the White Sox, the Tigers may reap quick profits in a new stadium. But what about the long run?

Unlike basketball, baseball depends on tradition. Its heritage is a strong selling point. Why has Baltimore's new stadium taken on the trappings of a classic ballpark? Because it is clear that many fans like the look and feel of the classic stadiums, that tradition and nostalgia sell. Rather than an ersatz classic, the Tigers have the real thing, and it's a park that Monaghan's customers favor keeping, according to every poll.

Over the long run, the Tigers could make more money in a renovated Tiger Stadium than in a new stadium, especially if they market the park's tradition and intimacy as the Red Sox and Cubs do. Tiger Stadium is a proven winner. A new stadium would be a high-stakes gamble with the stability of the franchise.

"The chemistry between a baseball team and a city is delicate," says Bob Buchta. "In their drive for the quick buck, the Tigers may be jeopardizing the entire foundation of their franchise's value. Pittsburgh used to be a great baseball town, but something was lost, and they stopped caring. Seattle, with their new stadium, can't generate real interest in baseball. The Tigers are taking for granted the connection that they've had with this city since 1901. Tom Monaghan and Bo Schembechler have shown that they don't understand that connection. They seem to think that selling baseball is like selling pizza. It doesn't work that way. People have to care about a baseball team. They have to feel that it's somehow theirs. And when management claims complete ownership of the franchise without regard for the feelings of the fans, they may come to realize too late that what they own isn't worth much."

With renovation, the Tigers could get the added revenues they seek from stadium amenities. With modifications in the stadium area, they could make money from parking. "At a much lower cost, they can have all the sky boxes, all the concessions, the larger clubhouses, and the expanded office space," says John Davids. "All the things they want in a new park, they can get much more easily and cheaply by renovating Tiger Stadium. Any city can build a SkyDome, or a new Comiskey Park, that are really inferior to places like Wrigley Field, and Tiger Stadium, and Fenway. But only two other cities have what we have in Detroit. The Tigers really should market that."

The Tigers take fan loyalty for granted, but their calculations don't allow for fans' demonstrated sentiment for the stadium—a sentiment that, like love for the team, translates into dollars and cents. And they think they can get a new stadium with all the toppings and have the public pay for it.

Rosemary Hogan believes that business should not be divorced from principle and from civic morality. "Whether the Tigers like it or not, they are part of this community. You have to drag them kicking and screaming, but they are part of the city. They are in one of the oldest neighborhoods in the city of Detroit. They have absolutely no idea of their impact on the community. And they've shown that they really don't care."

The Tigers "have very little input in terms of the black community," says Holley. Asked if Monaghan has given money to social or charitable programs in the city, Holley replies: "If he is, I don't know where it is. He gives to South America, you know. Maybe we ought to take a bunch of us over to South America and see what we can get, and bring it back."

Monaghan pursues his own profit and "doesn't care who it hurts," says Hogan. "He doesn't care how much it hurts the city. He just wants to get his bucks."

Asked about his "plantation basketball" criticism of the Pistons, Holley says: "I felt that something needed to be said. And I did, and I took a lot of criticism. Much of the white community felt it was unfair, because business is business. Well, the drug boys tell me business is business. The prostitutes tell me, 'It's just business.' If we deal with business with no real morality, business with no real ethics, business with no real responsibility, then how do I say to the drug dealers and prostitutes that you too have a responsibility not to do this, and not to do that?"

Business, says Frank Rashid, is "the new American theology."

CHAPTER 17

THE EMPTY THREAT

We don't want to leave. We're not trying to hold a hammer over anyone. But if a team meets the criteria of a distressed franchise, it is a possibility to switch cities. In the long run, if matters continue as they are, we'll probably meet that criteria.

— Bo Schembechler in the
Detroit News, *August 4, 1991*

It's time the fans stopped being held hostage. It's time we as fans said, 'You don't want to be here, then don't be here.' We'll put together an organization to get a new club. We are the fifth-largest media market. It may take a few years, but we'll have a new team here because the major leagues are not going to let the fifth-largest media market go away.

— Walter Briggs IV

Tiger Tale Number 6: If you don't build it, we'll skip town.

In late twentieth-century America, when corporations want the public to build them a new place of business, they know how to get it: threaten to leave town.

Since World War II, thousands of businesses and hundreds of thousands of jobs have left Detroit. The automakers and their suppliers have fled for cheaper labor markets. Detroit today is a desperate place — desperate enough to be blackmailed.

When General Motors said it needed a new plant, Poletown's homes and churches and shops were bulldozed. When Chrysler made the same demand, Detroiters paid to demolish houses and businesses, clear and clean up contaminated land, and build the company a new plant on the east side; each job promised at the Jefferson Avenue assembly plant cost Detroiters $48,828.

Sports team owners are expert at the blackmail game. When Baltimore Orioles owner Edward Bennett Williams demanded a new stadium, Maryland lawmakers caved in and allocated $16 million a year in lottery proceeds to build him one. The Illinois legislature approved a sweetheart deal for the White Sox after owners Eddie Einhorn and Jerry Reinsdorf threatened to take the charter American League franchise to St. Petersburg, Florida. Owners have made implicit or explicit threats in their quests for new stadiums in Cleveland, San Francisco, Minnesota, Milwaukee, Texas, and elsewhere.

Christopher Kittides of BEI is sanguine when asked if he approves of local government building a new physical plant for a private business. "Why are you subsidizing GM?" he asks. "That's the largest corporation in the world. They get tax abatements for Poletown, and Chrysler gets tax abatements on Jefferson, and on and on. We're talking multibillion-dollar corporations. If you look at the Tigers, they are a business, but they're nothing next to GM." The issue, says Kittides, is "whether government at any level should support private business. The track record is that we do it all the time."

Eugene McCarthy says it amounts to a form of tyranny. "They're having the same fight in Washington," he says, "over a new football stadium, as to how much city money should go into it. They all do it. The damn corporations shake down the states and the cities before they come in. General Dynamics is playing Maryland off against Virginia, and we've got a couple up in Minnesota, that say if you don't give us a tax break we'll go to North Dakota."

Given the "track record," it came as no surprise that the Detroit media by mid-1991 were parroting the line that the city would lose the Tigers if taxpayers didn't underwrite a new stadium. The surprise was that it wasn't the Tigers who were issuing the threats. Politicians were eagerly making them for the club.

When Monaghan bought the Tigers in 1983, he inherited the thirty-year lease binding the team to stay at Tiger Stadium until 2008. Shortly after the sale, talk of a new stadium began, but Monaghan pledged that the team would stay in Detroit. On May 22, 1986, Monaghan told reporters that a move to the suburbs was out of the question. "I don't think you have to worry about that," he said. "I've never thought a minute of moving them."

In an interview later that summer Mayor Young's press secretary,

Bob Berg, expressed confidence in Monaghan's commitment to Detroit. "I don't think there's any doubt that, if there is a new stadium, it will be built in the city," he said.

As Young pitched for a new stadium, Monaghan made clear that he expected the city to pay for it.

On January 17, 1988, *Free Press* columnist Bob Talbert reported this response from a Monaghan aide, Michael Rohde, when asked whether Monaghan should put seed money toward a new stadium: "Why should he? Tampa Bay will give him a new stadium free plus $15 million to sign the lease."

The next day reporters asked Monaghan where a new stadium might be built. He replied: "Anything is possible. Where it will be, heaven knows."

Monaghan's vow to keep the team in Detroit had lasted less than two years. From then on, Tiger officials took the position that they were considering many stadium sites in the city and various suburbs.

As it became apparent that the city and the Tigers were making little progress on a new stadium, reports about suburban sites surfaced periodically. Early rumors in 1989 had the Tigers moving to Ann Arbor, near Monaghan's base of operations. But there was strong local opposition to such a plan, as there had been to other Monaghan developments.

In January 1990 radio host Ron Cameron said he had inside information that the Tigers were planning to build a new stadium in Dearborn, at Ford Road and Southfield, on a large plot of Ford land. Tiger vice president Bill Haase denied the rumor, reiterating that the Tigers were looking at many sites.

Soon there was more speculation about other sites in the western suburbs. The Tigers did nothing to stifle the rumors. "Even if they never intended to leave Detroit," says Walter Briggs IV, "I'm sure that some of their efforts were directed at: How can I get people to think that I might leave so that I can get them to bend a little bit towards my way?"

In the spring of 1990, the Tigers surveyed corporate clients about their preferences in luxury suites and other amenities at a new stadium. Many Detroit season ticket holders did not get surveys, raising suspicions that the Tigers were skewing their poll in favor of suburban interests. On the form, firms could indicate whether they favored a downtown or a suburban site. Only those choosing a suburban site were asked to explain why.

225

On June 3, 1990, Haase told the *Free Press*: "We would like to stay in Detroit, but only if it makes sense and is the location which will best accommodate the majority of our fans."

Monaghan, when asked on WPZA on June 19 about financing for a new stadium, said: "I don't think the city's going to build it." He added that he assumed a new park would "be owned by some municipality and we would have some kind of option to buy it down the road."

Site speculation continued to abound. In September a new version of the Dearborn rumor circulated: The Tigers and the Lions were planning side-by-side baseball and football stadiums on the Ford land. It was said that Lion owner William Clay Ford was dissatisfied with the Silverdome. This rumor brought vehement denials all around.

In November the Greater Detroit Chamber of Commerce made a public push for the Michigan State Fairgrounds. The idea of a fairgrounds stadium, which had surfaced periodically since the 1940s, aroused little enthusiasm this time around.

In December a new location emerged as number one on the media's rumor charts. The Tigers reportedly were looking at Ford land in suburban Allen Park.

A strong backlash developed. In a survey in the *Dearborn Times-Herald*, readers opposed a new stadium, ninety-three percent to seven percent. Eighty-three percent of State Representative William Runco's constituents opposed a new stadium in Dearborn.

On February 4, 1991, the Novi City Council donned Tiger hats and unanimously passed a resolution in favor of renovating Tiger Stadium and rejecting any new stadium in their town. Novi reportedly had been high on the Tigers' list. Novi Mayor Matthew Quinn noted that "it is important for a major city like Detroit to remain viable" and that "Detroit has to remain great in order for the entire metropolitan area to remain as strong as it is." Councilman Tim Pope emphasized that "Novi as a community is part of Detroit."

"We hope that Novi will be just the first among many cities that will say no to a new stadium that would be bad for the new city and bad for the city of Detroit," John Davids of the Tiger Stadium Fan Club told the Novi meeting. His hopes were soon realized. Similar resolutions followed in Plymouth Township, Holly, and other suburbs.

A few weeks later, Monaghan's statement that Detroit was a bad baseball town increased suspicions that the Tigers were packing their bags. Many local leaders were angered. "If it's a bad baseball town, maybe we need to look and see if it could be a bad pizza town," says the

Reverend Jim Holley. "It's just unfair for business people like Monaghan to make statements like that, and at the same time profit from the city."

Wayne County Executive Ed McNamara and his deputy, Michael Duggan, entered the fray just as the Tigers seemed to have squandered any chance for public support for a new stadium by dismissing Ernie Harwell.

The Tigers had few solid arguments. The charade that the stadium was crumbling had been exposed. The Tigers had ignored the Cochrane Plan and had allowed public opinion to grow in support of renovation. Their arguments about needing a new stadium to compete had not carried the day.

Their best remaining weapon was a threat to leave town. But with suburbs balking, that threat seemed idle. There was no solid evidence that the Tigers had a new stadium deal anywhere. The leaders of Wayne County were gambling that they could get political mileage as the men who waged a heroic last-ditch campaign to save the Tigers for Detroit. They needed to convince the public that there was a real chance the Tigers would leave.

Duggan and his staff wined and dined influential opinion leaders to convince them that a new stadium was the only way to keep the Tigers from moving. For the first time, the Tiger Stadium Fan Club faced a formidable public relations foe. The fan club's former chief adversaries, the Tigers and the City of Detroit, never had mounted an effective media campaign. Now the fan club was outgunned. The volunteer organization could not match Wayne County's paid political punch.

The campaign intensified with Schembechler's rusty girder speech. He ruled out renovation and demanded that a new stadium be built at public expense. Though the forum was more prestigious and the talk more blunt, Schembechler in essence said only what Tiger officials had said for years: We want a new stadium, and we want the public to pay for it.

But for the first time, there were public officials ready to pick up the tab and hand it to taxpayers. And there was something else new too: a deadline. Schembechler announced that the Tigers would give civic leaders until August 1 to come up with an acceptable proposal for a new stadium.

Or else what? It was left unsaid. The media didn't ask the obvious questions. What would happen after August 1? Were the Tigers planning to leave town? Did they have a site in the suburbs? Did the Tigers think they could move out of Michigan?

Later, Duggan admitted that the August 1 deadline had been his idea. Not only was the county issuing the team's blackmail threats, it was setting the deadline for the payoff.

"He's doing corporate service, not public service," says Frank Rashid. "He's become the Tigers' PR guy. That's where our tax dollars go: to pay Duggan's salary to negotiate with us, on behalf of the Tigers."

At every opportunity, Duggan argued that the Tigers were ready to leave. Dutifully, columnist after columnist, editorial after editorial urged civic leaders to keep the Tigers in Detroit by coming up with a plan for a new stadium. Even news stories started from the premise that a new stadium was the only hope for keeping the Tigers.

"The Tigers aren't doing the blackmailing themselves," says Rashid. "They're letting the county officials and the media do the blackmailing for them, on the unproven assumption that the Tigers can leave whenever they want to."

When asked if the Tigers had ever threatened to leave, county officials said no. "The Tigers have never once threatened to take the team out of Michigan," said McNamara to anchorman Bill Bonds on WXYZ-TV.

"The Tigers weren't holding a gun to anyone's head," Duggan told the Detroit City Council on June 17. "They weren't asking for anything. We went to them. We said, 'We think it's important for you to stay.' "

Duggan's June 5 report to McNamara—really a piece addressed to opinion leaders—made the Tigers' threats more openly than the club had ever done. Duggan wrote that the Tigers were heading to the suburbs "not out of bad feelings for the city, but out of economic desperation following years of attendance that lagged seriously behind what their finish in the standings would justify." He reported that Schembechler "felt the neighborhood was safe" but "did not see any prospect for changing the perceptions of the public" to the contrary.

Duggan reported that Tiger officials "indicated that while they would like to stay in Detroit, they had to make the best business decision for the organization. Mr. Schembechler indicated that they would be pleased to stay in the city if we could show him it was the best business decision."

Duggan portrayed the city as helpless. He noted that Detroit had lost a hundred thousand jobs in the last two decades and said the city would lose many more if the Tigers left. He admitted that the Tigers employed only five hundred people, about half of them Detroit residents, but argued that "the loss of the Tigers will trigger another round of business exodus from the City from owners who will see the Tigers leaving as the last loss of hope."

Accepting all the team's phony arguments against renovation, and all Schembechler's claims of impending financial ruin, Duggan contended that the Tigers must have a new stadium. "Without a modern stadium to generate revenue for the team," he wrote, "the Tigers may be able to do much better financially in another city. We are foolish to leave the team in a position where they have no choice but to look."

But look where? Monaghan and Schembechler had made it plain that the Tigers were not going to pay for a new stadium. Most suburbs didn't seem eager to host the team, and there was little political support for public financing for a suburban stadium. The Tigers were legally bound to stay at Tiger Stadium until 2008.

Duggan waved aside such realities by hinting darkly of a secret suburban site. "A number of suburban sites the Tigers have looked at have been reported in the media," he said. "Others have not."

As for the lease, Duggan simply assumed that because the Lions and Pistons had found a way to leave the city, the Tigers could too.

In his report, Duggan called the supposed threat to move out of state "perhaps the most chilling prospect of all." He pointed to surprise moves by other sports teams—the NFL's Colts leaving Baltimore, the Raiders pulling out of Oakland—as evidence that the threat was credible. At a presentation before the Detroit City Council on June 17, he ticked off a list of potential suitors. In decreasing order of credibility, they were Washington, D.C.; St. Petersburg, whose new domed stadium had failed to secure a National League expansion franchise; Buffalo, which had all but dropped out of the NL expansion bidding; Orlando, where voters had approved a county hotel tax to finance a new stadium; and Phoenix, which according to Duggan was "prepared to levy a sales tax to build a baseball stadium should a team locate there."

Is it really possible that the Tigers could move out of Michigan? Tiger Stadium Fan Club leaders as well as many legal experts and baseball analysts say no, citing several crucial points:

The Tigers don't meet major league baseball's criteria for franchise relocation. To move out of the Detroit area, the Tigers would need the approval of baseball commissioner Fay Vincent, three-quarters of the American League owners, and one-half of the National League owners.

Vincent's criteria for relocating a franchise were listed in an article in the June 3, 1991, issue of the *Sporting News*, the weekly publication that has been called "baseball's Bible." They are: (1) the team must have severe financial problems linked to poor attendance or low broadcasting revenue; (2) there must be no local group available to buy the team; (3) there must be no prospective owner from outside the area who would keep the team in the area; and (4) there must be no aid or cooperation from state or local government available.

The Tigers do not meet any of these criteria. Hank Aguirre's December 1990 offer to buy the team made clear that there are legitimate buyers who would keep the Tigers in Detroit. Government help is obviously available. As for financial problems, the Tigers by Schembechler's own admission continued to be profitable. The best argument he could muster is that "in the long run, if matters continue as they are, we will probably meet that criteria."

Vincent said he was planning to appoint a committee of three owners to evaluate his policy on transferring teams, but he continued to state strong objections to franchise relocations.

The Tigers would be far back in line for franchise shifts. Vincent told the *Sporting News* that "our owners are concerned about the viability of several franchises. It's no secret Seattle is one of them; there are major concerns up there. Also, Cleveland could be a problem, if the team's stadium situation doesn't work out, and I'm greatly concerned about Dr. McMullen's inability to sell the Houston club to local interests."

The Seattle franchise, despite a more competitive team and increased attendance in 1991, faced trouble because of low local broadcasting revenues. The *Sporting News* reported in September 1991 that the Mariners were definitely going to move; it was only a question of when. In Houston, attendance and public support dwindled after McMullen auctioned off all the team's best players. Cleveland has been saddled for decades with a poor stadium, a losing team, and low attendance.

Vincent also could have included on his endangered list the following teams: (1) San Francisco, where voters turned down a new stadium and owners have been openly looking for a new location; (2) Montreal, where the stadium was falling apart and the team was sold in the summer of 1991 to a business-government consortium after rumors that the Expos were about to leave town; (3) Pittsburgh, with a small media market and a modern stadium, Three Rivers, that has become so despised that the city's mayor announced in September 1991 that she would like to see plans for a new baseball-only park for the Pirates; and (4) Atlanta, with chronic low attendance.

Baseball would never abandon a top media market such as Detroit. The Tigers not only are a charter member of the American League and one of baseball's most stable and successful franchises, they play in one of the biggest media markets in the nation. Today, broadcast revenues are the most important factor in team economics.

Monaghan would risk huge business losses if he moved the team out of state. Domino's Pizza is headquartered in Michigan. Would Monaghan risk the stability of his business by moving the Tigers out of state and suffering a backlash from Michigan pizza customers?

Moreover, would Monaghan move away from one of the most loyal fan bases and most baseball-crazy towns in America for the likes of a small market like St. Petersburg or Phoenix? The fragile state of baseball economics would make such a move extremely risky.

For these reasons, any Tiger threat to move out of state lacks credibility. Yet in the summer of 1991, the idea gained legitimacy through constant repetition in the media. It became officially sanctioned fiction. Voters' belief in such a threat's legitimacy is crucial to the new stadium effort.

In the wake of the Harwell firing and Schembechler's blustering demands for a new stadium at the team's chosen location, threats to move were producing a backlash. Many fans have become so enraged at Monaghan and the club that they have come to feel that Detroit would be better off to let the Tigers leave than to cave in to their demands. They express confidence that one of the other franchises looking to relocate would move in to fill the void.

"It's time the fans stopped being held hostage," says Walter Briggs IV. "It's time we as fans said, 'You don't want to be here, then don't be here.' We'll put together an organization to get a new club. We are the fifth-largest media market. It may take a few years, but we'll have a new team here because the major leagues are not going to let the fifth-largest media market go away."

On July 30 Schembechler called a press conference to reject the county's preferred new stadium site near Woodward Avenue in downtown Detroit and to insist that a new stadium be built in the Briggs

231

Community. Afterward, McNamara congratulated himself on his efforts to "save" the team for Detroit.

"I think that the Tigers have made a tremendous concession by agreeing not to look to the suburbs or to other states," he said on WJR in response to Schembechler's ultimatum, "and we certainly appreciate that position they've taken." The previous November, said McNamara, "the Tigers were out in Novi and Washtenaw [County] looking for sites, and now they're zeroing in on the inner city of Detroit, where we think they belong, and we're down now to is it Detroit or St. Petersburg, Florida? But where in Detroit are we going to put it? I think that's real progress, and I hope everybody looks at it that way."

Unfortunately for McNamara, not everybody saw it his way.

"The county has decided that whatever the Tigers insist on, the county is going to do," says the fan club's John Davids. "They can't say it publicly, but they're going to do whatever the Tigers want, because they've succumbed to the blackmail threat that the Tigers are going to leave."

The August 1 deadline passed with neither a bang nor a whimper. Two days later, Schembechler set a new deadline, telling reporters: "We don't want to leave. We're not trying to hold a hammer over anyone. But if a team meets the criteria of a distressed franchise, it is a possibility to switch cities. In the long run, if matters continue as they are, we'll probably meet that criteria."

Experts in sports law say Detroit should call Bo's bluff.

"Detroit needs to start using its political muscle," Gary Roberts, dean of Tulane University's law school, told the *News* for an August 9 story. "Rather than cower under the threat of the Tigers' leaving, you can say: 'We've got things that can hurt you just as bad.' "

Jim Gray of Marquette University's National Sports Law Institute told the *News* that a threat to reopen the question of baseball's antitrust exemption might make the Tigers back down. "Baseball is exempt from antitrust laws — for now," said Gray. "But it only takes one case to ruin it. And if the people in Detroit can exert pressure on Capitol Hill, that may be a way to get around this problem."

The opponents' major weapon is the Tigers' lease, which legal experts say contains unusually strong language. The lease's power is important because it bears directly on the credibility of the club's threats. If the city can stop the Tigers from moving to any other site, the Tigers lose their strongest leverage for a new stadium.

Michael Duggan was a lawyer specializing in leases before he held office. Duggan boasted that he would have no trouble showing the Tigers how to break their lease. "It is very doubtful the City could prevail in any legal action to try to get a court to order the team to spend another 17 years in this facility," wrote Duggan in his June 5 report to McNamara. "It would be foolish to bet the Tigers's future in the City of Detroit on a court ruling on this lease."

Sports teams and other corporations break leases all the time, but this lease, say legal experts, is extraordinarily strong. "There is a provision in the lease," Professor Matthew McKinnon of the Detroit College of Law told the *News,* "that states, if they do not play in Tiger Stadium, the city can get an injunction stopping the team from playing anywhere else."

In a July *Detroit Legal News* story, McKinnon said: "I don't think it would be very easy to get out of this lease. I'd rather be on the city's side of the litigation, based on what I know."

Duggan argued that the Tigers could get out of the lease because they had signed it based on promises for renovations that had not been fully delivered. Duggan said items such as an expanded commissary, a new ticket office, new parking lot, and entrance plaza were never made, and that repairs to the plumbing, roof, electricity, concourses, and other parts of the stadium had not been as extensive as the Tigers had expected.

Haase of the Tigers cites "things that were proposed and promised to us within that lease that never came into being. And that being the case, there may be some gaps there that would allow us to break that lease."

But McKinnon disagrees: "I don't think there's enough to say [the city] has breached the lease in a major way and we [the Tigers] can move out now," he told the *Legal News*.

Several legal experts affirm McKinnon's position.

Charles Moon, a prominent attorney, says: "I don't see anything in the lease which would allow the Tigers to leave. The city could insist on enforcement of the lease."

Attorney Steve Finegood argued on behalf of the Tiger Stadium Fan Club that the team's own actions had created the deficiencies in the renovations. "Those renovations weren't done because the Tigers didn't tell the city half the things that were wrong with the stadium," Finegood told the *Legal News* in July.

Moon says the lease allows the Tigers to sue if the city doesn't live up to its obligations to reimburse the club for repairs. "Right now the

Tigers could say to the city: 'Here's something we want to do. Will you finance it?'" he posits. "'If you can't finance it we'll advance the costs, and you reimburse us.' One of the things that makes Duggan's position weak is that the Tigers haven't done that. If they're so dissatisfied with the condition of the stadium as Duggan thinks they are, and as Schembechler at least insinuates, they should be making demands on the city to do things."

Finegood notes that the Tigers accepted the renovations as completed in 1984. According to information the fan club obtained under a Freedom of Information Act request, the Tigers have never notified the city that more work needs to be done.

McKinnon says Duggan has exaggerated the deficiencies in the renovations: "The things he lists in his report as not having been done are relatively small parts of the whole package. He says 'many of the promised renovations were not delivered.' But probably ninety-five percent of everything that was promised to be done was done."

McKinnon notes that a firm tenet of contract law holds that if one party "fails to do what they've promised to do, you can't walk away from the contract unless they've breached it in some major way. It would be really hard," he concludes, "to prove that there was a so-called serious or material breach that would allow the Tigers to put an end to the lease."

Furthermore, the statute of limitations for contracts is generally six years. Time has run out on the Tigers, says Finegood. McKinnon agrees. "It seems to me a lot of these things have gone way past the period of time where the Tigers could legitimately complain about them," he says.

If the Tigers tried to leave the stadium, and the City of Detroit moved to enforce the lease, it could cause a very long court battle. "No matter what the outcome of such a lawsuit would be," wrote Eric Pope in the *Legal News*, "McKinnon points out that it would take three or four years in the courts. . . . And in his opinion the Tigers couldn't commit themselves to a new stadium until after the legal issues surrounding the old lease had been resolved."

The legal issues might be rendered moot if Mayor Young were to let the Tigers out of their contract. But Moon says Young can't do that on his own. He says any change or termination of the lease would have to be approved by Detroit's City Council.

In September 1991 the Common Ground Coalition, a new organization of Detroit religious, business and community leaders opposed to a new stadium, began a petition drive to put a proposal before Detroit voters. The coalition's initiative would mandate that any changes in the Tiger Stadium lease be approved by the electorate.

Given this tangle of obstacles to any move by the Tigers, the questions facing the citizens of Detroit and Wayne County become: Can the Tigers really leave? If not, why are officials bluffing for them?

Ostensibly, Duggan's June 5 report was an objective "Evaluation of Wayne County's Options to Keep the Tigers." To those familiar with the issues, though, it reads more like a sales document or a legal brief. McKinnon takes this for granted. He notes that Duggan is a lawyer. Lawyers, he says, "are advocates for their side. That's what they're supposed to do. They're trying to persuade people that their position is the correct one. If I were on that side, and I wanted to have a new stadium, I would look for as many things wrong with the stadium, both from a legal and from an architectural standpoint, as I could find. And I would use that as the ammunition to justify my position."

The fan club, says Frank Rashid, asked Duggan to evaluate the Cochrane Plan "hoping that he would be a public servant. You do this with some skepticism, but you do it. You hope that Duggan is going to be tough for us, strong for the public. He's going to negotiate with the Tigers on our behalf. Instead, he's negotiating with the public on the Tigers' behalf. When Schembechler makes an ass of himself in public, Duggan defends him, composes whole apologias for the man, tells us what he really meant. Schembechler doesn't have to issue the blackmail threat; Duggan does it for him. Schembechler doesn't have to say the lease is weak. Duggan says the lease is weak. To me, when Duggan publicly criticizes the lease, that shows whose side he's on."

Tiger fan John Grindstaff is glad that the Tiger Stadium Fan Club brought the terms of the lease to light in 1990. "They're saying that the Tigers signed a lease," he says. The fan club is "trying to hoist them on their own petard. They're saying, 'Look, if you're so business-oriented, and so wed to the policy of business comes first, then take the one business idea that's above all else: that when you sign a lease you abide by it.' "

Thomas Shull of the Heartland Institute believes it's a matter of principle. "If Tom Monaghan were an honorable man," says Shull, "then he would stand by that contract. It is clear that he bought an organization that had promised to stay there thirty years."

Whether or not it's legal for the Tigers to break their lease, says Shull, "doesn't answer the question of whether it's decent."

CHAPTER 18

WHAT THIS CITY NEEDS IS MORE MILLIONAIRES AND LOW-PAYING JOBS

> We're not, in any sense of the word, sitting here wanting to create a situation where people feel that they are paying for a private business to continue on in their local area without realizing that there is an awful lot of economical benefits.
>
> — *Tiger vice president Bill Haase*

> Every day they would play a baseball game in a new stadium, you would be taking seven police officers off the streets.
>
> — *State Senator John Kelly*

Tiger Tale Number 7:
A new stadium is good for a city.

In city after city, officials have sold the public on taxes for new stadiums by arguing that what's good for the home team is good for the hometown. New stadiums, they contend, generate more investment, more businesses, more jobs, and more pride.

They said it in the early 1970s about a riverfront dome, and they are saying it in the early 1990s: A new stadium would be a big shot in the arm for Detroit.

"The so-called 'common man' will benefit more than big business from the stadium," argued stadium backer Tom Adams in 1972, "because it will provide a more attractive entertainment facility and, more importantly, create additional tax revenues for housing, education and other basic needs."

Twenty years later, the lofty rhetoric would soar even higher above the bombed-out landscape of Detroit's inner city. In a press release explaining his dismissal of the Cochrane Plan, architect Jerry Shea argued that downtown Detroit needs a new stadium "to remain a vital civic center in the United States, and that the State of Michigan itself needs downtown Detroit to remain a key player in the emerging global market place."

The whole world is watching, apparently, to see where Sparky Anderson will hang his jock strap in 1995 — the year by which Bo Schembechler has claimed the Tigers must have a new stadium.

Grandiose claims of economic spin-offs are needed to sell the public on paying for new stadiums because it's become clear that stadiums don't pay their own way.

"In the sixties, the multipurpose stadiums were publicly funded, and the argument was that these would pay for themselves," says architect Philip Bess. "Now, the rationale has changed. Now it's understood that they won't pay for themselves, but that they'll generate ancillary development."

The Tigers' Bill Haase recites the rationale a little defensively: "I think you have to look at what governments do . . . in order to entice other businesses to stay within their local area in order to keep the economy flowing. Whether people like to hear it or not, a sports franchise does do an awful lot for the local economy. . . . We're not, in any sense of the word, sitting here wanting to create a situation where people feel that they are paying for a private business to continue on in their local area without realizing that there is an awful lot of economical benefits."

But economists say that new stadiums do not benefit a city's economy. According to studies published by the Heartland Institute, American cities spent $750 million in the 1980s to build or renovate sports facilities and got nothing in return except wealthier sports owners.

Economist Robert Baade studied 1965–83 economic activity, including retail sales figures, in twelve cities with new stadiums. He found that a new stadium is more likely to reduce than to increase its city's share of regional income.

When people spend money on a ball game, they spend less on other entertainment such as movies or restaurants, Baade noted. A new stadium doesn't increase spending. It only shifts money, jobs and businesses around. "Perhaps a new restaurant will open up in the vicinity of a new sports stadium; it is, however, just as likely that an established restaurant fifteen blocks away will close its doors as a result," Baade wrote. "Is this what stadium proponents consider 'economic growth'?"

In Detroit many local businesses could be in jeopardy if Tiger Stadium were replaced. "It would hurt," acknowledges Tim Springstead, owner of Nemo's Bar on Michigan Avenue. Nemo's, with a long-established and loyal clientele, "will exist no matter what happens to the stadium," says Springstead. "But that's a portion of our business that we don't want to lose. We lost the Lions about fifteen years ago, and that hurt our business."

Others could be harmed more.

"If they move it I'll be out of business," says Michigan Avenue souvenir stand owner Tom Cross. "I've been doing this almost twenty years."

"There will be hundreds of people put out of work," says Peter Rosen, who sells peanuts outside the ballpark. A new stadium, says Rosen, would "eliminate all the people from the city from being able to make any money on the Tigers, so that Monaghan and big business can dominate the whole scene."

Bars, restaurants, and souvenir shops along Michigan and Trumbull thrive on ball game crowds. Restaurants and bars downtown and in nearby Mexican Town also benefit from baseball business. No matter what the site of a new stadium, these businesses would not be replaced around the kind of place the Tigers want: a temple of pure profit surrounded by an asphalt moat.

Around Tiger Stadium and other older, urban parks, people walk past businesses before and after the game. At new stadiums, people park on site and buy food, drink, and souvenirs inside the stadium. Businesses outside the parking apron are left to wither.

In an article in the September/October 1991 *Inland Architect*, Bess described the new Comiskey Park as "anti-urban":

> The bars, shops, restaurants, and other sorts of commercial street life that one would typically find around a traditional urban ballpark have been banished from the immediate vicinity of the new Comiskey Park; no pre-or post-game food and drink will be found, or allowed, within nearly half a mile of the stadium.

"A big parking lot in the city is not in the public interest," says Bess in an interview. "Everyone drives in, everyone drives out, there's no ancillary development in the neighborhood, and it's hostile to other kinds of uses."

Detroit's stadium backers of the early 1970s spoke of shops and restaurants mushrooming in the fertile economic turf around a domed stadium. Twenty years later, the buzzword was "enterprise zone." In a tacit acknowledgement that stadiums by themselves don't generate spin-off businesses, county officials proposed that the state give businesses special tax breaks and incentives to locate around a new stadium. Detroit and Wayne County officials created an Enterprise Zone Authority in the summer of 1991 to plan such an area.

Wayne County's Michael Duggan explained the idea to the Detroit City Council as "the most development friendly zone in the entire state of Michigan."

To the media, he painted a picture of a "Fairlane Mall-type development," referring to an upscale Dearborn shopping center, with shops, "ethnic villages," businesses, and even a golf course surrounding the stadium.

"The enterprise zone concept is quite fascinating to me," said Haase in a July 1991 interview. "I think it has a unique opportunity to make a community or an area very viable more than eighty-one dates out of the year that a baseball franchise would be operating. If you put together, as has been proposed, little ethnic villages with restaurants, shops, maybe a little shopping mall, a couple of businesses, and — depending on what kind of land you have available — even some kind of recreational activities, then what you're doing is creating an area that's usable more than eighty-one times out of a year. And I think that's great."

The "enterprise zone" would be an attempt to create artificially what already exists around Tiger Stadium. Critics wondered how businesses would thrive outside a new stadium's asphalt buffer.

"The development they're talking about, with this ring road, and a hundred acres of parking, is totally against any urban planner's idea of how to develop a city," says John Davids, architect of the Cochrane Plan. "You do not create a suburban island in an existing urban city, especially a mature city like Detroit."

A new stadium, says contractor Joe O'Neal, referring to the fortresslike Renaissance Center downtown, would be "another Ren Cen."

Walter Briggs IV worked as an accountant in the Renaissance

240

Center. "There's this fear of the city," Briggs acknowledges, "but it's an issue that can't be dealt with by the Tigers saying, 'We're going to build a wall around it,' because the Renaissance Center as an example is a disaster. We found out ten years later that we had to open it up to the city to get it to do what we intended to do.

"If that's what you're going to do, and you take the public money that you're going to spend on building a park like that and spend it instead on upgrading the community and investing in existing structures, you're going to do a lot more to bring people in the long run down to the city. We have to learn to take the existing structure, rebuild it, enhance it, improve it, renovate it."

Brian Tremain, a securities broker who lives in Corktown, says an enterprise zone is wishful thinking. "It doesn't make sense," he says. "How are you going to get restaurants there that are going to live off of eighty days a year of traffic? Why is it all of a sudden that the stadium is going to bring two million people, and it's going to enhance the neighborhood, when in fact for the last eighty, ninety years it's been bringing millions of people to the neighborhood, and it hasn't necessarily brought a Chi-Chi's or anything else?"

Even Haase changed his tune after county officials argued that a new stadium near Woodward Avenue downtown would revitalize the area. Schembechler was insisting on a site in the Briggs Community, surrounded by twelve to fifteen thousand parking spaces. "You just can't jump-start an area by sticking a stadium into it," Haase told the *Free Press* at the end of August. "The Briggs site has all that's necessary."

Stadiums do not function as economic catalysts, Baade has found. His examination of eight cities with new stadiums showed that the long-term effect of stadium building on a city's economy is to shift development toward the service sector. There is no growth, merely "realignment," Baade noted. Jobs are not created, but only diverted from manufacturing to service, from higher-skilled to lower-skilled and lower-paying occupations. There is no net economic gain. Spending on sports diverts spending from other leisure activities, and new business start-ups in the neighborhood of a stadium are negated by business failures in other areas of the city.

Diverting money from other businesses to finance a stadium creates inequities, argues Thomas Shull of the Heartland Institute. A tax on hotels and motels to finance a new stadium, as proposed by Wayne County officials, could disrupt the local economy, he says. "Low-

241

paying unskilled jobs are not bad in and of themselves," says Shull, "as long as you are not artificially creating a tremendous number of them where they are not needed or appropriate. Artificially injecting hundreds of millions of dollars into the economy to create a certain type of job runs the risk of distorting the real needs of the economy.

"If you have the county pouring millions of dollars out of businesses such as hotels and motels that have shown they are meeting real needs and dump that money into a stadium, all that does is provide a subsidy to someone who is already very wealthy. It's not clear that the market in this area is lacking either in millionaires or in low-skilled, low-paying jobs."

Citing no evidence to refute the Heartland Institute studies, officials contend that a new stadium would be a great deal for Detroit. "You do get your investment several times over from the development and revenue that's generated outside the stadium walls, so the community has to decide to make the investment," Duggan argued in the *Detroit News* of August 18.

There are studies claiming that stadiums generate economic growth for cities but Baade points out that they have occurred within the context of public officials trying to generate support for new stadiums. Officials have to argue that there are ancillary benefits, because cities lose big money on building stadiums.

Dodger Stadium in Los Angeles is the only major league baseball stadium built entirely with private money since 1923. It's also the only one of fourteen new stadiums to make money, according to another Heartland study, by economist Dean Baim. The other thirteen stadiums that Baim investigated cost more to build and operate than they took in. These publicly financed stadiums received government subsidies of $139 million, Baim calculated. The worst money loser was the Superdome in New Orleans, which lost $70 million in its first twelve years. The thirteen stadiums, on average, cost taxpayers $550,000 a year.

Baim's study does not include the biggest white elephant of all, Toronto's SkyDome. In 1990, in its first full year of operation, the SkyDome smashed the all-time major league attendance record by drawing nearly 3.9 million fans to Blue Jay games. Income from those games and seventy other events yielded an operating profit of $27.4 million (Canadian). But interest payments on construction, business taxes, and depreciation were $66.7 million, leaving Ontario taxpayers nearly $40 million in the hole. The stadium cost $578 million to build, four times the original estimate. By the end of 1990 the overall debt on the stadium had risen to $320 million and the interest on the debt was accumulating at the rate of about $100,000 a day. By September 1991, the debt was $345 million.

The SkyDome's financial bath has become a national scandal in Canada. Late in 1991 the Ontario government was negotiating a sale of its 51 percent share in the stadium. Provincial leaders insisted they would not "give away" the facility to private interests, but the *Financial Times of Canada* in September noted that sale of the province's stake likely would involve Ontario's "foregoing $12.6 million a year in revenue it needs to reduce its own deficit" and "would almost certainly involve waiving responsibility for the $60 million in lawsuits." The Stadium Corp. of Ontario was being sued by the dome's architect and the builder of its retractable roof, both of whom claimed the Crown corporation hadn't paid them in full.

"If the government is going to have investments out there, I'm not sure commercial sports enterprises are the best place for them," Ontario Treasurer Floyd Laughren told the *Financial Times*. "It's a strange priority for the government."

The SkyDome is an extreme example of how stadium boosters' financial projections collapse under the weight of reality. Huge cost overruns on new stadium construction are common. Though most stadiums generate enough revenue to meet operating costs, few make enough to scale the mountain of debt piled up on loans used to pay for construction.

Taxpayers are handed the bill. Residents of Pontiac and Michigan paid more than $11 million between 1976 and 1987 for deficits at the Pontiac Silverdome, and still pay about $800,000 a year.

Chances of a baseball-only stadium covering its operating expenses and construction debt are slim. Even the relatively inexpensive Astrodome in Houston must be booked 150 days a year just to break even. A stadium relying on eighty-one baseball games cannot meet costs.

"At today's costs, with a limited number of events, it just won't work," said Michael Poplar, executive vice president of Cleveland Stadium Corporation, in an August 1991 *Free Press* article. "You have to have a building leased ninety percent of the time."

In Detroit a new baseball stadium for the Tigers would face a crush of competition for other events. The area already has plenty of sites for concerts, revivals, and tractor pulls: the Pontiac Silverdome, the Palace of Auburn Hills, Joe Louis Arena, Cobo Hall, the Fox Theatre, and other smaller halls, plus three summertime open-air concert venues.

"If building a new stadium were going to be profitable for the city, then Tom Monaghan would actually be building it himself, because it would be profitable for him," says Lois Briggs-Redissi, the great-granddaughter of Tiger owner Walter Briggs. "It's obviously a losing deal, and he knows it."

Theoretically, sports fans could benefit from public subsidies for stadiums if owners passed on those subsidies in lower ticket prices. In practice, fans often pay ticket surcharges to help retire the construction debt.

Baim contends that stadium subsidies are a regressive redistribution of wealth. The burden of repaying bonds from general revenues falls on all taxpayers. Taxes on liquor or cigarettes—used in Cleveland to finance a new stadium and proposed by some county officials to help the Tigers—fall disproportionately on the poor, as do sales taxes and proceeds from state-run lotteries. In a sort of reverse socialism, the population at large subsidizes sports owners, who are among the nation's wealthiest individuals. Monaghan is one of four billionaires in Michigan, according to a *Fortune* 1991 survey.

"We've had twenty years of experience with the results of public subsidies for new stadiums, and seen cities like Pontiac that are in trouble because of that funding," says Walter Briggs IV. "It doesn't help the community. It doesn't bring in jobs or anything else, particularly if you build it with an asphalt pavement park around it. Cities are under a lot more financial pressure now. And cities recognize that their tax burden is big enough as it is."

In the Detroit area, taxpayers are skeptical. In a March 1990 poll, 69 percent of respondents said that if a new stadium were built for the Tigers, Tom Monaghan and the club should pay for it. Only 15 percent said taxpayers should foot the bill, and 11 percent said people who buy tickets or attend games should pay.

"It's wrong that the Tigers are out there saying, 'You guys have to pay for it,'" says Briggs. "They believe there's some government responsibility to do this, and I don't believe that's the case at all."

Briggs says he doesn't blame Monaghan "for trying to get every freebie he can, because he's running a business. But I as a fan or a taxpayer don't want to pay on his profit. The fact that we subsidize Pontiac doesn't make it right. There's a lot of things we are starting to realize about what government can and cannot do, and one of the things it cannot do is run that kind of facility."

Briggs recalls a conversation with Monaghan aide John McDevitt, in which he told McDevitt that it was not fair for the Tigers to expect taxpayers to pay for a new stadium.

"We provide benefits to those businesses around there," Briggs says McDevitt replied.

"Well, I'm sorry," Briggs responded. "You don't sit down and ask the Renaissance Center to be built by government because certain surrounding people gain benefits from it."

"It's the classic entitlement mentality of a socialist state, coming from a capitalist," says Brian Tremain. "To me, that's the real criminal element in it all, the thing that offends me the most."

Billionaires are not usually well loved, but Monaghan has earned special infamy around Michigan through a series of colossal public relations boondoggles. In a sleepy resort area called Drummond Island, he angered local residents with expansion of his vacation hideaway. Tales of conspicuously excessive parties at the island lodge did not endear him to the masses. Many Ann Arbor residents resent his reckless development of Domino's Farms and other property, and people living near Monaghan's headquarters hate the holiday traffic jams created by his huge corporate Christmas lights displays. "Monaghan is a public relations disaster," says Bert Gordon. "He's antagonized the whole Western world."

Monaghan's ostentatious displays of wealth in buying Bugatti automobiles, Frank Lloyd Wright buildings, and other costly trinkets haven't helped his public image. And in a speech at Madonna College, he said that it is exciting to be poor and that a family can live on an income of less than a hundred dollars a year by buying bulk food from the U.S. Department of Agriculture.

All that was bad enough. Then his underling, Bo Schembechler, fired Ernie Harwell and demanded that the public build the Tigers a new stadium.

"I don't see any goodwill coming from him other than 'Give me,' " said Councilwoman Kay Everett of Monaghan. "If I saw him not having all the accoutrements of a rich man, all the cars and all the various islands and all the things he can purchase. . . . You tell me you can buy an island and you can't buy a stadium?"

The Reverend Jim Holley voices a common sentiment. "If he's going to build a baseball country club, then he ought to be made to build it himself. And he can take it to Mars if he wants to. But he ought not to use public money for it."

"There's no question this will be a really tough sell," said Wayne County Commissioner Kevin Kelley in the *News* of August 18, 1991. "People are not happy with Tigers management, and they don't like the idea of subsidizing them."

Even Duggan recognized the problem. "There's a gut level feeling that if a billionaire owns a baseball team, the public shouldn't be paying for him to build a new stadium," he said in a radio interview. To soften this perception, Duggan emphasized that the Tigers would pitch in for a new stadium, but the arrangements remained vague well past the August 1, 1991, deadline Schembechler had imposed on city and county officials at Duggan's request. Schembechler indicated that the Tigers might be willing to chip in some revenues from rental of luxury boxes. There would certainly be ticket surcharges. And Haase mentions parking revenues as a possible source for repaying the bonds used to pay for construction. But clearly the deal depended on government finding most of the dough.

Duggan promised county taxpayers that they would hardly feel the pinch. So successful was he in his initial media blitz that the *News* of May 1, 1991, wrote a story with this lead: "Contrary to popular belief, the current proposal for a new Tiger Stadium in Detroit would not cost taxpayers any money." The article quoted Duggan as saying that "the taxpayers are not going to be on the hook for this stadium."

The county's initial plan was to use its residual authority from the riverfront dome fiasco of the 1970s to levy a five percent hotel/motel tax. But the idea ran into a buzzsaw of opposition.

Occupancy rates in the Detroit area in 1991 already were among the lowest in the nation, having declined since 1986 from 71.3 percent to 50 percent. The proposed 5 percent hike would make Detroit room taxes second only to New York's. Mayor Young had staked his costly expansion of Cobo Hall on the premise that the city could gain more convention business. Hoteliers argued that any additional tax could be fatal to their industry. "We have enough problems attracting conventions here because of Detroit's image problem without adding a prohibitive tax," said William McLaughlin, president of the Metropolitan Detroit Convention and Visitors Bureau, in an August 5 *News* article.

When the Greater Detroit Chamber of Commerce, one of the strongest backers of a new stadium, came out publicly against the hotel tax, it signaled severe problems for the county's financing package.

Officials went back to their drawing boards in search of other "painless" levies. Media reports said the county was considering a smaller hotel tax, a tax on luxury cars, and new levies on liquor, cigarettes, and restaurant meals.

But David Held, president of the Hotel Association of Greater Detroit, said surcharges on rental cars and alcohol would also hurt hotel patrons. "This is the purest form of taxation without representation," Held told the *Free Press* on August 1. "It's not going into administrative coffers to help us. It's going into private development. Why don't they have a $15 surcharge on each automobile sold? Why do they pick on the little guys?"

Putting together a financing package that would fly with voters was an iffy proposition. Opposition to stadium taxes has been mounting nationwide. Taxpayers have rejected stadium proposals in San Francisco, Oakland, and Miami. In Cleveland city voters rejected a stadium proposal but it passed countywide by a razor-thin margin.

A key element in selling taxpayers on a new stadium is the threat that if a financing package is turned down, the team may leave town in search of a better deal. In Detroit such a loss, Duggan and other officials argue, would be a psychological blow from which the city might never recover. "If you accept the fact that a baseball stadium is part of the basic infrastructure of a large community, then you have to invest in it," Duggan was quoted as saying in the August 13 *News*.

But Duggan's assertion is not a fact; it is an arguable premise. There is a general identification in the public mind between sports franchises and the vitality of a city, but a city can survive without a ball club. Washington, D.C., did not fall apart after its baseball teams left — twice. Milwaukee did not collapse without the Braves, and the arrival of the Brewers was not needed to revive it. Green Bay's occasionally great football team has never made Green Bay an important city.

Bess concedes that the new Comiskey Park was a success in drawing fans in its first year, but asks in *Inland Architect*:

> So, if and when the team performs poorly, and the new Comiskey Park comes to be recognized by White Sox fans as just another dressed-up suburban stadium ("Royals Stadium in drag" another critic has called it) hostile to all forms of urban life around it, fans, taxpayers and government officials may ask themselves again the question that has recently been suppressed: Have we paid too high a price for this sports franchise?

One question facing Detroiters is what price is worth paying to meet the demands of the Tigers. At a City Council meeting on June 17, 1991, Everett expressed skepticism. "As a citizen, I resent being held almost at gunpoint by someone who has a lot of money that I have to build a stadium for them," she said. "I don't want us to lose this team, but I don't want us also to mortgage this city or have this city held at a point where we have the second highest hotel/motel tax."

Everett also wondered aloud if the Tigers could be trusted not to break a lease for a new stadium. Duggan, who a few minutes earlier had bragged he could get the Tigers out of their existing lease with the city, told the city leaders: "If we do a competent job of negotiating the lease, we will follow the same pattern of virtually every stadium being built in the country, which is we will lock them into a long-term lease."

Shull of the Heartland Institute has his doubts. "If in fact it is possible for the Tigers to walk away from this contract, why would you want to get involved in another contract with them?" he asks. "No one in their right mind signs a contract a second time with someone who stiffed them the first time around."

Stadium deals around the nation are filled with examples of massive concessions to teams that grew dissatisfied with their initial contracts. The Philadelphia Phillies in the mid-1980s restructured their lease. The city agreed to give the Phillies $1 million for a new scoreboard and to let the team build twenty-three new baseball-only sky boxes. The City of Seattle forgave the Mariners rent from 1985 to 1987 and picked up all game-day expenses for that period, and the club got to keep forty percent of the revenue on all new baseball suites. The team got the right to cancel its lease if attendance fell below 1.4 million, and the Seattle business community had to launch a massive ticket drive to meet that figure.

If a city gives in to corporate blackmail, where does it stop? What happens the next time the business is unsatisfied?

Detroit gave the Tigers the renovations the club wanted in the 1970s, and the Tigers agreed to a thirty-year lease. Before half of the term had expired, they wanted a new stadium. What would happen if the county and city built the Tigers a new stadium and the team later wanted out of the deal? What would happen if the Tigers didn't draw those million more fans a year that Monaghan is counting on?

On July 30, 1991, Bo Schembechler called a press conference to say that the Tigers had "rejected . . . categorically" one of two city sites that the new Detroit-Wayne County Stadium Authority was about to

248

propose. In a radio interview following Schembechler's statement, Wayne County Executive Ed McNamara said:

"I think what he was only saying — I hope that's what he's saying — is that . . . the Briggs is certainly the one he favors, but he will objectively look at the Woodward site, but he wants a fair appraisal, an objective appraisal, of both sites."

"What's next? Guaranteed attendance?" asked Cochrane Plan designer Judy Davids incredulously after hearing McNamara's response. "Bo said he wants a deal just like the White Sox got — and they got guaranteed attendance."

The Illinois Sports Facilities Authority, the government agency that owns the new Comiskey Park, will get no rent from the White Sox if attendance fails to reach 1.2 million in any year during the first ten years of the team's lease. During the second decade, the authority must buy up to 300,000 tickets to make up the difference should attendance fall below 1.5 million.

The reliability of any deal with the Tigers is important in the light of the massive costs of a new stadium project. Taxpayers spent millions of dollars on Tiger Stadium's infrastructure — the roads, sewers and utilities that serve the ballpark. To duplicate that infrastructure at a new location would be expensive, and to demolish the old stadium would waste the money spent to develop the area for baseball.

If contractor Joe O'Neal is correct, new infrastructure costs would be $15 million and demolition of the current stadium would cost $10 million. Should the city fork out $25 million to replace assets that it already owns and that don't need to be replaced?

If a stadium were built in the Briggs community, the Tigers' preferred site in Detroit, or in any other residential area, there would be other painful costs in displacing residents from their homes. Again, what happened on the south side of Chicago is illustrative.

"The new Comiskey Park displaced nearly 80 privately owned residential buildings (approximately 220 households) for the stadium and its parking," wrote Bess in *Inland Architect*. "Those displaced were virtually all black people, working-class poor, and elderly persons on fixed incomes. Residences that remain — the Chicago Housing Authority's low-rise Wentworth Gardens and the T.E. Brown apartments, a church-sponsored mid-rise residential building for the elderly and handicapped that sits about a hundred feet from where the White Sox launch their post-home run and Saturday night fireworks — are separated from stadium property by eight-foot-high chain link fences."

"There's already so much housing stock taken from Detroit," says Pat Muldoon, who with her husband, Brian, is restoring a home in Corktown. "A lot went with the riots. A lot has gone in the last twenty years with the white flight. Homes are just neglected."

Corktown is a well-organized neighborhood designated a historic district. In the summer of 1991 the Briggs Community issued a neighborhood development plan to try to reverse its decline. At the same time, Schembechler insisted that leveling the Briggs neighborhood for a new stadium was the only way the Tigers would stay in Detroit.

Muldoon says Briggs "may not be as historic as Corktown, but it's a community that people have lived in thirty, forty, fifty years, and it's just as important to them as my neighborhood is to me. Whether it's a historic neighborhood or not, there are people there."

Sasha Roberts, director of F.O.C.U.S. Inc., a private nonprofit neighborhood service agency in the Briggs Community, calls the idea of building a new stadium "an atrocity." One built in Briggs "would cause added crisis to people who are already struggling daily. We have fifty-four seniors, most of them housebound, to whom we deliver food. Most of them probably would not survive relocation." Roberts takes offense at the belief that her neighborhood is blighted. "The media talk about our neighborhood as a desolate place, that all we are is crack houses, vacant lots, and abandoned buildings. That's not true at all." She notes that in 1991 her agency's programs served nearly three hundred Briggs Community children. "If F.O.C.U.S. and the schools and the church leave the neighborhood" because of a new stadium, she says, little will remain for the families not displaced. "There wouldn't be a whole lot left for the kids here except the streets."

Duggan told the City Council: "I would hope that if we get in any area where we have to relocate people, we will do it in a humane and sensitive manner."

"Obviously, it tugs at your heartstrings any time you're dealing with people who have lived in a community for a long time," says the Tigers' Haase.

To many in Detroit, a new stadium is a question of social priorities.

Securities broker Tremain, a leading member of the Tiger Stadium Fan Club, calculates the long-term cost of a city-financed stadium as over half a billion dollars, just for land acquisition and construction. If twenty-five-year taxable municipal bonds were issued for $200 million, a common estimate for land and stadium construction, the debt service would be $22.7 million a year. The project's cost over twenty-five years would be $567.5 million. This figure comes out to $62,000 per day, or $280,250 per game played at a new stadium.

"Every day they would play a baseball game in a new stadium, you would be taking seven police officers off the streets," says State Sen. John Kelly. He says it costs the City of Detroit about $40,000 to deploy each police officer. In 1991 the city laid off hundreds of police officers because of budget deficits.

Frank Rashid has no trouble coming up with a long list of items more deserving of government money than a new baseball stadium. "We have this sad infrastructure — roads and streets that go unpaved," he says. "The school system. The block upon block of abandoned, un-vital, poorly planned-out streets. An infant mortality rate that's a national disgrace. Problems with kids on dope. We have this crime problem in this town with young males, and we have just a piss-poor recreation program for kids. I can't send my kid to an organized sports league in Detroit. All the kids in our neighborhood go to Ferndale. In other cities, and certainly in suburban communities, they have all these wonderful advantages — all this publicly funded stuff that keeps kids off the streets, and gives them something to do."

On August 16, 1991, Detroit's recreation director, Dan Krichbaum, proposed closing eight of the city's thirty-two recreation centers because of budget cuts. Krichbaum also said the department would have to cut in half the city's swimming, gymnastics, boxing and basket-ball programs, and the summer playground program; close the Nature Center and all refreshment stands on Belle Isle, the city's foremost park; eliminate ice skating at Hart Plaza and reduce other outdoor skating programs; slash programs for senior citizens; and stop regular cleaning and mowing of seventy to eighty small play lots for children.

"Recreation has been hacked almost to death as it is," responded Jim Frazer, director of Cass Corridor Youth Advocates. "They don't have much going for kids now, compared to years past. Obviously, there's going to be more kids on the street, more who get hooked up with the dope people when they have no other place to go."

"We are shortchanging the youth in Detroit," says Roberts of F.O.C.U.S. "Nothing tells them that they're important. We're going to take their neighborhood, take their schools, waste public money on a new stadium, and not blink an eye at it."

Not only do Detroit's children lack recreation programs. The city's schools suffer from lack of money and a host of other problems. "We haven't built a new school in almost twenty years in this city," notes the

Reverend Jim Holley. "And yet you're asking our kids to compete. The suburban communities get something like about $5,600 per kid. We're at $1,800 to $2,100 per kid. And you want our kids to compete?"

In those ever-expanding suburbs, millions of dollars are spent to duplicate the wasted resources of the inner city. City streets, utilities, churches, schools, houses, and businesses have been abandoned and left to decay; the same things are built anew in the outer reaches of suburbia. Developers make money and public investments in the city are discarded.

"If you study the whole history of wealth in this country," says Rashid, "you see how an Al Taubman can become respected, because he has acquired wealth. But the way he's done it is by raping and pillaging the city, destroying the environment, building hideous malls all over southeastern Michigan."

Taubman, a wealthy developer, in the summer of 1991 was an envoy for Mayor Young in negotiations over a new stadium deal with Wayne County officials and the Tigers. The mayor, in office since 1973, has shown a penchant for tearing down and rebuilding the urban landscape. Young "has a kind of big-project mentality for what he thinks will revitalize the city," says Bess. "Obviously the best, or worst, example of that is the Renaissance Center, and its fortresslike quality. While it's certainly an icon on the Detroit skyline, it hasn't had the kind of positive economic impact on the city that everyone thought it would."

Does a city measure its vitality by the number of glitzy new buildings it can put up, or by the care it takes in preserving its heritage and its common ground?

"Tiger Stadium is clearly one of the good things about downtown Detroit," says Bess. "It's one of the things that people have a genuine affection for and a continuing loyalty towards. For whatever reasons, a lot of people and businesses apparently have just given up on Detroit and taken off. If Detroit is to continue functioning as a city, it has to have things in it that people care about enough to stay and invest in. If there is broad public support for renovating Tiger Stadium through the Cochrane Plan, or even another plan that would in any case cost substantially less money than a new stadium, it seems to me that's a very good reason to renovate."

In the film *Baseball's Heirlooms*, Chicago sportswriter Bill Gleason says, referring to the decision to replace Comiskey Park: "In Europe they preserve . . . their magnificent old buildings, but here we tear down everything. If we had a civilized society, these people would be sent to prison."

Explaining his desire to see Tiger Stadium renovated rather than replaced, structural engineer Robert Darvas says: "A nation that does not take seriously its history does not have much of a future either."

Nor a city.

CHAPTER 19

THE PEOPLE'S CONSENT

It would be just plain wrong to stand by and allow hundreds of millions of dollars to go into an unwanted, unneeded playfield for millionaires, when our children have so few clean, safe places to play.

— Frank Rashid

Tiger Tale Number 8: It's a done deal.

On July 25, 1991, *Detroit News* columnist George Cantor gushed over the grand entrance of wealthy developer Al Taubman into the political dogfight between Ed McNamara and Coleman Young over who would control a new stadium project.

"Al Taubman sat down at the table and suddenly there was no longer any doubt," wrote Cantor, a former Cochrane Plan supporter wooed successfully by Michael Duggan. "There will be a new stadium and one way or another it will be built in Detroit.

"If Taubman is in it far enough to be visible, it will be done. This is the one guy who can bang heads together and make it happen. He has the money and he has the marbles."

Two days later, the front page of the combined *News* and *Free Press* Saturday edition showed a huge picture of Young and McNamara grinning. They had just emerged from behind closed doors and announced a deal to form a city-county stadium authority. The message was clear: The people in power have decided. The deal is done. Tiger Stadium is gone.

The same columns had been written twenty years earlier. Politicians and developers were shaking hands and smiling. The deal had been cut.

255

There would be a new domed stadium on the riverfront—and it would revive downtown Detroit.

Plans in the early 1970s were much further along. The bonds to finance the stadium were ready to be sold. The site had been picked, the land had been acquired, the Tigers had signed a lease. There was no significant public opposition. There would be no vote of the people.

A few people filed a lawsuit, and the deal collapsed in weeks. Detroit never got its dome on the riverfront, and Tiger Stadium was saved.

This time around, the sell job is much harder. The experience of the seventies and eighties has made taxpayers wary of financing new stadiums. A well-organized and articulate opposition got the jump on the dealmakers. Those in power have failed to convince the public that the stadium is falling down. The Tiger Stadium Fan Club has demonstrated that renovation is feasible with the Cochrane Plan, and Gunnar Birkerts and Joe O'Neal have proposed another creative solution.

The Tigers and their public apologists have had limited success in selling taxpayers on a new stadium. The campaign to exaggerate the problems involved with the stadium's posts has been balanced by the fan club's success in publicizing Tiger Stadium's closest seats in baseball. Bo Schembechler's complaints about the Tigers needing a new stadium to be competitive have been met with plenty of healthy skepticism. And although some citizens do fear the stadium neighborhood and dislike the parking situation, most pin the blame for low attendance on the team's performance and the misguided policies of Tiger management.

The Tigers' public image plummeted so low after the firing of Ernie Harwell and Schembechler's belligerent new-stadium campaign that many citizens were wishing the Tigers a hearty "good riddance." Detroit City Council President Maryann Mahaffey said Schembechler's bullying tactics amounted to blackmail: "This is nothing but Bo and his machismo, whatever-I-want-I-get attitude. This is the power of money, that means you all have to knuckle under and kowtow. I think it's just the height of arrogance."

Many voters felt the same way. Stanley Jeziak of Dearborn Heights wrote the *News* a letter that was typical of dozens of others:

> The city of Detroit can't pick up its garbage, light its streets, or give police protection to its residents but is going to build a $200 million stadium so that millionaire performers can get their exercise and the

Tigers' owner can get even richer?. . . Spare the taxpayers. Let the Tigers go to Florida.

Officials argued that a new stadium would provide great economic benefits, but many people saw it as nothing more than glorified pickpocketing.

"Schembechler says the Tigers need a new stadium with plenty of parking, fenced, lighted, safe from crime, hard by a freeway — ergo, the Briggs site," wrote *Detroit News* columnist Nickie McWhirter on August 4, 1991.

> He says this will assure that the Tigers are "competitive."
> He doesn't say such a stadium so located will make it possible for the Tiger organization to reap parking revenues it has never before enjoyed, money now spread among Corktown entrepreneurs. He doesn't say that isolating baseball fans from downtown and nearby restaurants and bars will encourage them to eat and drink their fill in stadium refreshment centers, profiting the Tigers organization. He doesn't say that private suites and services will further enrich Tiger coffers or that the only competition he's talking about is competition for discretionary income — yours and mine.

On August 16, 1991, the *Free Press* summarized the public mood with an article headlined: RESENTMENT RISES ABOUT PAYING FOR A NEW STADIUM. "They're lighting up the lines of radio call-in shows, deluging newspapers with letters and besieging the offices of county politicians," wrote reporter William Kleinknecht. "They all have opinions about Tiger Stadium — and most of them are mad as hell. Grass-roots opposition to public financing for a new stadium seems to be mounting, and some experts say a botched public relations job by the Tigers and government officials must take its share of the blame."

Quips Frank Rashid of the Tiger Stadium Fan Club: "Tigers' public relations is an oxymoron."

Despite the relentless efforts of Wayne County officials and the local media's acquiescence in the campaign to squelch renovation, the public remained unconvinced. According to a scientific survey by Nordhaus Research published in the *News* of August 7, 1991, forty-seven percent of people polled in metropolitan Detroit still preferred renovating Tiger Stadium, and forty-one percent wanted to build a new stadium.

Support for renovation had fallen significantly, and no wonder:

Detroit's two newspapers and its major TV and radio stations had failed to investigate the arguments made by Duggan and BEI Associates dismissing renovation. The reports that had greased the skids for a new stadium deal were not scrutinized at all by the media. After the release of BEI's documents, nearly every story on the topic began from the premise that a new stadium was a fait accompli.

The argument that a new stadium is a done deal appears to be the last refuge of scoundrels. It enervates real debate over the merits of the arguments for saving or replacing the stadium. It convinces those not well versed in the issue that the battle is over. The "done deal" propaganda is the most crucial element of the stadium scam; it is the assault on hope. When people feel there is no hope, they lose their will to fight.

But even though the power brokers said the deal was done, and the media told the public what to think, the battle for Tiger Stadium was far from over when Young and McNamara shook hands.

Before the deal is done, the people must consent. Voters have to go along with the plan to give public money to Tom Monaghan to build an expensive new stadium and to tear down a national landmark.

Will fans agree to pay ticket surcharges for the next twenty-five years to help finance a baseball mall and wipe out a ballpark that holds their cherished memories? Will taxpayers approve a deal that could leave them holding the check when projected revenues don't cover the cost of construction of a new stadium? Can the Tigers break their lease with the City of Detroit? Will bond buyers be interested in a stadium bond issue if legal challenges are pending? Can the city find money and public support to acquire and clear the land for a new stadium?

In September 1991 an effort to guarantee the public the final say over the fate of Tiger Stadium was launched by the Common Ground Coalition, an amalgam of community groups including the Tiger Stadium Fan Club. The coalition began collecting signatures on petitions to put a proposal on the Detroit ballot to enforce the Tigers' lease with the city and to renovate Tiger Stadium. If passed, the initiative would give the citizens of Detroit the sole power to decide if and when to allow the Tigers to break their legal commitment to the ballpark.

As the 1991 season closed, the "done deal" was unraveling. On October 2, Bo Schembechler rejected two Detroit stadium sites proposed by public officials. Schembechler claimed the Tigers had been "dictated to" and said the club would now "start over" and entertain

258

offers from all comers in city and suburbs. "Frankly, it's almost like we've been kicked out of the city," he said.

As the negotiations degenerated into name-calling, several key arguments for a new stadium were collapsing. The idea that a new stadium would provide economic benefits for Detroit suffered a one-two punch. First, county officials and developers, trying to sell the public and the Tigers on their preferred site in the theater district downtown, reversed field and admitted that a new stadium in the Briggs Community surrounded by a huge parking lot would not spark economic development, even with the aid of an enterprise zone. Then Schembechler lashed out at the notion that putting the stadium in the theater district would revitalize downtown.

"There's a way to save the city but it's not through a baseball stadium," Schembechler told reporters. "That stadium is not going to bring business into your city. . . . Stadiums don't do that. That isn't the purpose of stadiums."

Asked by reporters why taxpayers should pay for a new stadium if it didn't bring economic benefits, Schembechler replied: "There's a tremendous pride in having a professional team in your town."

Many saw Schembechler's rejection of the Detroit sites as a way to pave the Tigers' way out of the city. Ed McNamara again began warning of the prospect of the Tigers moving out of Michigan, but Schembechler denied that was a possibility. "We're not leaving Michigan," he said. "I mean, not unless we're kicked out." Interviewed on WJBK-TV, American League President Bobby Brown said the league wanted the Tigers to stay in Michigan and would not approve a move out of state.

Michael Duggan, who a few months earlier had bragged the Tigers' 30-year lease with the city would be easy to break, now joined McNamara and Mayor Young in vowing to take the club to court if necessary to block any move out of the city. Officials even threatened to challenge baseball's anti-trust exemption. These pledges undercut the very blackmail threats Duggan and other officials had made earlier on the Tigers' behalf. If there were so many ways to force the team to stay in Detroit, why was it necessary for taxpayers to give the ball club a new stadium?

The open squabbling between Schembechler and county officials further jeopardized the chances of selling the public on bankrolling a new ballpark. Columnist Pete Waldmeir warned in the October 4 *News* that the players in the stadium debate were "approaching very, very thin ice." "People who once were passive about the new stadium and

259

the regressive taxes it inevitably will engender have been aroused by all the clamor," he wrote.

In a phone poll taken that day, WJR radio asked listeners whether they would support a hotel/motel tax and a restaurant tax to build a new stadium for the Tigers. The result: no, 177; yes, 17.

Tiger Stadium Fan Club leaders remain confident that public support for Tiger Stadium will prevent the destruction of a national treasure. In a 1991 speech Frank Rashid said: "We have little patience with those who say a new stadium is a done deal, or that nothing can be done to stop the wealthy, powerful people who would continue the wasteful, regressive legacy of disruption and destruction which have so marred this city and region. We have no patience with those who would simply give in and make Tom Monaghan the number one welfare recipient in the state, when our infants and children are going hungry, when our schools cry out for support, when drug abuse, homelessness and crime go unchecked. It would be just plain wrong to stand by and allow hundreds of millions of public dollars to go into an unwanted, unneeded playfield for millionaires, when our children have so few clean, safe places to play."

Without the people's consent, there is no done deal.

CHAPTER 20

BALLPARK VOICES

From interviews, public statements, newspaper and magazine articles, and the video *Baseball's Heirlooms*, here's what some notable and some ordinary people say about Tiger Stadium:

Former Tiger pitcher HANK AGUIRRE: It's a great stadium. The upper deck in right field is really my favorite spot. The ball flies out of there. I've seen a lot of facing home runs, and obviously over-the-roof home runs. I don't really think it's a big trick to hit it over the roof. Most people don't realize that the upper deck extends out into the playing field.

Retired financial analyst and consultant MARC J. ALAN of Grosse Pointe: These are critical times. People are hurting. The state has budget problems, the city has budget problems, and we're talking about building a new stadium? We'd do better to preserve some of Detroit's heritage.

Tiger manager SPARKY ANDERSON: We absolutely must have a new stadium if we expect to compete financially with Toronto and the Yankees. Sooner or later, everything becomes history. That's where old stadiums belong, in the history books.

I loved playing in Boston, but I would look those people straight in the eye and tell them they are being cheated by not having a new facility like Toronto and Comiskey.

New Yorker editor and baseball writer ROGER ANGELL: It's a wonderful example of a downtown urban park. One reason I feel apprehensive about the possible loss of Tiger Stadium is I don't trust baseball management to come up with something better. Whatever they come up with may be new and clean but it'll probably be worse. The people who build these new parks, they haven't thought much about what makes a ballpark wonderful.

One reason I'm suspicious about what management tends to go for is that there's always an attempt to gentrify baseball, to make it suburban, to make it safe and clean, to upscale the audience. The notion is we're going to get a better grade of fans, more affluent, a family crowd. I don't think that's necessarily true.

I don't think baseball should be dressed up. It should be easily accessible to fans of every level in our society.

Chicago architect and ballpark consultant PHILIP BESS: Tiger Stadium has grown by accretion, and you've got all kinds of very strange stuff going on on the outside: the vertical circulation, and the ramps on the outside hanging off of it, that are quite interesting, but not elegant. It's not an elegant kind of place. It's very authentic. It's a gritty, unique place with absolutely its own character and identity.

WALTER O. BRIGGS IV: I took my oldest son to his first game two years ago; he was three at the time. For six innings he was riveted to his seat — and we were sitting up behind a post, so they were not great seats. I tried to explain to him about when the stadium was built and all that. And now he asks me, "Can I go to my stadium?" I would hope that he would have the opportunity to have that kind of experience, to take his child.

Detroiter DAVID BROOKS: It's the best sports bargain in town. Four bucks to come to a major league sporting event just doesn't happen anywhere else. What's the cheapest Pistons seat right now?

Michigan Avenue peanut vendor MAJOR BROOKS: I think the worst person who could possibly have ever bought this team would be Monaghan. Anybody that's ever listened to the Tigers when they was a kid, and grew up listening to Ernie Harwell, couldn't possibly fire a man like that.

I think what they really could do is stay right here. They could renovate the stadium, and stay right here. Every time they get a spot they want to go, like in Dearborn, they don't want them. Out here in the Briggs Community, they don't want them.

Schembechler made this statement, right in the newspaper! He said that he wants customers, not fans. Now what kind of statement is that?

Tiger Stadium Fan Club member BOB BUCHTA: It is hardly in our interests to destroy a treasured baseball landmark in the name of luxury boxes, more expensive tickets, and high-priced parking and then ask taxpayers to foot the bill.

Congressman and former Tiger pitcher JIM BUNNING: Tiger Stadium ought to be used until it can't be used any more. I think it's a great place to watch a baseball game.

Ontario native ALEX CLUNIS: I've been a Tiger fan ever since I was a little kid.

When I take my kids, or Eva takes her nephews, she'll say, "I was here with your grandfather. We were in these seats; we were right here." And that's important to little kids. That's a real thrill for them: "I'm sitting in the same seat that my grandpa sat in, fifty years ago."

I've been in construction a long time now. Don't tell me you can put up a stadium for $135 million. You have to allow fifty percent right off the top for graft, greed, corruption, and general mismanagement of funds.

Actor JEFF DANIELS: It's a living, breathing museum of baseball history. In here, the ghosts of baseball's past mingle with the stars of today.

Longtime Tiger fan CATHERINE DARIN: I personally would prefer that they would just leave the stadium alone. I don't need suites and I don't like the idea of having suites around the stadium to accommodate people. If people want to watch baseball that way, it's up to them, and I suppose they can talk about baseball or whatever they want, but when you look at the boxes that are here now, they don't seem to be paying much attention to the ball game.

DETROIT FREE PRESS, *in an editorial on March 18, 1989:* One of the most truly unalloyed pleasures of a Michigan summer is a trip to Tiger Stadium. It looks like a ball field, it smells like a ball field, it enhances

263

the game. The country is full of plastic sports theaters. This region already has too many of them, too many built at public expense. The community has many needs that seem to command greater concern than a new or expensively renovated stadium.

Attorney BILL DOW: One of the biggest highlights of my whole life was the first time I entered Tiger Stadium. I was seven years old; it was 1962. It was a game against the Baltimore Orioles. Sad Sam Jones was pitching for the Tigers against Milt Pappas. Kaline was my hero. My only disappointment that game was that he was out with a broken collarbone, so I just saw him on the dugout steps. It was a real hot day. Norm Cash hit a long home run.

What really hit me was when I entered the stands I saw the green seats, the stark white uniforms, the green grass. It was such a beautiful thing to behold. Every time after that, whenever I would drive down Michigan Avenue, I could see those huge light standards and I'd just get so excited with anticipation.

Wayne County deputy executive MICHAEL DUGGAN, speaking to the Detroit City Council: Renovation of the existing stadium is the sentimental choice, but when it comes to spending taxpayer money in a responsible manner, renovation cannot be justified.

VICKI DUTTON of Petaluma, California: The thing I like about this stadium is that it doesn't have luxury boxes. It's more of a stadium for the people. In other stadiums, it's very difficult to get tickets; if you can get them, they're not necessarily the best seats. Those are always saved for companies.

MICHAEL FUNKE of Detroit: It's a great stadium. What other stadium has got double-deck bleachers? Nobody. Where else can I park three blocks away for nothing?

What Monaghan wants to do is to build another SkyDome. He just wants to make more bucks off of people, make it much more difficult for working-class people to make it to the ball game.

JOHN GRINDSTAFF of Detroit: There's nowhere in baseball where you can be in the upper deck and be this close to the play. There is no center field in baseball deeper than Tiger Stadium, yet in the bleachers you're still on top of the play—because of the way the ballpark's built. In order to do that, you've got to have poles. You hear Bo and everybody talking about these posts. Well, you've got to take the bitter with the sweet. In order to be on top of the game, you've got to have the poles.

I've been coming here for forty years, and I may not ever come back. If they build one like they built in Chicago, or Atlanta, or Cincinnati, or Pittsburgh, they won't see me. Because I've been there. That's no fun.

Tiger Senior Vice President/Planning and Operations WILLIAM E. HAASE: I love this ballpark as much as anybody. But I also realize, from working with the ball club as long as I've been here, that there are shortcomings. And it does present some problems when it comes to upkeep, and the enormous expenditure that we're continuing to see grow and grow and grow.

Tiger broadcaster ERNIE HARWELL: Tiger Stadium and the other ballparks that we see like it, I think, have character, not like the cookie cutters at some of the ballparks that you see. You don't know whether you are in Atlanta or Pittsburgh or Cincinnati or Des Moines or whatever; they're all designed alike.

In the older ballparks like Tiger Stadium, the fans are down close. They can see the guy sweat and hear him cuss. They're right on him, and they feel like they're in the game. And it's a more intimate feeling that they have of the players and the game. And I think it's great that these old parks can still stand up.

Tiger fan DOUG JEROME *of Midland, Michigan*: To me it's a gorgeous stadium. I'd hate to see it go. I don't know why they think they have to get something else. They renovated it, and to me there's nothing wrong with it.

Tiger Hall of Famer AL KALINE: There's nothing like playing in the old ballparks. The backgrounds are great, and there's some history to it. The fields are all different.

Tiger Hall of Famer GEORGE KELL: This is important, that the people be a part of the game. I like for the people to be right on top. I like to hear the people. At Tiger Stadium at third base, I could hear everything that was said over there. One day Hal Newhouser was pitching. He was getting rocked by the Boston club. He came over to back up third base,

265

and some fan was getting on him real good. And I said: "Hang in there, Hal. Don't worry about that guy." And I heard the guy say: "You're not doing too good yourself, Kell."

You name me any other city in America that's been through the trials and tribulations, the unemployment problems, that this city has . . . but yet they keep flocking to Tiger Stadium. And we say, "Well, they won't draw as well next year. They can't. They've got twenty to twenty-five percent unemployment." But they still come to Tiger Stadium. It is without a doubt one of the great sports cities of America.

Best-selling author ELMORE LEONARD: We always sat in the grandstands between home and third. Now, it would be section 217, reserved. Then it was the grandstands, and tickets were a buck-ten.

It's a real ballpark. The location has never bothered me. I've always liked the fact that you can get in and out of there so fast. Whereas at the Silverdome, or the Palace, you're stuck.

Detroit City Council president MARYANN MAHAFFEY: It would be ridiculous to replace it. It's a good stadium. Where else can you get this close to the field?

Former U.S. senator EUGENE McCARTHY: I'm generally inclined to always stay with the old parks. . . . If you have an old one, I don't think a new one does that much good.

Wayne County Executive ED McNAMARA, speaking to the Detroit City Council: The Tigers' bottom line is to make sure that they operate in a profitable way, and in the present facility that they now have, that is an impossibility.

Tiger owner TOM MONAGHAN: I've been the one in favor of the old stadium, but I keep getting beaten down with logic.

Corktown resident PAT MULDOON: People who work at the concession stands, or park cars, wouldn't be able to even get to another site, if it were to move out of here. A lot of people would lose their jobs if it were moved.

This enterprise zone, and this hoopla about the proposed "ethnic village" and all that, is smoke and mirrors. What we'll end up with is like Comiskey: You'll have a brand-new ballpark with a nice, big parking lot around it.

Parking lot attendant MARIO MUSCAT: I really like this old ballpark. I'd like to see them keep it. Anywhere you sit in the ballpark, you have a good seat. I've been to other ballparks where, face it, you need binoculars to sit in box seats.

Legal secretary EVA NAVARRO: My dad introduced me to baseball, the Tigers, Tiger Stadium. I don't think that we could have developed this close relationship if it hadn't been for Tiger Stadium—going to the games, the fun, the excitement, the sharing.

One day I was sitting in the upper-deck bleachers with my nephews, and the younger one, who was about nine at the time, turned to his brother and said, "You know, David? *Ty Cobb* played here." Kids appreciate these things. They know what we have. They'd like to keep coming.

We all know, if they build a new stadium, what that means. They're going to kill the tradition that we grew up with, the closeness of the field, and the intimacy of Tiger Stadium. You'll never get that in a new park, never.

They say that you build a new stadium, give them time, they'll forget, they'll come back. That's not true. We know what we have now, and there's no way that they could build one better. That's why we fight so hard to keep what we have.

Tiger Senior Vice President/Marketing and Communications JEFF ODENWALD: I think the best seats in the house are the upper-deck box seats. You can find me hiding up there quite often. . . . I like to walk up there. It's a great vantage point.

The family of four can still walk in here for a minimum of sixteen bucks. You can still walk into Tiger Stadium and not be sitting where you've got to phone your part in, but you can sit right there behind the left fielder or the center fielder or the right fielder, and you only have to pay four bucks.

DAVE OSINSKI *of* Warren: You can't get closer to the field than here. It's a real nice stadium. All it needs is proper maintenance.

I went to a game a couple years ago in San Diego. We had second-row box seats behind the plate, and it was in the third deck. And hell,

267

you are so far away. They're supposed to be good seats, but it's like looking at an ant in the batter's box.

These are probably the best seats in the upper deck, first base side. I can't imagine getting better seats than this. You're so close to the field, even in the bleachers, and it's the deepest center field in the leagues. You're still right on top of the action. You just can't beat it.

Architecture critic JOHN PASTIER: For baseball fans, Tiger Stadium is as sacred as a secular place can be. It is steeped in history and tradition. . . . Moving would destroy eighty-nine years of continuity, and fans and players alike would lose their tangible link to Ty Cobb and dozens of other legends, as well as Babe Ruth and hundreds of other visiting greats. Their presence suffuses Tiger Stadium, and cannot be transferred to a new location.

DENNIS PREWOZNIAK of Midland: You come to the game, and you think about all the great players that were here, all the Hall of Famers. You like to see the old stadium, and you like to see what it was like where the old greats used to play. I mean, Mickey Mantle played here.

Marygrove College Professor FRANK RASHID: Great cities retain a connection with their past. They build on it, they profit from it, they don't destroy that connection. If you're talking about building a great city, or even a viable one, the city will have to hang on to its past. And there is no single building that is more linked with the past of this town than Tiger Stadium. Losing it would be a great, great loss.

Too often in the past, the people of this city and region have remained silent while their lives were disrupted, their history destroyed, their tax dollars wasted—all in the name of something called "progress."

The auto companies called it "progress" when they urged the city to replace its quaint, efficient streetcars with ugly, wasteful buses. Planners told us it was "progress" to tear down old city hall and replace it with the disaster known as Kennedy Square. In the name of "progress," factories and freeways have supplanted distinctive old neighborhoods and uprooted their residents with little or no payoff to the city and its people.

Developers have invoked "progress" to destroy much of the natural environment of southeastern Michigan, while they profited from the abandonment of the central city. Obviously, we need a new definition of progress.

Singer MIKE RIDLEY: My dad once said, "The thing about this ballpark is that you can smell it two blocks away." You can smell the popcorn and the cigar smoke. You can hear the crack of the bat and the rumbling and the murmur of fans as they're walking in. You feel it before you actually go into the ballpark, before you see it, sometimes. You'd park the car and start walking toward the stadium, and you could smell the concession stands.

One of my memories of the ballpark is that some man was smoking a cigar. It seems like whenever I smell a cigar somewhere, I always think of Tiger Stadium.

New York writer CARL ROLLYSON: In a new stadium, a so-called modern or contemporary stadium, there just wouldn't be any of those peculiarities, those angles, the sense of closeness to the field, that you get in something like Tiger Stadium.

I wouldn't want to see the Detroit Institute of Arts moved out to Pontiac, just so that they could have a better parking facility or whatever, or the Detroit Public Library.

Kansas City Royals pitcher BRET SABERHAGEN: I think if you face-lift it, and give it some upgrades, it could be around for a while. If you go back and you think about the Polo Grounds and Ebbets Field, things that were great stadiums at one time, and they're torn down now, you can't see them no longer, all you can do is see pictures of them.

The Cochrane Plan is done very well. If you improve the stadium, people are going to come out and want to see the new additions.

My first win was against the Tigers, here, so I have some fond memories of Tiger Stadium. I think it's a good pitcher's ballpark, and it's a great hitter's ballpark as well. You have a lot of home runs. Fans want to come out and see some home runs hit, and they're going to see them when they come out to games here.

Tiger president BO SCHEMBECHLER: The Detroit Pistons play in a new facility that's second to none. The Detroit Lions are not playing in Tiger Stadium. They're playing in Pontiac. I don't see the Detroit Red Wings playing in Olympia. They're playing in beautiful Joe Louis Arena.

There's only one team that's playing in an old facility, and it's unfair for you to think that you can shackle us to a rusted girder in Tiger Stadium and expect us to compete and win, because it's not going to happen.

It's obvious to us we can't continue to function here. It's a losing proposition. We can't generate the money we need to insure a good baseball team that's going to compete.

Any money you put in here you're wasting. It's been proven that these old stadiums are not going to last. This has been one of the last ones to stand. By the end of this decade, Fenway Park and Wrigley Field will be gone. *Gone*.

Retired dentist DON SHAPIRO: A new stadium, I think, would appeal to grown-ups a lot more than to children, and I don't think the kinds of stadiums they build now are designed to have any magic. It's hard to get excited about chrome and carpeting and stuff. You're surrounded by it all the time, so it's not different from anyplace else you go.

But Tiger Stadium is different from places you go now. It's part of the charm of an old stadium that it is something out of the past. You don't enter stadiums anymore through cavernous, cement corridors.

We don't have much that's old anymore. We just have stuff that's broken down in Detroit. Very typically, somebody bought an old restaurant on Jefferson, called Little Harry's. It was one of the earliest examples of early French architecture. It was designated a landmark. But the new owners tore it down anyway, in the middle of the night. That happens all the time in Detroit.

Tearing down Tiger Stadium would be taking the last jujube away from the kid. We have what someone once called a dwindling portfolio of pleasures in Detroit. There isn't much left for us in Detroit. There are very few things that Detroit can rally around. The Tigers and Ernie Harwell mean a great deal.

Comedian THOM SHARP: The park is in the wrong hands. It's too bad. If you love baseball, how can you not love that ballpark, and want to see it saved and used? You know, when you have a guy who makes pizzas and another guy whose main job in life for twenty years was bullying nineteen-year-old kids, you've got great baseball men.

It's like a sick grandmother. "We can save her with this operation." And they go, "Nah, forget it." "Wait a minute! All she needs is this operation." "Yeah, I know. Nah, forget it. We'll get another grandma.

One that brings in more money and one where you can park under her."

I just can't figure it out. They have their minds made up. They are looking for all the reasons not to renovate it rather than reasons to do it. No one could build a theater like the Fox now, or the Fisher Theater or Orchestra Hall. And they are renovating other places. I don't understand why they can't say, "Hey! Let's do that with Tiger Stadium!"

Former Belleville mayor ROYCE SMITH: Billionaire ball team owners pay ball players two or three million a year; they ought to build their own stadium. It's still taxpayers' money for private enterprise. The Tigers I don't think are going anyplace. They should pay their own way.

Chicago-based comedian and former Detroiter TIM SLAGLE: Comiskey Park is a tragedy. I was there last year, I saw one game. I figured I had to see the park. There was nothing wrong with it. It was a little worn in spots. We were sitting in right field, and it was kind of funny, because the wall was pebbled; it was not smooth concrete, as you see now. At the top, near the rail, it was worn, shiny, smooth. Those rocks had been worn smooth by eighty or ninety years of people jumping up when they saw a ball hit, wanting to see if it was a home run. That's the kind of history that was just destroyed.

I went by it just about a week ago [July 1991]. They've been tearing it down for about three months. They have only half the stadium removed. Isn't it funny that they were telling the politicians that that stadium was ready to fall down at any moment?

Detroit Free Press *columnist* BOB TALBERT: A new stadium's larger concourses would allow for better and faster concession areas and the Tigers surely would expand the menu to include hamburgers, chicken and other items sold in competing stadiums.

Tiger Stadium is not user-friendly. But the new stadium the Tigers have in mind will be. Count on that.

Securities broker BRIAN TREMAIN: I'm enamored with the stadium. More importantly, since I came to Detroit in 1978, it's obvious to me that the city has very few jewels left in its crown. And the ones that have had grassroots movements, some of them have been able to be saved, most importantly Orchestra Hall. I got involved in that on day one.

271

We have so little fabric left in Detroit, and we have to save these pieces of fabric, so there's some tie-in to the past, some reason to come back, and to feel good about coming back to Detroit.

DR. EDWARD TURNER of Southfield: The Tigers, you see, don't belong to the Tigers. The Tigers belong to Detroit. They belong to the people. The stadium does not belong to the owner. The stadium belongs to the people. The only thing he's got are the ball players, and everybody knows ball players go and come. So what has he got? Nothing.

This involves tremendous taxes, a new stadium, tremendous taxes for something that is unnecessary, something that is to my way of thinking a monstrosity. Tiger Stadium is one of the greatest works of art, one of the greatest pieces of beauty, one of the most wonderful structures in the world.

Tiger Stadium Fan Club stalwart PATTY WARNER of Flint: The first time I went to Tiger Stadium was in 1985. To walk out and see all that grass, it was a magical experience. I was envious of the people who lived down there who could drive right across town to see a game. To be a Detroiter, to grow up with that ballpark, to hear all the wonderful stories about going to the game with your dad and granddad — what a great thing!

UAW member RANDY WESTBROOKS of Milan, Michigan: People in the past haven't appreciated great things like this until they're gone. And then they say, "I wish it was here. I wish it hadn't been destroyed."

They have some asinine notion that the facilities here aren't good for the players, and they can't do anything to improve it. They think the parking's bad. And they can't put in these expensive boxes with people paying ninety thousand dollars a year to have this box to entertain clients. It's not built for that. This was a ballpark built for working people, for working fans to come and walk in here and watch the Tigers play.

The Cochrane Plan is a viable plan. I feel like it wasn't given a real fair chance. The management of the Detroit Tigers had made their mind up that they wanted a new stadium, and they weren't going to accept anything less than that. They didn't look at renovation.

It's part of the American mystique: bigger, better. New is better than old, and it's more important to have a new, cookie-cutter stadium.

272

This field has personality of its own. This is part of the city, it's part of Michigan.

Political commentator GEORGE F. WILL: Tiger Stadium is a national treasure. I'm big on historic preservation generally. It's not like Monticello, where you can't change it and alter it and adapt it, but an awful lot of happy human experiences have occurred there, and you shouldn't casually discard it.

I can't speak to the urban effects — whether it anchors a neighborhood or is good for the city. I imagine it does both, but I can't prove that. I don't need to prove that, however, to make a sufficient case for preserving Tiger Stadium. You do not casually knock down something that much woven in with a city's and an industry's history.

Detroit mayor COLEMAN YOUNG: We're rebuilding a new city and there comes a time when we need a new stadium. And the only question before us is whether it's now, five years from now or ten years from now. Nobody in their wildest dreams expects that stadium to last beyond ten years. Most people say it will fall down in five. . . .

I think we need a new stadium. The old one, for all its nostalgic reminiscence, is about to fall down.

CONCLUSION

HEADING HOME

Tiger Stadium isn't fancy. There are no exploding scoreboards, cascading waterfalls, Hard Rock cafes, or ivied walls. You can't stay overnight, buy egg rolls, or sip martinis while swinging business deals during pitching changes. All you can do is watch baseball. During this century, that's what nearly 100 million people have done at Michigan and Trumbull.

Tiger Stadium's virtues are pedestrian: The seats are close to the field. Baseball is on center stage. Tradition fills every nook and cranny. The field is green and real and open to the sky.

Many say it is the best baseball park in the world.

"Unlike the ivy-clad perfection of Wrigley Field or the self-congratulatory ugliness of Fenway Park, 79-year-old Tiger Stadium represents the last remaining link with baseball before it became too self-conscious," wrote *Time*'s Walter Shapiro. "No park provides more of the sensual joys of the game itself. On a clear night, fans can hear the crack of the bat, the infield chatter and even the ball hitting the catcher's mitt in the Tiger bullpen down the third-base line."

Tiger Stadium is full of simple sounds, simple pleasures — sounds and pleasures that are fast disappearing behind the smoke and mirrors of orchestrated spectacle. Toronto's SkyDome bills itself as the "world's greatest entertainment center." Baseball games are played in the world's greatest entertainment center, but it's a little hard to see them from the fifth deck. Instead, you can watch the players' faces on TV, relax in the health spa, or go to a singles bar.

Too modern for your taste? Try Baltimore. Nostalgia is big business there. The Orioles' new stadium has an archway and brick walls that make it look like a real old-fashioned ballpark. There's even a warehouse beyond the right-field fence. Maryland's taxpayers are paying tens of millions of dollars a year for this fake antique. In return, they're getting a park where every upper deck seat is farther from the field than the most remote comparable seat at Tiger Stadium.

Tradition can't be manufactured. A heritage can't be imitated. No new ballpark could duplicate the spunky, gritty charm of Tiger Stadium. The place reeks of hot dogs, beer, and roasted peanuts. At a game, if you close your eyes and listen to the chatter on the field and the buzz of the crowd, you can easily imagine the stands filled with men in bowlers and ladies carrying parasols.

But Tiger Stadium's past represents only a part of its great worth. Today, there simply is no better place to watch big league baseball. Tiger Stadium has the closest seats and the fewest distractions. The huge, high circle of stands creates a grand interior world in an outdoor space. In that world, fans can share an intense common experience.

Detroiters know how to fashion an impressive product out of carefully orchestrated individual efforts. The city's favorite sport is a game where people in turn apply fine, delicate movements in a common purpose. The building that houses the town's game is a perfect metaphor for Detroit: sturdy, functional, enduring, inclusive, and accessible.

Metropolitan Detroit is a divided city. Within the space of a few miles are mansions of wealth and hovels of desperation. Race divides Detroiters. Class divides Detroiters. Culture and religion and geography and circumstance divide Detroiters. There is little common ground left.

But in Detroit there is still a place where people can unite. What happens inside the ballpark doesn't change the world outside. But inside there is a vision of a different world. In rare moments, there is common celebration of a dream come true, a triumph for all those who call themselves Detroiters.

It wouldn't be the same in a new ballpark. Modern stadiums don't bring people together. Their reason for being is to make money, and they do so by denying access to people who don't have the bucks and by assigning places according to status. In a new stadium, there would be few or no bleacher or cheap grandstand seats for teenagers, working families, and senior citizens on fixed incomes. Those without connections or corporate portfolios would find themselves sitting beyond the pale. The honchos in their luxury suites would hog all the good views.

The stadium scam has worked in city after city. The same lies have been told, the same threats have been made, the same promises have gone unfulfilled, and with the same results: The old parks gone. The cherished memories bulldozed. The common ground obliterated. Replaced by entertainment centers masquerading as ball fields. Wiped out for McStadiums with plastic fences and giant food malls and unobstructed seats in the stratosphere.

Places where a hero picked off third base would be met with the blank stares of vast indifference.

In Detroit the scam has met a more formidable foe. Tiger Stadium stands strong and proud. After four years of fighting, its defenders remain steadfast. They have something worth fighting for.

"I've been telling people Bo Schembechler is the Big, Bad Wolf," says Frank Rashid. "He huffs and he puffs but he can't blow it down, because we have the house made of bricks."

Much is at stake in the battle over Tiger Stadium. The fate of Fenway Park and Wrigley Field may hinge on what happens in Detroit. Detroit's own future will be shaped by the decision on whether to waste a treasured ballpark or preserve it, on whether to keep a common ground or shut out the average fan with another palace for the rich.

Baseball is the national pastime because we Americans have always felt the game is ours. In no remaining major league venue is that feeling more fully realized than in Tiger Stadium, the most accessible, the most democratic of ballparks.

"Through sport," wrote baseball commissioner Bart Giamatti just before his death in 1989, "we re-create our daily portion of freedom, in public."

That freedom rings down through the years at Michigan and Trumbull. From the days of the wildcat stands to the nights of the bleacher kazoos, baseball in Detroit has always been the people's game. And so it remains.

Afterword

SELF-INTEREST AND THE TIGER STADIUM FAN CLUB

Interviewed in the July 1991 issue of *Detroit Monthly* magazine, Tiger president Bo Schembechler had this to say about the Tiger Stadium Fan Club:

> Way overplayed for as much power as they wield. It's just too bad that you media people run to 'em, because there's a lot of self-interest there. They're not fans of the stadium or the ballclub. They represent themselves. They're all politically motivated. I think they want to run for some kind of office. The head of that outfit will be on the ballot before too long.

Schembechler does not allow for the possibility that the fan club's motives are sincere. He and his boss, Tom Monaghan, are such true believers in the American gospel of self-interest that they apparently cannot fathom how anyone could be motivated by anything else.

In February 1991 Tiger vice president Bill Haase, who had called the fan club's members "a bunch of parking-lot owners" — implying that they had a financial stake in the stadium's fate — told me: "I'm not looking into their motives. I think they're very sincere people, and I think they believe in what they're doing, but I don't think they see the whole picture either. . . . I love this ballpark as much as anybody, but I do see that at some point in time you've got to make some hard decisions that make sense."

Deputy Wayne County Executive Michael Duggan played the same patronizing tune in his June 5 report to his boss, Ed McNamara. Building a new stadium, he wrote, "is a painful decision, but we have got to be responsible with the tax dollars entrusted to us, even if the decision causes an emotional backlash among many baseball fans." Consideration of the renovation option, he said, was based on an "emotional attachment" to the old stadium, whereas the decision to replace it had been reached based on "objective facts." Never mind that a new stadium would cost in the hundreds of millions of public dollars; you're just being emotional.

Schembechler's *Detroit Monthly* claim could not be further from the mark. The fan club is a thoroughly likeable group of ordinary citizens whose only goal is to save the oldest and best stadium in baseball.

Frank Rashid, the fan club's most visible spokesperson, has often been taken to be the "head" of the "outfit." He comes from an extraordinary and extraordinarily close-knit, though far-flung, Lebanese family that instead of family reunions has family conventions, and that bills itself as "the oldest Christian family in the world." One of his sisters, Kathy, is an artist who worked on the restoration of the beautiful Orchestra Hall downtown—a reclaiming of urban life that Rashid likens to the Tiger Stadium cause. His youngest brother, Kevin, is another of the fan club's founders. "All my kids are cause-fighters," says their mother, Peg, proudly.

Rashid teaches English at Marygrove College in Detroit. He also lives in the city. In what spare time he has—besides the fan club and his job, he has two children to raise and care for—he plays softball and reads the *New York Review of Books*.

"We're just regular people," insists Judy Davids, who with her husband, John, designed the Cochrane Plan, the fan club's renovation proposal. Says John: "People in this area aren't used to people like us winning against people like Monaghan."

There is about the fan club an eminently appealing lack of guile. Eva Navarro, who remains girlish about her love for baseball and the Tigers, showed me her hoard of Tiger treasures one evening. They include dozens of ticket stubs, many with the game's score and pitching matchup written on them in her hand. Her most treasured stub is October 3, 1972, the night the Tigers wrenched the division title from the Boston Red Sox in the season's last game. She is careful to note that it was a Tuesday. The Tigers won that night (she looks at her stub), 3 to 1. "I climbed over the railing" when the game finished, she says, "and grabbed a little handful of dirt, which I still have. . . ." She cherishes also a letter from Ted Williams, typed on Washington Senators letterhead and addressed quaintly to "Miss" Eva Navarro, and a genuine, signed Norm Cash bat.

About Schembechler's comments she is passionate. "I'm a legal secretary," she says when asked about self-interest. "I've never had any political aspirations. We do represent the fans, because we are the fans. The Bill Haases and Bo Schembechlers are not the fans. Tom Monaghan, who flies in in his helicopter a couple of times a year, is not a fan.

"It's insulting," she says warmly, "because what he's saying is that nobody does anything for free. That there aren't people out there that care about something, that believe enough about something, that they're willing to take a stand and fight for it."

"There's no way they can get at the fan club," says Eva's friend Alex Clunis, "because the fan club has the fans' interests at heart. All they want to do is make sure that the issue gets to the people, because they know if the people have their way, there won't be a new stadium. Nobody wants one."

John and Judy Davids claim a "unique qualification" to design a renovation of Tiger Stadium that is hard to dispute. They have attended, says John, about five hundred games at Michigan and Trumbull. When they were young and poor and living in Ann Arbor, they drove to Detroit dozens of times a year to see the Tigers. For them the park's preferred seating is in the right-field bleachers, where people like "Baseball John" Miramonti hang out.

Baseball John is 38 years old and drives a Zamboni at an ice rink for a living. "The first time I came in this place," he says, "I was with Cub Scout Pack 454. I was sittin' in the upper deck in right field, and I was like, 'Wow!'

"I used to hitchhike here, from the freeway, to watch a ball game. Guys would pick me up — businessmen — and let me off at the park.

"It doesn't matter what problems you have in your life," he says. "You can come in here for four bucks. All you need is four dollars, and you've got yourself a place."

Like everyone in the right-field bleachers, it seems, Miramonti has a Kirk Gibson story. He tells of the time Gibson offered him a job. "I was sittin' out here in right field one day, really miserable and bummed out. I was so quiet that day, and Gibby noticed it.

"He goes, 'What's wrong?'

"I go, 'Aw, I need a job.'

"He goes, 'Go up there and get a piece of paper, and write down your phone number.' "

Baseball John has a bald, laconic sidekick who wears a leather jacket and a constant ironic smirk. "This is my buddy George," he says. "Kirk Gibson named him the Scary Guy."

Says George: "This is where the intelligentsia of the ballpark hangs out."

"Out here," opines Baseball John, "it doesn't matter if you're black or white, or purple, or whatever. And baseball is meant to be played where it's meant to be played, not in a fabricated piece of shit that they *call* a ballpark."

The right-field bleachers are "like home to us," says George. "We get loud and rowdy and stuff, but we have a good time."

"That's the highlight of my life," says Baseball John. "Being known as the guy who sits in the right-field bleachers. I love this place, man."

"Where else can you pay four dollars and be so close to the field?" asks Judy Davids. (Where, indeed, can you be offered a job by Kirk Gibson?) "If they build a new stadium, the cheap seats will be way up in the upper deck, and John will have to pay six dollars just to park his car. It's people like him who will be left out."

John and Judy Davids dedicated the Cochrane Plan to Baseball John.

The fan club, says Rosemary Hogan of Livonia, has been "a labor of love, and it's started a lot of friendships. Our main thing in common is baseball, the love of the game, and our love of the ballpark.

"I was raised with football," she says, "but in 1984 I got free tickets to Tiger Stadium, and I've been hooked ever since. It was going to Tiger Stadium that turned me into a baseball fan." Hogan says her first visit to Michigan and Trumbull was "mesmerizing."

The architect and ballpark expert Philip Bess told me, about the fan club: "I'm very sympathetic with what they're doing, and even more so with why they're doing it. That's really the key. They're doing it because they love it. They don't have any economic interest in it; it's a matter of affection."

"The fan club," Don Shapiro of West Bloomfield Hills told me when I interviewed him for this book, "all they have is ordinary Joes who love baseball, like me. There isn't much money. Good, dedicated people. No question."

The fan club's members are ordinary Joes, and they do have affection for the stadium: a very deep and abiding affection, springing from childhood visits and fond and important memories of their parents — usually their fathers. "My dad introduced me to baseball," says Eva Navarro. "I don't think that we could have developed such a close relationship if it hadn't been for Tiger Stadium.

"People ask me, 'Why are you doing this?' It's not that simple. I can't just say because I love baseball, because I love Tiger Stadium. I do. But if it hadn't been for that stadium, then I wouldn't have had an opportunity to develop this relationship with my father, which I cherish. I found a new friend: my dad. My other friends were dating, and going to drive-ins, and going to parties. I was going to the ball game with my dad."

But affection and love really are two different things. The fan club's members have affection for the ballpark as a place — an affection that is deep, and resonant, and shared by hundreds of thousands of Michiganders, and that in itself would be a sufficient reason not to replace Tiger Stadium. But they love the city of Detroit.

Love is not a matter of sentiment, but of action and sacrifice and doing what is right. The fan club talks about the just and wise use of public money; about where political power resides, and where it should reside; about urban blight and urban sprawl and the importance of urban institutions. They talk about the environment. Throughout southeastern Michigan, in the suburban communities to which most white people have fled, there has been "too much urban sprawl that has damaged the natural landscape," says Frank Rashid. "Some things, for that reason, belong in the city."

Though the fan club's history has not been devoid of internal disagreements, even conflicts (for example, while the Cochrane Plan was being developed, some members opposed any renovation proposal that would include sky boxes), it has been marked by an impressive, democratically achieved unanimity of purpose. (The large executive committee makes all decisions, sometimes not very quickly, and there is no elected or acknowledged leader. For the record, neither Frank Rashid nor Bob Buchta is the fan club's "president.")

When in late July 1991 Wayne County commissioner Arthur Blackwell suggested that a new stadium be built and that the present one be saved and used for Canadian football, the fan club was unimpressed. You can't have your cake and eat it too, says the fan club. There is no such thing as a painless tax; bonds do cost the taxpayers money; and the issue is not sentiment but the wisdom of spending $200 million or more for a new stadium to replace a priceless civic treasure, when there are any number of more pressing needs in the city of Detroit.

"There's a whole history in this town of not having adequate programs for youth," says Frank Rashid. "But we're building a playground for millionaires, and we're going to bend over backwards to do it, when Detroit's kids have so few clean, safe places to play that it's scandalous. Which is not to say that's the most important thing that has to be done. The real scandal in this town is the schools."

The fan club's leaders have learned the hard way that prevailing in public affairs is a matter of repeating oneself endlessly. They may be just regular people, but they are almost to a person extraordinarily intelligent and quick on the uptake. And they are chagrined at having to be buffeted in the fickle winds of the media's often puzzling sense of priorities.

The local press has been largely unhelpful through it all by being uncritical, and by caving in when its interests begin to be threatened. The media's space and attention span are both limited, so we are afflicted with Tom Gage's baseball column in the *News* (July 17, 1991):

> News: The local chapter of the American Institute of Architects, when asked by the Tiger Stadium Fan Club to make a judgment, declared Tiger Stadium obsolete.
> To which a fan club spokesman said: "Their arguments make no sense."
> Views: It's a losing battle, guys. But you know what, keep trying.
> The only sadder sight than the wrecking ball would be to know the ol' park fell without a fight.

Gage fails to mention that the chairman of the AIA committee that rendered the judgment, Jerry Shea, is vice president of a development firm (Kughn Enterprises of Southfield) that is on the site selection committee for a new stadium, or that Shea's failure to disclose that fact was a violation of an explicit provision in the AIA's code of ethics.

And Shea's committee's arguments do indeed make no sense. What is it that makes Tiger Stadium "functionally obsolete" — especially in the light of two serious renovation proposals, put forward by architectural and building professionals?

"The whole thing is a political football," says Michael Ferber of Jeffsan Inc. "And facts do get lost in a situation like that."

Gage's "losing battle, guys" remark is especially infuriating to fan club leaders. "I've gotten to where I really resent when people tell me to keep up the fight," Frank Rashid told me once. "They're saying, 'We're not going to help you, but keep screwing up your life, since you have nothing to lose.' "

And the issue is much more than "the ol' park" — though the importance of the building itself is not sentimental or trivial, and was the fan club's first reason for being. The point is, as the fan club has been saying all along, the just and wise use of public money; the city's last, best connection with its history; accessibility for ordinary people to public (and publicly subsidized) entertainment.

The fan club's leaders donate an impressive array of skills and unpaid time to the cause. Bill Dow is a lawyer, as is Steve Finegood. Both have provided important advice and knowledge on the stadium lease and other legal questions. John and Judy Davids are architectural professionals. Brian Tremain is a securities broker with the talent and nerve required for successful hobnobbing and networking. Frank Rashid, Bob Buchta, John Davids, Mike Gruber, and Eva Navarro are skilled at handling the press. Everybody licks envelopes, makes telephone calls, and hands out flyers at the park during home stands — all for no pay.

Not less important than any of the people who design comprehensive renovation plans or write press releases or go on talk shows is Catherine Darin. Catherine is a small, unprepossessing woman who saw her first game in Briggs Stadium in 1946, the year she immigrated from Ireland. Through all the fan club's crises and triumphs, Catherine has staffed the office at the Gaelic League (on Michigan Avenue, just west of the stadium), promptly filled orders for merchandise, opened mail that has come to the fan club's address (P.O. Box 441426, Detroit 48244–1426), relayed telephone messages (313-964-5991), and done all the things that must constantly be done. "Catherine has really been the backbone of the group at times," says John Davids.

"The fan club is honest," says Davids. "There's no one in the fan club who stands to benefit from this at all. I've said publicly on several occasions that I would donate the work that we've done to the city to renovate the stadium. How can they accuse us of being self-interested?"

(Contractor Joe O'Neal, whose brainchild, the Birkerts-O'Neal plan, would be a more radical renovation than the Cochrane Plan, expresses the same sentiment. "I don't have to build it," he told me in his office in Ann Arbor. "I just want to see that baby saved.")

"The thing that really outraged me was Bo's statements in *Detroit Monthly* where he said that we are politically motivated — that there's a lot of self-interest there," says Davids. "What the hell kind of self-interest is there here? We've all donated our work, and we all will continue to donate our work. What kind of self-interest is that? And then to make the slam that we are all going to look for political careers — it's complete garbage. We're architects and professors and teachers and photographers. We're not political wannabes. We're people who believe very strongly in the city of Detroit.

"The first thing the fan club was started on was really a baseball issue," he says. "We started because we thought Tiger Stadium was a great place. And it's a fantastic place. But very quickly, we knew that it was a lot bigger than a baseball issue. The big issue is social justice. The big issue is, Do we give one of the wealthiest men in this country two hundred million dollars of hard-earned public money, to the detriment of the city, just because he says he has to make more money?"

Mike Ridley became involved in the fan club because Thom Sharp asked him to produce his song "Don't Tear It Down." Ridley had written his song "Baseball," "with a lot of thoughts about Tiger Stadium and Ernie Harwell."

Like so many others, Ridley's first and fondest reason for wanting to save Tiger Stadium was personal. "I have so many fond memories of the Tigers," he recalls. "I used to fall asleep on my dad's bed. We'd sit there and listen on his little transistor radio, listening to Tiger baseball. So many fond memories."

Quickly, though, he found "that it really wasn't a baseball issue. It was a social issue. Things like fiscal responsibility and trying to remain true to our heritage. All of a sudden I had passion for a social issue. I hadn't had it since Vietnam.

"Why aren't people considering this as a social justice issue? Everyone's saying that we're standing in the way of baseball progress, which is not really the issue. They talk about the new Comiskey Park, and the new Baltimore park, about how we can have that. Well, we don't need that. Because you're going to drop, I bet when all is said and done, $250 million, and then everyone will say, Why did we tear Tiger Stadium down in the first place? And nobody will know why."

Like everyone in the fan club, Ridley is met on occasion with worldly-wise skepticism. He will be with "some of my real good friends, people who have been behind the Tiger Stadium issue. We'll talk, and all of a sudden I'll discover that they've lost their enthusiasm, their belief that we can save Tiger Stadium. Nothing really hurts me more than that."

Ridley predicts that "Tiger Stadium will be saved, will be renovated, everyone will be happy with it. We'll have saved a lot of money, and kept the oldest address in professional sports. And we will be able to say, 'I told you we could do it!' I like flying in the face of opposition."

Dr. Edward Turner expresses the same militant confidence. About the prospect of a new stadium, he told me: "I wouldn't allow it to happen. Frank Rashid and I, we'd go wherever they were going, and raise whatever stink needed to be raised. We wouldn't allow it. We'd lie down in front of the shovels."

Dr. Turner may have to make good on his promise, if the Tigers succeed in doing to the stadium what they did to Ernie Harwell. And their attitude toward views in opposition to theirs is now a matter of record.

On September 28 and 29, 1991, the last weekend Ernie Harwell was broadcasting games from Tiger Stadium, some fans in the bleachers tried to unfurl a banner reading "BO FIRED ERNIE. BO MUST GO." At each game, stadium security guards, backed by Detroit police officers, immediately tore down the sign. Told that what he was doing was illegal a police officer replied: "I know it's illegal, but we have to do it anyway."

Stephen Brunt of the *Globe and Mail* of Toronto remarked that the guards' action "demonstrates exactly the limits of free speech at Michigan and Trumbull."

Not exactly: On Sunday, the fans insisted that the guards return the banner to them. At the seventh-inning stretch they unfurled it again; this time it stayed up, and the entire bleacher section sustained a chant of "Bo must go!" until play resumed. The fans had defied Tiger management and the city police and had prevailed.

Charlie Vincent of the *Free Press* called what the guards and police had been ordered to do "incredibly small." The next day he asked Schembechler who had authorized it.

"Geez, I don't know," replied Schembechler. "Why do you ask that question now? Signs like that have been up all summer. It doesn't matter what we do. We can't do the right thing, and I don't mean in the fans' eyes. I mean the media. Whatever we do would be wrong."

That same week, Schembechler turned down two stadium proposals by Wayne County and City of Detroit officials, justifying his refusal to consider the deals by saying the Tigers had to do what was best for the fans. "We owe it to our fans, to our ball club, to seek options from other sources and for other sites," he said.

The Tiger Stadium Fan Club is not only the largest and most effective stadium preservation group ever, it is also by far the largest group of Tiger fans ever organized. "We haven't ignored the stadium fan club people in the sense that they may feel," says Haase. But the Tigers have been recklessly disdainful of the fans' desires regarding Ernie Harwell and the stadium. Time will tell whether their dangerous policy comes back to haunt them; sub-par attendance since 1988 can be seen as an early symptom of possible long-term fan disaffection.

The questions can fairly be asked: Who has the fans' interests at heart? And who is acting out of self-interest?

Ethan Casey
October 1991

APPENDIX 1

CHRONOLOGY OF MICHIGAN AND TRUMBULL

1875.	The City of Detroit replaces Woodbridge Grove with a farmers market.
April 28, 1896.	Detroit beats Columbus, 17–2, to inaugurate Bennett Park.
April 20, 1900.	Buffalo's Doc Amole pitches a no-hitter in the Tigers' first American League game.
April 25, 1901.	The Tigers score ten runs in the ninth inning to beat Milwaukee, 14–13, in the first major league game at Michigan and Trumbull.
August 30, 1905.	Ty Cobb debuts, doubling in a run in his first Tiger at-bat.
September 6, 1905.	Frank Smith of Chicago holds the Tigers hitless.
October 11, 1907.	Tigers lose their first World Series home game to Chicago.
October 14, 1908.	The smallest crowd in World Series history— 6,210—sees the Tigers lose to the Cubs, 2–0.
October 11, 1909.	Tigers lose World Series game before a record crowd of 18,277.

October 12, 1909. Tigers post first World Series win at home, 5–0, over Pirates.

April 20, 1912. Tigers beat Cleveland, 6–5, in eleven innings to dedicate Navin Field. Ty Cobb steals home to score the first run.

July 4, 1912. George Mullin pitches the first no-hitter by a Tiger.

August 30, 1912. Earl Hamilton of St. Louis holds the Tigers hitless.

June 3, 1918. Dutch Leonard of Boston hurls a no-hitter.

1922–23. Navin Field is double-decked, raising the capacity to 30,000.

May 13, 1924. A record 40,000 fans see Hooks Dauss beat the Yankees.

June 13, 1924. Fans join fight between Tigers and Yankees, causing forfeit.

June 8, 1926. Babe Ruth hits a 626-foot homer over the right-field fence.

April 19, 1927. Ty Tyson does the first radio broadcast from Navin Field.

July 18, 1927. Ty Cobb gets his 4,000th hit playing for Philadelphia at Detroit.

September 24, 1928. Only 404 fans see Tigers play Red Sox.

October 8, 1934. A record 44,551 watch Tigers lose World Series sixth game.

October 9, 1934. Bleacher fans pelt Cardinals' Ducky Medwick with produce and debris, forcing him from the game. Routed 11–0, the Tigers lose the series.

October 7, 1935. Before a record 48,420, the Tigers win their first World Series. Goose Goslin drives in Mickey Cochrane with the winning run in the ninth.

April 22, 1938. After a three-year expansion, the park is rededicated as Briggs Stadium with a capacity of nearly 56,000.

September 9, 1938. The Detroit Lions debut at Briggs Stadium, beating Pittsburgh 16–7 before 17,000 fans.

May 4, 1939. Ted Williams hits the first homer to clear the stadium roof.

October 6, 1940. A record crowd of 55,189 sees Bobo Newsom shut out the Reds in the World Series.

July 8, 1941. Ted Williams's two-out, ninth-inning homer gives the American League a thrilling 7–5 victory in the first All-Star Game in Detroit.

October 5, 1945. A new record 55,500 is on hand as the Cubs beat the Tigers, 3-0, in the third game of the World Series.

July 20, 1947. The all-time biggest home crowd — 58,369 — jams the park for a doubleheader against the Yankees. Part of the crowd stands in the outfield.

June 15, 1948. Night baseball comes to Detroit; Athletics beat Tigers, 4–1.

June 20, 1948. Cleveland's Bob Feller hurls a no-hitter.

August 9, 1948. The Tigers draw an all-time record night-game crowd of 56,586.

September 26, 1948. All-time record for a single day game is set: 57,888.

June 23, 1950. The Tigers beat the Yankees, 10–9. All nineteen runs are the result of home runs. Detroit hits a record-tying four home runs in one inning.

July 10, 1950. Tigers Vic Wertz and George Kell homer, but the National Leaguers clout four round-trippers and take the All-Star Game, 8–3.

May 15, 1952. Virgil Trucks pitches a no-hitter against Washington before only 2,215 fans. The Tigers need a ninth-inning home run by Wertz to win the game, 1–0.

December 27, 1953. The Lions beat the Cleveland Browns, 17–16, to win the NFL championship.

December 29, 1957. The Browns rout the Lions, 59–14, in the NFL championship game before 55,263 fans.

June 17, 1958. The Tigers' first black player, Ozzie Virgil, makes his debut in Detroit and goes 5-for-5.

January 1, 1961. Briggs Stadium is renamed Tiger Stadium.

June 27, 1961. For a twi-night doubleheader against the Chicago White Sox, the contending Tigers draw 57,271, the record crowd for a twi-nighter.

April 13, 1962. In an Opening Day game played in a snowstorm, Tiger pitcher Frank Lary pulls a leg muscle running out a triple. The injury leads to arm problems that end his career.

June 24, 1962. In a seven-hour game, then the longest in baseball history, the Yankees beat the Tigers in twenty-two innings, 9–7, when journeyman Jack Reed hits the only home run of his career.

August 3, 1962. The Minnesota Twins' Harmon Killebrew hits the first homer ever over the left-field roof, off Jim Bunning.

September 28, 1964. An all-time stadium record crowd of 59,203 sees the Lions lose to Green Bay, 14–10.

August 11, 1968. Gates Brown wins both ends of a doubleheader against Boston before 49,087 with a fourteenth-inning homer and a ninth-inning single.

September 14, 1968. Denny McLain becomes the first thirty-game winner since 1934. Willie Horton's single in the bottom of the ninth wins the game.

September 17, 1968. The Tigers clinch their first pennant since 1945 on a Don Wert single in the bottom of the ninth to beat New York, 2–1.

October 7, 1968. The most famous single play in the history of Michigan and Trumbull: Willie Horton throws out Lou Brock at home plate. The play turns around the World Series as the Tigers rally from a 3–1 deficit to win the title.

July 13, 1971. Reggie Jackson's blast off the light tower on the right-field roof leads the American League to a 6–4 victory in the All-Star Game.

October 3, 1972. The Tigers beat Boston 3–1 to win the American League Eastern Division title.

October 10, 1972. Joe Coleman strikes out fourteen and shuts out Oakland in the first American League Championship Series game ever played at Tiger Stadium.

April 17, 1973. Steve Busby of Kansas City pitches a no-hitter.

July 15, 1973. Nolan Ryan, hurling for the Angels, pitches a no-hitter. Norm Cash brings a table leg up to the plate to face Ryan.

November 28, 1974. Before 53,714 fans, the Lions play their last game at Michigan and Trumbull, losing to Cleveland, 31–27.

May 15, 1976. Mark Fidyrch wins his first start, beating Cleveland 2–1.

June 28, 1976. Before a national television audience and a capacity crowd, Fidrych dispatches the Yankees 5–1 and "Birdmania" reaches its peak.

February 1, 1977. A fire destroys the press box and part of the third deck at Tiger Stadium.

July 13, 1977. Detroit Mayor Coleman Young announces the Tigers will sell the stadium to the city for one dollar and lease it for thirty years, enabling the city to procure a federal grant to finance a renovation of the ballpark.

June 17, 1980. A day after bleacher fans pelt Milwaukee center fielder Gorman Thomas with bottles, the Tigers close the bleachers for two weeks.

September 18, 1984. The Tigers beat Milwaukee to clinch the Eastern Division title.

October 5, 1984.   Milt Wilcox shuts out Kansas City, 1–0, to finish a Tiger sweep in the American League playoffs.

October 14, 1984.   Kirk Gibson scores the winning run on a pop-up to the second baseman and later homers off Goose Gossage as the Tigers beat San Diego to win the World Series.

October 4, 1987.   Finishing the season with a dramatic sweep of the first-place Blue Jays, the Tigers win the division title as Frank Tanana beats Toronto, 1–0.

April 20, 1988.   About twelve hundred people show up on a cold, rainy Wednesday night to encircle Tiger Stadium for the first-ever human hug of a ballpark.

October 13, 1988.   Over objections from the City of Detroit, a state board of review approves the Tiger Stadium Fan Club's petition to place Tiger Stadium on the National Register of Historic Places.

March 16, 1989.   Tiger owner Tom Monaghan endorses a proposal for a new stadium. Three days later, hundreds march around Tiger Stadium in protest. The proposal is quietly dropped.

January 22, 1990.   The fan club unveils the Cochrane Plan, a $26 million proposal to preserve and modernize Tiger Stadium.

June 10, 1990.   At the second hug of Tiger Stadium, over a thousand fans again surround the ballpark in a show of determination to save it.

June 28, 1990.   Nelson Mandela, African National Congress leader, addresses a crowd of 49,000 at the first political rally in the ballpark in over twenty years.

August 25, 1990.   Cecil Fielder becomes only the third player to hit a home run over the left-field roof at Tiger Stadium.

December 20, 1990. In a stunning press conference at Tiger Stadium, Hall of Fame broadcaster Ernie Harwell announces that the Tigers are dismissing him after the 1991 season.

April 8, 1991. Fans boycott Opening Day to protest Harwell's ouster and the club's plans to replace Tiger Stadium. As hundreds stage a protest rally along Michigan Avenue, attendance at the opener, normally a sell-out, is only 47,382.

April 22, 1991. In a speech to the Economic Club of Detroit, Tiger president Bo Schembechler demands that civic leaders come up with a plan to build a new ballpark for the Tigers by August 1. He says the club has ruled out renovation.

June 10, 1991. The National Trust for Historic Preservation places Tiger Stadium on its annual list of most important endangered historic places. It is the only sports facility ever so designated.

June 26, 1991. Mickey Tettleton hits his second home run over the right field roof within a week.

August 1, 1991. Detroit Mayor Coleman Young and Wayne County officials announce the formation of a city-county stadium authority to help build a new stadium. The Tigers' "deadline" passes without a financing plan and with the club and politicians deeply at odds over a stadium site.

September 14, 1991. The newly formed Common Ground Coalition launches a petition campaign to give Detroit voters the decisive power to enforce the city's lease with the Tigers and preserve Tiger Stadium.

September 30, 1991. Ernie Harwell broadcasts his final game from Tiger Stadium.

APPENDIX 2

ATTENDANCE AT MICHIGAN AND TRUMBULL

Table 2–1. Attendance at Tiger Regular Season Home Games

Year	Attendance	Team W-L Pct.	League Average (a) Attendance	Difference
		At Bennett Park		
1901	259,430	.548	203,540	+ 55,890
1902	189,469	.385	288,141	− 98,672
1903	224,523	.478	302,909	− 78,386
1904	177,796	.408	406,605	− 228,809
1905	193,384	.516	418,195	− 224,811
1906	174,043	.477	394,862	− 220,819
1907	297,079	.613	443,098	− 146,019
1908	436,199	.588	453,595	− 17,396
1909	490,490	.645	464,154	+ 26,336
1910	391,288	.558	411,343	− 20,055
1911	484,988	.578	407,789	+ 77,199
Total	3,318,689		4,194,231	− 875,542

(a) Average attendance for other American League teams

297

At Navin Field

1912	402,870	.451	408,680	−	5,810
1913	398,502	.431	446,900	−	48,398
1914	416,225	.523	333,052	+	83,173
1915	476,105	.649	279,797	+	196,308
1916	616,772	.565	405,016	+	211,756
1917	457,289	.510	408,408	+	48,881
1918	203,719	.437	214,897	−	11,178
1919	643,805	.571	430,062	+	213,743
1920	579,650	.396	643,521	−	63,871
1921	661,527	.464	565,543	+	95,984
1922	861,206	.513	573,307	+	287,899
1923	911,377	.539	527,316	+	384,061
1924	1,015,136	.558	605,758	+	409,378
1925	820,766	.526	623,726	+	197,040
1926	711,914	.513	600,096	+	111,818
1927	773,716	.536	548,462	+	225,254
1928	474,323	.442	535,266	−	60,943
1929	869,318	.455	541,879	+	327,439
1930	649,450	.487	576,611	+	72,839
1931	434,056	.396	492,748	−	58,692
1932	397,157	.503	390,868	+	6,289
1933	320,972	.487	372,177	−	51,205
1934	919,161	.656	263,492	+	655,669
1935	1,034,929	.616	379,011	+	655,918
1936	875,948	.539	471,853	+	404,095
1937	1,072,276	.578	523,366	+	548,910
Total	16,998,169		12,161,812	+	4,836,357

At Briggs Stadium

1938	799,557	.545	522,304	+ 277,253
1939	836,279	.526	492,046	+ 344,233
1940	1,112,693	.584	617,298	+ 495,395
1941	684,915	.487	603,863	+ 81,052
1942	580,087	.474	517,161	+ 62,926
1943	606,287	.506	441,469	+ 164,818
1944	923,176	.571	553,569	+ 369,607
1945	1,280,341	.575	614,297	+ 666,044
1946	1,722,590	.597	1,128,370	+ 594,220
1947	1,398,093	.552	1,155,425	+ 242,668
1948	1,743,035	.506	1,345,152	+ 397,883
1949	1,821,204	.565	1,272,778	+ 548,426
1950	1,951,474	.617	1,027,270	+ 924,204
1951	1,132,641	.474	1,107,148	+ 25,493
1952	1,026,846	.325	1,038,143	− 11,297
1953	884,658	.390	868,488	+ 16,170
1954	1,079,842	.442	977,503	+ 102,339
1955	1,181,838	.513	1,108,733	+ 73,105
1956	1,051,182	.532	977,500	+ 73,682
1957	1,272,346	.506	989,125	+ 283,221
1958	1,098,924	.500	885,301	+ 213,623
1959	1,221,221	.494	1,132,605	+ 88,616
1960	1,167,669	.461	1,151,265	+ 16,404
Total	26,576,898		20,526,813	+ 6,050,085

At Tiger Stadium

1961	1,600,710	.623	951,367	+ 649,343
1962	1,207,881	.528	978,575	+ 229,306
1963	821,952	.488	919,171	− 97,219
1964	816,139	.525	935,446	− 119,307
1965	1,029,645	.549	870,124	+ 159,521
1966	1,124,293	.543	1,004,716	+ 119,577
1967	1,447,143	.562	1,098,853	+ 348,290
1968	2,031,847	.636	1,031,727	+ 1,000,120
1969	1,577,481	.556	959,751	+ 617,730
1970	1,501,293	.487	962,167	+ 539,126
1971	1,591,073	.562	934,317	+ 656,756
1972	1,892,386	.551	867,832	+ 1,024,554
1973	1,724,146	.525	1,064,496	+ 659,650
1974	1,243,080	.444	1,073,110	+ 169,970
1975	1,058,836	.358	1,102,781	− 43,945
1976	1,467,020	.460	1,199,162	+ 267,858
1977	1,359,856	.457	1,406,130	− 46,274
1978	1,714,893	.531	1,447,313	+ 267,580
1979	1,630,929	.528	1,595,465	+ 45,464
1980	1,785,293	.519	1,546,520	+ 238,773
1981[b]	1,149,144	.550	993,603	+ 155,541
1982	1,636,058	.512	1,649,568	− 13,510
1983	1,829,636	.568	1,704,724	+ 124,912
1984	2,704,794	.642	1,635,126	+ 1,069,668
1985	2,286,609	.522	1,711,201	+ 575,408
1986	1,899,437	.537	1,790,253	+ 109,184
1987	2,061,830	.605	1,939,655	+ 122,175
1988	2,081,162	.543	2,032,190	+ 48,972
1989	1,543,656	.364	2,177,354	− 633,698
1990	1,495,785	.488	2,218,190	− 722,405
Total	47,314,007		39,800,887	+ 7,513,120
1991	1,641,661	.519		
Total	48,955,668			

(b) Strike season; Tigers played only 109 games

300

Table 2-2. Postseason Attendance

Year	Event	Games	Attendance
1907	World Series	2	18,676
1908	World Series	3	29,929
1909	World Series	4	63,410
1934	World Series	4	171,409
1935	World Series	3	142,553
1940	World Series	3	162,159
1945	World Series	3	163,773
1968	World Series	3	160,902
1972	AL playoffs	3	129,047
1984	AL playoffs	1	52,168
1984	World Series	3	156,001
1987	AL playoffs	3	149,117
Total		35	1,399,144

Table 2-3. All-Star Games

Year	Attendance
1941	54,674
1951	52,075
1971	53,559
Total	160,308

Table 2-4. All-Time Totals — Regular Season

Years	Where	Attendance
1901–91	Home[a]	95,849,424
1912–91	Home[b]	92,530,735

[a]Includes Burns Park (Sunday games, 1901–9), Bennett Park, Navin Field, Briggs Stadium, Tiger Stadium.

[b]Includes Navin Field, Briggs Stadium, Tiger Stadium.

The estimated all-time major league baseball attendance at Michigan and Trumbull through 1991 was 97,164,635. This figure includes All-Star games and postseason play but excludes ten percent of the 1901–09 attendance as allowance for games played at Burns Park (244,241 total).

Table 2-5. Lowest Major League Attendance Marks (1983–1990)

Team	Low Recent Attendance	(Year)	Winning Percentage That Year	Year Before
Cleveland	655,181	(1985)	.370	.463
Pittsburgh	735,900	(1985)	.354	.463
Seattle	813,537	(1983)	.370	.469
San Francisco	818,697	(1985)	.383	.407
Atlanta	848,089	(1988)	.338	.429
Minnesota	858,939	(1983)	.432	.370
Chicago White Sox	1,045,651	(1989)	.463	.441
Texas	1,102,471	(1984)	.429	.475
New York Mets	1,112,774	(1983)	.420	.401
Montreal	1,128,981	(1986)	.484	.522
Houston	1,184,314	(1985)	.512	.494
Cincinnati	1,190,419	(1983)	.457	.377
Milwaukee	1,265,041	(1986)	.478	.441
Oakland	1,294,941	(1983)	.457	.420
San Diego	1,454,061	(1987)	.401	.457
Chicago Cubs	1,479,717	(1983)	.438	.451
Detroit	1,495,785	(1990)	.488	.364

APPENDIX 3

HALL OF FAMERS AT MICHIGAN AND TRUMBULL

(Note: This list does not include Negro Leaguers who may have played in Navin Field or Briggs Stadium, or managers, such as Casey Stengel, who appeared at Michigan and Trumbull, but never as players.)

Hank Aaron	1971 All-Star Game; 1975–76 Brewers
Luis Aparicio	1956–73 White Sox-Orioles-Red Sox
Luke Appling	1930–50 White Sox
Earl Averill	1939–40 Tigers; 1929–39 Indians
J. Frank Baker	1908–22 Athletics-Yankees
Chief Bender	1903–14 Athletics, 1925 White Sox
Yogi Berra	1946–65 Yankees
Jim Bottomley	1936–37 Browns
Lou Boudreau	1938–52 Indians-Red Sox
Roger Bresnahan	1901–2 Baltimore
Lou Brock	1968 World Series
Three Finger Brown	1907–8 World Series with Cubs
Jesse Burkett	1902–5 Browns-Red Sox
Roy Campanella	1951 All-Star Game
Rod Carew	1967–78 Twins; 1979–85 Angels

Frank Chance	1913–14 Yankees, 1907–8 World Series with Cubs
Jack Chesbro	1903–9 Yankees-Red Sox
Roberto Clemente	1971 All-Star Game
Ty Cobb	1905–26 Tigers; 1927–28 Athletics
Mickey Cochrane	1934–37 Tigers; 1925–33 Athletics
Eddie Collins	1906–30 Athletics-White Sox
Jimmy Collins	1901–8 Red Sox-Athletics
Earle Combs	1924–35 Yankees
Stan Coveleski	1912, 1916–28 Athletics-Indians-Senators-Yankees
Sam Crawford	1903–17 Tigers
Joe Cronin	1928–45 Senators-Red Sox
Dizzy Dean	1934 World Series with Cardinals
Ed Delahanty	1902–3 Senators
Joe DiMaggio	1936–51 Yankees
Hugh Duffy	1901 Milwaukee
Johnny Evers	1907–8 World Series with Cubs
Red Faber	1914–33 White Sox
Bob Feller	1935–56 Indians
Rick Ferrell	1929–47 Browns-Red Sox-Senators
Elmer Flick	1902–10 Athletics-Indians
Whitey Ford	1950–67 Yankees
Jimmy Foxx	1925–42 Athletics-Red Sox
Frankie Frisch	1934 World Series with Cardinals
Lou Gehrig	1923–39 Yankees
Charlie Gehringer	1924–42 Tigers
Bob Gibson	1968 World Series with Cardinals
Lefty Gomez	1930–42 Yankees
Goose Goslin	1934–37 Tigers; 1921–33,38 Senators-Browns
Hank Greenberg	1930–46 Tigers
Clark Griffith	1901–7 White Sox-Yankees; 1912–14 Senators
Lefty Grove	1925–41 Athletics-Red Sox
Bucky Harris	1929, 1931 Tigers; 1919–28 Senators
Gabby Hartnett	1935 World Series with Cubs
Harry Heilmann	1914–29 Tigers

Billy Herman	1935 World Series with Cubs; 1941 All-Star Game
Harry Hooper	1909–25 Red Sox-White Sox
Rogers Hornsby	1933–37 Browns
Waite Hoyt	1930–31 Tigers; 1919–31 Red Sox-Yankees-Athletics
Catfish Hunter	1968–79 A's-Yankees
Ferguson Jenkins	1974–81 Rangers-Red Sox-Rangers
Hughie Jennings	1907, 1909, 1912, 1918 Tigers; Tiger manager 1907–20
Walter Johnson	1907–27 Senators
Addie Joss	1902–10 Indians
Al Kaline	1953–74 Tigers
Willie Keeler	1903–9 Yankees
George Kell	1946–52 Tigers; 1943–46 A's; 1952–57 Red Sox-White Sox-Orioles
Joe Kelley	1902 Baltimore
Harmon Killebrew	1954–75 Senators-Twins-A's
Ralph Kiner	1955 Indians; 1951 All-Star Game (Pirates)
Chuck Klein	1935 World Series with Cubs
Nap Lajoie	1901–16 Indians-Athletics
Tony Lazzeri	1926–37 Yankees
Bob Lemon	1941–58 Indians
Freddie Lindstrom	1935 World Series with Cubs
Al Lopez	1941 All-Star Game; 1947 Indians
Ted Lyons	1923–46 White Sox
Mickey Mantle	1951–68 Yankees
Heinie Manush	1923–27 Tigers; 1928–36 Browns-Senators-Red Sox
Juan Marichal	1971 All-Star Game
Eddie Mathews	1967–68 Tigers
Willie Mays	1971 All-Star Game
Willie McCovey	1971 All-Star Game
Joe McGinnity	1901–2 Baltimore
John McGraw	1901–2 Baltimore
Bill McKechnie	1913 Yankees

Joe Medwick	1934 World Series (Cardinals); 1941 All-Star (Dodgers)
Johnny Mize	1949–53 Yankees; 1941 All-Star Game (Cardinals)
Stan Musial	1951 All-Star Game
Mel Ott	1941 All-Star Game
Satchel Paige	1948–53 Indians-Browns
Jim Palmer	1965–84 Orioles
Herb Pennock	1912–34 Athletics-Red Sox-Yankees
Gaylord Perry	1972–77 Indians-Rangers; 1980 Rangers-Yankees; 1982–83 Mariners-Royals
Eddie Plank	1901–17 Athletics-Browns
Pee Wee Reese	1951 All-Star Game
Sam Rice	1915–34 Senators-Indians
Robin Roberts	1951 All-Star Game; 1962–65 Orioles
Brooks Robinson	1955–77 Orioles
Frank Robinson	1966–71 Orioles; 1973–76 Angels, Indians
Jackie Robinson	1951 All-Star Game
Red Ruffing	1924–47 Red Sox-Yankees-White Sox
Babe Ruth	1914–34 Red Sox-Yankees
Ray Schalk	1912–28 White Sox
Joe Sewell	1920–33 Indians-Yankees
Al Simmons	1936 Tigers; 1924–44 Athletics-White Sox-Senators-Red Sox
George Sisler	1915–28 Browns-Senators
Duke Snider	1951 All-Star Game
Tris Speaker	1907–28 Red Sox-Indians-Senators-Athletics
Willie Stargell	1971 All-Star Game
Sam Thompson	1906 Tigers
Joe Tinker	1907–8 World Series with Cubs
Dazzy Vance	1934 World Series with Cardinals; 1915 Yankees
Rube Waddell	1902–10 Athletics-Browns
Honus Wagner	1909 World Series with Pirates
Bobby Wallace	1902–16 Browns
Ed Walsh	1904–16 White Sox
Zack Wheat	1927 Athletics
Hoyt Wilhelm	1957–69 Indians-Orioles-White Sox-Angels

Billy Williams	1975–76 A's
Ted Williams	1939–60 Red Sox
Early Wynn	1939–63 Senators-Indians-White Sox
Cy Young	1901–11 Red Sox-Indians

APPENDIX 4

TEN SILLIEST REASONS FOR TEARING DOWN TIGER STADIUM

10. *The blustering fib.* It's obvious the damn thing's falling down. (Coleman Young)

9. *The quack prognosis.* The arteries and veins inside the stadium are clogged and bleeding. Rust and decay inside the bowels of the stadium is an inoperable ulcer. (Bob Talbert, *Detroit Free Press*)

8. *Protecting the public purse.* Renovation of the existing stadium is the sentimental choice, but when it comes to spending taxpayer money in a responsible manner, renovation cannot be justified. (Michael Duggan)

7. *The menu.* A new stadium would allow the Tigers to serve hamburgers and chicken. (Bob Talbert)

6. *Blaming the victim.* Detroit all of a sudden has become the worst baseball town in the country. (Tom Monaghan)

5. *Self-interest.* The manager's office is too small. (Sparky Anderson)

4. *The facile analogy.* Cobb, Gehringer and Kaline didn't last forever. (John Lowe, *Detroit Free Press*)

3. *The voice of realism.* They're going to need a new stadium so they may as well get on with it. (Joe Falls, *Detroit News*)

2. *The long view.* It's only a building. (Frank Tanana)

QUEEN OF DIAMONDS

1. *The really long view.* They're preserving the Colosseum in Rome, but they're not playing any games in it. (Bo Schembechler)

(Adapted from the December 1990 "Unobstructed Views," the newsletter of the Tiger Stadium Fan Club)

SOURCES

Alexander, Charles C. *Ty Cobb*. New York: Oxford University Press, 1984.

Angell, Roger. *Five Seasons*. New York: Popular Library, 1978.

_____. *Season Ticket: A Baseball Companion*. Boston: Houghton Mifflin Company, 1988.

_____. *The Summer Game*. New York: Popular Library, 1978.

Baade, Robert A. "Is There an Economic Rationale for Subsidizing Sports Stadiums?" Heartland Policy Study no. 13 (Feb. 23, 1987). Chicago: Heartland Institute.

Baade, Robert A., and Richard F. Dye. "The Impact of Stadiums and Professional Sports on Metropolitan Area Development." *Growth and Change* (Spring 1990).

Baade, Robert A., and Laura J. Tiehen, "An Analysis of Major League Baseball Attendance, 1969–1987." *Journal of Sport and Social Issues* 14, no. 1 (1990): 14–32.

Baim, Dean V. "Sports Stadiums as 'Wise Investments': An Evaluation." Heartland Policy Study no. 32 (Nov. 26, 1990). Chicago: Heartland Institute.

Benson, Michael. *Ballparks of North America: A Comprehensive Historical Reference to Baseball Grounds, Yards and Stadiums, 1845 to Present*. Jefferson, N.C.: McFarland & Company, 1989.

Bess, Philip. *City Baseball Magic: Plain Talk and Uncommon Sense about Cities and Baseball Parks*. Pub. *Minneapolis Review of Baseball* and the Ballparks Committee of the Society for American Baseball Research, 1989.

_____. "Mall Park: New Comiskey Park and the State of the Art," *Inland Architect* 35, no. 5 (Sept./Oct. 1991): 32–41.

Betzold, Michael. *Tiger Stadium: Where Baseball Belongs.* Detroit: Tiger Stadium Fan Club, 1988.

Bingay, Malcolm W. *Detroit Is My Home Town.* New York: Bobbs-Merrill Company, 1946.

Chadwick, Alex. *Illustrated History of Baseball.* New York: Bison Books Corp., 1988.

Conot, Robert. *American Odyssey.* New York: William Morrow & Co., 1974.

Falls, Joe. *Baseball's Great Teams: Detroit Tigers.* New York: Collier Books, 1975.

_____. *So You Think You're a Die-Hard Tiger Fan.* Chicago: Contemporary Books, 1986.

Giamatti, A. Bartlett. *Take Time for Paradise: Americans and Their Games.* New York: Summit Books, 1989.

Hawkins, John. *This Date in Detroit Tigers History.* Briarcliff Manor, N.Y.: Stein and Day, 1981.

Johnson, Arthur T. "Economic and Policy Implications of Hosting Sports Franchises: Lessons from Baltimore." *Urban Affairs Quarterly* 21, no. 3 (March 1986): 411–33.

Klobuchar, Amy. *Uncovering the Dome.* Prospect Heights, Ill.: Waveland Press, 1982.

Lowry, Philip J. *Green Cathedrals.* Cooperstown, N.Y.: Society for American Baseball Research, 1986.

McCallum, John D. *Ty Cobb.* New York: Praeger Publishers, 1975.

McGraw, Bill. "The First Time," *Detroit Free Press* Sunday magazine (April 5,1987).

_____. "One Hundred Years of Baseball in Detroit: Remembrance and Celebration." *Detroit Free Press* Sunday Magazine (April 5, 1981).

Moss, Richard J. *Tiger Stadium.* Lansing, Mich.: Michigan Department of State, 1976.

Pastier, John. "The Business of Baseball." *Inland Architect* (Jan./Feb. 1989): 56-62.

_____. "Rescue Operation: Plans to Save Tiger Stadium." *Inland Architect* 35, no. 5 (Sept./Oct. 1991): 42–49.

Peterson, Harold. *The Man Who Invented Baseball.* New York: Charles Scribner & Sons, 1973.

312

Peterson, Robert. *Only the Ball Was White*. Englewood Cliffs, N.J.: Prentice-Hall Inc., 1970.

Reicher, Joseph L., ed. *The Baseball Encyclopedia*, sixth ed. New York: Macmillan Publishing Co., 1985.

Reidenbaugh, Lowell. *Take Me Out to the Ball Park*. St. Louis: The Sporting News, 1983.

Sullivan, George, and Cataneo, David. *Detroit Tigers: The Complete Record of Detroit Tigers Baseball*. New York: Macmillan Co., 1985.

Thorn, John, and Pete Palmer, eds. *Total Baseball*. New York: Warner Books, 1989.

Veeck, Bill, with Ed Linn. *Veeck — As in Wreck*. New York: Simon & Schuster,1989.

Voelker, Don. "Michigan and Trumbull Before Baseball." *Michigan History* (July/Aug. 1989): 24–31.

INDEX

Aaron, Hank, 101
Abbott, Juliana Philinda, 22
Adams, Tom, 85, 91–93, 237
African-American Night, 73, 122
Aguirre, Hank, 162, 230, 261
Alan, Marc, 96–99, 261
Albert Kahn Associates, 148
Alderson, Sandy, 215
Alexander, Dale, 58
Alexander, Doyle, 3
All-Star Game, 63, 68, 101, 105, 127, 189, 291–93
Allgaier, Ron, 182
Altrock, Nick, 42
Amadori, Tony, 182
American Association, 27
American Institute of Architects, 166, 171–72, 284
American League Championship Series
of 1972, 103
of 1984, 117
of 1987, 7–10, 126
American League
founding of, 32
Amole, Doc, 32, 289
Anaheim Stadium, 87, 183
Anderson, Sparky, 101, 110, 111, 158, 160, 238, 261, 309
Angell, Roger, 101, 129, 182, 262
Angus, Sam, 34
Antietam National Battlefield, 136
antitrust exemption, 211, 232, 259
Armour, Bill, 35
Astrodome, 87–88, 90, 96, 128, 243
Atlanta-Fulton County Stadium, 87
Auker, Eldon, 46

Baade, Robert, 203, 216, 238–39, 241–42
Baim, Dean, 242, 244
Baker Bowl, 59, 87
Baltimore Colts, 229
Baltimore Orioles, 80–82, 224, 264
Banks, Ernie, 72
Barrett, Jimmy, 33
Barrow, Ed, 35
baseball economics, 209–221
Baseball's Heirlooms (film), 252, 261
Batchelor, E. A., 40
Beaubien, Joseph, 21
BEI Associates, 142–45, 164–69, 174, 176–77, 258
Bell, Jim, 71
Bench, Johnny, 101
Bennett, Charlie, 26–27, 30, 40, 44
Bennett Park, 11, 29–38, 104, 289
Berg, Robert, 141, 145, 225
Berger, Horst, 140
Bess, Philip, 201, 216, 239–40, 247, 249, 252–53, 262, 282
Bingay, Malcolm W., 34, 42, 50, 53, 55, 62
Birkerts, Gunnar, 173–74, 256
Birkerts-O'Neal plan, 144, 167, 173–77, 187, 285
Black, William, 99
Blackwell, Arthur, 283
Blanchard, James, 147, 150, 163
Blue, Vida, 103
Bob D. Campbell & Co., 138, 164
Bonds, Bill, 228
Book-Cadillac Hotel, 50
Boston Braves, 86

Boston Red Sox, 10, 73, 79, 82, 102, 175, 214, 216–17, 220
Boswell, Thomas, 182
Boulevard Park, 27
Braves Field, 86, 129
Bridges, Tommy, 52
Briggs, Spike, 66, 69, 70
Briggs, Walter O. Sr., 17–20, 42, 43, 45, 47, 55–57, 60, 62, 65, 67, 69–71, 77, 115, 122, 127, 180, 184, 188, 208, 243
Briggs, Walter O. III, 18, 56, 62, 65–66, 70–71, 90, 108, 144, 200, 214
Briggs, Walter O. IV, 42, 56, 156, 212, 223, 225, 231, 240–41, 244–45, 262
Briggs Community, 90, 121, 176, 232, 241, 249–50, 257, 259, 263
Briggs Stadium, 55–76, 77, 89, 152, 156, 285, 290–92
first night game at, 67
Briggs-Redissi, Lois, 244
Brink, Peter, 136
Bristah, Jim, 193
Brock, Lou, 3, 83–84, 292
Brookens, Tom, 11
Brooklyn Dodgers, 71, 87
Brooks, David, 191–92, 262
Brooks, Major, 262
Brooks, Scott, 191–92, 194
Brooks Lumber Company, 116
Brouthers, Big Dan, 26
Brown, Bobby, 259
Brown, Gates, 71, 78–80, 122, 292
Brown, Orville, 49
Brunt, Stephen, 287
Bruske, Paul Hale, 40
Bryan, William Jennings, 209
Buchta, Bob, 88, 133–34, 142–44, 148, 150, 154, 156, 164, 167–68, 174, 178, 183–85, 201–02, 208, 220, 263, 283, 285
Buelow, Fritz, 33
Bunning, Jim, 67, 69, 263
Burns, Ed, 43–44
Burns, Jack, 46

Burns, James D., 32, 34
Burns Park, 32, 34, 302
Busby, Steve, 293
Busch Stadium, 87

Cain, Bob, 70
Cameron, Ron, 225
Cammeyer, William, 30
Campbell, Jim, 79, 94, 111, 113, 116, 124, 139, 164, 205, 208
Campus Martius, 24
Candlestick Park, 87
Canseco, Jose, 121
Cantor, George, 178, 255
Carey, Paul, 16, 183
Carrigan, Bill, 41–42
Cartwright, Alexander, 23
Casey, Doc, 33
Cash, Norm, 1, 78–80, 264, 281, 293
Cass Corridor Youth Advocates, 251
Cass Farm, 24
Cauffiel, Lowell, 139–142, 144, 148
Cavanagh, Jerome, 89, 91–92
Charles S. Davis Associates, 148
Checker Cab Company, 11, 49
Chicago Cubs, 10, 35, 51–52, 64, 117, 123, 130, 175, 205, 217, 220
Chicago Road, 22
Chicago White Sox, 70, 74, 124, 130, 137–139, 192, 217, 219–220, 224, 249
Chicago White Stockings, 25
Child, Charles, 149
Chiquita Bananas, 192
Chrysler, 224
Cincinnati Red Stockings, 25
Cincinnati Reds, 63, 110
Clark, Dick, 191
Clemente, Roberto, 101
Cleveland, Clyde, 198, 203
Cleveland Browns, 292
Cleveland Indians, 71–72, 75, 77, 86, 104
Cleveland Stadium Corporation, 243
Clunis, Alex, 263, 281

Cobb, Ty, ix, 7, 11, 35–37, 40–41, 43–45, 74, 267–68, 289–90, 309
Cobb's Lake, 41
Cobo, Albert, 69
Cobo Arena, 198
Cobo Hall, 91, 243, 246
Cochrane, Mickey, 47, 50, 52, 74, 101, 290
Cochrane Plan, 143, 151–72, 177, 187, 217, 227, 235, 238, 240, 249, 252, 255–56, 269, 272, 280, 282–83, 285, 294
Colavito, Rocky, 75, 78
Cole, Bert "King," 44
Coleman, Joe, 292
Colias, Ted, 14, 16–19, 49–51, 58, 62–63
Columbus Senators, 29–30
Comiskey Park, 38, 124, 128, 130, 137–139, 165, 183, 215, 252, 271
Comiskey Park (new), 181–84, 190, 206, 217, 219–20, 239, 247, 249, 261, 267, 286
Common Ground Coalition, 235, 258, 295
Connie Mack Stadium, 87
Connor, Edward, 90
Conway, Alice, 14–17, 48–50
Conway, Ella Echternkamp, 15–16
Conway, Jim, 14–16, 19–20
Conway, Jimmy, 15
Conway, Lefty, 15, 20
Conway, Neal, 13–17, 19–20, 67
Conway, Robert, 19
Cooperstown, 62, 185
Corktown, 15–16, 22, 48–50, 63, 69, 121, 124, 199, 241, 250, 257
Coughlin, Father Charles, 64
Couzens, James, 44
Craven, Bill, 180
Crawford, Sam, ix, 35–36
Crosley Field, 38, 63, 66, 87, 129
Cross, Tom, 239
Cutler, David, 61

Daniels, Jeff, 263

Darin, Catherine, 65–66, 78, 152, 199, 263, 285
Darvas, Robert, 173–74, 176, 185, 253
Dauss, Hooks, 44, 290
Davids, John, 115, 151–57, 220, 226, 232, 240, 280–82, 285–86
Davids, Judy, 115, 151–54, 157, 249, 280–82, 285
Davidson, William, 149
Davis, Charles B., 109
Dean, Dizzy, 82
De Bartolo, Edward, 138–139
Debs, Eugene V., 191
Deer, Rob, 183, 212
DeFran, Jeff, 151
Dembski, Peter, 4
Dequindre Park, 62
Detroit Base Ball Club, 24–25
Detroit Building Authority, 109
Detroit Chamber of Commerce, 89, 91, 94
Detroit City Council, 178, 229, 235, 240, 250, 264, 266, 281
Detroit Creams, 27
Detroit Lions, 18, 60–61, 70, 78, 89–91, 94, 103, 107–109, 110, 127, 198, 226, 239, 269, 291–93
Detroit Pistons, 5, 107, 110, 125, 197–98, 204, 218, 221, 262, 269
Detroit Red Wings, 3, 107–108, 110, 125, 194, 197–98, 204, 269
Detroit Renaissance, 93
Detroit Stars, 62
Detroit Tigers
  origin of name, 27
Detroit-Wayne County Enterprise Zone Authority, 240
Detroit-Wayne County Stadium Authority, 248
Detroit Wolverines, 25–27
Detroit Wolves, 62
DeWitt, Bill, 75
DeWitt Law, 75, 77
DeWitt-Spaulding Lumber Company, 23
Dillon, Pop, 33

DiMaggio, Joe, 72
Doby, Larry, 71–73, 122
Dodger Stadium, 86–87, 177, 183, 242
Domino's Pizza, 113, 115, 131, 150,
    156, 161, 173, 198, 231, 245
Doran, Wayne, 165
Doubleday, Abner, 23, 30, 62
Dow, Bill, 81, 167, 264, 285
Dowling, Pete, 33
Duffy, Hugh, 33
Duggan, Michael, 127, 163–78,
    186–87, 197–98, 200–02, 209–10,
    227–29, 233–35, 240, 242, 246, 247,
    250, 255, 258–59, 264, 279, 309
Dumka, George, 282
Dutton, Gary, 189
Dutton, Vicki, 189, 264
Dzadowski, Sam (Patsy O'Toole), 62

Early Risers, 24
Easter, Luke, 71
Eastern Market, 28
Ebbets Field, x, 38, 57, 87, 129, 140,
    182, 269
Economic Club of Detroit, 143,
    177–79, 185, 209–10, 295
economic impact of stadiums, 237–52,
    257, 259, 261, 266, 284, 286
Einhorn, Eddie, 130, 137–38, 223–24
Eisenhower, David, 82
Elberfeld, Kid, 33
Ellison, Jeff, 191–92, 194
Elysian Fields, 23
Engle, Clyde, 35
Engler, John, 163
"enterprise zone," 240, 266
Eugene V. Debs Memorial Kazoo
    Night, 190–94
Evans, Darrell, 3, 7–12, 110, 115, 117,
    126, 127
Everett, Kay, 245, 248
Ewald, Dan, 160

F.O.C.U.S. Inc., 250–51
Falls, Joe, 309
Faust, Scott, 141

Feliciano, Jose, 83
Feller, Bob, 72, 290
Fenway Park, 38, 39, 57, 82, 88, 128,
    130, 140, 175, 188, 194, 206, 214,
    216, 220, 273, 277
Ferber, Michael, 169, 284
Fetzer, John, 76, 77, 91, 94–96, 101,
    103, 108, 111, 113–15, 122, 208
Fidrych, Mark, 3, 5, 7, 11, 104–105,
    293
Fielder, Cecil, 12, 190, 294
Fifield, Jack, 39
Finegood, Steve, 233–34, 285
Fireman's Field Day, 79
Flood, Curt, 84
Flood v. Kuhn, 211
Forbes Field, 38, 87, 129
Ford, Henry, 29, 37, 42
Ford, William Clay, 89–91, 94–96,
    226
Ford Auditorium, 188
Ford Land Development Corporation,
    165
Ford Motor Company, 55
Fort Pontchartrain, 21
Foxx, Jimmy, 47
franchise relocation criteria, 230, 259
Frazer, Jim, 251
Freehan, Bill, 3, 79, 83–83, 121
Frisk, Emil, 33
Fryman, Woody, 102
Funke, Michael, 264

Gaedel, Eddie, 70
Gaelic League Irish-American Club,
    133, 285
Gage, Tom, 284–85
Gaule, Dan, 17–19, 49
Gehrig, Lou, 61
Gehringer, Charlie, ix, 16, 44–46, 309
General Motors, 223–24
Giamatti, A. Bartlett, 277
Gibson, Bob, 9
Gibson, Josh, 72
Gibson, Kirk, 11, 110, 116–19, 281–82,
    294

Gladding, Fred, 78
Gleason, Bill, 252
Gleason, Kid, 33
Goldy, Purnal, 78
Gordon, Bert, 51, 55, 58–60, 101, 245
Gordon, Lou, 95, 98
Goslin, Goose, ix, 52, 290
Gossage, Goose, 117–18, 294
Grant, Jim "Mudcat," 72
Gray, Jim, 211, 232
Greater Detroit Chamber of
  Commerce, 226, 246
Green, George, 29, 31
Green, Pumpsie, 73
Greenberg, Hank, ix, 11, 16, 19, 46,
  56, 59–60, 63–65, 72, 74
Greene, Sam
Grenesko, Don, 175
Gribbs, Roman, 92, 93, 107
Grieve, Tom, 217
Griffith Stadium, 87, 129
Grindstaff, John, 60, 81, 194, 235,
  264
grounds keepers, 13–20, 30, 43
Gruber, Mike, 133, 285

HOK Sports Facilities Group, 142,
  148–50, 152, 158, 163, 166, 169,
  177, 217
Haas family, 215
Haase, Bill, 123, 142, 144–45, 154–58,
  164, 199–201, 217, 225–26, 233,
  237–38, 240–41, 246, 250, 265,
  279–88
Hack, Stan, 52
Hall of Famers at Michigan and
  Trumbull, 303–07
Hamilton, Earl, 290
Haney, Bob, 144
Hanlon, Ned, 26
Harris, Bucky, 47
Harwell, Ernie, 7, 76, 77, 80–83, 155,
  160–63, 196–97, 207–08, 227, 231,
  245, 256, 262, 265, 270, 286–88,
  295
Hastings Street, 75, 79

hay market, 22–23, 29
Heartland Institute, 210, 235, 238,
  241–42, 248
Heilmann, Harry, 43
Held, David, 247
Helms, Bubba, 120–21, 123
Henderson, Rickey, 104
Hendrick, George, 103
Henneman, Mike, 4
Hernandez, Willie, 110
Herndon, Larry, 11, 110, 118, 126
Hoffa, Jimmy, 71
Hogan, Rosemary, 218, 221, 282
Holley, Jim, 198, 218, 221, 227, 245,
  251
Holmes, David, 95
Holmes, Ducky, 33
Horton, Brian, 119
Horton, Willie, 3, 78–80, 83–84, 121,
  122, 292
Hotel Association of Greater Detroit,
  247
House of David, 50
Hubbell, Carl, 35
Hubert H. Humphrey Metrodome, 9,
  130
Hudson's department store, 198
Hunkin & Conkey, 39
Huntington Avenue Grounds, 31
Husting, Bert, 33

Iacocca, Lee, 213
Iffy the Dopester, 50
Ilitch, Mike, 107, 113
Illinois Sports Facilities Authority,
  138, 249
Independence Hall, 136
International League, 27

Jack Murphy Stadium, 87, 130
Jackson, Reggie, 101, 103, 121, 293
James, Bill, 128
Javier, Julian, 83
Jeffsan, Inc., 154, 168–69, 284
Jennings, Hughie, 36, 37, 43
Jerome, Doug, 265

Jeziak, Stanley, 256
Jimmy Foxx Spite Fence, 47
Joe Louis Arena, 107–08, 202, 243
Johnson, Ban, 27, 32
Johnson, Walter, 35
Jones, Sad Sam, 264

Kaline, Al, ix, 4, 69, 79, 81–84, 102,
  151, 264–65, 309
Kaline's Corner, 69
Kansas City Athletics, 86
Kansas City Monarchs, 62
Kansas City Royals, 117
Kaufman, Ruth, 161
ka-zinga, 60
Kell, George, 19, 68, 265, 291
Kelley, Kevin, 246
Kelly, John, 237, 251
Kelsey, John, 43, 45
Keyworth Stadium (Hamtramck
  Stadium), 62
Killebrew, Harmon, 69, 101, 292
Kimm, Bruce, 105
Kingdome, 130, 214
King's fairgrounds, 24
Kittides, Christopher, 145, 164–69,
  171, 173, 175–76, 224
Kleinknecht, William, 257
Knorr, Fred, 70–71, 111
Koch, Larry, 161
Kozlowski, Mark, 211
Krauklis, Harijs, 153
Kresnak, Jack, 198
Krichbaum, Dan, 251
Kuenn, Harvey, 2, 74, 75
Kughn, Richard, 172, 284
Kukula, Patricia, 165

Ladies Day, 1, 31, 78, 219
Lajoie, Bill, 159, 162, 196, 208
Lake Front Park (Chicago), 31
Landis, Kenesaw Mountain, 43, 51
Lane, Ray, 81
Lapides, Max, 48, 50, 59, 61, 67, 68,
  79, 203, 219
La Russa, Tony, 215

Lary, Frank, 11, 292
Laughren, Floyd, 243
Layne, Bobby, 61
League Park, 87, 129
Lee, Manny, 3
Lemon, Chet, 110, 122
Leonard, Dutch, 290
Leonard, Elmore, 266
Letterman, David, 160
Lewis, Wrangler, 49
Linder, Carl, 192
Lolich, Mickey, 78, 79, 84
Louisiana Superdome, 242
Lowe, John, 309

Mack, Connie, 47, 51
Mack Park, 62
Mahaffey, Maryann, 193, 256, 266
Mandela, Nelson, 293
Mantle, Mickey, 68, 69, 268
Maris, Roger, 75
Market Opinion Research, 200–02
Marketing Resource Group, 150
Martelle, Scott, 191
Martin, Billy, 101–02
Matchick, Tommy, 2, 81
Mausi, Shahida, 158
Maxwell, Charlie, 75, 78
May, James, 21–22
Mayberry, John, 121
McAuliffe, Dick, 79, 80
McCarthy, Eugene, 82, 191–93, 224,
  266
McCarthy, Joe, 194
McDevitt, John, 132–34, 139–42, 245
McKinnon, Matthew, 233–35
McLain, Denny, 79, 80, 82, 83, 102,
  104, 292
McLaughlin, William, 246
McLeod, Alex, 30
McNamara, Ed, 163–65, 175, 186–87,
  198, 227–28, 232, 249, 255, 258–59,
  280
McWhirter, Nickie, 257
Meade, John, 190
Medwick, Joe "Ducky," 51, 82, 290

Memorial Stadium, 86

Metropolitan Detroit Convention and Visitors Bureau, 246

Meusel, Bob, 44

Michigan State Fairgrounds, 89, 91, 226

Michigan Supreme Court, 98–99

Miller, Canfield, Paddock & Stone, 97

Milliken, William, 91–93, 98

Milwaukee Braves, 86

Milwaukee Brewers, 117

Milwaukee County Stadium, 86

Minnesota Twins, 9, 126, 130

Minoso, Minnie, 74

Miramonti, John, 281–82

Miranda, Constancio, 140

Monaghan, Susan, 155

Monaghan, Tom, 8, 113–16, 123–24, 131–33, 135, 137, 141, 144, 147–52, 154–57, 159–60, 162–63, 173, 184–85, 193, 195–200, 202–09, 211–13, 215, 220–21, 224–27, 229, 231, 236, 239, 243–46, 248, 258, 260, 262, 264, 266, 279, 281, 294, 309

Monroe, James, 22

Montreal Expos, 130, 143, 231

Moody, Blair, 96–99

Moon, Charles, 91, 99, 233–35

Moriarty, George, 41

Morris, Jack, 3, 11, 110, 159–60, 162, 197

Morris, Steve, 129

Moten, Emmett Jr., 147

Muldoon, Pat, 250, 266

Mullin, George, 69, 290

Municipal Stadium (Cleveland), 57, 69, 86, 136

Municipal Stadium (Kansas City), 86

Murphy, Ed, 190

Muscat, Mario, 267

Nance, Doc, 33

National Association, 25

National Basketball Association, 107, 213

National Football League, 60–61, 70, 213

National Hockey League, 107

National League
Detroit franchise in, 25–27, 30
formation of, 25

National Park Service, 136

National Register of Historic Places, 136, 150, 294

National Sports Law Institute, 211, 232

National Trust for Historic Preservation, 136, 295

Navarre, Francis, 21

Navarre, Robert, 21

Navarro, Eva, 101–03, 267, 280–81, 283, 285

Navin, Frank, 14, 34–38, 39, 41–44, 47, 50, 51, 77, 127, 184, 208

Navin Field, 39–53, 56, 57, 140, 156, 206, 290

Negro Leagues, 62

Nemo's Bar, 239

New York Yankees, 34, 44, 45, 68, 75, 78, 82, 116, 212–15

Newhouser, Hal, 63, 64, 67, 121, 265

Newsom, Bobo, 63, 291

Nixon, Julie, 82

no-hitters, 69, 289–93

Nordhaus Research, 257

Northrup, Jim, 78, 79, 84

Northwestern League, 27

Oakland Athletics, 86, 103, 121, 215

Oakland Raiders, 229

Oakland-Alameda County Coliseum, 87

obstructed view seats, 32, 179–90, 256, 265

Odenwald, Jeff, 123, 161, 177, 186–87, 204–07, 218, 267

O'Leary, Charlie, 35

O'Neal, Joe, 173–77, 219, 240, 249, 256, 285

Olympia Stadium, 107
Olympic Stadium, 130, 143, 231
"Opera Under the Stars," 50
Orchestra Hall, 188, 271
Oriole Park at Camden Yards (new
    Baltimore stadium), 182, 220,
    275–76, 286
Orr, Edward, 23
Osborn Engineering Company, 39, 56,
    129, 144, 180, 185
Osinski, Dave, 118, 119, 199, 267
O'Toole, Patsy (Sam Dzadowski), 62
Owen, Marv, 51

PASS cable, 203–04
Paige, Satchel, 62, 72
Palace of Auburn Hills, 110, 149, 172,
    218, 243, 266
Paparella, Joe, 75
Pappas, Milt, 264
Parrish, Lance, 110
Pastier, John, 88, 128–29, 136, 138,
    143, 149–55, 165–66, 168–71,
    174–76, 179–81, 183–84, 187, 268
People Mover, 176
Pepper, Jon, 182, 219
Petry, Dan, 110
Philadelphia Athletics, 47, 86
Philadelphia Phillies, 248
Pierce, Billy, 121
Piersall, Jimmy, 75, 77–78
Poletown, 223–24
Polo Grounds, 31, 38, 87, 129, 182,
    269
Pontchartrain Hotel, 92
Pontiac Silverdome, 91, 94, 95, 103,
    107, 110, 144, 226, 243, 266
Pope, Eric, 234
Pope, Tim, 226
Poplar, Michael, 243
Prebenda, Ron, 85, 96–100
Prewozniak, Dennis, 268

Quinn, Matthew, 226

R.F.K. Stadium, 87

Rashid, Frank, 131, 133–34, 154, 196,
    209–11, 213, 221, 228, 235, 251–52,
    255, 257, 260, 268, 277, 280,
    283–85, 287
Rashid, Kathy, 280
Rashid, Kevin, 280
Rashid, Peg, 280
Rather, Dan, 193
Ravitz, Mel, 125
Recreation Park, 25–27
Redmond, Herbie, 122
Reed, Jack, 292
Reinsdorf, Jerry, 130, 137–38, 224
Renaissance Center, 85, 98, 107,
    240–41, 245
Reuther, Walter, 71
revenue sharing, 212–13
Ricci, James, 206
Rice, Grantland, 52
Richardson, Hardy, 26
Ridley, Mike, 84, 162, 166, 269,
    286–87
right-field overhang, 56–57, 149
Rivard, Dorothy, 14–16, 19, 20, 62
riverfront dome, 85, 91–100, 103, 128,
    135, 163, 237, 240, 256
Riverfront Stadium, 87, 88
Roberts, Gary, 232
Roberts, Sasha, 250–51
Robinson, Dave, 160
Robinson, Frank, 101
Robinson, Jackie, 71, 73
Rogell, Billy, 89
Rohde, Michael, 225
Rollyson, Carl, 73–74, 188, 269
Rosen, Peter, 207, 239
Rossetti, Gino, 172, 178
Rossetti Associates, 108, 124
Royals Stadium, 128, 183, 247
Rowe, Jack, 26
Runco, William, 226
Ruth, Babe, 7, 44–45, 47, 59, 268,
    290
Rutherford, Doug, 79
Ryan, Nolan, 7, 293

Saberhagen, Bret, 269
Sachner, Paul, 136
St. Boniface Church, 50, 200
St. Louis Browns, 65, 70, 72, 86
St. Louis Cardinals, 3, 9, 50–51,
  83–84
Salsinger, Harry, 45
San Diego Padres, 117–18
San Francisco Giants, 11, 73
Sauk Trail, 21
Save Our Sox, 130
Saylor, Jack, 61
Schacht, Al, 42
Schaefer, Germany, 1, 5, 35, 36, 42,
  104
Schembechler, Glenn E. "Bo," 142,
  143, 156, 158, 163–64, 167, 173–74,
  177–79, 185–87, 189, 198–200,
  206–07, 209–10, 212–14, 219–20,
  223, 227–32, 235, 238, 241, 245–46,
  248–50, 256, 258–59, 263–64,
  269–70, 277, 279–81, 285–87, 295,
  310
  rusty girder speech, 143, 177–79,
  185, 200, 209–10, 212, 214, 227,
  269–70, 295
Schu, Rick, 197
Seattle Mariners, 212, 214, 230, 248
Selis, Stewart, 202
Shapiro, Don, 39, 46–48, 51, 58–59,
  64–65, 79, 101, 102, 207–08, 270,
  282
Shapiro, Walter, 183, 189, 273
Sharp, Thom, 162, 199, 270, 286
Shea, Jerry, 166, 172, 238, 284
Shea Stadium, 87, 184
Shea's Bar (Casey's), 61
Sheridan, Pat, 9–10
Shibe Park, 37, 68, 87, 129
Shine, Neal, 159–60
Shrine of the Little Flower, 64
Shuck, Brenda, 94
Shull, Thomas, 210–11, 235–36,
  241–42, 248
Sinclair, John, 151–52, 158
Skowron, Bill, 75

SkyDome, 131, 134, 149, 180–81, 189,
  214, 220, 242–43, 264, 275
Slagle, Tim, 195, 271
Smith, B. Ward, 96–98
Smith, Frank, 289
Smith, Lyall, 67, 89
Smith, Mayo, 83, 101
Smith, Royce, 96, 97, 99, 271
Snowflake House, 154
Snyder, Ralph, 109, 139
South End Grounds, 31
Sparma, Joe, 82
Sportsman's Park, 14, 38, 87, 129
Springstead, Tim, 239
stadium financing, 237–38, 242–44,
  246–48, 250, 257–58, 260, 263,
  271–72, 276, 283–84, 286
Stallings, George, 27, 30, 34
Stanford Research Institute, 93, 96
Stanley, Mickey, 78, 79, 83
Staub, Rusty, 101
Stearns, Frederick, 26–27
Steinbrenner, George, 215
Sterling, James, 154
Stevens, Bill, 41, 42, 43, 45
Stewart, Dave, 121
Strange, Doug, 197
Stubbs, Franklin, 212
Sweany, Robert, 93
Swearingen, Dale, 129, 144, 180, 185
Sweeney, Ann, 181, 190
Swift, Jack, 49

Talbert, Bob, 142, 143, 144, 158, 225,
  271, 309
Tanana, Frank, 3, 293, 309
Taubman, Al, 252, 255
Teamsters, 71
Tettleton, Mickey, 295
Texas Rangers, 176, 217
Thomas, Gorman, 111, 293
Thompson, Sam, 26
Thompson, William G., 25
Three Rivers Stadium, 87, 88, 181,
  231
Tiehen, Laura, 203, 216

Tiger Stadium, 1–5, 7–12, 77–84, 90, 94, 101ff.
  attendance at, 196–208, 215–16, 219, 228, 256, 266, 288, 300, 302
  hugs of, 140, 157, 294
  lease, 108, 114, 124, 144, 166, 193, 224, 229, 232–36, 248, 256, 258–59, 285
  parking at, 90, 108, 176–77, 199–202, 206–07, 257, 266
  renovation of, 107–10, 114, 124–25, 132–35, 139–41, 144, 147–78, 187, 217, 220, 227, 229, 233–34, 248, 257–58, 263–64, 270, 272, 280–81, 283–84, 287, 294–95, 309 (See also Birkerts-O'Neal plan and Cochrane Plan)
  seating proximity, 265–68, 275, 276
  structural integrity of, 127, 132–34, 137–45
Tiger Stadium Fan Club, 127, 131, 133, 135, 137, 140, 148, 150, 152–57, 162–64, 167, 196–97, 201, 209, 218, 226–27, 230, 233, 250, 256–58, 260, 279–88, 294, 310
Tighe, Jack, 70–71
Timmerman, Tom, 78
Toronto Blue Jays, 3, 9, 125–26, 197, 203, 242
Torre, Joe, 101
Trammell, Alan, 11, 110, 114, 153
Tremain, Brian, 241, 245, 250, 271, 285
Trout, Dizzy, 68
Trucks, Virgil, 69, 291
Trumbull, John, 22
Turner, Edward, 72–73, 121–22, 272, 287
Turner Construction Company, 141–43, 148
Tyson, Ty, 290

Union Grounds, 30
United Auto Workers, 71, 194

Van der Beck, George Arthur, 27–30

Vasiloff, Ronald, 199–200
Veach, Bobby, ix
Veeck, Bill, 70–71
Veryzer, Tom, 105
Veterans Stadium, 87, 88, 143
Vincent, Charlie, 287
Vincent, Fay, 230–31
Virgil, Ozzie, 73, 79, 121, 292
Vitale, Pat, 165
Vitt, Ossie, 63

Waddell, Rube, 36
Wagner, Honus, 37
Wakefield, Dick, 18–19
Walden Pond, 136
Waldmeir, Pete, 259
Walker, Gee, 78
Warner, Patty, 272
Washington Senators, 64, 102, 281
Wayne County, 8, 143, 144, 163, 165, 171, 173, 175, 227, 241–42, 252, 257, 295
  hotel-motel tax, 8, 95, 164, 241–42, 246–48, 260
Wayne County Board of Auditors, 95
Wayne County Stadium Authority, 85, 92, 95
Weeghman Park, 38, 206
Wert, Don, 78, 82, 292
Wertz, Vic, 68, 291
Westbrooks, Randy, 77, 80, 119, 194, 272
Western League, 27, 32
Western Market, 23
Whitaker, Lou, 7, 10, 110, 122, 153
White, Deacon, 26
Wilcox, Milt, 294
Wildcat stands, 11, 29, 31–32
Will, George F., 147, 157, 212–13, 273
Williams, Dick, 118
Williams, Edward Bennett, 224
Williams, G. Mennen "Soapy," 99
Williams, Ken, 197
Williams, Ted, 18, 63, 281, 291
Wilson, Earl, 79

Wilson, Michael, 123
Wilson, Willie, 117
Wineman, James, 94
Woodbridge, Dudley, 22, 23, 28
Woodbridge, Leverette, 22
Woodbridge, William, 22
Woodbridge Grove, 22–23, 289
World Series
　of 1887, 27
　of 1907, 36, 42, 289
　of 1908, 36, 289
　of 1909, 37, 289–90
　of 1934, 50–52, 82, 290
　of 1935, 51–53, 55, 56, 290
　of 1940, 63, 291
　of 1945, 64, 291
　of 1968, 2, 3, 9, 83–84, 292–93
　of 1984, 117–20, 123, 294
World War I, 42

World War II, 17, 19, 59, 63–64, 66
Wrigley Field, 38, 56, 58, 66, 70, 123,
　128, 130–31, 140, 175, 183, 188,
　205–06, 220, 273, 277

Yankee Stadium, 57, 69, 130, 174–75,
　215
Yawkey, Thomas A., 35
Yawkey, William C., 34
Yawkey, William H., 34–36
York, Rudy, ix, 63
Young, Coleman, 108, 108, 110,
　125–27, 131–35, 137, 141, 145,
　147–48, 152, 158, 163, 173–74, 225,
　234, 246, 252, 255, 258–59, 266–67,
　293, 295, 309
Young, Matt, 212

Zetlin, Lev, 140–42